Law, Governance and Technology Series

Volume 79

The *Law, Governance and Technology Series* is intended to attract manuscripts arising from an interdisciplinary approach in law, artificial intelligence and information technologies. The idea is to bridge the gap between research in IT law and IT-applications for lawyers developing a unifying techno-legal perspective. The series will welcome proposals that have a fairly specific focus on problems or projects that will lead to innovative research charting the course for new interdisciplinary developments in law, legal theory, and law and society research as well as in computer technologies, artificial intelligence and cognitive sciences. In broad strokes, manuscripts for this series may be mainly located in the fields of the Internet law (data protection, intellectual property, Internet rights, etc.), Computational models of the legal contents and legal reasoning, Legal Information Retrieval, Electronic Data Discovery, Collaborative Tools (e.g. Online Dispute Resolution platforms), Metadata and XML Technologies (for Semantic Web Services), Technologies in Courtrooms and Judicial Offices (E-Court), Technologies for Governments and Administrations (E-Government), Legal Multimedia, and Legal Electronic Institutions (Multi-Agent Systems and Artificial Societies).

Fabiana Di Porto · Oreste Pollicino
Editors

Law and Politics of Virtual Worlds

How NFTs and Metaverse are Reshaping Legal Systems

Springer

Editors
Fabiana Di Porto
University of Rome UnitelmaSapienza
and LUISS University
Rome, Italy

Oreste Pollicino
Bocconi University
Milan, Italy

ISSN 2352-1902 ISSN 2352-1910 (electronic)
Law, Governance and Technology Series
ISBN 978-3-032-08540-5 ISBN 978-3-032-08541-2 (eBook)
https://doi.org/10.1007/978-3-032-08541-2

This Springer imprint is published by the registered company Springer Nature Switzerland AG
The registered company address is: Gewerbestrasse 11, 6330 Cham, Switzerland

Contents

Introduction

Fabiana Di Porto and Oreste Pollicino

Abstract Non-Fungible Tokens (NFTs) and virtual worlds (often referred to as the metaverse) are at the core of future Internet. With increasing investments in these technologies, the growth of this expanding sector has drawn new developments in the global economy, such as decentralised finance (DeFi) or personalized health. Being more than just a parallel reality made of virtual spaces, the metaverse shows its capacity to shape the real world and has raised interest at policy and scholarly levels. In the European Union and the U.S., the debate focuses on potential risks for the public, from the processing of personal data by companies, to social and health implications, along with market distortions and the protection of fundamental rights.

Although books on virtual worlds, NFTs and the metaverse exist, they either provide practical primers without a legal perspective or, if they are legal scholarly books, they are focus on a specific sector (e.g. cryptocurrencies, smart contracts, etc.). This book "Law and Politics of Virtual Worlds" aims to fill the gap by providing a comprehensive overview of the legal issues raised by virtual worlds, NFTs and the metaverse in the different domains. This book explores the potential of these technological developments to challenge established legal notions in different legal fields, ranging from public, financial, intellectual property, contract, and competition laws. To do so, it adopts a fully innovative perspective, bringing together two perspectives: that of leading scholars and of policy makers, which views are contrasted to offer the reader a wider picture of what virtual worlds of the future might resemble. The book builds on a series of seminars that took place on April-May 2022 at Luiss University of Rome, which triggered wide participation from the public. Given the novelty of the subject and proposed methodology, this work seeks to reach the interest of a wider audience than just legal scholars.

F. Di Porto (✉) · O. Pollicino
University of Rome UnitelmaSapienza, Rome, Italy
e-mail: fabiana.diporto@unitelmasapienza.it

Bocconi University, Milan, Italy

O. Pollicino
e-mail: oreste.pollicino@unibocconi.it

F. Di Porto and O. Pollicino (eds.), *Law and Politics of Virtual Worlds*, Law, Governance and Technology Series 79, https://doi.org/10.1007/978-3-032-08541-2_1

The book is structured in six parts.

1 Defining Virtual Worlds, Metaverse and NFTs: A Public Law Perspective

Part I sets the scene by providing definitions of key concepts and explores issues of governance and how constitutional law and the protection of individual rights might be affected. It starts with a policy paper titled *Navigating Virtual Worlds, The European Way* by Roberto Viola and Filomena Chirico from the European Commission. The chapter explores Europe's approach to the development and regulation of the metaverse, and the implications of Web 4.0 on society and governance. The metaverse, characterized by immersive digital worlds and digital twins of real entities, has the potential to revolutionize various sectors like health, education, finance, and democratic participation. The fusion of real and digital worlds will transform human experiences and societal structures. In this framework, Europe aims to lead in shaping Web 4.0 by ensuring that the development of virtual worlds is guided by fundamental rights, principles, and regulations. The authorshighlight how the EU is focused on embedding values such as openness, security, and trust from the outset, preventing issues like closed ecosystems and corporate domination seen in earlier digital developments. The global market for virtual worlds is expected to reach over €800 billion by 2030, with significant job creation around Extended Reality (XR) technologies. However, the rise of virtual goods, NFTs, and digital assets introduces challenges in property law, jurisdiction, and rights, which Europe seeks to regulate early on. They speak of regulatory readiness to mean that the EU's Digital Services Act (DSA) and Digital Markets Act (DMA) already provide a solid regulatory framework to address the challenges of virtual worlds, since these laws aim to maintain fairness, transparency, and user rights in the increasingly immersive and interconnected digital landscape. They stress the importance of the European vision for the metaverse, that focuses on a fair, secure, and interoperable digital space that respects users' rights, while ensuring that the metaverse serves the public good and is not monopolized by corporate interests.

Chapter 2, titled *The Metaverse: Interoperability as Governance* by Fabiana Di Porto and Daniel Foà provides a comprehensive analysis of existing definitions for virtual worlds and the metaverse, and focuses on interoperability and its relevance for the metaverse. As per the definitory level, the authors identify three stages of development of the metaverse: Birth (separated virtual worlds), Infancy (interconnected and interoperable worlds), and Maturity (a fully-functioning metaverse that coincides with the web 4.0). Interoperability, defined as the ability of different systems to work together, is critical for both technological (hardware/software) and societal interactions in the metaverse, as it ensures the seamless exchange of information across digital platforms, contributing to better governance. There are several challenges to attain interoperability: because the metaverse today consists of siloed virtual worlds, with varying degrees of immersiveness and synchronicity, interoperability is essential for connecting these worlds into a fully functioning yet mature metaverse. Interoperability mandates exist primarily for public sectors (e.g., the European Interoperability Framework), while private sector interoperability is largely governed by market forces and standard-setting organizations (SSOs). There are nonetheless legal frameworks, such as the GDPR, the DMA and Data Act, that address certain aspects of interoperability, particularly in terms of data portability and access to operating systems and hardware components. However, they remain sector-specific and limited in scope. To establish the seeds for a future governance of the metaverse, collaboration between governments, regulators, and the private sector is vital, so to develop interoperability standards for the metaverse. The chapter suggests that partial interoperability (i.e. limited to identity and currency) should be pursued now; while full interoperability should be established at a later stage. The choices made about interoperability will shape the development of the metaverse and determine who controls its key components. Hence, a targeted regulatory approach would be preferable, instead of general regulations that could hinder innovation. The creation of interoperability standards should involve multiple stakeholders, including international bodies, governments, and private companies.Issues of governance of the metaverse are further developed in Chapter 3 *Metaverse: Yet Another Jeopardy for the Constitutional Social Contract?* by Riccardo Vecellio Segate, which explores the metaverse's potential to disrupt global digital governance, with significant implications for constitutional law. The metaverse could revolutionize governance in digitized environments by challenging the existing constitutional frameworks that define the public and private realms. It raises complex jurisdictional issues, especially related to conflict-of-laws controversies and cross-border digital governance. Traditional constitutions, which are territorially bound, may become obsolete in the metaverse, a space where legal entitlements and the relationship between citizens and the state might be profoundly altered. The notion of social contracts, foundational to constitutional law, could be replaced or transformed due to the decentralized and privately managed nature of the metaverse. The metaverse's transnational nature challenges the traditional jurisdictional boundaries of nation-states. The Chapter questions how current constitutions could accommodate these digital environments or whether new constitutional discourses are necessary to handle conflicts that arise in virtual spaces. The privatization of governance in the metaverse, through standards adopted solely by corporations, risks threatening the effectiveness of constitutional norms and may deepen inequalities by creating a digital elite and further eroding public governance. As citizens increasingly interact in virtual spaces, the protection of privacy, digital rights, and human autonomy will need new safeguards, potentially at the constitutional level. The chapter highlights concerns over corporate surveillance and the potential erosion of human rights in the metaverse. Although the metaverse represents an opportunity, it raises a risk for constitutional frameworks, potentially pushing towards a global governance system that may either reinforce or undermine constitutional protections. There is, therefore, an urgent need to discuss the creation of a global or metaverse-specific constitutionalism to address the governance challenges posed by enhanced virtuality. The role of constitutions as a binding social contract may be weakened, necessitating a rethinking of their relevance in the context of digitally powered societies. It is important to take a proactive, imaginative scholarly approach to anticipating the constitutional challenges of the metaverse rather than reacting after they arise.

2 NFTs and Financial Markets: What Regulatory Gaps?

Part II provides a composite picture of the legal notion of NFTs in financial markets law and how they may affect the development of the metaverse. A first take is provided by Paolo Chiocca and Irene Tagliamonte, respectively commissioner and civil servant at the Consob (the Italian regulator for financial markets). Their policy-oriented Chapter 4, titled *The New EU Framework for Crypto-Assets: Recent Developments and Main Challenges Ahead*, discusses the evolving regulatory landscape for crypto-assets within the European Union, focusing on the Markets in Crypto-Assets Regulation (MiCAR) and its implications. The crypto-asset market has experienced significant volatility, exemplified by events like the collapse of TerraUSD and FTX. This has highlighted the need for a robust regulatory framework to prevent systemic risks. According to the authors, MiCAR is designed to regulate various types of crypto-assets, including cryptocurrencies and NFTs, with the aim of protecting investors, ensuring market integrity, and fostering financial stability. MiCAR applies principles of technological neutrality, proportionality, and "same activity, same risk, same regulation." Defining the scope of MiCAR, especially for NFTs and decentralized finance (DeFi) protocols, remains a challenge. MiCAR lacks clear definitions in some areas, which could lead to regulatory arbitrage and loopholes, especially for decentralized services like DAOs. MiCAR includes provisions to prevent market manipulation and fraud in crypto markets, similar to those in traditional financial markets. However, adapting these rules to the unique characteristics of blockchain and decentralized systems is complex. Indeed, EU regulation of the crypto-asset market aims to address the risks posed by decentralized finance and volatile crypto markets. While it provides a comprehensive framework, challenges remain in fully adapting to the decentralized nature of blockchain technology. Global cooperation and continued regulatory updates will be necessary to ensure a stable and secure market for crypto-assets.

Two more scholarly Chapters follow that also analyse NFTs. Chapter 5 *New Horizon for Financial Law and Policy: Non-Fungible Tokens in the Metaverse*, by Joseph Lee explores the role of NFTs in the evolving metaverse and their implications for financial regulation and law. The Chapter highlights how NFTs, though traditionally seen as unique digital assets, are increasingly being treated as financial assets, requiring regulatory frameworks to govern their use in decentralized markets. Current financial laws, including EU regulations like MiCA, do not fully encompass the complexities of NFTs, especially "fractional NFTs", which can function similarly to traditional financial instruments. This creates a need for new legal structures and regulations. In this regard the author discusses how blockchain technology and Decentralized Autonomous Organizations (DAOs) are becoming central in NFT governance, offering opportunities for collaborative regulation through smart contracts and decentralized platforms. As NFTs become more prevalent in the financial landscape, legal frameworks must evolve to include new concepts of ownership and property rights, while also fostering innovation and protecting market integrity. The future of financial law on NFTs should be shaped by a combination of private law, regulation, and emerging technologies such as blockchain.

A third perspective is proposed in the scholarly Chapter 6, by Filippo Annunziata, titled *NFTs and EU Financial Markets Legislation.* It analyzes the impact of the MiCA regulation on the evolving NFT market. Although MiCA was not designed specifically for NFTs, its provisions will affect NFT markets. It categorizes NFTs as crypto-assets but does not subject them to the same level of regulatory scrutiny as other tokens like stablecoins. However, "fractional NFTs" and NFTs issued in large series may fall under MiCA's regulatory scope. Moreover, the EU's approach to NFTs under MiCA focuses on protecting consumers, but the framework remains ambiguous regarding hybrid tokens and NFTs that could potentially qualify as financial instruments. Uncertainties in the final text of MiCA persist that would suggest to prompt future EU regulations tailored specifically for NFTs, so to keep the evolving market and development of NFTs safe.

3 The Challenges of IP Law

Part III focuses of novel concepts of properties brought about by NFTs and the tokenization of art and creativity, and explores how intellectual property rights (IPRs) are challenged in the metaverse.

Chapter 7, titled *NFTs: Copyright Profiles—and Beyond*, by Giovanni Cavani and Gustavo Ghidini explores the intersection between NFTs and copyright law, highlighting the legal challenges and implications surrounding this rapidly growing market. The creation of an NFT does not inherently confer copyright protection on the associated digital content: simply tokenizing a work of art does not provide new copyright protections if the content was not already protected by copyright. NFTs can be classified as legal assets, but purchasing an NFT does not transfer copyright ownership of the work it represents. Buyers only acquire rights to the digital token, not to the reproduction or commercial exploitation of the underlying content, unless specifically stated in a smart contract. The immutability of blockchain creates difficulties in enforcing copyright infringement claims. Once a work is tokenized and placed on a blockchain, it becomes challenging to remove or alter it, even in cases of proven infringement. Furthermore, the anonymity provided by cryptocurrency transactions in the NFT market creates a potential for money laundering. The use of NFTs for illegal financial activities is a growing concern due to the lack of effective regulation and traceability in blockchain-based markets. The Chapter concludes that while NFTs present new opportunities for digital art and assets, they also raise significant legal challenges, particularly in copyright and intellectual property law. Regulatory frameworks need to evolve to address issues related to ownership, IPRs and financial risks associated with NFTs.

The second Chapter (no. 8) is a policy paper titled *NFTs and IP: Easier Said than Understood*, by Stefania Ercolani. It explores the complex relationship between NFTs and IP law, particularly focusing on the legal and practical challenges posed by NFTs. NFTs typically do not include IPRs over the digital content they represent. Instead, they often provide only limited rights, such as access to or display of the digital asset. The absence of clear regulations around NFTs leads to various risks, including copyright infringement, misappropriation, and plagiarism. Buyers may unknowingly purchase NFTs linked to copyrighted works without proper IP rights, resulting in potential legal disputes. NFTs are often governed by smart contracts, but these contracts rarely transfer full intellectual property rights. Instead, they grant narrowly defined licenses for non-commercial personal use, while the original creator retains IP ownership. Enforcing copyright in the NFT space is difficult, especially when marketplaces do not monitor or verify the legitimacy of the NFTs they sell. Cases of plagiarism, piracy, and wash trading (inflating NFT prices through self-dealing) are prevalent. Many NFT platforms, such as OpenSea, operate under terms that limit legal liability, placing the burden on buyers to verify the authenticity and legality of the NFTs. The Chapter concludes that the current NFT ecosystem is fraught with legal uncertainty, especially regarding intellectual property rights. Without clearer regulations and better enforcement mechanisms, both creators and buyers remain vulnerable to exploitation and fraud in the NFT market. The development of comprehensive IP laws adapted to NFTs and their integration into the metaverse will be essential for the future.

Chapter 9 is the last of the series devoted to IPRs. *The Uncanny Token*, by Brian L. Frye originally explores the nature of NFTs and how they challenge traditional notions of art and the art market. In the author's view, NFTs are best described as digital ledger entries that represent ownership, but not necessarily of a physical object. The Chapter argues that the art market has always functioned similarly, with artworks acting as tokens representing an artist's career rather than as objects of intrinsic value. Frye suggests that NFTs reveal a truth long obscured by the traditional art market — that it is fundamentally a market for "clout" or reputation rather than a market for objects. This realization makes people uncomfortable, as it strips away the perceived authenticity and artistry of the market. The Chapter contends that the NFT market is akin to a securities market, where collectors invest in the future value of an artist's career rather than in the physical or aesthetic qualities of the artworks themselves. Overall, NFTs challenge our understanding of art by exposing the art market's underlying economic mechanisms. They reveal that both the art and NFT markets are primarily about investment in reputation and brand, not the inherent value of objects. Frye argues that this transparency could benefit artists by creating more direct and efficient systems for selling and benefiting from their work.

4 NFTs and Smart Contracts: Questions of Property Law

Part IV is devoted to blockchain-driven smart contracts and the way these tools can further the exchange of NFTs: both legal and technical guarantees need to be endorsed for smart contracts to ensure that the code incorporates the highest protection for consumers and lowest risks of code bugs.

Chapter 10 *Smart Contracts, NFT Trading, and Weaker Party Protection*, by Andrea Stazi examines the legal implications of smart contracts and NFTs, focusing on their opportunities, challenges, and the protection of weaker parties in these decentralized markets. Smart Contracts are self-executing contracts written in code that do not require human intervention. They are immutable and operate automatically, but this rigidity can pose challenges, especially in disputes where judicial intervention may be necessary. NFTs can be understood as digital assets that represent ownership of physical or digital items. However, while they offer opportunities for creators to monetize digital content, they also present risks, including fraud and challenges in ensuring consumer protection. In both smart contracts and NFT transactions, the protection of weaker parties, such as consumers, is a concern. The anonymity of blockchain and the complexity of smart contracts make it difficult to apply traditional consumer protection laws effectively. Issues like unfair terms and lack of transparency are harder to manage in a decentralized environment. Current legal frameworks, particularly in the EU, need to adapt to address these challenges, ensuring that consumers are adequately protected in decentralized markets. Chapter 11 *Non-Fungible Tokens (NFTs), Smart Contracts, and Contracts: The Need for Legal and Technology Assurances*, by Joshua Ellul and Ioannis Revolidis explores the intersection of NFTs, smart contracts, and legal frameworks. It highlights that while NFTs are primarily technological solutions for managing digital rights, they introduce complex legal questions about what ownership they really entail, especially when considering technological failures. First, NFTs are viewed as smart contracts that could imply a legal contract, raising concerns about their legal status and ownership claims, particularly when tied to physical assets. Legal clarity is necessary for the interpretation of NFTs, especially in scenarios where they are used to claim ownership of physical goods. There is a pressing need for both legal and technological assurances to address gaps where technology alone cannot guarantee compliance or protection, such as bugs in smart contract code. The Chapter emphasizes the importance of contract law in providing certainty and legal remedies when NFTs fail to operate as expected, especially in cross-jurisdictional contexts. The authors conclude that neither legal nor technological solutions alone can fully support NFTs. Instead, a combined approach, utilizing both technical safeguards and legal assurances, is essential to enable NFTs to achieve their full potential.

5 Competition Law and the Metaverse

The challenges put by the metaverse to competition law and policy are at the core of Part V.

Chapter 12 *Virtual Worlds and Competition Issues: Same Problem, Same Solution*, by Jacques Moscianese and Fabrizio Di Benedetto explores the emerging competition landscape in the metaverse, focusing on two potential outcomes: the coexistence of multiple virtual worlds or the dominance of a single virtual world. The authors draw parallels between the evolution of payment card schemes and the search engine market to highlight the risks of market tipping and monopolies.

The metaverse could evolve into either a market with multiple virtual worlds competing or one dominated by a single player, akin to Google's dominance in search engines. Without interoperability between platforms, users could be "locked-in" to a single virtual world, unable to switch easily, reducing competition and innovation. The authors argue that interoperability is crucial to ensuring healthy competition, similar to the banking industry's payment schemes that allowed cross-platform services. They conclude that interoperability is essential for fostering competition and preventing monopolistic outcomes in the metaverse. The application of the Digital Markets Act could play a vital role in maintaining a competitive market, ensuring that no single player dominates the space, and protecting both users and businesses from lock-in effects.

Chapter 13 is a policy paper that closes Part 5. *Metaverses, Digital, and Competition Law: What's New?* by Andrea Pezzoli discusses the challenges that the metaverse may pose to competition law. It aims to determine whether current competition law tools are adequate for addressing these new issues and how competition authorities might need to adapt. While the challenges are similar to those faced in digital markets, Pezzoli argues that traditional competition law tools are still largely relevant but must be continuously updated to remain effective. For instance, market definition in the metaverse is complex, and traditional measures like market shares may be inadequate to assess market power due to blurred boundaries and the decentralized nature of virtual worlds. The importance of data and interoperability in the metaverse is emphasized, with concerns about how dominant platforms could monopolize data and exclude competitors. Collaboration between competition authorities and data protection agencies is necessary to address these issues. Pezzoli concludes that while existing competition law remains relevant, it requires continuous updating to handle the unique features of the metaverse. There is also a need for cooperation between competition and data protection authorities to ensure effective regulation of the metaverse environment. The temptation to introduce overly ambitious regulations should be avoided until there is a better understanding of the metaverse's evolution.

6 Privacy and Data Protection Concerns for the Metaverse

Part VI features a focus on data protection issues in the metaverse and offers a view on the path forward for the metaverse. Chapter 14 *Data Protection Challenges and Privacy Issues in the Metaverse dimension* by Laura Greco examines the challenges for the application of data protection regulations, by exploring the possible configurations of the relationships between data subjects, controllers and processors (and terms for exercising the relevant rights) in the light of the characteristics of virtual worlds and the interactions therein.

Chapter 15 *Exploring the Metaverse: Opportunities, Risks, and the Path Forward*, is authored by Angelo Mazzetti from Meta and discusses the rapid development of the metaverse, its potential social and economic impacts, and the necessary steps for its responsible growth. The reason for this chapter is, again, to provide the reader with a wider (possibly conflicting) range of views on a highly sensitive issue.

7 Theorizing the Metaverse: Lessons from the Past

The metaverse promises significant advancements in fields like healthcare, education, and entertainment. It could revolutionize how people interact online, making experiences more immersive and realistic through technologies like virtual reality and augmented reality. The economic potential of the metaverse is vast, with estimates suggesting it could be worth trillions of dollars globally in the coming decade. Despite the potential benefits, the metaverse also presents challenges, including concerns over data privacy, the monopolization of platforms, and the risk of further reducing physical social interactions in favor of virtual ones. To ensure that the metaverse fosters innovation while minimizing risks, collaboration between tech companies, regulators, and users is essential. Standards and rules need to be developed in parallel with technological advancements to address issues like privacy, safety, and accessibility. To harness its full potential and minimize harm, the development of the metaverse should be guided by lessons learned from previous technological advances, involving a collaborative effort from all stakeholders, including industry leaders, regulators, and users.

NFTs and the metaverse are at the forefront of digital innovation, with the potential to reshape sectors as diverse as finance, education, and personal identity. These "digital space" challenge traditional legal frameworks, including constitutional law, by creating new environments where digital assets, such as NFTs, hold real-world value and implications. In the following we wish to explore the perspectives through which the so-called virtual space, even immersive like the metaverse, can be connected to the real space.

We believe it is important to consciously reflect on this point, asking which theory of space is best suited for the metaverse, using it as a laboratory to understand, more generally and in relation to other digital ecosystems such as artificial intelligence, the dynamics and distortions that may characterize how we approach spaces that appear disconnected from the physical ones. In reality, these spaces increasingly represent privileged places where not only our social interactions develop, but also the combination of voices and perspectives that form the genetic code of the public discourse.

7.1 Early Views: The Utopian vs *Dystopian Approaches*

A first theory of space that has been (and still is widely) used to address this topic is the dichotomy between utopian and dystopian approaches. This dichotomy, for instance, characterizes the debate over opportunities and risks of artificial intelligence. However, we deem that it is misleading as it constitutes one of the most dangerous traps one may falls into. The reason is that both approaches share a weakness: they view the "virtual" space—in this case, the metaverse—as entirely disconnected from the real world. An "elsewhere" that shares nothing with the tangible reality in which we live.

Drawing lessons from the past, the utopian approach prevailed in the debate over the nature of cyberspace: this new digital dimension promised a horizon of freedom, primarily from state control. It was an entirely disconnected space where the well-being and self-regulation of the emerging community were to be ensured. As time showed, this vision represented a big misunderstanding (of course easy to recognize in hindsight) of the nature of cyberspace.

Consider John Perry Barlow's 1996 Declaration of Independence of Cyberspace,[1] which solemnly addressed States in this way: "*Governments of the World, weary giants of flesh and steel, I come from Cyberspace, the new home of Mind. On behalf of the future, I ask you of the past to leave us alone. You are not welcome among us. You have no sovereignty where we gather.*"

National actors, in this vision, are elsewhere, unable to proclaim their sovereignty or extend the enforcement of legal norms into an idealized space as a separate territory.

More than twenty-five years later, it is easy to conclude that history has revealed a reality far different from what Barlow hoped for. And this is for at least two reasons. First, nation-states have shown not only that they can regulate but also "over-regulate" cyberspace, which, it is always worth remembering, is made up not only of bits but of physical infrastructure and underwater cables, thus an "atomic" dimension that is part of the analog world from which Barlow (self-)proclaimed an unrealistic independence. Consider how non-democratic regimes have managed to create Great Firewalls, as in the Chinese case and, more recently, the Russian one following the invasion of Ukraine, where virtual walls and strategies of disinformation and censorship have caused very real and significant injuries to the exercise of freedom of expression and the right to information.

[1] Barlow (1996).

The second reason for the slow decline of the utopian view, lies in the fact that what was supposed to be, according to Barlow's utopian vision, a new world free from constraints and powerful interests, where the user community would be able to self-regulate according to a common value framework, has turned out to be a space quite accessible to private powers. These powers have certainly influenced that process of self-determination by users, which was supposed to be the cornerstone upon which the space imagined by the web pioneers was built.

Due to the influence of these initial, in retrospect quite naive, positions, early commentators exploring the arrival of cyberspace and its legal consequences frequently referenced the difficulties that a global network capable of connecting individual users located in different jurisdictions and with virtual communities linked to various legal systems would pose for the claim of territorial control of activities and conduct, a core postulate of state sovereignty. Particularly in U.S. legal doctrine, there was an immediate recognition of a contrast between proponents of a cyber-anarchist vision and those who contested the normative and descriptive premises of this thesis. The positions opposing state regulation, possibly inspired by a "libertarian bias" inclined to view public regulation of "new" phenomena with suspicion, were based on the perceived superiority of self-regulation in cyberspace. This vision was influenced by certain challenges in applying rules conceived for a physical world and territorial boundaries, such as the uncertainty users might face in identifying the applicable rules within the various domains/sites where their conduct occurred (the absence of "notice").

These concerns, as we know, soon gave way to views not hostile to state regulation, which gained traction also due to early judicial decisions in the United States acknowledging that the peculiarities of cyberspace did not prevent conduct occurring within it from being governed by already existing legal standards developed to regulate the "world of matter." In fact, as noted in a study from many years ago, it was precisely the response of U.S. courts to the anarchic orientation first mentioned, by asserting their jurisdiction over cases involving Internet disputes, that confirmed the existence of "adjudicators" within a space previously thought immune to state intervention. This could suggest a somewhat paradoxical scenario where "*the area of Internet law, long considered the most emblematic expression of national law's limitations in facing globalization challenges, would, by contrast, prove to be one of the few fields of law still encapsulated in national law, where not only a global approach but even a transnational one may prove inadequate.*"

A third reason for the declining relevance of utopian theories that support cyberspace self-regulation is represented by the evident challenges posed by market evolution. If, initially, users could venture into "perfect competition" among virtual platforms-communities with their own rules—thus allowing for a competitive market arrangement to coexist with a similarly "free" one of self-imposed rules—today profound changes have altered this apparent linearity, creating an oligopolistic structure where undisturbed competition among community-based, self-imposed rules is unlikely to appeal to proponents of a cyber-anarchic approach. These ongoing transformations are even more systemic, as they involve not only antitrust tools (which are evolving in the new European framework, even allowing for ex ante intervention, unimaginable for competition law purists) but also the very tools and nature of constitutionalism, which must remain faithful to its genetic mission of limiting power, even when this power appears in variable shapes and arrangements.

An antithetical perspective to the utopian is the dystopian one. Both views share share the inclination to consider the metaverse in particular, and cyberspace in general, as a spatial dimension entirely disconnected from the physical, real, or atomic one. However, in dystopian views, the new digital context, whether the metaverse or, currently, artificial intelligence, is portrayed as the most terrifying and catastrophic possible space, often associated with an undefined existential risk. It is evident that this is another theory of space unhelpful for our purposes, as it amplifies a narrative of separation and disconnection between two environments (the physical one and the one "founded" by the technology in question) that are instead very close and often overlapping in terms of the exercise of identity and numerous fundamental rights of the individual/user. Additionally, this perspective fails to recognize the opportunities and benefits the new digital context could bring, instead dramatically magnifying risks and shadows.

7.2 A Second Perspective: The "Istopian" Approach

As an immediate response to the dystopian and utopian approaches described in the previous section, another perspective has emerged, particularly rooted in relevant American jurisprudence, not only from the Supreme Court. We could categorize this specific theory of space as isotopy, which allows the identification of a set of redundant semantic categories that enable a uniform narrative. Applied to our context, this means identifying a continuum, without any particular discontinuity, between physical space and virtual space.

Consider how in the United States, issues related to online content control have been addressed. Specifically, one of the main problems that legal scholars and other law practitioners had to face involved the risk that the network, thanks to its ease of access, would become a vehicle for prohibited or otherwise restricted content in the "real world," effectively creating a free zone that could evade the prohibitions imposed by the legal system. This problem is well illustrated by the famous narrative surrounding the cyberporn panic, which was the origin of the first attempt at cyberspace regulation, enacted in 1996 by Congress with the Communications Decency Act. This Act, besides regulating intermediaries for the first time, introduced certain restrictions on online access to manifestly offensive and indecent content, in response to the aforementioned concerns. The following year, the United States Supreme Court declared these provisions unconstitutional under the First Amendment, as they imposed excessive and disproportionate limitations on the constitutionally guaranteed right of adults to access explicit content. The *Reno v. ACLU* decision[2]

[2] SCOTUS, Reno v. ACLU, in 521 U.S. 844 (1997).

is noteworthy not only because it represents a bold defense of freedom of expression in the face of a significant interest like child protection, but also because it marked a development in understanding the new medium and its characteristics, recognizing the digital realm as possibly the space for realizing Justice Holmes' 1919 metaphor of the marketplace of ideas.[3]

In effect, using the isotopic parameter mentioned earlier, it simply applies to the new digital space those same characteristics foundational to physical space, in a perspective of complete continuity. Indeed, the decision in question defines the Internet as "the new free marketplace of ideas," effectively forcefully applying to this new virtual reality a metaphor conceived decades earlier for physical space.

That decision could not foresee that soon the digital reality would radically alter its characteristics, evolving into an oligopolistic dimension unknown at the time. Perhaps this still idealized and pluralistic view of the Internet—a medium that, according to the Supreme Court, was not seen as benefiting from content regulation any more than it would without a specific regulatory framework—may have influenced the case's outcome.

More recently, in the *Packingham* case,[4] the Supreme Court went even further than the "digital reissue" of the free marketplace of ideas coined in *Reno*, asserting that "*While in the past there may have been difficulty in identifying the most important places (in a spatial sense) for the exchange of views, today the answer is clear. It is cyberspace—the 'vast democratic forums of the Internet.*"

This firm stance, perhaps somewhat naïve and at times risky, draws an analogy between the classical agora of the physical world and the exchange of ideas that may (or may not) be guaranteed by the (less free) digital agora.

The aforementioned attempts to redefine the role of platforms, especially social networks, carry profound implications concerning the values at play in digital space, with which the new "powers" must inevitably engage. Equating a social network with a public service or a "State" is not a neutral operation, as it involves imposing a set of guarantees typically associated with the actions of public actors. While on paper, this operation could represent a step forward in terms of protection, it also conceals certain pitfalls. Specifically, subjecting private entities to the same standard of protection required of public actors could lead to complex consequences for certain European strategies, especially concerning content that is not illegal but may become subject to removal or other technical measures. It is no coincidence that Justice raised this concern in his concurring opinion in the *Packingham* case,[5] criticizing the overly casual language with which the Supreme Court opinion suggested that the Internet and social networks in particular constituted the new "public forum" of digital reality, without weighing the normative implications of this dictum.

More recent developments suggest a revisitation of the assumptions that previously underpinned this view. The notion that regulation could be detrimental and

[3] SCOTUS, Abrams v. United States, in 250 U.S. 616 (1919). See, specifically, Justice Holmes' *dissenting opinion*, 624 ss.

[4] SCOTUS Packingham v. North Carolina, in 582 U.S. ___ (2017).

[5] See fn 4.

result in outcomes affecting the degree of protection for freedom of expression seems to have given way to concerns over the exponential growth of influence over free speech wielded by digital giants, as exemplified by Justice Thomas's words.[6] There appears to be a growing fear that it is necessary to preserve free speech from the very actors operating on the web, who are no longer the competing virtual communities that initially populated it (capable of maximizing freedom of expression by providing alternative spaces) but rather a few powerful economic entities whose moderation standards affect a vast audience of users/individuals. Perhaps Thomas's words are a warning to "*save the First Amendment from digital platforms*." This may indicate the first cracks in the long-standing idea that cyberspace represented the achievement of a true marketplace of ideas. In reality, this is a metaphor no longer compatible with the digital landscape, where "private powers" have established themselves, rendering the marketplace of ideas not free, but rather conditioned by concentrations of power. Note that this refers not solely to economic power, which can be countered with competition law, but to private power that impacts the overall sustainability of the democratic system, for which the only effective tools are found within the arsenal of constitutional law.

It is evident that the spatial theories just described, while capturing certain aspects of the interconnections between physical space and virtual space, fall short either by excess or deficiency, since they either dramatically amplify the distances (utopia and dystopia) or they completely eliminate them (isotopy).

7.3 A New Perspective: Heteropia

Perhaps there is a third way linked to a spatial theory that may be better suited to the context and the interconnections of the metaverse. Specifically, Michel Foucault's concept of heterotopia[7] may be especially useful here, referring to those spaces with the unique characteristic of being connected to all other spaces but in such a way as to invert the set of relationships they themselves designate, reflect, or mirror. This definition is very useful because, on one hand, it brings out the connection between physical space and virtual space, which is a defining feature of this relationship, and on the other, it highlights the importance of the emergence of a new element capable of inverting power dynamics and perspectives of interconnection.

So, what is this inverting element in the context of Hetheropia?

It refers to the process of "transfiguration" that has characterized the major digital platforms, which have transformed from economic actors into true powers, with their own right, and the response this transformation demands of modern constitutionalism. To remain faithful to its original mission of limiting power, constitutionalism is now compelled to find new configurations for action with regard to the metavese. Specifically, the aforementioned inversion is also geometric, as it shifts

[6] See fn 3.

[7] Foucault (2000).

from the vertical geometry of the classic authority-versus-liberty relationship to a horizontal dimension. Here, the objective is to find the most appropriate tools to limit and contain the private power held by large tech platforms, while also relying the concept of digital sovereignty,.

To be clear, this is not the first time the issue of the relationship between public law and private power has arisen, nor is it the first time that private entities, in practice, regulate certain markets—consider sports federations, for example—with such influence over a particular economic sector that they hold, de facto, power in a broad political sense.

However, the discontinuity and thus the significance of private power in the new digital context stem from two reasons. The first is quantitative: the pervasiveness of digitalization, the mechanisms of algorithmic automation, and the vast amount of data available to define profiling processes and even anticipate user preferences have granted the major multinational digital corporations an unprecedented global influence. The second novelty is qualitative, if we may call it that way, as it affects the scope, pluralism, and freedom of public debate, as will be further examined. There has never been a situation like the one occurring in the digital realm. This is where private entities with such significant dominance over a particularly unique market—the "market of ideas", to paraphrase Holmes's legendary metaphor of the free marketplace of ideas—are able to influence public debate so effectively. For the major platforms, as has been argued recently, "*fostering a large community—similar to a public sphere—is key to the business model.*"[8]

Building on Habermas,[9] there is a need to recreate the conditions and prerequisites for a functioning public sphere within the digital ecosystem and the metaverse. This is noteworthy because, evidently, it intertwines with the issue of power concentration in the hands of private entities (which, as noted, often exercise quasi-constitutional functions in practice).

Balkin[10]'s aspiration suggesting an idealistic model of a digital public sphere where social media—private entities primarily operating according to market logic—should voluntarily, at least regarding the U.S. context, pursue semi-public objectives seems rather optimistic, bordering on unrealistic. In Balkin's view, social media private platforms should facilitate public participation in politics, culture, and the arts; second, they should organize a public forum on the web to encourage the exchange of ideas; and third, they should take care of the ways in which public conversation is conducted and moderated.

It is hard to imagine this scenario becoming a reality, especially since, as mentioned earlier, we are witnessing a phenomenon largely in the opposite direction: the dissolution of social formations, at least the traditional ones, in cyberspace, with all the negative consequences that the absence of intermediation by intermediate communities can have on the exercise of power (and its abuse) and the weakening of the individual's position, who is increasingly immersed in the Internet in a context

---

[8] Maduro and de Abreu Duarte (2021) (Last accessed 1 April 2025).

[9] Habermas (1991).

[10] Balkin (2020).

of individualism, but also of solitude, ultimately making them more vulnerable to power, whether public or private.

From this perspective, the analogies the Supreme Court has drawn between the space controlled by private entities on the Internet and the classic public forum, the cradle of public discourse in the analog context, are quite delicate and, in many respects, controversial, especially if such metaphorical language is to be given prescriptive and not merely descriptive weight.

References

Balkin M (2020) *How to regulate (and not regulate) social media,* Knight Institute, *Occasional Paper Series* 1, New York NY

Barlow JP (1996) A declaration of the independence of cyberspace. EFF, Davos

Foucault M (2000) Spazi altri. I luoghi delle eterotopie. Mimesis, Milano

Habermas J (1991) The public sphere. In: Mukerji C, Schudson M (eds) Rethinking popular culture. Contemporary perspectives in cultural studies. University of California Press, Berkeley/Los Angeles, pp 398–404

Maduro MP and de Abreu Duarte F (2021) Regulating big tech will take pluralism and institutions, 07 October. https://www.euronews.com/2021/10/07/regulating-big-tech-will-take-pluralism-and-institutions-view

NFTs and Metaverse: Definitions, Governance and Constitutional Issues

Navigating Virtual Words, the European Way

Roberto Viola and Filomena Chirico

Abstract The online experience as we know it is changing rapidly. The real and the virtual will merge as never experienced before and become intertwined. The concept of virtual worlds is not new, but only now has it become both technically feasible and economically interesting, especially for tech giants. This paper explains and discusses the European Union's approach to virtual worlds, augmented reality and the "Metaverse". The EU's objective is to ensure that private incentives to innovate develop freely by embedding from the outset the rules and values that are fundamental to our societies. In this context, interoperability and open standards remain key to this vision. By the same token, enhanced attention from regulators is needed to avoid replicating in the new "virtual world" the problems that have impacted the current online experience. Fortunately, the EU has already modernised its regulatory system for the supervision of very large platforms and gatekeepers with the Digital Services Act and Digital Markets Act.

1 Introduction

The metaverse has been at the centre of attention in recent times not only as the next big thing which big tech companies were fast to jump on, but also the one to which regulators were looking to square the circle between promised opportunities and the various doubts as to how it would be developed: Whether it would be an open

The authors are, respectively, Director-General of the Directorate-General for Communication Networks, Content and Technology at the European Commission and Head of Unit for Digital Markets at the same Directorate-General. The views and the opinions expressed in the article belong solely to the authors and do not necessarily reflect the view of the European Commission.

R. Viola · F. Chirico (✉)
Directorate-General for Communication Networks, Content and Technology, European Commission, Brussels, Belgium
e-mail: filomena.chirico@ec.europa.eu

R. Viola
e-mail: roberto.viola@ec.europa.eu

F. Di Porto and O. Pollicino (eds.), *Law and Politics of Virtual Worlds*, Law, Governance and Technology Series 79, https://doi.org/10.1007/978-3-032-08541-2_2

world, whether there would be one or many virtual worlds etc. In September 2022, European Commission President Ursula von der Leyen, announced on the occasion of her State of the European Union address[1] a new initiative on 'virtual worlds', those worlds that compose the Metaverse. It is indeed logical that we do not talk about a new world, but rather about many new worlds that will replace today's virtual reality on the internet.

This new reality will be a very different one from what we know today. Today's internet is still predominantly bi-dimensional. While we are already talking about 'web 3.0' as a projection of the experience of browsing as we know it, with an augmented reality built on top of the current web content and experience, the future 'web 4.0' connecting all those virtual worlds will have a more transformative impact on our reality and on our capabilities as humans. The future web 4.0 will create a virtual dimension in which everything and everyone will have a digital version of themselves, a faithful reproduction based on an unprecedented amount of data representing an individual, an entity, a landmark building or a machine: Their 'digital twin'.

In the future web 4.0 the expectation is that the real and the virtual will merge as never experienced before, with a set of digital twins that will make it seamless to pass from the digital experience to the real and back, with a range of very significant consequences in many important areas of our lives – from medicine to learning, engineering, finance and complex systems. The real world and the digital world are becoming intertwined and indivisible.

While the concept of virtual worlds is not new, only now has it become technically feasible and economically interesting. It is therefore not surprising that the European Heads of State and Governments, at the March European Council called for the European Union to stay at the forefront of Web 4.0 development.[2] The European Commission responded to this call in July presenting a new strategy for Europe[3] outlining the steps to be taken to reap the new opportunities while anticipating and mitigating those risks that can be already foreseen.

2 The European Vision

The first generation of the Internet developed mostly in an uncoordinated and unregulated manner. This was the translation of the vision of the Internet of the 90s, as enshrined in John Perry Barlow's Declaration of the Independence of Cyberspace[4]:

[1] See https://state-of-the-union.ec.europa.eu/state-union-2022_en. Accessed February 18, 2026.

[2] European Council conclusions, 23 March 2023.

[3] Communication from the Commission to the European Parliament, the Council, the European Economic and Social Committee and the Committee of the Regions of 11.7.2023: *An EU initiative on Web 4.0 and virtual worlds: a head start in the next technological transition*, COM (2023) 442/ final,

[4] https://www.eff.org/cyberspace-independence. Accessed February 18, 2026.

a world that is both everywhere and nowhere, where identities may be distributed across many of jurisdictions, where legal concepts of property, expression, identity, movement, and context do not apply.

Fast forward 20 years and it is inevitable to acknowledge that despite laudable approaches and objectives of decentralisation and openness, we are faced with an online world where digital harassment and suppression of freedoms are not exceptional events, a world of closed ecosystems, with the prevalence of proprietary systems and corporate digital gatekeepers.

Against the reality of today's Internet, the EU is the first jurisdiction that recognised the need of a digital "constitutional" moment, to acknowledge the transformative impact of digital technologies on our society and reassert what should have been obvious but wasn't: that people's rights and our societies' fundamental principles apply also in the digital space. And this is the basis for having in the 2020s a rather different Declaration: the European declaration on digital rights and principles.[5]

To be sure, Europe's engagement with the digital world has started even before the Declaration. The EU has already taken bold steps and introduced a new groundbreaking horizontal framework to control and curb the most egregious violations of rights online and to reestablish a safe, open and fair digital environment. Yet this came after many concerns and issues had manifested themselves. With new developments coming via immersive technologies, metaverses and web 4.0, Europe is committed to shape this next frontier at the outset, embedding Europe's digital rights and principles in the new worlds *from the beginning* and preventing, rather than correcting, abuses and unfairness. The European vision is one of virtual worlds that are open, trustful and secure, where the rule of law – and not the rule of the algorithm – reigns and with the ultimate objective to give everyone a fair chance to participate and to reap the emerging opportunities.

3 The Metaverse in Concrete

If we look more in detail into the ongoing and expected developments in the virtual worlds, many new technologies and applications are already being developed in various societally important areas such as health and education as well as in various industrial sectors such as automotive, manufacturing or logistics. One of the authors already referred to this ongoing evolution as *ambient computing,*[6] a seamless integration of computational elements in an environment where everything is interconnected, which allows the intelligent management of the environment in which the user is immersed. Building a workplace with both ergonomic and sustainable features would be mainly a task for intelligent robots, a medical check could be performed

[5] https://digital-strategy.ec.europa.eu/en/policies/digital-principles. Accessed February 18, 2026.

[6] Roberto Viola and Luca De Biase "Il codice del futuro. La carta europea dei diritti digitali e il senso dell'innovazione", Il Sole 24 Ore – Norme e Tributi 2023.

on the perfectly accurate digital twin of an individual, programmable payments for spare parts of a machine could be triggered and performed by the machine itself.

The potential of the developments just briefly sketched above is very significant. Even if as of today there is not yet a "killer" application, i.e. a use case triggering a paradigm shift, it is clear already that as more content and applications are offered, more and more people will find it interesting and useful to engage with it. In virtual-real worlds, citizens will have the chance to become increasingly active in democratic life – provided that they do not experience the threats to their freedom that are unfortunately common in today's online life. Companies, large and small, will have new opportunities to develop innovative content, products and services – provided the space is not controlled and limited by old or new private gateways to the virtual worlds. Public authorities and governments may provide public services in areas such as health and education, and foster scientific research or actions to control climate change through infrastructures in the metaverses – provided sufficient data are made publicly available for the pursuit of the public interest.

While all of this has an obvious societal value, it also brings with it clear commercial interests. With an estimated growth in size of the global market for virtual worlds to over €800 billion by 2030[7] and over 860.000 jobs to be created around Extended Reality Technologies (XR) in next couple of years,[8] the impact that virtual worlds are going to have on the economic incentives of private companies cannot be underestimated. In particular, the same type of incentives we have seen in the bi-dimensional Internet may likely emerge to create private systems and proprietary solutions or to relax the needs of control and protection of rights, with the objective of boosting growth and profits.

The EU's objective is to ensure that private incentives to innovate and expand in the virtual worlds are nourished and develop freely by embedding from the outset the rules and values that are fundamental to our societies.

Let us look at some examples of how the new technological developments relevant for the metaverse interact already with the existing European regulatory framework.

First, as new markets open up for virtual goods and services, there are relevant implications as regards for example the interaction between new marketplaces offering this new type of goods and services and the rights attached to these virtual objects, perhaps through non-fungible tokens (NFTs), QR codes, ledgers or other technologies that have not yet been invented.

The very nature of these goods – i.e. their interconnection at a global level – raises questions of property law, the issue of jurisdiction, the role of competent authorities and the applicable law.

NFTs, ledgers and similar technologies have already transformed the way digital assets are owned and exchanged by creating a unique proof of ownership for digital assets, which are themselves unique. These technologies have numerous potential

---

[7] https://www.bloomberg.com/professional/insights/data/metaverses-80-billion-etf-assets-by-2024-virtually-a-reality/. Accessed February 18, 2026.

[8] VR/AR Industrial Coalition – Strategic paper, available at https://data.europa.eu/doi/10.2759/197536. Accessed February 18, 2026.

applications in the metaverse. Proof of ownership will have an enormous importance for assets that only exist in a digital form: virtual land, virtual objects, and – with growing importance already today – digital art.

All digital assets in the metaverse including products, services and any other items could be attached to an NFT. In this context, NFTs – and the items to which they are attached – may fulfil different functions and thus be looked at from different perspectives, from intellectual property protection, online platforms supervision or financial markets regulation. If a non-fungible token represents a bond, the token could qualify as investment instrument[9]; if such emerging NFTs marketplaces were to trade in crypto assets, they would be covered by the relevant European legislation,[10] while if they were to "sell" NFTs in exchange of ordinary or digital currencies, they would be subject to the same obligations as ordinary online marketplaces selling physical goods.

Moreover, in virtual worlds where everything may become tokenised with fungible, nonfungible, hybrid or composable-NFT tokens, a new economy might be generated focusing on NFT markets and creators. Here again, the question of whether decentralised and interoperable services will prevail rather than traditional and centralised systems, or a mixture of the two systems.

In this context, whatever the model, the European vision is and will remain one where interoperability and open standards are key, enabling the seamless use of identities, avatars, data, virtual assets and experiences as well as the associated rights across platforms and networks.

Second, as people interact in an increasingly immersive way in the virtual worlds, such digital interactions are likely to take an even more personal and enhanced nature than today – approaching and mixing with the physical experience. Algorithms influencing people's choices and behaviours will be much more pervasive than in the current context: Machines that control other machines that control other machines and compute and interact with each other.

By the same token, illegal activities and content, identity thefts, cyber bullying and harassment may thus have an even larger impact than today, especially on children, on vulnerable users or minorities.

Against an existing lively ecosystem of start-ups and innovators in the most advanced technological elements or in sectoral areas, such as online gaming, big technology conglomerates are positioning themselves in regard to the metaverse and new artificial intelligence systems and are already investing the enormous capital they are able to mobilise in order to occupy this space.

Fortunately, the EU has already modernised its regulatory system for two-dimensional digital technologies which appears largely fit also for the developments

---

[9] So-called MiFID II, Directive 2014/65/EU of the European Parliament and of the Council of 15 May 2014 on markets in financial instruments and amending Directive 2002/92/EC and Directive 2011/61/EU.

[10] So-called "MiCA" Regulation (EU) 2023/1114 of the European Parliament and of the Council of 31 May 2023 on markets in crypto-assets, and amending Regulations (EU) No 1093/2010 and (EU) No 1095/2010 and Directives 2013/36/EU and (EU) 2019/1937, *OJ L 150, 9.6.2023, p. 40–205.*

we are observing: the new rules for the supervision of very large platforms and gatekeepers, the Digital Markets Act[11] and Digital Services Act[12] were conceived from the start as a horizontal and future-proof legislations which can also apply to the three-dimensional and to the four-dimensional Internet, ensuring protection from illegal content, a fairer system that does not only favour large players, enhanced transparency of algorithms and so on.

For the first time, supervision of the biggest digital intermediaries is centralised at the European level, to leverage the weight of a single market of 27 countries and joining forces with digital regulators across the Union. While the first enforcement actions are already ongoing, particular attention will be devoted to emerging trends and behaviours.

In this context, it is worth mentioning also the new European Digital Identity system[13] – the basis for an interconnected public European e-wallet. Also this system has been designed with this evolution in mind: to offer to all individuals a unique and secure way to prove their identity, to give everyone full control over their most personal data, controlling how much information they want to share when they are interested in being part of an online experience. In other words, putting in the hands and under the control of each of us the key to our "digital twin".

4 Conclusion

As the Internet of the 90 s, today virtual worlds and the metaverse are bringing about yet another landmark change to the way we live our lives and opening up new avenues for both personal and economic development.

Compared to the past, Europe has a vision of the expectations and benefits stemming from digital developments and has modern and future-proof regulatory instruments aimed to increase trust in technologies, to offer to everyone fair chances online and to reassure everyone that our rights and values will be respected in all dimensions of the online worlds. The journey is only at the beginning. These tools can (and must) be applied and if needed adapted to put the web in four dimensions at the service of all Europeans.

[11] Digital Markets Act Regulation (EU) 2022/1925 of the European Parliament and of the Council of 14 September 2022 on contestable and fair markets in the digital sector and amending Directives (EU) 2019/1937 and (EU) 2020/1828, in *OJ L 265, 12.10.2022, p. 1–66.*

[12] Notably the Digital Services Act Regulation (EU) 2022/2065 of the European Parliament and of the Council of 19 October 2022 on a Single Market for Digital Services and amending Directive 2000/31/EC in *OJ L 277, 27.10.2022, p. 1–102.*

[13] https://commission.europa.eu/strategy-and-policy/priorities-2019-2024/europe-fit-digital-age/european-digital-identity_en. Accessed February 18, 2026.

The Metaverse: Interoperability as Governance

Fabiana Di Porto and Daniel Foà

Abstract Interoperability is what allows different systems to communicate, both on technological (e.g. hardware and software) and societal grounds (i.e., to connect users' experiences over internet or ease collaboration between institutions). To achieve the seamless exchange of information, interoperability entails the establishment of standards and technical requirements that could either be realized through spontaneous efforts by market participants or imposed by the law.

Building on the assumption that technical specifications are key to make interoperability happen, this chapter aims to show that interoperability plays a fundamental role in realizing the metaverse and shaping its governance.

More specifically, we show that interoperability is the watershed between existing walled virtual worlds (i.e., the building blocks of the metaverse), and a mature, fully-functioning metaverse. Even more, interoperability contributes to define the very governance of virtual environments and the markets the metaverse creates. Hence, striking a balance between industry-defined standards and regulatory intervention is essential to define a good governance.

The paper is the result of a common effort by the authors. However, Fabiana Di Porto drafted Sections 1, 2.1, 5 and 6.2 while Daniel Foà Sections 2.2, 3, 4 and 6.1. The authors contributed equally to the Conclusion

---

F. Di Porto (✉) · D. Foà
University of Rome UnitelmaSapienza, Rome, Italy
e-mail: fabiana.diporto@unitelmasapienza.it

University of Bari "Aldo Moro", Bari, Italy

D. Foà
e-mail: daniel.foa@uniba.it

F. Di Porto and O. Pollicino (eds.), *Law and Politics of Virtual Worlds*, Law, Governance and Technology Series 79, https://doi.org/10.1007/978-3-032-08541-2_3

1 Introduction

The notion of interoperability is multifaceted and not clearly defined, being it relevant in different areas and for diverse purposes.[1] The European Commission has elaborated the concept in both legal frameworks and policy documents. However, the idea behind interoperability is not new, nor is it confined to technical and digital realms only.

In nature, there are many examples of interoperability: for instance, animals have developed the ability to change their biological properties to make communication with peers possible. Chameleons are one of those. They can manipulate the distance between nanocrystals encapsulated in their skin to change their color, from a darker to a lighter one. Besides camouflage, these different colors serve to communicate: brighter colors display aggression to other chameleons, while darker ones mean the intention to submit or "give up". Without such biological changes, chameleons would not possibly interact with each other.

Unlike animals, humans employ language to communicate. While a phenomenal tool, language falls short to make people speaking different idioms communicate. As the Italian novelist Italo Calvino once penned: "*The limit between two languages is a wall that cannot be crossed*".[2] Translation is thus the type of interoperability people speaking different languages use to communicate.[3]

We have notable examples of interoperability in fine arts too. The famous statue Apollo and Daphne by Antonio Canova displays the nymph turning herself into a tree so to make her non-interoperable with the god, thus escaping his sexual assault.

The specific definition of interoperability may vary depending on the context and the exact legal document being considered. Definitions exist that are either sector-specific or general in nature. They stress especially the technical layer of interoperability, since they either identify it as the ability to share and reuse IT solutions, thus allowing different IT systems to work together seamlessly, or they see it as a means to achieve data exchange.[4] In this latter sense, interoperability is understood

---

[1] For an overview of the definitions of interoperability adopted in the literature, see Bourreau et al. (2022, p. 13 ff.); Berg (2024, pp. 1–5).

[2] Calvino (1972, p. 54). The same concept is expressed in his novel "If on a Winter's Night a Traveler" (purporting that language is a barrier between people, and that it is ultimately impossible for two languages to truly understand and communicate with one another). "*We were two tongues that could not understand one another, two languages that could not be translated, two words that could not be made to mean the same thing.*" Calvino (1979, p. 33).

[3] Same Calvino said: «*Without translation, I would be limited to the borders of my own country. The translator is my most important ally. He introduces me to the world*»: Interview with I. Calvino, The NYT Magazine, 10.07.1983, Sect. 6, p. 23.

[4] See European Commission (2017a, p. 4) which reads "'sharing and reuse' of IT solutions is a necessary condition for interoperability to apply in practice in a Digital Single Market, where citizens and businesses can seamlessly access public services and undertake activities online". It echoes the definitions in the doctrine that considers interoperability as the ability to make two systems interact with each other, through the definition of standards: Berg (2024, pp. 1–5); Farrell and Saloner, (1985, pp. 70–83).

in the overly-famous GDPR,[5] which Article 20 grants data portability: in fact, portability inherently requires interoperability between systems to facilitate the transfer of personal data across service providers.

Early sectorial definitions can be found in network regulation, such as energy, telecom and satellite networks. For instance, the European Electronic Communications Code (EECC) conceives interoperability as the ability of different electronic communications networks and services to work together seamlessly, regardless of the technologies used (Recitals 144 and ff., Article 39).[6] Technological neutrality is also required for satellite systems by Article 2(1) of Regulation (EU) 2021/696,[7] as well as for electricity systems by Article 18(1) of Regulation (EU) 2019/943.[8] Article 20(1) of Directive (EU) 2019/944 on wholesale energy markets[9] adds two more features to interoperability, namely: the exchange between IT systems requires data to flow "*in a standardised and automated manner*", hinting that standardization should couple interoperability efforts, and that the outcome of such standards should be a transfer of data that does not require human intervention to work.

In all the above-mentioned cases, interoperability is an intermediate step to achieve better accessibility of services, as well as market competitiveness.[10] In other words, the rationale pursued by regulation is always pro-competitive, and aimed at favoring switching by customers. More sectoral rules have been established in the context of the EU digital strategy (e.g., in the Digital Services Act[11] and the Digital Markets Act[12]) and EU data strategy (namely: the Data Act[13] and Data Governance Act[14]). Albeit resulting in a fragmented set-up, such provisions are an unquestionable starting point for establishing what interoperability is.

Concerning definitions of general nature, the European legislator has over time repeatedly intervened on interoperability, making it a principle of good governance.

---

[5] See Regulation (EU) 2016/679 of 27 April 2016 General Data Protection Regulation (GDPR), in OJ L 119, 4.5.2016, see Recital (68).

[6] Directive (EU) 2018/1972 of 11 December 2018 establishing the European Electronic Communications Code, OJ L 321, 17.12.2018.

[7] Regulation (EU) 2021/696 of 28 April 2021 establishing the Union Space Programme and the European Union Agency for the Space Programme, OJ L 170, 12.5.2021.

[8] Regulation (EU) 2019/943 of 5 June 2019 on the internal market for electricity, OJ L 158, 14.6.2019.

[9] Directive (EU) 2019/944 of 5 June 2019 on common rules for the internal market for electricity and amending Directive 2012/27/EU, OJ L 158, 14.6.2019.

[10] Pflücke (2023, p. 270 ff).

[11] Regulation (EU) 2022/2065 of 19 October 2022 on a Single Market for Digital Services and amending Directive 2000/31/EC (Digital Services Act), OJ L 277, 27.10.2022.

[12] Regulation (EU) 2022/1925 of 14 September 2022 on contestable and fair markets in the digital sector and amending Directives (EU) 2019/1937 and (EU) 2020/1828 (Digital Markets Act), OJ L 265, 12.10.2022.

[13] Regulation (EU) 2023/2854 of 13 December 2023 on harmonised rules on fair access to and use of data and amending Regulation (EU) 2017/2394 and Directive (EU) 2020/1828 (Data Act), OJ L, 2023/2854, 22.12.2023.

[14] Regulation (EU) 2022/868 of 30 May 2022 on European data governance and amending Regulation (EU) 2018/1724 (Data Governance Act), OJ L 152, 3.6.2022.

In the context of public affairs and public services, in fact, interoperability means the ability of institutions to work together seamlessly. For instance, Article 67(3) TFEU sees interoperability as a means to "*contribute to a high level of security within the area of freedom, security and justice of the Union, including the maintenance of public security and public policy, and safeguarding security in the territories of the Member States*".[15]

The most recent application of interoperability as a principle of inter-institutional collaboration can be found in the European Interoperability Framework (EIF) 2017,[16] where the concept becomes key for establishing European public services across Member States. In this framework, interoperability is the "*Ability of organisations to interact towards mutually beneficial goals, involving the sharing of information and knowledge between these organisations, through the business processes they support, by means of the exchange of data between their ICT systems*". The EIF outlines interoperability as encompassing legal, organizational, semantic, and technical layers and provides 47 recommendations for public administrations to ensure effective interoperability of their digital services.[17] The adoption of EIF marks a decisive step forward in the definition of a common ground for interoperability among public services, that is suitable for promoting greater investment while realizing increased efficiency.

More recently, new (and more far reaching) rules on interoperability have been adopted in the context of the Interoperable Europe Act,[18] a regulation aimed at facilitating cross-border data exchange, with the goal of achieving a full digitalization of key public services by 2030. Complementary to EIF policy is regulation of electronic identity tools: Article 11a of the eIDAS 2.0 Regulation ensures cross-border interoperability of electronic identification schemes between Member States, which are vital for the provision of public services.[19]

---

[15] https://home-affairs.ec.europa.eu/policies/schengen-borders-and-visa/interoperability_en (Last accessed 30 April 2025).

[16] See European Commission (2017b, p. 3 ff).

[17] On legal Interoperability see https://joinup.ec.europa.eu/interoperable-europe/legal-interoperability (Last accessed 30 April 2025). Other legal and policy instruments that collectively frame the European Union's approach to ensuring interoperability in the digital public sector further include: (1) Directive (EU) 2019/1024 of 20 June 2019 on open data and the re-use of public sector information (OJ L 172, 26.6.2019), which aims at making public sector data interoperable, open, and accessible across borders within the EU (see esp. Article 5 encouraging the use of open standards and formats to ensure data interoperability); and (2) the eGovernment Action Plan 2016–2020, which outlines how interoperability should facilitate cross-border digital services within the Digital Single Market (European Commission 2016).

[18] Regulation (EU) 2024/903 of 13 March 2024 laying down measures for a high level of public sector interoperability across the Union (Interoperable Europe Act), OJ L, 2024/903, 22.3.2024, noting that "*The existing informal cooperation should be replaced by a clear legal framework to enable interoperability across different administrative levels and sectors and to facilitate seamless cross-border data flows for truly European digital services that strengthen the internal market.*" (Recital (1)).

[19] Regulation (EU) 2024/1183 of 11 April 2024 amending Regulation (EU) No 910/2014 as regards establishing the European Digital Identity Framework, OJ L, 2024/1183, 30.4.2024.

What is noticeable of the EIF is the prominent role it gives to the Interoperable Europe Board,[20] a body composed of representatives from Member states and the EU Commission charged to facilitate strategic cooperation and to drive the further development of cross-border interoperability in the Union. In its capacity, the Board can request the Interoperable Europe Community (a network of public and private stakeholders, civil society organizations and academics) to contribute by providing expertise and advice.[21] This governance set-up has yet to prove capable of achieving results; however it is worth noticing as it has established organizations tasked with fostering interoperability among public institutions, which are complex subjects.

Overall, the above definitions highlight five key elements of interoperability: (1) seamless operation, where systems should work together without significant technical barriers; (2) technological neutrality, meaning that interoperability should not be dependent on the specific technologies employed; (3) data exchange, whereby the ability to exchange information between systems is essential; (4) standardization, meaning that the use of common standards can facilitate interoperability; and (5) institutional capacity-building principle, meaning that interoperability applies to social interaction among institutions becoming a building block of good governance.

At the same time, such interoperability schemes have limitations, in that they are targeted at the public sector only. As per the private one, the only relevant EU provisions are those of the European Regulation on standardization..[22] The latter relies on three Standard Setting Organizations (SSOs)[23] to establish European standards. In such regard, the Commission can request that one or more of these SSOs draft either a European standard or European standardization deliverable within a set deadline, determining the content requirements to be met and a deadline for its adoption. The elaboration of standards is market-driven, thus falling in a mandated self-regulation scheme,[24] given that the SSOs are private actors representing the industry. The EU Commission is only tasked to assess if the standards drafted by the said SSOs meet its initial requests. If this is not the case, it can (Art. 11) raise formal objections to harmonized standards and – possibly – request their revision. However, this power is subject to a significant procedural constraint, which undermines its effectiveness: the Commission does not hold the capacity to make its own independent assessment. Instead, it is up to a Member State or the European Parliament, who consider that a harmonized standard does not entirely satisfy the requirements to inform the Commission thereof. Only at that stage, the Commission can, after consulting the committee set up by the corresponding Union harmonization legislation, or after

---

[20] Art. 15 Interoperable Europe Act.

[21] Art. 16 Interoperable Europe Act.

[22] Regulation (EU) 2022/2480 of 14 December 2022 amending Regulation (EU) No 1025/2012 as regards decisions of European standardisation organisations concerning European standards and European standardisation deliverables, OJ L 323 of 19/12/2022, 1–3.

[23] The Commission can ask three SSOs to develop standards to support EU legislation and policy: the European Telecommunications Standards Institute (ETSI), the European Committee for standardisation (CEN), and the European Committee for Electrotechnical Standardisation (CENELEC).

[24] Ayres and Braithwaite (1992).

other forms of consultation of sectoral experts, take the decision not to publish, to withdraw or maintain the standards with restrictions. Evidently, this is a very cumbersome process (likely to delay the adoption of standards) that gives a lot of power to political bodies (Member States and the EU Parliament) and the stakeholders participating in the SSOs. Alongside these procedural pitfalls, there is also a lack of authority of the EC to verify the actual compliance with the developed standards: because the standards are incorporated into EU legislation, it is the latter to establish the compliance schemes. Most often, the assessment of compliance is in the hands of national certification bodies, which are, again, private actors.

What is lacking is a strong framework where standards are set and their enforcing authorities clearly identified. To understand why it is so important for the private sector to have rules and authorities entrusted with strong powers to boost interoperability within the EU, we use the example of the metaverse, a network of interconnected and interoperable virtual worlds[25] that coincides with the web 4.0[26] and allows the seamless movement of digital assets[27] from one platform to another.

After setting the stage and defining the metaverse by using a three-phase approach (Sect. 2), this chapter investigates what type of interoperability should be pursued for what layers that make up the metaverse (Sect. 3). We then analyze the existing legal framework, made of both antitrust and regulation, to see how it affects interoperability in the metaverse (Sect. 4). After assessing if the current frameworks are fit for the challenges the metaverse poses (Sect. 5), we turn to the question of how interoperability for the metaverse should be designed to ensure its good governance, and who are the actors that should take the lead of standardization initiatives (Sect. 6). Section 7 concludes.

[25] According to the Commission, virtual worlds are "Persistent, 3D, real-time, immersive environments, blurring the line between real and virtual, for socialising, working, learning, making transactions, playing and creating", European Commission (EC 2023c, at 3).

[26] Defined as "4th generation of the World Wide Web where physical and digital worlds are seamlessly blending, enabling more intuitive and immersive experiences. Making use of advanced artificial and ambient intelligence, internet of things, virtual worlds and extended reality capabilities, web, real objects and environments are fully integrated and communicating between each other through more collaborative, decentralised and user-centered approaches" (Ibid. fn. 25).

[27] In such a technological environment, among the pursued objectives is the transfer of assets between 'worlds', even if they are managed by different entities, guaranteeing minimum levels of user experience and non-degradation of the transferred assets.

2 Why Interoperability is Essential for the Metaverse

2.1 *Defining the Metaverse*

As of today, no consensus exists on how to define the metaverse.[28] Early definitions[29] frame virtual worlds (a term that the scholarship often uses as a substitute for the metaverse) as a user experience that is: (1) immersive[30] and three-dimensional (3D); (2) synchronous (or real-time)[31] and persistent.[32]

At the core of those definitions lies the blending of real and virtual realities, the degree of which varies depending on the enabling technologies by which they are powered (captured under the 'extended reality', or XR label).[33] These key elements, however, are still not enough to distinguish it from its building blocks: the virtual worlds. Policymakers at the regional and global levels[34] have in fact acknowledged that interoperability across networked platforms managing virtual worlds constitutes a distinguishing third characteristic. Hence, pursuing interoperability is not just a matter of exchanging data among platforms, but is essential to build a fully-functioning metaverse, through the connection of its parts (the virtual worlds).

The European Commission's definitions of virtual worlds and metaverse adopt a three-phased approach. Broadly, the EC defines virtual worlds as "*persistent, immersive environments, based on technologies including 3D and extended reality (XR), which make it possible to blend physical and digital worlds in real-time, for a variety of purposes such as designing, making simulations, collaborating, learning, socialising, carrying out transactions or providing entertainment*".[35] The metaverse,

[28] For a comprehensive literature review, see Di Porto and Foà (2023, p. 8 ff).

[29] (Ibid, fn 28).

[30] It refers to the type of experience that virtual worlds enable and is composed of: in-web presence, indicating the idea that virtual worlds may enable experiences not "in front of the web" but "within the web", and sensoriality. See Balcerak Jackson and Balcerak Jackson (2024, p. 18 ff).

[31] It refers to the ability of virtual environments to allow users to communicate and interact in real time, or in ways that make them feel as if they were in a common environment; for instance, in medical rehabilitation, patients experience greater proximity with their care givers. Different devices and technologies allow for diversified degrees of synchronicity. See Tarr et al. (2018, p. 1 ff).

[32] Meaning that virtual worlds continue to evolve even when users are not connected to them, and the consequences of such evolution are perceived by/affect the user when connected again. See Allen (2022).

[33] On the notion of extended reality see also European Commission (2022b), passim.

[34] World Economic Forum WEF (2023, at 3): "The metaverse is an "immersive, interoperable and synchronous digital world" where interoperability is meant to enable "data to circulate via interoperable infrastructure, of participants to move themselves, their assets and creations across platforms and experiences".

[35] European Commission (2023b, p. 1). Instead, the European Commissio's (2023c) SWD's Glossary defines 'virtual worlds as "Persistent, 3D, real-time, immersive environments, blurring the

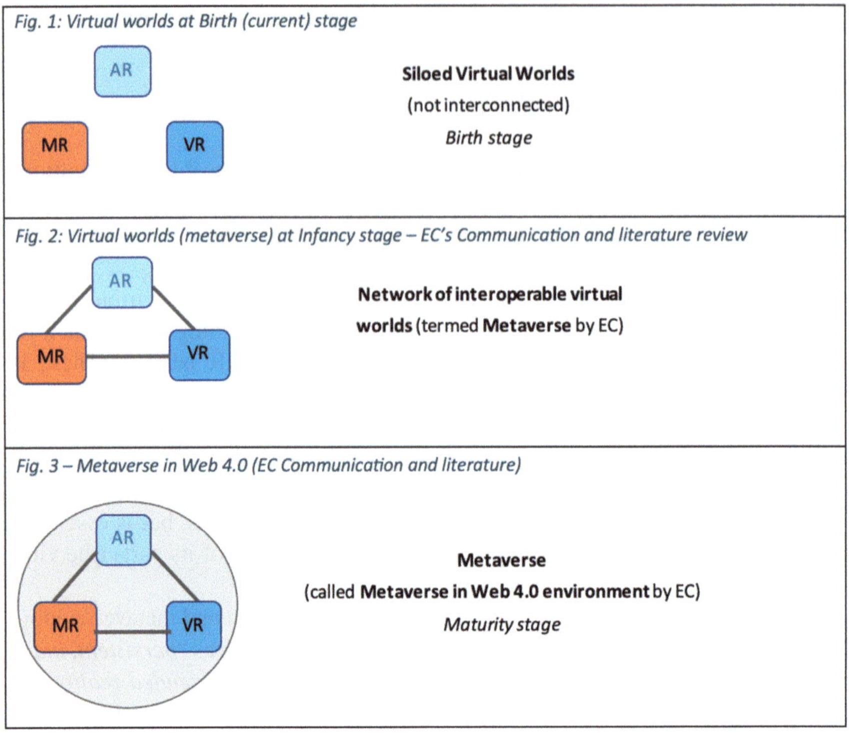

Fig. 1. Stages of development of virtual worlds. *Source* Di Porto, et al. (2024, CERRE Report, 10).

instead, is defined as "*Interoperable network of virtual worlds*".[36] From those definitions it results that interconnection and interoperability are effectively key, but they are associated to more mature stages of development of virtual worlds, rather than being a characteristic of present ones.

To make those definitions workable, it is possible to distinguish between three different stages of development of virtual worlds leading to the metaverse: Birth, Infancy and Maturity (see Fig. 1).

At Birth (the present stage), virtual worlds are siloed, and each allows for a given type of user experience, enjoying different degrees of immersivity, synchronicity, and persistence, enabled by state-of-the-art technologies.[37]

line between real and virtual, for socialising, working, learning, making transactions, playing and creating" (p. 87).

[36] See (European Commission 2023c, at 86) (Glossary).

[37] Those, include, e.g. include augmented reality (AR), virtual reality (VR), and mixed reality (MR), but not necessarily emerging ones (such as brain-computer interfaces).

The EC emphasizes the need to foster interoperability to create a "network of interconnected virtual worlds".[38] This network, that would mark the Infancy stage, is misleadingly labelled by the EC "the metaverse".[39] Not to mix up the two notions, we deem it preferable to term this Infancy phase simply as a network of interoperable virtual worlds, where interoperability should be fostered to enable "*the seamless use of identities, avatars, data, virtual assets, experiences or environments and the associated rights across platforms and networks*".[40] By accepting this distinction, virtual worlds can no longer be misunderstood or mixed-up with the metaverse, the latter being a development of the former.

Indeed, the EC identifies a third and more advanced stage, that we term Maturity, where – thanks to the realization of the Web 4.0[41] – infant virtual worlds will fully integrate in one environment that coincides with the next generation web.[42] Such integration allows a fully-functioning metaverse, and should be "*powered by open and highly distributed technologies and standards that enable interoperability between platforms and networks and freedom of choice for users*".[43] Hence, to achieve this fully-functioning metaverse, "*the Commission, in cooperation with Member States and stakeholders, will engage with key organisations active in the development of standards for open and interoperable virtual worlds and Web 4.0.*"[44] Table 1 summarizes these findings.

2.2 *Interoperability and the Metaverse*

As can be grasped from the above reasoning, to realize a truly unified user experience, in an interconnected system, globally accepted interoperability standards are needed.[45] This goal may be achieved all at once or through intermediate steps; even more importantly, it can be accomplished either through top-down initiatives or by market participants themselves developing standards.

---

38 European Commission (2023b, at 11).

39 European Commission (2023c, at 3).

40 European Commission (2023b, at 11).

41 European Commission (2023b, at 1): "virtual worlds are an important part of the transition to Web 4.0": "[...] the expected fourth generation of the World Wide Web". Using advanced artificial and ambient intelligence, the internet of things, trusted blockchain transactions, virtual worlds and XR capabilities, digital and real objects and environments are fully integrated and communicate with each other, enabling truly intuitive, immersive experiences, seamlessly blending the physical and digital worlds". Also policy papers emphasize the need to distinguish three phases of development of virtual worlds, that culminate in the Web 4.0-type of Metaverse. See Hupont Torres et al. (2023, p. 11 ff).

42 Trunfio and Rossi (2022, p. 103).

43 European Commission (2023b, at 4).

44 Ibid.

45 Morse and Stein (2022).

Table 1. Phases of development of virtual worlds

	BIRTH	INFANCY	MATURITY
TIMESPAN	NOWADAYS	MID RUN	LONG RUN
DEGREE OF INTERCONNECTION AND INTEROPERABILITY	Siloed virtual worlds	Interconnection/ interoperability of virtual worlds	Interconnected/ interoperable virtual worlds within one environment that coincides with the web
TERMINOLOGY EMPLOYED BY THE EC	Virtual worlds	Metaverse	Metaverse in Web 4.0
PREFERABLE TERMINOLOGY	Virtual worlds	Net of interconnected/ interoperable virtual worlds	Fully-functioning metaverse

As highlighted, the evolution of virtual worlds is marked with high uncertainty as to how and when they will materialize. Therefore, it is not yet clear what type of standards should be used, for what components of virtual worlds and who should make this happen.

While some industries can successfully function even if economic actors are completely isolated and do not have any (technical, semantic, etc.) communication mechanisms in place, in others their absence would impede the actual development of the market or cause a decisive detriment to its growth. The metaverse must undoubtedly be included in the latter category as interoperability is needed to make its layers work seamlessly: indeed, it is necessary for the proper functioning of communication networks and it is required to allow one asset to move freely from one 3D space to another (be it an avatar, a Non Fungible Token – NFT – an Artificial Intelligence (AI)-generated content). Its relevance is not limited to the technical side, though, it being necessary to increase social engagement, as people will participate and interact on a given virtual world if others also do so (network externalities).

Without interoperability, each virtual world would remain a walled garden and no network or unified metaverse would exist. Therefore, interoperability is central to its existence but also to its governance, to materialize and further develop.

For the metaverse to materialize all the involved players need to agree on a tremendous number of standards.[46] And because technology is evolving at a high speed and the path to the metaverse could last decades, the industry should keep collaborating for long time to go. Coopetition[47] may be key: in order to establish a functioning and successful metaverse, collaboration among competing firms is desirable, as the

[46] See e.g. the Metaverse Society; Open Metaverse Interoperability Group; Metaverse Standards Forum. References on the main standardisation initiatives are available at https://metaverserea lity.ieee.org/publications/newsletter/have-i-got-some-metaverse-standards-for-you (Last accessed 30 April 2025).

[47] See Brescia Morra and Vangelisti (2021, pp. 47–62).

metaverse is first of all a cooperative environment where enhanced experiences may exist only if sharing and mobility between virtual worlds is granted.

It follows that establishing interoperability standards equals to featuring the metaverse's very structure and governance.[48] Many variables must be taken into account, including who will be in charge of defining interoperability standards and, even before that, what layers and features they should cover.

3 Interoperability for What Layers of the Metaverse?

Looking at its most widespread value-chains, we can identify three layers composing virtual worlds[49]: (1) protocol infrastructure, which includes networks that provide connectivity, hardware devices for access (like VR headsets or smart glasses), and computing platforms; (2) software platform applications, like decentralized blockchain technologies, network engines, graphic engines and modelling platforms, as well as operating systems; and (3) user experience software applications, including the virtual worlds apps, virtual goods, digital identities (like avatars) and payments.

3.1 *The Protocol Infrastructure Layer*

Concerning the protocol infrastructure layer (1), today many big tech firms have developed their own visors and headsets functional to accessing and interacting within their virtual worlds. These operators often attempt to integrate their services within their own existing ecosystems for smartphones, suite of office tools (e.g. Microsoft)[50] or by attempting to leverage their dominance in the Web 2.0 to expand in other markets (e.g. Google).[51] The result of these moves may be a fragmented market made of competing ecosystems, that are managed by large tech companies. However, if common standards are developed, devices such as visors, virtual and voice assistants may become interoperable and therefore usable in different virtual worlds.

---

[48] This is the definition given also by Bushell (2022, p. 7).

[49] Cosenza (2022).

[50] There are many examples in which the EU Commission has found big tech companies to have adopted abusive conducts, e.g., Microsoft Teams (https://ec.europa.eu/commission/presscorner/detail/en/ip_24_3446) (Last accessed 30 April 2025) which has now reached the statements of objections phase.

[51] See Bundeskartellamt, B6-55/20, *Meta Quest/Meta,* November 2022; available at https://www.concurrences.com/IMG/pdf/23_11_2022_oculus.pdf?102923/6164e156275d3f4759fef721cc3374f498773b2fb64914f2d51b4fd6ad970f75 and, with specific regard to Google, see case AT.40099 Google Android (https://competition-cases.ec.europa.eu/cases/AT.40099) (Last accessed 30 April 2025).

3.2 The Software Platform Applications Layer

As per software platform applications (2), it is still uncertain whether a centralized or decentralized architecture will prevail. If a centralized one, then end-user contract terms will be relevant to establish interoperability, as well as IPRs. If a decentralized one, then we should consider that the underlying blockchain might encounter limitations if the number of transactions increases rapidly, potentially thwarting the effectiveness of interoperability.[52]

3.3 The (Software) User Experiences Applications

Lastly, software user experiences applications (3) include virtual worlds apps, virtual goods, identity schemes behind avatars and payments. The items included in this layer are those where the lack of interoperability is immediately perceived, as it directly affects users' experience and their perception of the value of their digital assets. Reaching a high degree of interoperability in this layer would allow a smooth transfer of goods, avatars and experiences between virtual worlds. At present, lacking proper interoperability between software apps, technical solutions have been developed to allow payments on platforms using cryptocurrencies different than the one promoted and used by the platform itself. This is possible thanks to wrapping of cryptocurrencies through a software on a specific network and then connect the crypto-wallet to an NFT sales portal.[53]

The distinction of virtual worlds in different layers highlights that spillover effects can exist that may hinder the transition towards the metaverse: for instance, tokens like skins for avatars created in one virtual world may lose quality if transferred to another one (where such transfer is technically possible). That would suggest that minimal quality standards for application graphics characteristics are desirable, so to ensure the smooth transfer of assets from one platform service to another. Instead, standards of this kind are not currently in place, nor do interoperability specifications exist allowing communication between different virtual worlds' operating systems, applications and devices.

Assuming that operators are in the best position to collaborate and set standards, how could public authorities help support the process? If no incentives exist for market participants to interoperate, should public authorities intervene? If so, when would that be desirable to avoid stiffing innovation while at the same time leading virtual worlds towards the metaverse? And what type of regulatory intervention should public authorities prefer?

---

[52] To counter this weakness, sidechains may be used.

[53] Moreover, today there are attempts to facilitate interoperability between blockchains (e.g., Cosmos, Lamina 1). On this topic, see Wang (2021).

4 European Law on Interoperability

In EU law, there are multiple legal sources aimed at promoting interoperability, which can be either horizontal or sectorial. First, the fundamental regime is set forth in the above-mentioned Regulation (EU) 2022/2480,[54] which however does not grant the EU Commission self-standing authority to elaborate or assess the standards produced by the SSOs and does not provide it with enforcement powers in relation to their correct implementation. More rules are established in the cited EIF, which however only applies to public administrations.

4.1 Regulation: The DMA and Data Act

In addition to those horizontal frameworks, sectoral regulatory disciplines exist which are relevant for digital markets, such as the DMA and the Data Act. Also EU competition rules apply that could result in interoperability being mandated on market participants. Antitrust enforcers can indeed impose interoperability as a remedy for anticompetitive behavior; at the same time, competition laws can limit undertakings' initiatives on standardization, as cooperative agreements could amount to a restriction of competition leading to foreclosure.

Considering this broad set of European regulations, we will analyze them in more detail, distinguishing between provisions pertaining to vertical and horizontal interoperability.[55] Vertical interoperability pertains to communication within one virtual world. In this regard, the DMA entrusts developers with the right to access operating systems and hardware capabilities of gatekeepers.[56] In particular, companies such as app or device developers, that use the services of a gatekeeper (such as an app store) to distribute their apps, must be able to access the relevant operating systems

[54] See fn 22.

[55] Bourreau et al. (2022, at 14 ff).

[56] To date, the large operators designated as gatekeepers under the DMA are: Alphabet (for the Google Play app store, maps and shopping services, the Chrome browser, advertising intermediation, the Android operating system, YouTube for video sharing and Google search for search engines), Amazon (for the marketplace and advertising intermediation), Apple (for the app store, the Safari browser and the iOS operating system), ByteDance (for the social network TikTok), Meta (for the social networks Facebook and Instagram, for messaging services messenger and WhatsApp, for advertising and commercial intermediation, through Meta Marketplace) and Microsoft (for the social network LinkedIn and the Windows operating system) (designated on 6 September 2023 (the decisions can be found at the following link: http://europa.eu/rapid/pressReleasesAction.do?reference=IP_23_4328). On 29 April 2024, the Commission also designated Apple as the gatekeeper for its tablet operating system (iPadOS) (see Decision: https://ec.europa.eu/commission/presscorner/detail/en/ip_24_2363). On May 13, 2024, Booking was also designated gatekeeper for the online intermediation service Booking.com (https://ec.europa.eu/commission/presscorner/detail/en/ip_24_2561). In total, twenty-four "core platform services" provided by these companies have been designated (Last accessed 30 April 2025).

of gatekeepers free of charge (Art. 6(4) DMA).[57] This is to allow developers to capitalize on network effects, i.e. to be able to take advantage of the user base present in the basic service of the gatekeeper (the app store) to be able to spread their own applications or devices.[58]

A further reference to interoperability is included in Art. 6(7) DMA, under which the gatekeeper is required to allow service and hardware providers to "*effective interoperability ... with the same hardware and software components accessible via operating system or virtual assistant ... that are available for the services or hardware provided by the gatekeeper*". Also in this case it is a question of vertical interoperability, and not horizontal, since third party access to software and hardware components is mandatory only if the gatekeeper uses them *for its own services or products.* In other words, interoperability operates only if the gatekeeper is vertically integrated, i.e. active both in the essential facility, or bottleneck (e.g., the operating system or the hardware and software components of a marketplace) and the downstream market (e.g., the app store or the resale of products, respectively). A relevant exception to this duty to access exists that allows the gatekeeper to take measures to avoid interoperability compromising the integrity of its operating systems, virtual assistants and hardware or software components provided by the gatekeeper.

This access duty aims to prevent the technical "downgrading" of the app stores of smaller competitors, allowing the latter to have access to the functionalities (hardware and software) of the gatekeeper's operating system. The rule must be read in conjunction with Art. 6(3) DMA, according to which end users must be able to "easily change" a preset service, such as an app store, and allows competitors to request users to become the default provider.

The DMA does not cover horizontal interoperability, the latter being explicitly mentioned by the Data Act instead. This Act entrusts the Commission with the power to adopt binding standards with regard to interoperability[59] between cloud and edge computing services; however, this is limited to services "*of the same service type*". Technically, the Data Act gives the Commission the power to promote horizontal interoperability between "data spaces" (Art. 33), and between "data processing

[57] Pursuant to art. 6(4) DMA, the gatekeeper is required to allow "the installation and effective use of third-party software applications (apps) or software application stores (app stores) that use or are interoperable with its operating system". This allows third parties to access such software applications or app stores "by means other than the relevant core platform services of that gatekeeper". The gatekeeper is required to allow users to set third-party services (apps and app stores) as default (instead of gatekeeper services), making this choice easy. See Bourreau (2022, at 5).

[58] According to Scott Morton (2023): "Rival app stores could then take advantage of the indirect network effects of [gatekeepers] because, at the moment of entry, they will already have a large installed base of developers available. App store access to those network effects promotes contestability. By joining a network that already has many users and many developers, a rival app store or payment method is well-positioned for adoption by both sides".

[59] Art. 2(40) Data Act defines interoperability as "the ability of two or more data-based services, including data spaces or communication networks, systems, products, applications or components to process, exchange and use data in order to perform their functions in an accurate, effective and consistent manner".

services" (Art. 35).[60] While European data spaces consist of common standards to make mono or multi-sectoral databases interoperable, so to share or process data jointly,[61] "data processing services" are essentially cloud and edge computing.[62]

As per regulatory powers, the Data Act allows the Commission to adopt 'essential requirements' on a number of relevant features of data spaces (Art. 33(1))[63] including Application Program Interfaces (or APIs). In regulatory terms, these requirements are assimilated to harmonized standards and therefore binding.[64] In addition, the EC can request SSOs to adopt harmonized interoperability standards (that comply with its own essential requirements). When exercising this power, a form of mandated self-regulation,[65] the EC shall implement principles of openness, transparency, and technology-neutrality and ensure the widest participation of stakeholders, as laid down in EU Regulation on standardization.[66]

Hence, the Data Act will affect horizontal interoperability in virtual worlds, but only to a limited extent, given that Art. 35(1), imposing interoperability obligations on data processing service providers, specifies that they must be services "*of the same service type*". This phrase means that interoperability can be prescribed by the Commission only if it is functional to offer identical services. So it can be arranged between two cloud gaming services, but not between cloud intended for gaming and cloud intended for virtual worlds in the health sector. If we think that digital currency is the tool that allows the movement of objects between virtual worlds, we understand the importance of reconsidering at least the specification relating to services "of the same type". Given the current Birth phase and the one we intend to reach (Infancy), it would be desirable for the law to promote the definition of interoperability standards for services other than cloud and edge computing.

However, despite the said limitations, we believe that this provision is a valuable one. In fact, in specifying the objective of standards, Art. 35(1)(b) of the Data Act expressly mentions the need to "*enhance portability of digital assets between different data processing services that cover the same service type*", which could imply that interoperability between cloud and edge computing of virtual worlds operating in the same sector is included and therefore promoted.

---

60 See Art. 2(1)(8) Data Act defining Data processing services as 'a digital service that is provided to a customer and that enables ubiquitous and on-demand network access to a shared pool of configurable, scalable and elastic computing resources of a centralised, distributed or highly distributed nature that can be rapidly provisioned and released with minimal management effort or service provider interaction;'.

61 Art. 33(1), Data Act. See also https://joinup.ec.europa.eu/collection/semic-support-centre/data-spaces (Last accessed 30 April 2025).

62 Kramer et al. (2023, at 79).

63 For example, content and quality; data structure; licenses and means to enable interoperability of data sharing contracts.

64 If adopted in conformity with EU Regulation 1025/2012.

65 Baldwin et al. (2011, p. 137, 146 ff).

66 Fn 22 above.

4.2 Antitrust

EU competition rules pertaining to interoperability apply essentially in two cases: either they establish interoperability as a remedy in cases of abuses of dominant positions (art. 102 TFEU), or they are the object (or effect) of an agreement between parties aimed at setting standards for technologies, goods and services.

To evaluate whether interoperability can be imposed by competition authorities as a remedy, it will first be necessary to assess if any undertaking enjoys a dominant position (in any of the relevant layers of the metaverse) and abuses of it through active (e.g., self-preferencing or tying[67]) or omissive conducts aimed at discouraging new entrants. When such circumstances occur, interoperability may be forced to bring the abusive conduct to an end.

The effects of such remedies are hard to assess as ecosystem competition dynamics may be affected.[68] Hence, competitive assessment should consider the specific phase of development of virtual worlds (above, Sect. 2.1). At Birth, due to the existence of siloed virtual worlds, the likelihood of having ecosystems is high, that may generate "glue anticompetitive effects".[69] Hence, mandating interoperability as a remedy to an abuse of dominant position perpetrated by siloed virtual worlds' operators may be necessary to lead to the Infancy stage. Establishing if dominance might exist at Infancy or Maturity stages is challenging, but it is still valuable to consider, already now, if virtual worlds might be dominated by a handful of players, or one of its features tipped, as warned by the Commission.[70]

Second, competition law deals with situations in which market players act in a coordinated manner to set standards. In fact, the intrinsically cooperative character of the metaverse makes interconnection of platforms and services desirable and necessary for its full development. However, such agreements may potentially restrict competition, thus breaching Article 101 TFEU. In this case, both "Horizontal Guidelines"[71] and the new Block exemption regulation[72] would apply. In practice, unless they are covered by the Block Exemption, agreements are assessed through the Horizontal Guidelines. Accordingly, early-stage agreements (e.g., those stipulated at Infancy stage) that serve to create a technology are outside Article 101(1) TFUE, if no exploitation exists.

---

[67] An example is the Amazon Buy Box case. See Commission Decisions of 20 December 2022, Cases AT.40462 – Amazon Marketplace, and AT.40703 – Amazon Buy Box, C(2022) 9442 final, in OJ C 87, 9.3.2023, p. 7–11.

[68] Hovenkamp (2021, p. 1955 ff).

[69] Lianos et al. (2024, p. 12 ff).

[70] See European Commission (2023a), at 10, highlighting that the "risk of having a small number of big players becoming future gatekeepers of virtual worlds, creating market entry barriers and shutting out EU start-ups and SMEs from this emerging market". More broadly on the topic, see Di Porto (forthcoming).

[71] European Commission (2023d).

[72] European Commission (2023e).

For agreements that fall within Art. 101 TFEU, the Block Exemption applies. Among other things, it exempts from 101 TFEU agreements that present the following features: (1) there is no joint exploitation of the outcome; (2) access to the shared data is indispensable for output; and (3) adequate compensation exists. If joint exploitation exists, agreements are exempted if (4) the output is indispensable and (5) is protected by IPRs or know how. It follows that early-stage agreements like the ones stipulated by Microsoft and Apple with OpenAI,[73] leading the first to incorporate generative AI in its ecosystems, might be scrutinized under antitrust rules. The same could happen for the multiyear agreement between Microsoft (Azure) and OpenAI for the exclusive provision of cloud services to the latter.[74] Such scrutiny could help shed light on gatekeepers' leveraging of their economic power into new and emerging technologies, expanding their market power in other layers of the metaverse.

Outside the cases covered by the Block exemptions, a thorough assessment would be required to evaluate whether such agreements are covered by Article 101(3) TFEU. The boundaries of permissibility are very thin, even if collaboration to interoperate is considered essential for the transition to the Infancy stage. However, such collaboration may result in a prejudice to users and competitors. For instance, the EC should assess whether, through such agreements, ecosystems' leaders *de facto* set or control standards for interoperability resulting in forms of abuse of dominance.

Moreover, cooperation between firms leading to information exchange at any layers of virtual worlds may occur in the context of regulatory initiatives. For instance, regulation or public authorities may mandate undertakings to share information with other firms. In such cases operators do not enjoy discretion in deciding what information to share with other competitors). Being the 2023 Horizontal Guidelines silent about mandated sharing, enforcement problems may arise due to the parallel application of antitrust rules and regulation.

5 Limitations of Existing Legal Provisions on Interoperability

From the above we learn that existing legal provisions on interoperability offer only partial solutions to the quest for working interoperability models (except for the rare cases of virtual worlds operated by public administrations and those providing public services). The DMA contains relevant provisions, but they only cover vertical interoperability, and solely address gatekeepers. Although the DMA gives new entrants the right to access gatekeepers' operating systems as well as software and hardware components, this applies only if the gatekeeper uses them for its own services or

[73] See for reference https://openai.com/index/openai-and-apple-announce-partnership/ (Last accessed 30 April 2025).

[74] The Commission found the agreement between Microsoft and OpenAi not to be subject to EU merger rules because Microsoft does not hold a controlling share in OpenAI. However, the Commission will continue monitoring the agreement, especially due to its exclusivity clauses.

products, i.e. if it is vertically integrated. The right of the gatekeeper to limit access on security or technical grounds (Art. 6 (7) and Art. 7 (9) DMA) further hampers interoperability as opportunistic behavior may arise.

As per the Data Act, it does address horizontal interoperability (Art. 35(1)), but it applies only to virtual worlds operating in the same industry (e.g. in health, but not in health and finance taken together). Lacking equivalence between service types, only antitrust rules would apply on a case-by-case basis, meaning that interoperability among virtual worlds operating in different areas is not fostered but only "defended" *ex post*.

Also, the Data Act and DMA raise legal intricacies due to the parallel application of antitrust rules that may hinder the evolution to the forthcoming stages. Hence, both regulations are insufficient to ensure effective interoperability, prompting to further regulatory intervention, lacking which obliged parties may well provide under-optimal interoperability tools to applicants, thus frustrating the regulatory rationale. From a strict regulatory point of view, more explicit provision should be adopted for horizontal interoperability between different virtual worlds, encouraging the adoption of standards, in collaboration with businesses.

Overall, a more comprehensive framework is needed to facilitate automated and real-time migration of content from one virtual world to another. For example, an avatar created on a gatekeeper's virtual world "A" encompasses the individual's identity, but it is also associated with a wallet, which may in turn contain assets and values of other types (think of NFTs or currency). To seamlessly move identities, assets, and currency from virtual world A to another (B), today the user can only employ data "portability" (Arts. 20 GDPR and 6(9) DMA). However, data portability qualifies as an individual right, that is left to the will of the individual user. Although portability is free of charge and the gatekeeper required to provide technical tools to facilitate it, it is unlikely that the implementation of the metaverse could leverage solely on the individual's desire to switch provider. A mechanism that would ensure the migration of data in an automated and real-time manner (like e.g. an API) whenever the user intends to move, even transiently, between one virtual world and another would be preferable.

The consequences of the current approach can be appreciated also with reference to the movement of 'money' among virtual worlds. Today the only possibility for the user to 'exchange' money is to liquidate tokens (not the currency) purchased in virtual world "A," and subsequently purchase tokens having an equivalent value in virtual world "B". Such mechanism, however, would not guarantee the perfect equivalence of value or experience in virtual worlds "A" and "B," since the tokens (e.g., an avatar's skin or a medical equipment used and "trained" in the "A" world) might not be recognized or work properly in the world "B". Similarly, the currencies obtained in "A" might have a different 'purchasing power' in "B", evidently limiting mobility between virtual worlds. Horizontal interoperability should therefore be regulated more analytically. In fact, if the goal of the Infancy phase is to enable the seamless and unrestricted movement of digital identities, tokens, and currency between virtual worlds, then communication between these worlds should be encouraged, already at the level of operating systems, as well as applications and devices.

6 Who and How Should Ensure Interoperability for the Metaverse?

The governance of virtual worlds and the metaverse should be distinguished from the operational aspects of interoperability. While the former relates to the ability of one or more bodies to lead the process of interoperability standardization; the latter refers to the precise identification of the layers for which interoperability standardization is desirable and optimal.

6.1 The Optimal Degree of Interoperability

Establishing the degree of interoperability that is likely optimal for virtual worlds is a complex task, as it may vary depending on the layer considered (above, Sect. 3).[75] Ensuring the existence of basic standardization can help to guarantee that entry by competing virtual worlds is possible and may prevent the development of closed worlds, which could hold back innovation. Nonetheless, as the JRC suggests, "*at present, it is not possible to converge around a single reference architecture, set of interoperability standards and building blocks for virtual worlds.*"[76]

A fundamental reason for the difficulty of establishing unlimited interoperability is the general uncertainty that exists about what the future features of these worlds and how much differentiation would be socially desirable.[77] Also, mandating interoperability for *all* features may limit the technological development of new solutions – thus restricting the growth of virtual worlds. Similarly, imposing early requirements on horizontal interoperability on components (like avatar features and ability to cross from one virtual world to another) that are highly differentiated and where players are innovating to compete, especially at Birth stage, may affect innovation and incentives.

Having said that, there are layers for which interoperability standardization is desirable already at the current stage for at least two reasons: (1) because it may help

[75] As a sidenote, it is worth noting that interoperability in telephone or banking networks, which have many fewer features than virtual worlds, have already proven complex.

[76] Hupont Torres et al. (2023, at 47).

[77] For example, in the context of be gaming worlds or historical worlds, there may be token products that are suited mainly to that world (or type of world) and not to all worlds. Similarly, avatars in one game world may not be appropriate for another. The desired restriction on the use may come from token makers (for instance, luxury bag makers not wanting their bags to be used in violent situations) or from other users (participants in a historical Rome world not wishing to see any modern goods among users, for example). This means that not only platforms but also at times users and token providers may not want interconnected movements of goods across worlds. Requiring the possibility of universal movement to be possible could distort legitimately desired options of users to rest in a coherent environment, making the potential for movement across virtual worlds or lack thereof seem to be an important feature for users to understand if they are purchasing or investing within a given virtual world.

broadening the user base; and (2) because it would realize the communication among different user experiences, that is indispensable for moving from Birth to Infancy.

For user experiences (*supra* Sect. 3.3), certain features may be easier to standardize than others. As the EU Commission suggests,[78] a good candidate is that of accepted tradeable forms of value for transactions (equivalent to currency). User authentication techniques for digital identities is another area where common standards could relatively easily be developed. Standardization of these specific elements is already ongoing within the Institute of Electrical and Electronics Engineers (IEEE),[79] and the Commission is eager to intervene in this regard to allow some degree of commonality across virtual worlds.[80]

Similarly, with regard to software platform applications (above Sect. 3.2), quality standards for visualization of media (images, video, etc.) are also naturally prone to standardization: the activity of ISO[81] in this regard is illuminating and could be considered for future embedding into the European standardization schemes. On the other hand, government-mandated software-based virtual world interoperability and perfect movement of tokens between them may be less desirable, and even counterproductive, at an early stage of the innovation cycle. That stems from the value of encouraging maximum innovation, which is difficult to predict, and may need IP protections to motivate.

As per the device layer (above, Sect 3.1), implementing interoperability at this level could help different devices and interfaces being used to access several virtual worlds. In this scenario, establishing open, cross-device, and consumer-centered standards may reduce market fragmentation while making virtual worlds an economic and societal success. To make this happen the Commission could consider the ongoing work of the IEEE,[82] as well as the International Electrotechnical Commission (IEC), which sub-committee IEC/TC 100 has developed standards for VR equipment and systems.[83]

---

[78] See European Commission (2023c, at 6).

[79] See e.g. the IEEE P3812.2 Standard for General Requirements for Identity.

[80] European Commission (2023c, at 6).

[81] See ISO/IEC JTC 1/SC 29 "Coding of audio, picture, multimedia and hypermedia information" (available at https://www.iso.org/committee/45316.html) (Last accessed 30 April 2025) which contains the well-known JPEG and MPEG standardization as well as other initiatives on interoperability standardization for efficiently coded media (e.g. synchronization, presentation, storage and transport of single or combinations of media and related security and privacy management): European Commission (2023g).

[82] See IEEE P3322 Guide for Comfort Requirements for Extended Reality (XR).

[83] See IEC TR 63308:2021 Virtual reality equipment and systems (available at: https://webstore.iec.ch/en/publication/64217) (Last accessed 30 April 2025). The IEC has also set a working group on the metaverse (WG 12: Multimedia systems and equipment for metaverse), aimed at defining the metaverse and equipment from a technical and standardization perspective.

6.2 Interoperability as Governance: What Role for the EU Commission?

From a governance standpoint, given the transnational dimension of the metaverse, interoperability deeply relates to the ability of the Commission to capture multi-stakeholder global consensus. As the JRC observes, "*the standardisation landscape is still highly fragmented and is rapidly evolving with multiple competing initiatives (both open and proprietary) that are attempting to provide and promote interoperability solutions for virtual worlds.*"[84]

The present scenario shows indeed a plethora of initiatives, where distinct groups are working to develop open interoperability standards for the metaverse: besides the already-mentioned IEEE, IEC and ISO, the World Wide Web Consortium (W3C) has created a "Metaverse Interoperability Community Group"[85]; other major organizations pursuing the same mission include the Open Metaverse Foundation[86] and the Metaverse Standards Forum.[87] Some of these initiatives have a very relevant size and count the most prominent stakeholders among their members.[88] These initiatives show the strong willingness of market operators to collaborate in order to set common standards for the metaverse. However, they also demonstrate the urgent need for a collective and synergetic effort.

These fora represent a prolific breeding ground which could support the European Commission's effort to identify the areas and layers in relation to which market operators deem standardization necessary, thus enabling it to exercise its powers under the EU Regulation on standardization in a more informed manner. However, because these fora do not account as European SSOs within the meaning of the Standardization regulation, their input would hardly translate into EU legislative proposals. It follows that all discussions among stakeholders taking place therein might only provide the Commission with a sound acceptability of the standards, but cannot per se translate into binding ones.

On its side, the European Commission has shown its willingness to lead the governance of standard setting for the metaverse by releasing a statement on 14 September 2022. There it asserted that '*Similarly, to the European Bauhaus, we will launch a creative and interdisciplinary movement, aiming to develop standards, increase interoperability, maximising impact with the help of IT experts, regulatory*

[84] Hupont Torres et al. (2023, at 48).

[85] https://www.w3.org/community/metaverse-interop/ (Last accessed 30 April 2025).

[86] https://www.openmv.org/ (Last accessed 30 April 2025).

[87] The description they propose of their activity states "[t]he Metaverse Standards Forum brings together leading standards organizations and companies for industry-wide cooperation on interoperability standards needed to build the open metaverse. The Forum will explore where the lack of interoperability is holding back metaverse deployment and how the work of Standards Developing Organizations (SDOs) defining and evolving needed standards may be coordinated and accelerated".

[88] E.g., the Standard Metaverse Forum has more than 2400 member organizations and features members as Microsoft, Meta, Huawei, Adobe, Nvidia, Qualcomm (https://metaverse-standards.org/) (Last accessed 30 April 2025).

experts citizens' organisations and youth'.[89] In that goal, it has commenced "The Virtual and Augmented Reality Industrial Coalition",[90] a platform for structured dialogue between the European VR/AR ecosystems and policymakers. In the same vein, through the 2022 amendment of the EU Standardization Regulation 2015, the EU tried to reinforce the role of European SSOs in the global arena by requiring that mandates addressed by the Commission to the SSOs be handled only by national standardization bodies from the EU (and EEA) member states. This requirement is meant to avoid undue influence of actors from outside the EU in the decision-making processes for the development of standards for key areas.

The Commission's ambition to lead the design of interoperability standards for virtual worlds is outspoken,[91] Its stated policy goal is to shape the "*metaverse according to European values, principles, rules and strategic interests: trustful, secure, respecting EU legislation*".[92] The industry seems to welcome the idea of the Commission playing a central role, as the feedback provided to its call for evidence show[93].

On papers, the Commission is well equipped to guide the standard setting for the metaverse, provided that Art. 10 of the Standardization Regulation entrusts it with significant powers over the definition of standards required of the SSOs. Building on that, the Commission could request the SSOs to "europanize" the standards international bodies (like IEEE, ISO, ITU, etc.) are developing in relation to the identified layers of virtual worlds (Sect. 6.1).

"Europanizing" means to revise those standards to make sure they comply with the European policy vision. The latter consists of pursuing a secure, open, and interoperable metaverse built on European values, supporting innovation, and protecting EU data. In practice, the European SSOs should be tasked to assess international standards to make sure that they reflect three pivots: (1) ensuring a human-centric design (in terms of safety and adherence to European values with interoperable standards); (2) allowing European technological leadership (meaning to help the local industry becoming leader in key technologies like VR, AR, and advanced materials within a robust ecosystem), and (3) ensuring infrastructure development to address connectivity demands for the metaverse's growth.

---

[89] European Commission, People, technologies & infrastructure – Europe's plan to thrive in the metaverse, Blog of Commissioner Thierry Breton, 14 September 2022

[90] European Commission (2023f).

[91] European Commission (2023b, at 11) (recalling that it is crucial for the EU to be present in the development of virtual worlds and their governance, and lead the way through the setting of open standards by reinforcing the EU Strategy on Standardization and drawing on the work of the High-Level Forum on European Standardization) and 14: "[The] *multi-stakeholder process will aim to address both virtual worlds' interoperability system and the essential components underpinning the functioning of virtual worlds, such as rights management, transactions in virtual worlds, and identity management, as well as topics related to the industrial uptake of virtual world solutions.*".

[92] European Commission (2023g, at 169).

[93] See the replies of stakeholders to European Commission (2023a) and the subsequent Communication on virtual worlds: European Commission (2023b).

Ensuring a human-centric design (1) means that the standardization effort must be aimed at guaranteeing human dignity and safe spaces, in line with European values. It must therefore be ensured that virtual worlds are a safe place, where interactions do not evade the rules applicable in the real worlds. An example would clarify the concept of "Europanization" of interoperability standards to make them human-centric. To protect individual rights means to grant privacy and data protection, to ensure liability in case of wrongdoing by both individuals and virtual worlds' providers, to grant a minimum level of cybersecurity.[94] What if an individual is banned from a virtual world for having committed a fraud and logs into another one to continue perpetrating frauds? If no communication exists between the two worlds that enables information of the ban to migrate, the individual would be free to do so, even if she uses the same digital identity (avatar).

This can be achieved in particular by introducing standardization in the software platform application layer (above, Sect. 3.2).

One solution to that would be to integrate the data on misbehavior and ban "by design" in the communication standard between the two virtual worlds. Embedding such information in the code of identity schemes (layer Sect. 3.3, above), the software application layer (above Sect. 3.2) or the access device (layer Sect. 3.1) could result in a safer experience for others, since they will be made aware that they are interacting with a fraud doer who was banned in another virtual world. The proposed solution would consist in imposing interoperability of the relevant layers of different virtual worlds and requiring each virtual world to acknowledge sanctions and bans imposed on the user by other providers (and/or public authorities). It should be noted that such a solution is not unfamiliar to international standards organization, which too emphasize that the design of user experiences and interaction paradigms require the application of human-centred design processes.[95]

Finally, to make the standardization requests by the Commission effective, its powers should be strengthened. First, it should be allowed to operate autonomous scrutiny on the deliverables presented by the SSOs, with no need to wait for an impulse from the Member States or the European Parliament. The current procedure under Article 11 of the EU Standardization Regulation ultimately slows down the entire process, weakening the Commission's leading role in standardization (and in the transition to the Infancy phase of virtual worlds).

---

[94] European Commission (2022a)

[95] See, ISO 9241-210:2019. Ergonomics of human-system interaction — Part 210: Human-centred design for interactive systems. https://www.iso.org/standard/77520.html (Last accessed 30 April 2025).

7 Conclusion

In this paper we analyzed the distinctive features of the metaverse in its various stages of development (Birth, Infancy and Maturity), highlighting the pivotal role of interoperability, for both fostering the metaverse and ensuring its good governance. Our investigation shows that full interoperability between virtual worlds does not exist yet and that, with respect to certain components like infrastructure and connectivity, it is desirable, although resource intensive. We further suggest that to promote the protection of fundamental rights in the metaverse, such protection should be incorporated by design into the standards' technical specifications.

As per the type of regulatory intervention, we showed that the adoption of general interoperability standards is not advisable, while partial interoperability (i.e. limited to certain components of virtual worlds) is, even at the current stage. The analysis of existing interoperability disciplines reveals that the current framework constitutes a valid starting point, though it is deficient, due to legal inconsistencies and the fact that it does not target all players involved in the metaverse value chain.

Finally, as per who should establish standards to ensure that interoperability between virtual worlds proceeds effectively, we recommend that the EU Commission is identified as the initiating entity. However, since virtual worlds will become more and more immersive (in Web 4.0) with the consequent exponential circulation of data (personal and otherwise), the widest involvement of stakeholders (regulators, companies, users, universities, civil society) is needed. In this context, the European Commission should put more effort into being able to take the lead in the standardization process currently underway. It should at least try to intercept the global consensus by referring to the existing work of international SSOs and then mandating European SSOs with the task of "europenizing" their standards. That would result not only in a multi-stakeholders approach, but also in a good practice of governance whereby virtual worlds ensure the protection of fundamental rights – which might otherwise be overshadowed in fully industry-led initiatives – from the outset.

References

Ayres I, Braithwaite J (1992) Responsive regulation: transcending the deregulation debate. Oxford University, Oxford

Allen K. (2022) Why the metaverse depends on a better understanding of persistent virtual worlds. https://cloudwars.com/metaverse/why-the-metaverse-depends-on-a-better-understanding-of-persistent-virtual-worlds/. Last accessed April 10, 2025.

Balcerak Jackson M, Balcerak Jackson B (2024) Immersive experience and virtual reality. Philos. Technol 37:19. https://doi.org/10.1007/s13347-024-00707-1

Baldwin R et al (2011) Understanding regulation: theory, strategy and practice. Oxford University Press, Oxford

Berg C (2024) Interoperability. Internet Policy Rev 13(2):1–10. https://doi.org/10.14763/2024.2.1749

Bourreau M. (2022) DMA horizontal and vertical interoperability obligations, Cerre issue paper, November 2022, at 14. https://cerre.eu/wp-content/uploads/2022/11/DMA_HorizontalandVerticalInteroperability.pdf. Last accessed April 10, 2025.
Bourreau M. et al. (2022) Interoperability in digital markets, CERRE Report, March 2022. https://cerre.eu/wp-content/uploads/2022/03/220321_CERRE_Report_Interoperability-in-Digital-Markets_FINAL.pdf. Last accessed April 10, 2025.
Brescia MC, Vangelisti MI (2021) Digital payments market: standardization and coopetition. In: Falce V (ed) Financial innovation tra disintermediazione e mercato. Giappichelli, Turin
Bushell C. (2022) The impact of metaverse on branding and marketing. https://ssrn.com/abstract=4144628. Last accessed April 10, 2025.
Calvino I (1972) Invisible cities. Einaudi, Turin
Calvino I (1979) If on a winter's night a traveler. Einaudi, Turin
Cosenza V. (2022) *L'ecosistema del metaverso*. https://osservatoriometaverso.it/lecosistema-del-metaverso/. Last accessed April 10, 2025.
Di Porto F. and Foà D. (2023), Defining virtual worlds: main features and regulatory challenges, Issue paper, CERRE–Centre for regulation in Europe, July 2023. https://papers.ssrn.com/sol3/papers.cfm?abstract_id=4507397. Last accessed April 10, 2025.
Di Porto F., Foà D. and Ennis S. (2024) Emerging virtual worlds: implications for policy and regulation, report, CERRE–Centre for regulation in Europe, February 2024. https://cerre.eu/publications/emerging-virtual-worlds-implications-for-policy-and-regulation/. Last accessed April 10, 2025.
Di Porto F. (forthcoming) Competition and virtual world
European Commission (2016) Communication EU government action plan 2016–2020 accelerating the digital transformation of government, Brussels, 19.4.2016, COM (2016) 179 final)
European Commission (2017a) ISA2. The sharing and reuse framework for IT solutions fostering collaboration among public administrations
European Commission (2017b) Communication "European Interoperability Framework" COM/2017/0134 final
European Commission (2022a) European declaration on digital rights and principles, 15 December 2022. https://digital-strategy.ec.europa.eu/en/library/european-declaration-digital-rights-and-principles. Last accessed April 10, 2025.
European Commission (2022b) Extended reality: opportunities, success stories and challenges (health, education), September. https://digital-strategy.ec.europa.eu/en/library/extended-reality-opportunities-success-stories-and-challenges-health-and-education. Last accessed April 10, 2025.
European Commission (2023a) Call for evidence for a non-legislative initiative on virtual worlds, Ref. ARES (2023)2474961 of 5 April 2023. https://ec.europa.eu/info/law/better-regulation/have-your-say/initiatives/13757-Virtual-worlds-metaverses-a-visionfor-openness-safety-and-respect_en. Last accessed April 10, 2025.
European Commission (2023b) Communication on "An EU initiative on Web 4.0 and virtual worlds: a head start in the next technological transition", 11.7.2023, COM (2023) 442/final. https://digital-strategy.ec.europa.eu/en/library/eu-initiative-virtual-worlds-head-start-next-technological-transition. Last accessed April 10, 2025.
European Commission (2023c) Staff working document, 2023, 250 final, 11.7.2023. https://digital-strategy.ec.europa.eu/en/library/staff-working-document-citizens-panel-report-virtual-worlds#:~:text=This%20Staff%20Working%20Document%20(SWD,citizens'%20panel%20on%20virtual%20worlds. Last accessed April 10, 2025.
European Commission (2023d) Guidelines on the applicability of Article 101 of the treaty on the functioning of the European Union to horizontal co-operation agreements (2023/C 259/01)
European Commission (2023e) Regulation (EU) 2023/1066 of 1 June 2023 on the application of Article 101(3) of the treaty on the functioning of the European union to certain categories of research and development agreements
European Commission (2023f) The virtual and augmented reality industrial coalition, 11 July 2023

European Commission (2023g) The rolling plan for ICT standardization. https://joinup.ec.europa.eu/collection/rolling-plan-ict-standardisation/rolling-plan-2023. Last accessed April 10, 2025.
Farrell J, Saloner G (1985) Standardization, compatibility, and innovation. Rand J Econ 16(1):70–83.
Hovenkamp H (2021) Antitrust and platform monopoly. Yale Law J 130:1952–2273
Hupont Torres I. et al. (2023) Next generation virtual worlds: societal, technological, economic and policy challenges for the EU, JRC. doi:10.2760/51579 (also referred as JRC (2023))
Kramer J. et al. (2023) Data act: towards a balanced EU data regulation, CERRE report, March 2023. https://cerre.eu/publications/data-act-towards-a-balanced-eu-data-regulation/. Last accessed April 10, 2025.
Lianos I. et al. (2024) Towards a legal theory of digital ecosystems, faculty of Laws University College London Law Research Paper No. 16/2024, Amsterdam Law School Research Paper No. 2024-22, Amsterdam Centre for Transformative private law Working Paper No 2024-01. https://ssrn.com/abstract=4849340. Last accessed April 10, 2025.
Morse A. and Stein S. (2022) The metaverse is on the way. https://www.virtualrealitymarketing.com/guides/the-metaverse-is-on-the-way-heres-what-you-need-to-know/. Last accessed April 10, 2025.
Pflücke F (2023) Interoperability in the EU: Paving the way for digital public services. In: Hofmann, Pflücke (eds) Governance of automated decision-making and EU law. Oxford University Press, Oxford
Scott Morton F. (2023) Digital market act designations: the interoperability of Google Android, November 2023. https://www.bruegel.org/analysis/digital-market-act-designations-interoperability-google-android-0#footnote5_z737yu1. Last accessed April 10, 2025.
Tarr B et al (2018) Synchrony and social connection in immersive virtual reality. Nat Sci Rep 8:3693. https://doi.org/10.1038/s41598-018-21765-4
Trunfio M, Rossi S (2022) Advances in metaverse investigation: streams of research and future agenda. Virtual Worlds 1(2):103–129. https://doi.org/10.3390/virtualworlds1020007
Wang G. (2021) SoK: exploring blockchains interoperability. https://eprint.iacr.org/2021/537.pdf. Last accessed April 10, 2025.
World Economic Forum WEF (2023) Interoperability in the metaverse, January. https://www3.weforum.org/docs/WEF_Interoperability_in_the_Metaverse.pdf. Last accessed April 10, 2025.

Metaverse: Yet Another Jeopardy for the Constitutional Social Contract?

Riccardo Vecellio Segate

Abstract If ever implemented, the metaverse is set to revolutionise the governance of cross-border modes of "living" in digitised environments. Alongside sector-specific disruptions, others may cut across multiple legal areas as overarchingly as to encompass citizens' constitutional entitlements. Stemming therefrom are dilemmas which warrant both domestic and global responses, including: the relationship between "the private" and "the public" under modern Constitutions; the metaverse as a multi-jurisdictional setting where fast-paced conflict-of-laws controversies will proliferate both quantitatively and complexity-wise; and the jurisdictional technicalities related to policy elaboration and enforcement in the virtual reality, with special emphasis on the transnationality of international-human-rights-law safeguards. Constitutions themselves as a social contract are undergoing transformation to accommodate trends such as time-shrinking, relational dematerialisation, Westphalia's disarticulation, and the public repercussions of State-sanctioned but privately managed communication infrastructure, which are being catalysed or upscaled by metaverse-provided experiences. Ubiquitous as it is, the metaverse might exhaust the territorially bound, constitutional social contract, defying the rationale for any social contract at all. How would an "international law of the metaverse" keep Constitutions current in virtuality-powered societies? The balance of power between natural and legal persons, the rule of law, and the very effectiveness of constitutional norms, might find themselves challenged as drastically as never before.

The metaverse as a potential disruptor for global digital governance, and its implications for domestic and supranational constitutional discourses in the age of post-Westphalia.

R. Vecellio Segate (✉)
University of Groningen, Groningen, The Netherlands
e-mail: r.vecellio.segate@rug.nl

F. Di Porto and O. Pollicino (eds.), *Law and Politics of Virtual Worlds*, Law, Governance and Technology Series 79, https://doi.org/10.1007/978-3-032-08541-2_4

1 Introduction

> The major digital and green transformations we embarked on together have only taken on additional importance as we have grappled with pandemics, lockdowns and now a war on our border. This is about building a better future for the next generation and making ourselves more resilient and more prepared for challenges to come. […] We will continue looking at new digital opportunities and trends, such as the metaverse.[1]

What laws should govern the conduct of avatars (and the users instructing or "dressing" them) in the metaverse? How to respond and remedy to torts and crimes committed in the virtual reality? Addressing these questions through a 'sliding scale of harm inflicted to both the metaverse community and the real-world community'[2] has been recommended, and it indeed reads like a viable option. But what about the jurisdiction over such "metaversan[3] community"?

In the so-called "real world", most often it is the Constitution that stipulates the boundaries of the legal order, identifies the laws which will be applied according to a predetermined hierarchy, and defines the jurisdictional competence of institutions and subordinate laws themselves. How could current Constitutions expand their mandate so to encompass the metaverse? Would they need to be radically rethought? Are we warranting a global and metaverse-specific constitutionalism—or constitutionalist discourse—to address the challenges of enhanced virtuality and avatar interaction? Could such constitutionalism be digitised, or made "smart", for example by requiring each action which is performed in the metaverse be recorded in a blockchain for evidentiary and accountability purposes,[4] run by a decentralised autonomous organization (DAO)? Caution is called for here, as automation is not necessarily a value-add when it comes to the Constitution, which is intrinsically human. The risk is that '[w]hen smart technologies govern all human conduct (of course in certain spaces), our conventional thinking about the authority of the law as we know it, and the demand for respect for the law, becomes obsolete[5]', which would be *a fortiori* problematic for a Constitution as the highest legal authority. A Constitution "made smart" would not necessarily serve the authoritative, symbolic, and unifying purposes for which Constitutions are generally enacted in the first place.[6]

---

[1] European Commission 2022a, p.3.

[2] Cheong 2022, p.9.

[3] Languages are gradually accommodating the lexicon that revolves around the Metaverse. There is no established rule for adjectives, but for the time being, I will mention "metaversan" or "metaversic" matters and affairs interchangeably, to mean they are "related or pertaining to or characteristic of the Metaverse".

[4] *See also* Pate 2022, p.188; Wu and Zhang 2023.

[5] Kasiyanto and Kilinc 2022, p.303.

[6] Salient and imaginative literature has painted fairly forward-looking observations on this point. I will only refer the reader to the following piece, which is just a blogpost but a well-written one: Wolfram 2016. On the idea of a humanity-aiding super-AI "for good", *refer to* Tegmark 2015.

In light of the weight of such open dilemmas for both our daily lives and the role of law within society, it is "slightly" disconcerting to find that scant to no scholarly literature exists on the potential constitutional consequences arising from the widely expected establishment of the metaverse as a key information and communication technology (ICT) revolution for the decades to come. A few writings and other materials from non-governmental (NGOs) and governmental organisations do exist to explore the question of whether we need a Constitution for the metaverse,[7] but these are explicitly sided, and anything but overarching: they might provide immediate policy reactions of some practical use, but fail to frame the metaverse against "epistemological" trends in how we produce, classify, evaluate, and build claims on foundational legal knowledge around constitutional concepts such as the "State" and its "jurisdiction". And yet, there must be reasons for this lacuna. One of them also represents my essential premise for this chapter: whenever we discuss the metaverse, we have no clue what we are actually descanting about.[8]

When general-use virtual-reality (VR), augmented-reality (AR), and mixed-reality (MR) applications—together composing the so-called "extended" reality (XR) for "spatial computing"—started to be engineered and then eventually marketed around twenty years ago, almost no one really picked up the "revolution" they were supposedly bringing about. Succumbing to lack of interest from consumers and regulatory pressure from e.g. privacy watchdogs, their market eventually plummeted – though research thereabout never ceased. The Covid-19 pandemic and related surveillance through digital behavioralism have redefined humans' aterritorial "remote urbanism"[9] and enabled the leap forward of these data-intensive technologies[10] – and yet, we are still mostly unaware of what their combined technological effect, i.e. the metaverse, will look like, for our cognition as well as for the legal systems we crafted to govern ourselves. Some say it is a typology of wearable or embodied neuro-reality whereby not only the content of the reality we perceive, but also the modes of its perception itself (and our cognitive accommodation thereof) will undergo transformation[11] – 'a shift from the Internet of things to the Internet of bodies that will make every controlling process remarkably cheap'.[12] And yet, besides conceptual hints or techno-scientific details, at this stage we cannot even be sure of whether many alternative metaverses will be established, or just one (at least in a "federated" fashion) – nor, for that matter, are we anywhere close to know who is going to populate it/them, and when. In fact, the metaverse seems hyped in public discourse just like, to exemplify, the blockchain, non-fungible tokens (NFTs), the Internet of Things (IoT), digital identity wallets, generative artificial intelligence (genAI), vibe-coding tools, or virtual/crypto currencies are; but differently from them, we know even less about what it would look like and how it would function, from both a regulatory and a

[7] *Watch e.g.* 92NY Belfer Center 2022.

[8] *Read also* Alexander et al. 2022.

[9] *Explore further at* Allam et al. 2022.

[10] *See* Bibri and Allam 2022, p.724.

[11] *Read e.g.* Properzi 2019, p.261.

[12] Mattei 2024, p.23.

technical perspective.[13] Sustainability issues are at stake, too, both environmentally and for the cohesiveness, fairness, and governance of our societies.[14]

To begin with, Westerners tend to link the idea of technological progress with emancipation and democracy, but let us consider the dilemma of autocracies: to what extent will they ever join a common enterprise towards developing a shared metaverse? As I write, local applications of VR/AR abound worldwide in any technologically skilled jurisdiction (that is, whatever the latter's domestic political arrangement), but if we are to imagine a globally interconnected virtual space where real-world citizenships lose currency, i.e. sort of a supranational parallel reality inhabited by avatars with biunivocal correspondence with world citizens, then this sounds closer to a West-powered project – and not even: it might be a reflection of aspirant techno-dominance on the part of business ecosystems (but not necessarily regulators) in the United States (US),[15] with some residual interest from those in the European Union (EU)[16] and the United Kingdom (UK),[17] as well as in "West-aligned" jurisdictions such as South Korea, Japan, Australia, Israel, and—to some extent—Singapore.[18]

I find it difficult to bet on the fact that for example China, whose constitutional discourse on e.g. data protection differs so remarkably from the Western one,[19] and which consistently rejects "universalist" approaches to core state attributes such as "jurisdiction",[20] could ever converge towards a biunivocally accessible world whereby Western avatars unrestrainedly entertain conversations with Chinese ones, and vice versa – and the users behind them. True that we could apply to the metaverse what States already pursue in other areas, that is some type of "international democracy" whereby no matter whether they are domestically democratic or not, they still democratically participate to decision-making in international fora across a number of global dossiers. This means that certain States may be granted voting rights internationally (eg within an international organisation or more information platforms of global governance) on a given topic despite they have never domestically enacted democratic procedures to address issues in that very same field (or even at all).[21] In this case, States might agree on a democratic system of governance for the metaverse insofar as common "spaces" or "aspects" thereof are concerned, to then manage their own "part" of the metaverse by themselves – even autocratically, should they so wish. Equally true indeed is that e.g. China would not be new in joining standard-intensive multilateral projects of digital infrastructure-building and regional connectivity while maintaining strict Internet restrictions and content censorship at

---

[13] *Read also* Buchholz et al. 2022; Tabassum et al. 2025.

[14] *Read e.g.* Masi 2025; Tiwari et al. 2025; De Giovanni 2023.

[15] *Check* Piscione and Drean 2023; Anderson and Rainie 2022. *Cf* Cosgrove 2023, p.5.

[16] *Check for instance* Europol 2022b; Mangada et al. 2022, p.32.

[17] *Refer eg to* Woods 2022; Howe 2022; Murgia and Bradshaw 2022.

[18] *See also* Dolata and Schwabe 2023, p.251; Roquet 2023.

[19] *See* Vecellio Segate 2022a.

[20] For a topical (though *ratione materiae* distant) exemplification, refer to Vecellio Segate 2022e.

[21] Although in another field, to grasp this concept one may *refer to* Vecellio Segate 2020b, p.204.

home;[22] hence, it could consider acting the same way towards the metaverse,[23] as yet another expression of its hypersecuritised techno-consumerism domestically and disguised-as-Confucianist "harmony" internationally.[24] Nevertheless, the metaverse might not work through compartmentalisation, in that its revolutionary momentum would fade that way.

As it should stand clear by now, we know almost nothing about the shape the metaverse will take – it is indeed no surprise that to guess the legal implications of interactions among avatars, scholars tend to tap into science-fiction.[25] If anything, this underscores the urgence of imaginative, "future-proof" scholarship and critical reflection that makes the most of scholars' "autopoietic potential" in anticipating issues rather than trying to fill the gaps later – once it might prove *too* late. Because of the central spot filled by the "constitutional discourse" within the texture of our organised societies, time has come to imagine a few metaversan scenarios and what their influence on constitutions worldwide might be.

In truth, we cannot safely affirm what a "Constitution" is, either, with this concept perpetually standing on the edge between effectiveness and formalistic rhetoric. Corporations shaping Internet governance have frequently navigated such an edge, e.g. when dealing with Chinese authorities in restricting Internet access, tracking cyber dissidents, and filtering out politically sensitive contents, despite freedom being highly regarded in China's written constitutional text.[26]

These two premises—that generalising on Constitutions' effective role within a legal order's hierarchy of sources, as well as on the metaverse's impending shape, is risky an exercise—may hopefully illustrate the reason why scholars or policymakers tabling a discussion around the "Metaversian constitution", do not really have a hint of what their discussion is or should be about. These rather shaky foundations represent the starting terrain of the present chapter.

The chapter unfolds as follows. Section 2 introduces the reader to the risks inherent to a catalysis of one phenomenon which is already transforming regulation, and could do so to unprecedented degrees if the metaverse succeeds as the next frontier technology in digital communication: privatised standardisation, with legislative time-shrinking in the background and the displacement of the Constitution as the primary reference point for legislators and citizens alike. Section 3 delves deeper into the risks just expounded, to survey the main substantive ways in which the metaverse could displace the Constitution by either "transcending" or "reformulating" the rights and obligations typically enshrined therein. Depending on the legislative and regulatory domain, the metaverse could either make the Constitution—in the long run—negligible and obsolete or, most plausibly, induce a resolute process of normative accommodation whereby "traditional" rights and obligations are rephrased and rebalanced

[22] *See* De Gregorio and Radu 2022, pp.84–85; *cf* Coccoli 2017, pp.229–230.

[23] *Read further* Hung 2022.

[24] *Check eg* Chen 2022; Warner 2022; Interesse 2022.

[25] *Check e.g.* Cheong 2022, pp.3–4.

[26] *See* Rothschild 2013, pp.151–152.

with the purpose of prioritising the metaversic logic of power, participation, communication, and engagement. Section 4 offers a specular analysis on the procedural and formal side: in what ways is the metaverse set to redefine the Constitution formally and procedurally? This (admittedly succinct) inspection encompasses the Constitution's "drafting style" and its relationship with the changing nature of the State, but it also explores the "constitutional moment" with its related approval and ratification procedures, alongside the procedures for amendment and overhaul of the constitutional text. It comments on the Constitution as the keeper of a legal order, and how this function may be overturned or anyway dramatically altered by the techno-dystopian reshuffle of legal orders themselves – in this case, be it through metaversic orders "parallel" (ie alternative) to the state-centric one, or via wider decentralisation or, most saliently, polycentric trends reinforced by the metaverse and the inherent "multiplication" of arenas and dimensions it conceptually brings with it. To put it bluntly, in a "pick-and-choose" regulatory arena and space for life action, the fragmentation of values, ideas, and "realities" can only further the weakening and capture that the State is already experiencing across most regions – and the decentralisation or "peripheralisation" of its Constitution, too, as a result. If that is the case, no wonder that "jurisdiction"—ie the State's (and its constitutional organs') ability to "speak the law"—as both a practice and a doctrine will warrant rethinking in the face of severe challenges. These are discussed in Sect. 5. In fact, the weakening of the State and its Constitution implies that their territorial and normative borders, too, become more porous to the oversized influence of cross-jurisdictional platforming and its special needs. As soon as *sui generis* interests—including those leading to granting "legal personality" to avatars—displace the generality of the Constitution *de iure* or even only *de facto*, and as the Constitution-enshrined rights progressively turn non-actionable (more than they already are), the "constitutional State" and all discourses attached thereto will need to abdicate in favour of either anarchy or hybrid public-private techno-driven autocratic forms of civil governance (not *government*, indeed) for humans and avatars. Section 6 draws on both sections 4 and 5 to illustrate how the metaverse could redefine constitutional procedures (Sect. 4) while disrupting the centralised ability of the State to "speak the law" (Sect. 5): it all depends on the metaverse's cognitive impact, the "transfigured" transplant of legal devices and transactions onto metaversic orders where the effect of those devices is distorted, and the perpetuation, duplication, and exacerbation of all law-dependent shortcomings that constitutional societies are already experiencing – both quantitatively (when the current legislation-dependent societal shortcoming, eg inherited privilege, is replicated in the metaversic order) and qualitatively (when the current problem acquires new and possibly even more perilous facets because of and/or through its readoption in the metaverse as well). Against this backdrop, special mention is credited to matters of constitutional voting *through* and *about* the metaverse. Section 7 sheds a ray of light: legislators start gaining (and socialising) awareness of the above, and planning rudimentary responses thereto, both substantively (eg via incorporating "neurorights" within their Constitutions) and procedurally (eg via conceiving of new constitutionally sanctioned voting systems that could find application in the metaverse as well). Questions remain, however, as to whether the global governance of these challenges is anywhere near to be fed with insights and solutions because of individual States' own uncoordinated initiatives – especially with reference to the issues of jurisdictional authority and apportionment that are so core to the metaverse as a disruptor of constitutional orders domestically and vis-à-vis each other under international law. In light of this encouraging but still insufficient—and possibly misguided as to what its focus should be—constitutional response by States to the metaverse, it is probably worth looking back to the social contract and global constitutionalism, and checking what conceptual and operational toolboxes have been developed thereunder to address this and similar disrupting moments. This is precisely what Sect. 8 succinctly aims to offer, with its appraisal of trends that interpret the redefinition of the State and its Constitution as a reflection of surreptitious adjustments in the public-private stakes of social contracting. What seems endangered here is the very foundational idea (no matter how often unimplemented) that society is one and public, with its key infrastructure of power and institutional circuitries to be somewhat accountable to citizens and subject to their ability to rewrite them out of common aspirations. Section 8 is indeed wrapped-up with a rhetorical question: if via the metaverse (quite a few decades from now, I would say) we replace the UN's P5 with the Big Tech and let them decide the fate of our global village, what have we accomplished towards a shared humanity that dreams ahead and accounts for its own survival as opposed to that of a few (now even private) entities? We shall make sure metaversic governance leads us to fairly different outcomes than this. Otherwise, as concluded in Sect. 9, what we risk facing is the obsolescence not only of the State and its institutions, but of the Constitution as a guiding star in troubled waters and, with it, the very notion that the social contract depends on a shared destiny that the people entrust into at least one piece of legislation that applies to all citizens and binds them to some form of legally shaped structure – no matter how imperfect is has always proven to be. Before abating what humanity has achieved, it is probably worth tabling a discussion on whether any stateless, pluricentric, and/or a-Westphalian alternative is going to walk us any farther, any better – and in whose ultimate interest.

2 The Standard-Setting Privatised Governance of Digital Rights

I will delve more closely into both the Constitution and the metaverse *infra*, but one preliminary matter to deal with is the general dilemma posed by new technologies which privatise (in full or in part) our access to fundamental, actionable rights. They privatise said rights' elaboration, delivery (execution, enforcement), and all disputes connected thereto, factually replacing the constitutional ecosystem of safeguards, procedures, and hierarchies in place, and depriving public life of power and meaning.[27] Granted, the alarm bell is frequently sounded on this, but dangers for the legal order do not always necessarily follow, or at least they are not necessarily as

[27] *See also* Bassini 2019, pp.184–185.

cataclysmic as first announced. After all, that of (juridical, and perhaps more specifically constitutional) "time-shrinking"[28] is a phenomenon we have been witnessing for quite a while already (i.e. for decades, if not—though less intensively—centuries). However, I tend to subscribe to the idea that the metaverse could in fact embody a dramatic disruption, an abrupt acceleration in terms of privatisation of the public good and of social relations thriving therein. This has been long enunciated in sci-fi literature as well (with special reference to the works by Neal Town Stephenson), which is often to the front in capturing social change and its robotised dystopic momentum.[29]

One of the concerns at stakes is that of leading towards the parcellation of reality into a multilevel living dimension, whereby the metaverse starts as a free "liberating" project to then actually turn into a multi-speed device that ends up drawing a new divide between the élite and the rest. Equally alarming would be either a metaverse for the élite and locked-out-from-the-metaverse life for those who cannot afford it, or, most probably, a you-get-what-you-pay-for technological solution whereby census-based social classes will be populating the metaverse, mostly replicating (and arguably worsening) those fractures that already so evidently sort humans into castes within any society[30] – and particularly the American one, which would serve as the barycenter of this whole enterprise. Social elevators might shift from educational attainments and hardworking attitudes to a scored subservience to the worldviews of unelected and unaccountable technofeudalists and the bureaucracies (starting indeed with universities) they are able to capture. In the first scenario (i.e. a metaverse-shaped reality for the élite versus an off-metaverse life for all others), a significant fraction of decision-making would be subtracted from public scrutiny and, with it, from the Constitution itself. Facing irrelevance towards the élites that preside over most global affairs transnationally, the Constitution would lose momentum and somehow dry up, losing pragmatic momentum and transplanting itself to the periphery of the legal order – instead of becoming the beating heart of an all-comprehensive neo-constitutional order.

For the time being, talks allude to the idea that digital services and public procedures such as marriages will be held (also?) in the metaverse, but what if one day the metaverse remains the only forum to hold core publicly relevant (and often constitutionally regulated) discussions, such as institutional hearings, parliamentary working sessions, or political-party meetings? Speaking at an innovation gathering named "TechLaw.Fest 2022", Singapore's then-Second Minister for Law, Edwin Tong Chun Fai, confirmed that he saw no reason against even legal advice and dispute resolution being provided through the metaverse in the near future[31] – and similar opinions circulate widely across governmental departments, regulators, and courts in East Asia. Is thus seems fair to wonder how this shift not only in *locus* per se, but in technology (and thus in hidden distributions of digital and non-digital

[28] *Refer also to* Ranchordás and Roznai 2020; Neuwirth 2024, p. 150.

[29] *Refer to* Venanzoni 2020, p.7.

[30] *Read also* Egliston and Carter 2021.

[31] *Read* Tong 2022.

power) most poignantly, will alter the landscape of access to justice, i.e. to what extent it will exacerbate existing divides (think of economic barriers but also information asymmetries) that already hinder the full realization of this constitutionally protected right. Needless to state, hybrid solutions are foreseeable, too; nonetheless, granting a "tier-B choice" (just like remote conferencing for those who cannot afford or are denied visas to travel – leaving environmental rubrics aside) would itself deepen societal fractures which keep widening at alarming speed.

Subsumed under juridical debates lie profound sociological transformations. To what extent is the metaverse an aesthetic conundrum rather than a wholesale attempted redefinition of the geometries of power? Constitutional implications could not prove more remarkable. First, one needs to grasp whether the metaverse is more of a top-down imposition pushed-for by a de facto monopolistic cartel of big techs, i.e. a technology nobody was truly longing for but will anyway encompass and phagocytise the prerogatives of traditional legal orders, or if it expresses instead a genuine interest on the side of a society which is desperately looking for escape routes and ways out from the centralised (publicists would call it "Westphalian") constitutional order made of States which no matter how internally administered, have a written or "dispersed" constitution as their apex. Is the metaverse a reaction to the downsides of such a centralisation, somewhat a symptom of disaffection towards its rules and of disappointment about its rulers? Will it challenge the constituted order, the status quo? Of course, it may embody both phenomena combined, so that it all turns into a matter of assessing odds, and especially of forecasting the overall outcome, expressed as potential consequences for Constitutions as we know them today. All considered, the metaverse is plausibly going to become neither a platform for neo-enslavement, nor the epitome of a new renaissance; in any event, it is urgent to assess how both forces are shaping the supposed need for a metaverse for us all to "live" in.

Prima facie, one could argue that analogous concerns and dynamics were already at play with the cyberspace, but this would be inaccurate a predicament. For better or worse, the cyberspace was conceived as a project of horizontal freedom, underpinned by some degree of digital anarchy and anonymity, but ended up being managed by a network of US-tied public-private partnerships such as the Internet Corporation for Assigned Names and Numbers (ICANN), infrastructured by a handful of corporations, and placed under the jurisdiction of States. Nowadays, cyberspace governance is indeed a contested terrain and a playing chessboard for geopolitical alliances and reposturing moves.[32] Hence, what differentiates it from the metaverse is that with the latter we would *already be starting* from a fairly codified private ecosystem whereby major corporations take the lead – importantly, the size (profit-wise and measured by market-share) these corporations exhibit is not comparable to that of the firms running the Internet back in the days. In sum, the starting scenario is worryingly unbalanced to favor conglomerates of private actors and the formulas for "social" contracts they advertise under the patronage of what has been called the 'model of benevolent dictatorship'.[33] Besides this, as (socio-legal) scholars and policymakers,

[32] *See* Vecellio Segate 2019.

[33] Leenes 2019, p.133.

our duty is to oversee not only the starting point, but the direction it will be heading to, what the metaverse will become over the years. The Internet was born horizontal and free to be later wrapped into compenetrated state and corporate geometries at once; the metaverse is already born heavily corporatised, yet it could even grow worse as its leadership and ownership evolve.

It is unlikely that the metaverse succeeds in readjusting the balance between constitutional powers or the functioning of those state institutions exercising such powers, unless it calls for a more foundational rethinking of the formal texture of the State, starting with the Constitution, understood narrowly as a legal text but also as the supreme reference of those values in which our social contract is grounded.[34] But the law, and with it the Constitution, feeds itself with spaces, displays its own geography, and is channeled through infrastructure.[35] The relationship between citizens and the constituted power articulates itself around institutionalised infrastructure granting citizens access to the law and its "lived life", so that they can live it, too, integrating themselves within the constitutional texture. All those interactions and "sharing" activities which occur in the metaverse will then be more pointedly framed as an exchange of that information and negotiation of the boundaries of those liberties that make or keep citizens an active component of their complex organised society. With reference to just-mentioned articulation, the relevant question might be: if not the metaverse alone, but a "metaversic model" more comprehensively, is what our societies tend to and are leaning towards, what will a Constitution be for? More roughly, would still we be needing any Constitution at all? Indeed, the "virtual" component of our lives would be regulated by service providers themselves, while the "offline" component of our living, attracted as it may be to the black whole of financialised privatisation, would be less and less a prerogative of traditional constitutional organs. Worse, even: the remaining (i.e. non-metaversic) part of our life would remain anchored to a Constitution whose guarantors (i.e. traditional public institutions) are increasingly captured by interests of an élite which is not even domestic, but transnational, and which is as such unwilling to attend to the interests of the average citizen.[36] Then again, is the "Constitution" the most appropriate term of comparison to assess the ways in which the metaverse might attempt to disrupt the traditional constitutionally entrusted rights and obligations?

What seems plausible is that a metaverse-intensive world would be governed by a capillary network of soft laws in the form of technical standards,[37] in such a way that those standards will define what one can or cannot do, is or is not granted access to, in a virtual ecosystem of standardised transactions, communications, operations, and perhaps even beliefs. They are "soft" in the sense that for the time being, no court of law would immediately enforce, in the real world, metaversic rights or duties deriving from such corporation-set standards, but if the metaverse is going to absorb a significant fraction of our daily living, the impact would be appreciable nonetheless.

[34] *See for example* Cern et al. 2012 or Raffield 2000.

[35] *Explore e.g.* Ducuing 2020, Kingsbury 2019, as well as Van Den Meerssche and Gordon 2020.

[36] *Check extensively* Vecellio Segate 2022d.

[37] See eg Hossain et al. 2025; Hemphill 2023

It might well be the case that the metaverse will serve as the definitive disruptor of the "soft" versus "hard" law dichotomy, and force lawmakers and policymakers to conceive of their outputs on a continuum of shades – and enforcers to follow-up accordingly; after all, 'limitations inherent in binary concepts of regulation are found in the context of technology and innovation generally. Not surprisingly, many novel industries and technologies are now qualified as oxymora, such as [...] "virtual reality"'.[38]

In fact, technical standards in the digital realm have a long history of *de facto* exceeding their "soft" configuration and being enforced onto citizens and organisations as if they were hard laws, which is constitutionally and epistemically problematic as the place of standards within the "hierarchy of legal sources" remains unsettled. And yet, as a minimum, this enforcement has mostly been backed or operated by state authorities and institutions (mainly law-enforcement agencies and courts) themselves – think e.g. of factually binding cybersecurity requirements framed as standards in China,[39] which are going to be enforced by an increasingly demanding and empowered Cybersecurity Administration.[40] The problem with metaversic standards instead is that *no single State*, endorsement aside, could actually enforce any of the standards "softly promoted" by metaverse providers, simply because such a technology is premised to create a supranational meta-reality where the distributional effects of any legally relevant action cannot be catered for by any single state authority alone. Once more, it is a matter of extent. First, one could be tempted to argue that societies are in fact able to supranationally agree on common technical standards – think e.g. of standard-essential patents in the telecommunications sector – and indeed, scholars have advised that '[c]ountries can incorporate issues concerning[, for instance,] the compatibility and security of metaverse technical standards into trade and technology agreements'.[41] Second, one could object that cooperation among jurisdictions is already intense when it comes to Internet governance and to certain classes of cybercrime. Both these arguments are valid in the abstract, but if the metaverse truly runs the way many apparently assume it will run, then our daily living "on" and "through" it would prove so massive that neither ad-hoc (or even structural) cooperation among jurisdictions on the enforcement side, nor the sharing of common standards on technological technicalities only, would suffice. Indeed, the "standards" at stake in the metaverse would impact the very way in which citizens can express their "being social" within a community whose boundaries are set not so much by tradition or the constitutional order of a State, but by the private rules, expectations, and policing actions of a corporation (or, most probably, a transnational cartel thereof) – including self-auditing as a misleading form of

[38] Neuwirth 2022a, p.45.

[39] *See* Vecellio Segate 2020a, p.656 ftn.49.

[40] *Refer to* Roberts et al. 2022.

[41] Yang 2023, p.8.

policy enforcement.[42] Facts based on such fictitiously "soft" laws are then adjudicated through equally fictitiously "soft" proceedings, with legal persons (including machines) arbitrating relatively small claims[43] under the privatised regime stipulated with (or more accurately, by) the corporation itself – the metaverse provider, in this case.

This privateness is problematic for a number of reasons. If standards are universalised, this is likely to happen out of imposition by the most powerful corporate conglomerate (most often one which can reap the benefit of regulatory capture with the most powerful governments) rather than owing to a consensual quality-based agreement alone – as it already occurs in cognate technology-intensive domains.[44] If standards are not integrated, instead, the Metaverse is unlikely to become what commentators seem to suppose it is set to become,[45] i.e. a global virtual arena for interactive engagement, transactions, and service-provision among avatars and the users behind them. Although decoupling is not (yet) abiding to the most extreme agenda most were expecting it to follow, it is still happening to a degree that would threaten the sharing of technical standards among jurisdictions.[46] Phrased differently, either a private entity proves powerful enough to impose its metaversan standards worldwide, or public entities will plausibly pursue a decoupling agenda – not just in supply chains, but in technical standardisation as well; self-evidently, either scenario is suboptimal: we would rather need States to take leadership of these developments and work towards common standards in a transparent and independent fashion – no chance this is going to happen within a few years. Meanwhile, leading standardisation bodies such as IEEE are promoting human rights agendas alongside traditional human rights organisations, up to issuing joint reports on metaversic rights;[47] this is an interesting development, whose implications are worth paying attention to.

3 Transforming the Constitution: Substantive Implications

The above has introduced the general framework within which Constitutions and the "upcoming" metaverse would swing. But what are the substantive constitutional profiles at stake? With no claim of exhaustivity, I will now peruse a few of them. Some will sound like the "metaversisation" of traditional human rights, but warnings have already been issued to caution against using "normative equivalence" by design as a tool for policing the digital realm: "translating" offline (or even current Internet's)

---

[42] For a telling piece on the misleading contours of internal auditing (though in another field), *refer to* Spahr 2011; *refer further to* Vecellio Segate 2020c, p.10 ff.

[43] *See also* Moreira and Vecellio Segate 2021, p.527.

[44] *Refer eg to* Vecellio Segate 2024a; Vecellio Segate 2024c.

[45] *Read also* Zalan and Barbesino 2023, p. 3.

[46] *See* De Gregorio and Radu 2022, p. 69.

[47] See eg Council of Europe and IEEE 2024.

human rights into the metaverse requires at times not solely equivalence, but recontextualisation, reprioritisation, and even reconceptualisation when applicable – in short, customised vision. Indeed, if

> the unique features of cyberspace put in question the desirability and feasibility of an automatic extension of offline human rights to cyberspace [...] because cyberspace represents a substantially different interactive environment, dissimilar to the context against which traditional human rights treaties and standards were developed,[48]

this is all the more true for the "pro" version of the Internet itself, i.e. the metaverse.

The first substantive matter of constitutional relevance to consider involves privacy rights in the metaverse.[49] I was writing in the Introduction that increased corporate surveillance due to pandemic lifestyle's intensive recourse to digital technologies has characterized the come-back of VR as a potentially disruptive technology. Such a surveillance, aimed at data exhaustion and behavioral extraction, flows into a broader trend that registers corporations take on public roles (including security, communication, dispute resolution, or those an ancient agora would have played) "free of charge" in exchange for data to feed their profitable analytics. One of the consequences is that public authorities often try to react by increasing in turn their own surveillance over what data is exchanged and how, reclaiming control over the communication process and, as a necessary corollary, the very infrastructure channeling it.[50] This occurred e.g. with the Internet:

> The predominant role of decentralized and unaccountable entities exercising powers mirroring public authority would look like a legitimate ground for state actors to expand their authority online. The challenges raised by private powers would appear as a legitimate ground to increase powers by restricting the freedoms of the private sector. This trend leads to increased surveillance and control. In this light, attempts by state actors to regain authority by impacting the architecture of the Internet represent powerful ways to regulate the digital environment.[51]

In fact, having the State join Internet regulation, which was saluted as strengthening electoral accountability,[52] has simply caused the State to align itself to the Big Tech and the transnational élite revolving therearound in surveilling citizens for tax, welfare, "security", and other proclaimed objectives.[53]

No one can tell how the metaverse will work yet, but if it will be powered by the same infrastructure enabling today's Internet, it is safe to assume that the aforementioned tendency will just increase in magnitude. Nevertheless, even by the most conservative estimations, billion more data points await to be collected thanks to the metaverse. The latter will plausibly require extraordinary computing power, data centres, and capillary network coverage, which means that it is probably wiser

---

[48] Dror-Shpoliansky and Shany 2021, p. 1281.

[49] *Read also* Blitz 2021, p.384.

[50] *Refer extensively to* Mainwaring 2020.

[51] De Gregorio and Radu 2022, p.86.

[52] *See e.g.* Flew 2022, p.299.

[53] *Refer extensively to* Vecellio Segate 2022d, especially Chapter 1 and Part Four.

to assume it will rely on an alternative infrastructure, including satellite-delivered Internet or even a completely different digital infrastructure yet to be engineered. Whatever the infrastructure though, the "catching-up game through surveillance" between public and private entities will most probably remain a constant. Notable here is that public and private entities are not as distinguishable as one might assume: they stand closer to a public-private power conglomerate[54] that accounts for the preferences and priorities of a transnational élite which endeavors to surreptitiously capture public and private actors alike.[55]

One of the consequences of surveillance is the chilling effect on citizens' behavior, which, in turn, strips customary laws of genuineness, in that the law is going to be tailored to traditions which stem from fear rather than spontaneous social organizing around commonly recognized values and practices. One dilemma, then, is whether such "denaturalised" customs would only invest the metaverse, or would rather be transplanted onto the "real word" (and thus incorporated into non-metaverse laws as customs, for example) as well. Does the surveillance of avatars chill the behavior of the users behind them with reference to their choices and actions in the off-VR, non-metaverse dimension of living? More research, also from cognitive psychology and other soft sciences, is urged on this point. An interesting angle this could be looked at from is labour law,[56] on how to make sure that constitutional principles of workers' dignity do not fall into obsolescence in the wake of metaversic workplaces and job tasks – when not "workers" altogether.[57]

Still along the lines of data protection, but resuming the debate on infrastructure, one question arises as to whether data portability—ie, interoperability as provided for in e.g. Article 20 of the General Data Protection Regulation (GDPR) or Article 50(2) of the Artificial Intelligence Act (AIA)—could be operated cross-infrastructure, or the metaverse and the "old" Internet running through different infrastructure would stay mutually incommunicable and siloed.[58] There are indeed several possible derogations from one's right to data protection within the EU, and their assessment is usually phrased in proportionality terms.

Notably, proportionality functions as a quasi-constitutional analytical tool at the intersection between public exceptionalism and fundamental rights, even beyond the data-protection realm.[59] For example, when will law-enforcement agencies be afforded the right to lawfully search our metaverse, just like today they strive to gain

[54] *Refer eg to* Vecellio Segate 2024b.

[55] *Refer extensively to* Vecellio Segate 2022d, especially Chapter 1 and Part Four.

[56] *Check also* Donini and Novella 2022, p.12.

[57] Tommasi et al. 2025.

[58] Thus, the constitutional-level problem with portability is not limited to the apportionment of jurisdiction narrowly conceived, as other publications report – *check e.g.* Madiega et al. 2022, p.5. Indeed, the question does not only concern *what the relevant fraction of a shared infrastructure* is (i.e. which State can exercise jurisdiction thereover), but more fundamentally *what infrastructure* should a jurisdiction be concerned with. Another data-portability (albeit quite different) issue, fraught with competition implications as well, concerns the interoperability between "metaverses" – if more than one are going to be developed; *refer to* Hunt 2022.

[59] *See extensively* Dalla Corte 2022.

access to smartphones, social-media profiles, or cloud storages? This question draws significance from a long history of policy and court constitutional-level debates on the boundaries between reasonable expectations of privacy and the sovereign right to access citizens' privately stored data and metadata.[60] And indeed, more generally, data protection is first and foremost a constitutional safeguard based on general principles of law – especially in Europe.[61] The data-access issue was mentioned from the law-enforcers perspective, but think of criminal defendants who are barred from subpoenaing technology providers and manufacturers for the contents of other individuals' electronic communications[62]: the problem will reiterate itself with regards to the metaverse, just higher in magnitude because of the qualitative comprehensiveness of the data that can be recorded therein compared to traditional online chats or social media. Said recorded data might even be uploaded to the "darkverse" (conceptually the same as the dark web)[63] and encourage scams, data brokerage, and illicit blackmailing activities.

There is then the whole discussion on "neurorights",[64] which cannot be elaborated on in detail here,[65] but surely impacts the constitutional safeguards we have to devise prior to the metaverse affirming itself in the market. Think, for instance, of the problem of affective computing and biometrics to accurately elaborate human or avatar responses to subliminal stimuli[66]: this will deserve dedicated regulation up to the constitutional level – exactly because we are entering a wholly novel terrain of rights directly inspecting and safeguarding our most intimate psychoneurological sphere. It seems worth recalling, in this respect, that the issue does not lie with *intermediation* per se,[67] meaning that to be problematic is not necessarily the fact that a VR application intervenes between the citizen and their socio-political responsibility, rights, and duties. In fact, *disintermediation*, too, might prove hazardous in that it alters the edgy balance among constitutional functions, prerogatives, and limitations. One exemplification is that of devices whose (claimed) ability to read our thoughts in the metaverse potentially translates into them communicating such thoughts to law enforcers without filter nor screening. Such agencies would then be made aware of our supposed thoughts (or those of our avatars, assuming—without conceding—they will get any closer to meta-consciousness, one day) and deploy them against us for investigatory purposes or perhaps even trying to tender them as evidence in criminal court proceedings.[68] This would raise serious concerns in terms of both legitimacy and accuracy, which are well known about digital evidence more generally[69] but in this

[60] *Refer e.g. to* Garon 2022, pp.56–63.

[61] *See* European Union Agency for Fundamental Rights 2018, pp.27–28;242–243.

[62] *Refer also to* Wexler 2021, p.2724.

[63] *Refer to* Huq et al. 2022, p.8. *See also* Julian 2022 or Verardi 2022.

[64] Brown 2024; Kellmeyer 2022.

[65] Bublitz 2025.

[66] *Read further* Martin 2022, pp.252–256; Vecellio Segate (2024d).

[67] It is not so with the traditional Internet, either; *refer e.g. to* Piana 2021, pp.45–46.

[68] *Check generally* Kraft and Giordano 2017.

[69] *See e.g.* Vecellio Segate 2021.

case, too, would be amplified in the metaverse and call for a remarkable rethinking of certain constitutional entitlements from a "neuro" perspective. Mentioned unfiltered reading abilities would be enabled by brain-computer interfaces powering "neuro-reality"[70] – which potentially exhibits profound implications for the constitutional human-rights discourse.[71]

Some implications of delving into human rights from a neuro perspective cannot be scrutinised at length here, but deserve to be mentioned briefly. As alienating as it might sound, the first is the right to … die; to die "definitely", meaning that holograms or anyway *post mortem* VR reproductions of ourselves in the form of avatars should be banned or discouraged. As a minimum, they should be subjected to strictly informed *ante mortem* consent. While we are still alive, it is also essential that our identity and autonomy are not interfered with by virtual realities, which would somewhat disable us as functional citizens. This right has been termed to "psychological continuity",[72] and is part of wider entitlements inherent to our mental sphere of action and reflection vis-à-vis the virtuality of VR/AR applications and their potentially disruptive cognitive momentum.[73] Mental health is one cardinal component of the right to health, which should be enhanced rather than compressed with the advent of the metaverse.

More to the societal side, certain rights are linked to ensuring that virtuality does not disrupt the democratic project – whatever "democracy" actually means, which is in itself highly debatable.[74] In the US, public actors are constitutionally required to be a platform for free speech under the First Amendment, so that identifying the metaverse as a public agora would stand as a primary step forward towards VR's democratisation – thus partly offsetting the threat the metaverse represents for healthy (… assuming they ever are so) democratic interactions in the digital prism.[75] Non-discrimination, too, bears a collective dimension, particularly algorithmically speaking, in that it entails safeguarding the identity and autonomy of citizens both individually and as components of natural or artificial groups.[76] Fair process is arguably common good as well, particularly in criminal courtrooms, where trials are "constitutionally" held on behalf of the State as a whole: providing judges with virtual tools to assess defendants should not lower the human inquisitory, exculpatory, and cross-examinatory requirements. More lightly, the right to a "fair process" should not be discounted digitally, either; an issue which had already presented itself with

---

[70] *Explore further at* Paiva Andrade 2019.

[71] *See generally* Fuselli 2020.

[72] Ienca 2021, p. 43. However, *check* Olson 1999.

[73] *Read further* Ligthart et al. 2022a; Ienca and Andorno 2017; Bujić et al. 2020; Ganschow et al. 2021; Lake 2020; Ligthart et al. 2022b.

[74] see Piergiorgio Odifreddi, *La democrazia non esiste. Critica matematica della ragione politica* (Rizzoli 2018).

[75] *Read further* Huq 2023.

[76] *Read extensively* Vecellio Segate 2022c.

Facebook and the like,[77] but which risks becoming unsustainable in the metaverse[78]: the exclusion therefrom might be tantamount to being rejected almost "corporeally" from an entire dimension of the private and social living. Specularly, the metaverse should not impair, delay, or complexify citizens' right to legal remedy and legal action, nor should it worsen those taxation trends which already see the wealthy get away with exceptionality regimes while the 99% struggles to make ends meet across most countries. Property rights (though probably to be framed under contract and land law as opposed to property law[79]) are also at stake[80]: they acquire constitutional dignity not solely owing to their potential interfaces with international human rights law (IHRL), for example with reference to the right to housing and speculations in the housing market, but also for relatively smaller items due to terms-of-service contracts 'called end-user license agreements, which claim to define the members' rights in their in-world assets',[81] and which might be enforceable in real-world jurisdictions based on actions performed in the (common?) metaverse – and vice versa. To put it otherwise, it was claimed that

> [t]he most important legal instruments governing free speech on the Internet today are not derived from the Constitution, but from contract law—the terms of service governing the relationship between Internet companies and their customers.[82]

This statement holds validity insofar as the "traditional" Internet is concerned, but because terms of service in the metaverse might operate as meta-jurisdictional switching devices, they are somehow elevated to constitutional significance. The last societally relevant policy area shaped by human rights and potentially impacted by the metaverse that I would like to mention here is that of security provision, understood as patrolling and more generally concerned with the question of enforcing more porous "borders", but also as cybersecurity and the physical safety of those who might be overexposed to real-world harm while operating in the metaverse, and would as such required additional protection – i.e., higher protection than it would have been the case had they not populated and performed through the metaverse. This calls *inter alia* for the identification of specially protected categories, including of course children but others, too, which might be more "metaverse-specific", so to write.

Again in the public realm, another portfolio of implications from the rise of the metaverse relates to the highest-ranked public-servant positions and their public status and standing, which may ultimately affect the balance of powers and the wider dynamics at stake between constitutional-level organs and offices. The risk is not new to the metaverse, of course: the boundaries between official and unofficial,

---

[77] Out of massive (and still growing!) literature from all possible scholarly standpoints, *check at least* Gillespie et al. 2020; Sander 2020; Gorwa et al. 2020; De Streel et al. 2020; Heldt and Dreyer 2021; Keller 2022; Quintais et al. 2023; Langvardt 2018.

[78] *See also* Wheeler 2023.

[79] *Read* Hutson et al. 2023, p. 4.

[80] *Consult* Part V *in* Barfield and Blitz 2018.

[81] Moringiello 2010, p.171.

[82] Citron and Richards 2018, p.1357.

and related procedural and substantive demarcations among powers both domestically and under public international law (PIL), have already turned porous because of extensive social-media posting and networking by officials such as Heads of States, key ministries, career diplomats, apex-court judges, and other high-ranked civil servants. However, the "identity replication" that avatars represent may well mark a step forward in that direction, compenetrating officiality and informality to unprecedented levels – thus also triggering unprecedented incidents, including deepfake-caused ones.[83]

More to the market side, immediate concerns are raised by the metaverse with regards to antitrust policies: conjecturing the metaversan Constitution will embody a section on competition law modelled after real-world state and supranational (quasi-) Constitutions such as the Treaty on the Functioning of the European Union (TFEU), how could multiple providers stay compliant and diversify the market? Put differently, if all (or most) metaverse providers are factually compelled to cooperate because the metaverse is supposed to be inherently collaborative as both a technology and a concept,[84] how could they refrain from forming a cartel by definition? Implications in the competition law domain are uncountable, and they encompass issues of algorithmic collusion and data "ownership" that will, however, not be examined here because their immediate consequences are less relevant at the constitutional level.[85]

Intellectual property rights (IPR), too, might be shaped by the metaverse to an extent that calls into question the Constitution. For example, a complex debate is held on whether AI-generated artworks are copyrightable: while the answer generally lies in the negative, some Constitutions (like the US one) are silent on whether copyrightable works shall be human-made, and the metaverse might reignite such a discussion by allowing for a previously unthinkable amount of art generated by non-humans (i.e. avatars, in this case) to be produced and marketed at relatively low cost.[86] Another IPR-related debate involving both the metaverse and the Constitution, again in the US, concerns the boundaries between art (protected under the First Amendment) and trademark infringement, trademark dilution, and cybersquatting regarding NFTs.[87]

Beyond specific fields though, there exist other inspections which are rather fundamental, challenging the rationale of the entire conception of the role of law within societies – which is usually shaped by and mirrored in the Constitution. For example, I will mention *infra* that avatars might be granted legal personality. One of the risks inherent in this choice is that certain crimes go unprosecuted just because users (i.e. real-world citizens) commit them through avatars or because such crimes are only

---

[83] *Refer further to* Europol 2022a.

[84] *Read* Murphy et al. 2021.

[85] On these (and other) "less constitutional" aspects of competition law for the metaverse, *read more at* Megale 2022; Grac-Aubert and O'Brien 2022; Gleiss et al. 2023, p.191.

[86] *See* Nanobashvili 2022, p.247.

[87] *See* Judge Jed Rakoff's memorandum in *Hermès International v. Rothchild*, U.S. District Court for the Southern District of New York, Case No. 22-cv-384 (May 18, 2022). *Read further* Murray 2022, p.12 ff. Roibu 2024; Yarmak 2025.

committed virtually. Of course this reads like unacceptable a perspective, but certain criminal-law intellectuals might well argue that besides retributivism, if criminal law is fundamentally premised on security concerns,[88] then punishing criminal avatars would not be concerning enough to trigger a legal response in the traditional criminal justice circuit. In other words, one's understanding of criminal law's theoretical essence—which undoubtedly *is* a constitutional-level debate—suffices to deliver two opposite conceptions about the convenience for criminal law to encompass crimes committed by avatars. I find it essential to specify that even if a response were triggered, crimes that are perceived as "grave" in the off-metaverse reality might turn out "soft" when committed in/through the metaverse, and the other way round. Over time, this might erode century-long constitutional traditions whose founding values propagate into criminal codes and shape back the constitutional discourse. Put differently, criminal law's substantive criteria for prosecuting and convicting an individual are grounded in value-based discourses whose highest synthesis is represented by the Constitution – although the latter is not too frequently cited explicitly in criminal courts.[89] Values translate into principles, which are then applied to "fill" the substantive priorities and hidden "hierarchies of harm" criminal law is construed upon; this is evidenced both domestically and internationally.[90] Think of human dignity as a fundamental societal value,[91] or take e.g. the principles of proportionality[92] (already recalled *supra*) and non-retroactivity.[93] To exemplify, in the UK, certain values emanating from ordinary statutes like the Human Rights Act shall be understood as bearing constitutional force and translating into constitutionally safeguarded principles of justice.[94] And in Canada,

> this overarching logic of constitutional analysis even touches upon *mens rea* requirements, with proportionality between the degree of moral fault and the gravity of the crime/seriousness of the penalty becoming a principle of fundamental justice and the constitutional measuring stick for constitutionally acceptable levels of fault.[95]

One implication is that if the metaverse succeeds in reshuffling the perception of the degree of gravity of certain crimes, it will also mark a contribution to constitutional discourses so far as the values criminal law draws inspiration from are concerned. Another implication is that a metaversan criminal law grounded in a privatised metaversan criminal discourse risks situating priority with corporate managerialism rather than societal virtue. In fact,

[88] *See also* Vecellio Segate 2022b.
[89] *Read further* Hoque 2021; Bilionis 1998.
[90] *Refer e.g. to* Heinze 2018.
[91] *See* Barak 2015, pp.103–113.
[92] *Read further* Nieto Martín 2019.
[93] *See* Kryvoi and Shaun 2021; Martinico et al. 2019, p. 505.
[94] *Refer to* Singh 2013, pp.18–19.
[95] Berger 2014, pp.9–10.

> the administration and enforcement of criminal law should be so structured that lay citizens take part in it and see their sense of justice at work in it, rather than left wholly to officials and experts acting on the instrumental reasons characteristic of bureaucratic control[96];

this bureaucratization of the criminal process is already widespread in the non-virtual reality, and a corporatised criminal law grounded in metaversan constitutions would plausibly exacerbate the problem. It is perhaps worth highlighting that not only the substance, but also procedural facets of criminal law are called into question by the Constitution and principles (more or less legitimately) derived therefrom.[97] This trespass into procedural matters flows naturally into the next section, dedicated to the formal profiles of the constitutional practice and discourse that are most plausibly going to be impacted by the metaverse. Nevertheless, the distinction between substance and form is obviously not always as neat.

4 The Constitutional form vis-à-vis the Metaverse

Will the metaverse "speed up" the Constitution, conferring *concinnitas* (elegant lightening) to it? Constitutional texts are still conceived with a sense of institutional *gravitas*, and yet in practice institutions seem to be irreversibly condemned to play the role of followers in catching-up games between reality (e.g. technological development, indeed) and the regulation thereof. Up to this time, we have used to reckon the Constitution as somehow external to the regulatory pace, as if responsive regulation was solely other laws' affair, in a way that "the guardian does not run after the runners". Truth is that the Constitution, as well, informs the action of responsive regulators and shapes the related responsive regulatory channels and responsive regulations. This is not to claim that a slower pace and some inflexibility are never to value[98]: the problem is that when everything seems fated to proceed at high speed, regulation needs to adapt (unless it is persuasive enough to invert reality's direction) or will be forced to abdicate its role in favour of more "efficient" platforms, where the debate is subtly or overtly privatized but that are perceived by civil society and businesses as more streamlined and thus preferable as "temporary" solutions[99] – such arrangements normalizing and crystallising over time. Responsiveness, understood here as response rapidity, is a key variable not solely in lawmaking, but even more in our way to conceive the law and its functioning within society, so much that higher or lower legislating pace may alter the way people "live" their relationship with the law and its representatives. A fitting example is the introduction of hybrid regimes in lieu of systems which one could once define of candid civil law. There is no such

---

96 Kleinfeld 2017, p.1457.

97 *Check e.g.* Aviram 2018; ECtHR 2019, pp.8;25–29;32–34.

98 And indeed, *check* Perrone 2020, Burbules 2020, Nicholas 2020, van Klink 2018.

99 *See also* Venanzoni 2020, p.9.

thing as a pure civil-law system anymore,[100] and the metaverse will just accelerate their hybridization/heteroconvergence process.

To keep pace with the technological takeover of public spaces, times, and social *mores*, codes of law need more and more to take in the influx of judicial "fill-ups" from both domestic and foreign (as well as international) jurisdictions: this is transforming civil-law systems into hybrid ones, whereby judges exercise not only case-by-case discretion but also leave a permanent interpretative trace in the legal system itself, factually integrating or even redefining the meaning to be attached to terms, procedures, categories of our living together, all the way up to constitutional norms. It is indeed through judicial activism operated by much stressed and under-pressure judges[101] that international standards are gradually but certainly penetrating the constitutional texture of several domestic jurisdictions in the form of standards and principles—like the precautionary one[102]—which are customarising much faster than it once happened. Will the metaverse further catalyse this already hyper-accelerated reality, putting judges (and legal systems, all the way to the Constitution) under further interpretative, (mal)adaptive strain? One preliminary operation is to sort customs generally from those specifically emanating and applicable to the metaverse only (should we call them "metaversan customs"?), to then wonder to what extent the latter may amend the former, in what (legally substantiated) ways, and more widely what room is there for virtual customs within the formal hierarchy of sources. For instance, should avatars' actions over time contribute to the formation of customs, perhaps if employed/deployed by public administrations? – doctrinally speaking, it is the State that originates and sanctions customs under PIL, not citizens' behaviors or opinions per se. Hard to tell, but any reasonable answer would also depend on whether avatars' decisions are AI-powered rather than human-supervised to an appreciable degree.

Another dossier is worth spending some thoughts on concerns the long-term response to the long-lived conundrum of the receipt of international law within domestic legal orders, often mediated by constitutional judges upon intervention of constitutional clauses.[103] In so-called "dualist systems" where public international law needs parliamentary or executive "domestication" before turning domestically enforceable, the metaverse might "come first" and *de facto* extend a quasi-global law as far as the rights and duties of avatars—"digital citizens"—are concerned. Broadening the scope of this abstraction, one could start speculating on the potential large-scale circulation of values across the metaverse, which would soon acquire the role of norm producer and super-spreader; a panacea for globalisation, but *which* globalisation? One that is freely adopted and sought after, or one which works by elitist imposition of "the market"? The one which pursues a common denominator across several approaches to "the public", or the one which serves as a sounding board for type-approved thinking?

---

[100] Just for the sake of exemplification, appreciate the case of Italy: Infantino 2013.

[101] *Read for instance* Francot and Mommers 2017.

[102] *Check* Venanzoni 2020, p.12.

[103] *See* Petersen 2009; Ndulo 2021; Ginsburg et al. 2008; HLR 2016; Böckenförde 2022.

One more dilemma concerns the boundaries of self-governance. In the metaverse, from a constitutional perspective, self-governance in an expression of informational self-determination, which stands as an established right across many "Western" jurisdictions,[104] but might foster more controversy in less individualistic legal cultures. That on metaversan governance is, in fact, a longstanding debate, which in literature has already drawn attention to.

> two sometimes conflicting fundamental normative claims: that the development of autonomous consensual governance in virtual communities ought to be encouraged, and that territorial [S]tates should limit autonomy where it offends against the values of the territorial community.[105]

The problem of governance lies at the crossroads of two delimitations: that between the governance of the metaverse by its own community versus State institutions, and that between such a community and the corporate owners/managers presiding thereover. Emphasis should be placed on "self"-governance of the metaverse not metamorphosising into a surreptitious private district whose rules of sociality are factually top-down imposed – no matter the participatory propaganda being propelled to the contrary effect. If the metaverse truly "runs itself", we will have two "public" constitutional communities one aside the other – whose members can however be said to mostly coincide. In the reverse scenario, i.e. that of a metaverse whose community is only rhetorically self-governed while in fact falling trapped into organised machineries of private ordering, we would obtain instead a private community which tries to subtract constitutional prerogatives from the state community (which I am assuming here, for the sake of readability, to be "public" – despite phenomena of transnational elitism, regulatory capture of institutions and decision-making processes alike, and so forth).

Let me now re-enter for a moment the domain of criminal law, but from a more theoretical standpoint. Preoccupations are often voiced to caution against the metaverse serving as a safe playground for activities which would be criminalised in the off-metaversan, institutionalised society. However, besides certain common tenets, each jurisdiction tends to criminalise the most absurd items, in a fairly randomised distribution of nonsense. If the metaverse is populated by avatars and as long as crimes committed among avatars bear no implications in the "real world"—plus, trusting that users voluntarily subscribe to this wild lawless land—why should any constitutional regime step in? No human being decides where to be born: once they are born somewhere, a social contract (and a constitutional regime, in most cases) will be applied to them and forced upon them. What if they prefer to at least retain full capacity of joining "another world" where rules they are bound to as citizens stop applying? What if they want to opt for a different criminal code, given that they have come to life after choosing none of them, and their beliefs might best suit a different one from that of their jurisdiction of citizenship? They might be yearning for sort of a "safe harbor" from prosecution, just like capitalist élites have been

---

[104] *Refer e.g to* European Union Agency for Fundamental Rights, p.18 ftn.1.

[105] Suzor 2010a, p.22.

finding in tax havens and offshore financial centres (that are widely held to exploit the obsolescence of Westphalia) a safe "lawful" capital conduit for decades, impoverishing ordinary taxpayers and public finances across all jurisdictions. Any group of people who acquires the chance to do so, will naturally tend to seek privilege, a "better life", exceptionalism, or "escape" where "normalcy" as applicable everywhere else is reversed or neglected. In other words, what if the masses, the "ordinary citizens" spot and seek in the metaverse a catharsis from their subordination-by-birth-to-a-preset-citizenship condition? What if they deliberately aspire to defying the constitutional regime by joining the metaverse, as they feel like constitutions codify legal orders which besides high proclaims, most often end up privileging the already privileged and perpetuating villain structures of subjugation? Indeed,

> where informed consent does exist, then concerns about predictability or substantive fairness are likely to be greatly alleviated. There must be room for participants who consensually choose to participate in communities whose rules may seem strange or arbitrary.[106]

This cannot be chosen "in real life" (norms cannot be violated within a certain community just because some among the latter's members mutually renounce to their rights – and indeed, authorities established via self-regulation do not fall within the scope of judicial authorities in, e.g., the—formerly—European Court of Justice's case-law[107]), but what about a virtual community of avatars, whose users seek exoticism or liberation, whatever the expression thereof? Who are "we" to saturate all pores? This legal-philosophy issue, alone, would deserve an entire—and quite extensive—treatise. On the more practical side, the first problem relates to who is going to check whether consent was given, was truly "informed", or was not subsequently revoked or renegotiated. The second is the external effect of this "self-regulation" onto all other members of the "real society" that those who self-regulate are part of in the offline world. The third is slightly more conceptual, and invests the advisability (but *whom for?*) of decentralising the constitutionally bound social contract to such an extent that self-contained meta-legal atoms can be independently devised therein. Furthermore, can a community truly establish and enforce its own rules? Is a system of self-governance even conceivable, or concretely achievable? Being it accountability, representation, direct election, output legitimacy and other geometries thereof,[108] or any other permanent or *á la carte* mechanism, there always seems to be a screen between "the people" and the exercise of their decision-making potential within any given community. Take the example of any technology-intensive online community:

> The emphasis on consent in t[he] conception of the rule of law also illustrates a key tension between the internal norms of a community and the contractual terms of service. The contractual documents that purport to govern virtual communities are somewhat problematic in that they are rarely designed to encourage readability and understanding. Moreover, they often conflict with the social norms within the community, usually because of discretionary enforcement, but also because norms within the community are continuously evolving through participation, whereas the written terms are unilaterally set in advance by

[106] Suzor 2010b, p.1880.

[107] *See* Custers et al. 2022, p.101.

[108] *Explore* Schmidt 2020, pp.25–8; Piattoni 2010, pp.210–227; Steffek 2015; Strebel et al. 2019.

> the provider. As the community cultivates a separate understanding of the norms than is set out in the contractual documents, real questions of consent arise when the provider attempts to enforce the conflicting contractual provisions.[109]

Could the same not be said of a constitutional regime, were it to be identified as the regulatory *locus* for digital realities as well? The metaverse community would fast arrange for its own standards of behavioral acceptability, including its distinct worldwide-in-scope separation of powers, while the Constitution would keep speaking the self-referencing lexicon of the "offline" reality.

The constitutional discourse is crafted out of legal statuses such as "citizenship" and transactional capital in the form of non-negotiable—because somewhat assumed—societal trust in the abstract "justness" of the public authority of state institutions and the laws governing their prerogatives, functions, agency, and hierarchy. One feature linked to it is that of coercion; for Kelsen, for example, the constitutional text needs neither be just, nor necessarily on-the-ground effective: it needs to be valid. His *Grundnorm* is assumed as valid and complied with because of the "recognition" other norms tribute to the hierarchy of norms themselves within any given jurisdiction, and this grants the Constitution a binding status which no other norm can defy and no ruler can negotiate. However, from the perspective of any single citizen, such a construction is imposed upon them *ab initio* rather than chosen or consensually arranged: leaving aside subsequent acquisitions of citizens, each individual is born within a constitutional arrangement whose chrisms are attached thereto until citizenship is potentially relinquished. If we accept this definition of "Constitution" (i.e. *the apex of a binding hierarchy of norms associated to any given individual at birth within the applicable jurisdiction and enforced throughout their lifetime unless citizenship is relinquished*), then we shall also accept that speaking of any "Constitution" for the metaverse is *prima facie* meaningless as it could only apply to an individual upon the latter's voluntary subscription. However, it is not this simple. Indeed, different would be the case of a metaverse whose adherence to were indispensable for a citizen to "perform" their offline citizenship, i.e. to exercise their rights and duties to such an extent that metaverse deprivation would equate to being placed outside the circuits of sociality, and at the periphery of the protection of the law. In such a case, where the metaverse takes on the semblance of an "extension" of one's citizenship, participation would be factually coerced onto the individual, and the legal form of said coercion could well amount to a Constitution. No matter if the metaverse can cater for the individual's needs, or if it abides to principles (or even mere aspirations) of justice[110]: in Kelsenian terms, what matters is that the *ordinamento* as it is construed delegates to it prominence over the regulation of essential aspects of our social living. In other words, the metaverse's Constitution would be "validated" by its very existence as the apical normativity over a fundamental sphere of life, and naturally trusted under the commonly share belief that no other regulatory option or solution is available. At that point, the question would be not so much about *whether* we could speak of a "Constitution for the metaverse", as it would be

[109] Suzor 2010b, p.1881.

[110] *See* Paz 2015, p.82.

about the legal relationship between such a Constitution and the "offline" one – all the more considering that the one for the metaverse would be univocal globally, while the "off-metaverse" reality would keep being regulated through multiple jurisdictionally intensive constitutional (Constitutions) and meta-constitutional (Bills of Rights, Basic Laws, Charters of Rights and Freedoms, etc.) texts. Regarding such a relationship, the justice systems of the metaverse versus the real world would need to cooperate strategically and uphold the principle of *forum non conveniens*, in addition to the recognition of anti-suit injunctions (from metaversic courts to real-world courts and the other way round,[111] based on competence and political deference) whenever cooperation in principle does not produce the desired outcomes. This, too, is a constitutional-level procedural dossier.

5 A doctrinal Dispute Over the Competence to *ius dicere*

Let me now inspect the depths of metaversan law: matters of jurisdiction, and especially of apportionment thereof among mega-corporations, among sovereigns, and between the two. How to apportion jurisdiction over data? Can the traditional PIL doctrines on jurisdiction be recycled for the purpose of regulating the metaverse? Does the *lex lata* suffice? This is not the right avenue to comprehensively assess jurisdictional options for the metaverse, or to compare those options with the current management of the cyberspace, but preliminary indications can indeed by derived by the long history of States trying to assert their jurisdiction over state and non-state actors acting across (relevant fractions of) the Internet, thus understood as both "online activity" and "network infrastructure". More analogical work is urged in this area, just like it starts surfacing with regards to competing assertions of jurisdiction over digital data as well as wrongdoings stemming from algorithmic decisions.[112]

To appraise (or anticipate solutions to) jurisdictional conflicts, apart from cyberspace analogies, the first step is to decide whether avatars can be granted legal personality, i.e. the ability to sue and to be sued and consequently to claim the protection of the law, cascading from the highest text which is indeed the constitutional one. Should they be granted legal personality separate from that of their users, then speaking of a metaversic Constitution would make more sense. The two other options are that we extend users' legal personality as to encompass their avatars as well (interpreting the latter as a sort of "shadow personae"[113]), or that we dismiss avatars' legal personality *in toto*. And if legal personality is granted to avatars (either directly or by extension), the law would need to clarify whether to be addressed are actions by

---

[111] An alternative is that 'si possa giungere ad una Corte dei diritti dei metaversi, frutto di una "federazione" (più che di una semplice collaborazione) fra membri di corti nazionali, con competenze proprie' – Di Porto 2022, p.14.

[112] Johns and Compton 2022; Shurson 2025; Berman 2018.

[113] In that case we could even speak of avatars in natural-person paradigms, as if they had consciousness, particularly if linked real-time through neural networks; *refer to* Cheong 2022, pp.7–8.

users with potential effect on avatars, actions by avatars with potential effect on users, or them both. It is true that the issues of legal personality and accountability were raised in scholarship with regards to robots as well,[114] and certain commonalities cannot be disputed, but the shift here is marked by the strict relationship between a single human being and their *only one* official avatar which would operate "on their behalf" in the cyberspace.[115] In some sense, the Constitution would then regulate *inter alia* the relationship between the user and himself/herself in the form of an avatar. These are all issues of legal status which never really rose to prominence with the traditional Internet, so that drawing by analogy from the latter for the sake of jurisdictional analysis is only of limited auxilium. It assists in PIL jargon though, not only with regards to the international responsibility of States under international law (which is obviously reflected onto constitutional checks-and-balances), but in order to assess how States would apportion jurisdiction over private liabilities in multi-jurisdictional cases (which are going to represent the large majority of instances in a metaversan dimension).

Curiously, someone proposed to "corporatise" the legal personality of avatars, that is, to treat them legally as if they were corporations.[116] Their main argument is that *nulla osta* in principle towards granting constitutional rights to avatars as an extension of their human users, even in the extreme circumstance a human decides to "extend" themselves through *multiple* avatars. Indeed, their claim is that this ubiquity is already happening, and is already somewhat protected by constitutional entitlements to registering e.g. a residence and several domiciles.[117] However, identifying different possible *but at any given time mutually exclusive* locations for a human body does not seem quite as revolutionary as agreeing onto situating more extensions of a human being in a virtual world where each of such extensions would produce legally relevant acts *even simultaneously*. In the former case, the potential existence of a human is multiplied, but such a human continues to be physically located at one place at any given time, while with the metaverse we could somehow "duplicate" and "multiply" the potential lives of each human being, producing legal effects through interaction, social participation, and, if applicable in the future, even meta-citizenship.[118]

---

[114] *See* ibid., p.6. *See also* Vecellio Segate and Daly 2023, pp.3–4;24; Callari et al. 2024, pp.12–13.

[115] Of course, this is to assume that each human being corresponds to one single avatar, and that such an avatar does not take decisions on its own; different are the cases of avatars powered by deep-learning, and of avatars managed by robots in the real world – which, however, could be in turn operated by a human being. *Read further* ibid., pp.11;22. Stylised corporate avatars might exist, too – and they would however ultimately respond to humans, such as corporate managers. To complexify things, every citizen might also be allowed to manage multiple multiverse accounts expressing more than one avatar, e.g. a personal one for one's private life and a business one for the same person's professional undertakings. Or avatars could even be completely disjointed from real-world identities – this is however unlikely, otherwise there would be no leap forward from the current Internet, where no one is forced to uphold or "continue" their real identity, and thus no genuine sense of community can be built.

[116] *See e.g.* ibid., pp.13–14.

[117] *Read e.g.* Zack 2007, pp.244–246.

[118] This is theoretically sound but might prove problematic in practice: if democracy is participation and participation requires time, attention, effort, interest, and care, shifting them onto "another

Hence, although I would refrain from fully subscribing to the afore-recalled "corporatising" proposal for constitutional discourses on avatars, the recourse to "piercing the corporate veil" as an analogy to grasp the boundaries between avatar and user liability[119] might hold discrete promise. What is more, one interesting conceptual element that can be extrapolated from such a comparison (i.e. that between avatars and corporations as legal persons) concerns the "a-Westphalianness" of multinational corporations (MNCs) under the (still current?) Westphalian design of the global order, which could be made recourse to by analogy to understand the geometry of tomorrow's metaverse. Think of Westphalian exceptionalisms such as the tax-avoidance schemes elaborated by MNCs through vast networks of capital conduits, bureaucratic triangulations, and incorporated subsidiaries: they are physically part of the Westphalian order, i.e. they are territorially placed within specific States, and yet they functionally operate outside the regulatory and conceptual scope of Westphalia – through its blind spots, somehow.[120] We run the risk that the metaverse ends up working in the same way: as the top exception to a system (Westphalia) which is exceedingly outdated, rather than as the catalyst of new modes of integrated, fair, and functional global governance. It would extend "above" and "through" Westphalian constitutional regimes, in a self-contained regulatory envelope, without trying to heal their obsolescence, but simply pursuing yet another unhelpful, elitist exceptionalism thereto.

Additionally—and this observation might well have featured in the previous section on the formal implications of the metaverse for the constitutional discourse—accurately apportioning jurisdiction according to pre-set rules is of the essence to promptly gather and appraise evidence of torts and crimes.[121] While such instances might not directly involve the Constitution, most legal orders uphold, in their constitutional texts, general norms applicable to the handling of evidence, including fairness (right to defence, assurance against self-incrimination, equality of arms, comprehensive and impartial investigation, etc.). As long as the metaverse remains governed by traditional publicists' jurisdictional rules which were not conceived for it, such fairness cannot be guaranteed. And the promise of deploying avatar witnesses, lawyers, prosecutors, or judges does not sound reassuring, either.

---

reality" might exhaust those energy and time capitals that were previously deployed for the offline (or off-metaverse, more precisely) world and its politics and struggles. Because human cognitive resources and will power are on average fairly limited and inconsistent, this may translate into "diluted citizenship" as opposed to doubling the citizenship and participatory potentials. Such an outcome seems especially worrisome if large categories of users, as recalled by Henz 2022 (p.3), actually conceive of the metaverse as an escaping strategy before anything else.

[119] *Check* Cheong 2022, pp.18–19. On liability, perhaps certain aspects of the newly proposed civil liability rules from European Commission will find application to the metaverse as well. *Check* European Commission 2022b.

[120] *Read extensively* Vecellio Segate 2022d. For an introduction to (and problematisation of) "Westphalia" and its "post-" under PIL and theories of global governance, one classic reference source is Falk 2002.

[121] Shurson 2025.

6 The Constitution as a Process: Drafting and Voting in the Metaverse?

I shall now turn to the pulling effect that the metaversan technological revolution would have on Constitutions' elaboration and structure. As a start, we may imagine that Constitutions will be rediscussed (or even first drafted) in the metaverse, wishing for a closer and less mediated involvement of the populace into all participatory phases—a concept that was first experimented with in the context of elections and party politics, and interpreted in literature as either "digital populism"[122] or "platform politics".[123] Risks for democracy are inherently served, however, any time a technology platform becomes a potential language—almost never neutral, supposing "neutrality" even exists—whose toolbox is deployed to convey messages aimed at shifting consensus and votes.[124] One could rebut that the same applies to TVs or social media, and yet the magnitude (i.e. both penetration rate and cognitive impact) does not seem quite the same. If '[d]igital communication has [already] transformed the ways citizens interact between themselves as well as how citizens observe and approach political institutions',[125] the metaverse holds potential to mark an even more radical shift and expose all the risks of outsourcing civil participation to the mediation of immersive technology platforms and the predicaments of remoteness. For one thing, we could not "withdraw" from the metaverse—which is engineered to be as immersive as feasible—as easily as we do from other technologies, also because in such a parallel reality, many daily-life functions would be performed "there" – hence, "environmental noise" (eg propaganda through the metaverse)—so to write—might prove more cognitively impactful and thus harder for individuals to ignore.[126]

In terms of legal doctrines and procedures, the metaverse might prove a noteworthy game-changer, too.[127] To exemplify, legal transplant (from jurisdiction to jurisdiction as much as from field to field) might occur more extensively and rapidly than ever before, both among metaverse users and from metaverse to non-metaverse legal orders. The first scenario would contribute to the creation of a meta-law for the metaverse which could cement into a Constitution (debated and drafted by other human metaverse users or—if they ever acquire sufficient intelligence—avatars themselves through machine learning on behalf of their human twins), while the second identifies the metaverse as a driving force for the circulation of legal values expressing normative influence onto real-world constitutional orders. The acceleration of transplant phenomena could eventually contribute its share towards international law shifting

---

[122] Bedock and Cappellina 2024.

[123] Tronconi and Bailo 2025.

[124] Think of subliminal techniques – *read more at* Neuwirth 2022b. No surprise a call has been voiced for the US to ensure that addictive algorithms are given no room for thriving in the corporate metaverse; *see* Mathiyazhagan et al. 2022.

[125] Thiel 2023, p.74.

[126] *Read further* Rosenberg 2022; Bojić 2022; Rosenberg et al. 2023; Madiega et al. 2022, p.6.

[127] *Refer eg to* Nicholson et al. 2025; Raposo 2024.

towards harder expressions of global governance and from there, finally, to some embryonic semblance of "global law".

More concretely, the textual structure of Constitutions, encompassing their declared aim and organised priorities, would be altered as well, witnessing a "rebalancing transition" within Constitutions about what to focus on the most, and the rest – with the metaverse depreciating certain matters, while warranting the inclusion or upshifting of others. This is also due to potential metamorphosis in the legislative process itself, which would stand closer to contracting between citizens and private third parties (which would—at least initially—be mostly foreign) than to the traditional bargaining affair among national legislators as expressive of political parties. Even assuming the latter is left untouched, their relative standing could be slightly resized, in that citizens would also live part of their lives in another dimension whose "constitutionalism" is else from the state one.

I should also account, at least in passing, for the main geopolitical moves that the consolidation of the metaverse as a daily-use technology would instigate – starting from the potential role of data in the European constitutionalisation process. One necessary premise is that pooling together personal data, and recombining their location and interconnections, their shape and hierarchies, conveys alternative ideas of the (actual and ideal) public order, which is a set of rules operating within space and time coordinates, and whose ultimate reference is the Constitution. Far from being just an abstraction, the law manifests itself through infrastructure and spaces, and is nurtured through concrete situations which not only "happen", but were first "imagined", "foreseen", or "aspired to" by lawmakers for specific spatial contexts and enforced by authorities proportionately depending on every given situation. Thereby the reason why immersing citizens in virtuality might produce constitutionally appreciable long-term outcomes as well: the perception of legality, legitimacy, truthfulness, gravity, relatedness, causation, inference, correlation, and several more, might change. This is why, for instance,

> [w]hen training in a [virtual environment], it is important to have an understanding of the tech nological variables that can be sacrificed without degrading learning effectiveness transfer to the real world. One of these variables is *environmental fidelity*, which can be understood as the fidelity of mapping from a real-world space to a computer-generated virtual replica.[128]

The other way round is equally salient: mentally mapping juridically meaningful spaces, situations, actors, feelings, and occurrences after experiencing or encountering them in VR might not produce the same legal expectations or perceptions that would have been produced had those encounters occurred in reality first. It seems wise to admit that

> [l]ike no other software, virtual worlds give the user a sense of *being inside* them. The projected metaverse also aims to provide an immersive experience of being somewhere else. It is then worth looking back to the discussion on virtual worlds, as they are able to create new environments for building social normative orders on top of them.[129]

[128] Murcia-López and Steed 2016, emphasis in the original, in-text citations removed.

[129] Pałosz 2022, pp.1880–1881.

Building normative orders (just like the European one) is a convoluted and progressive project to be delivered through an agenda whereby legislative and technical endeavors are pursued coherently and drive one another. Consider the dataspaces project of the European Commission[130]: could data integration (that is, a single European space for data sharing) spillover onto further political integration (Heidebrecht 2025), just like a single market for goods and services has partly shaped a common European destiny decades earlier? And would the "legal hardening" of this data-driven integration concretise into specific European quasi-constitutional clauses, that could steer the European project in a federal direction? In other words, could policymakers rely on data governance as a leverage for a *digital* constitutionalism,[131] and thus ultimately translate it into real-world politics to further the European integration process, strengthen a European identity, and craft a common purpose ahead? Too early to say, but Brussels' efforts remind us of the truth that States are no longer the only (or even key) public actors shaping the future of digital constitutionalism: certain supranational institutions—such as indeed the European Commission—pursue their own agenda, which is, so to write, "more than—or else from—the sum of their constituencies". That the EU tries to compensate for its political fragmentation in a narrow sense with a struggle to retain its primacy as the atypical superpower *par excellence* through the regulation of global markets (particularly in the digital ecosystem),[132] is extremely telling of the driving force data can represent politically, and makes it unpredictable the extent to which they will enforce their own agenda without letting States ride free about deciding on metaversic governance. The European Commission and Parliament seem indeed well intentioned to erect a "buffer zone" between European citizens and surveillance capitalism,[133] under the guise of a common space of digital constitutionalism that draws on democratic aspirations, legal pluralism, and liberal values generally.[134] No doubt a quasi-constitutional order is already at play within the EU, with the subsidiarity principle set to define who will have the final say regarding the metaverse. Beyond Brussels, however, supranational actors which are closely watching out on the metaverse are many and in competition with each other: the European choices will make it easier to forecast the role others will try to carve out for themselves within this novel policy chessboard.

I have already elaborated *supra*[135] on the way a wide marketisation of the metaverse might cast new light on norm diffusion, legal globalisation, and the reception of international norms within domestic orders. On a more substantive take, how should Constitutions accommodate those PIL orientations that inevitably stem from socio-economic rights and global developmental discourses, such as the principle

---

[130] *Check* European Commission, 'A European Strategy for data', https://digital-strategy.ec.europa.eu/en/policies/strategy-data (Accessed on 26, Nov 2025).

[131] *See also* De Gregorio 2021, and more extensively De Gregorio 2022a. *Check also* the same author 2022b.

[132] *Refer also to* De Gregorio and Radu 2022, pp.83–84.

[133] *Check eg* Czarnocki 2022; Stanger 2022.

[134] *See* De Gregorio and Radu 2022, p.86.

[135] Mainly at sections 3–5.

of economic justice, wealth-redistribution doctrines, and the obligation to address world poverty? Constitutions worldwide have been representing the linkage between all these tensions and aspirations to social justice between domestic orders and the international policy space, endeavoring to balance fair developmental action internationally with all substantive limitations and institutional restraints lying on the domestic side. The metaverse will plausibly attract further complications. Indeed,

> [v]irtual worlds are serious revenue generators. Gucci, for instance, ran its own 'Gucci Garden Experience' event in the Roblox online platform in May 2021. Players were able to try and purchase fashion accessories for their avatars. The digital 'Queen Bee Dionysus' bag was listed for 475 Robux, which was equivalent to $5. But it was eventually sold for $4115. This was real money as players would need to purchase Robux, the virtual currency of Roblox using real money.[136]

One could truly wonder if this whole ordeal is needed on a global stage where inherited poverty, class and caste humiliation, conflict over natural resources, perpetual crisis (ie, the "permacrisis"), structural scarcity, a loneliness pandemic, as well as inequality already reign unhindered. Of course, billionaires, the luxury sector, as well as surveillance conglomerates like Palantir or Paragon Solutions profit from the current legal regime (e.g. corporate tax avoidance, regressive tax systems, weak data-transfer safeguards, and trickle-down economic "doctrines") regardless of the metaverse, but we are here addressing humans who are bored, capricious, and wealthy enough to spend in the thousands just to dress up *their avatars* in branded fashion rather than themselves or fellow humans in need. Multiply this for millions of transactions, and you get the cardinal representation of the dystopian amalgamation of emptiness, waste, and ultimately self-extinction that humanity risks diving into.

What interests me for the sake of this chapter is that the constitutional text will stand right to the core of these challenges: how to ensure that the metaverse does not further exacerbate all those trends which run in the opposite direction compared to the goals and standards set by the "world community", e.g. through international human rights declarations and treaties?[137] This is not to say that Constitutions necessarily run against structural privilege: this usually succeeds in a very narrow sense only, and indeed the exacerbating real-world inequalities brought about by deregulated neoliberalism all happened while Constitutions were in place and supposed to direct legislation as to protect citizens from these excesses of power-concentration. An overwhelming majority of Constitutions across all regions (and especially in Western liberal democracies) failed dramatically in this respect, but this is no discount to the thesis that without them, societal values would have been betrayed to an

[136] Cheong 2022, p.5.

[137] Needless to remark, this quandary also fits the more general PIL debate on how to ensure that IHRL obligations are binding onto private parties directly, regardless of state mediation (i.e. independently from the accession/ratification to/of the relevant human-rights treaty by the State) – an issue which Cabedo (2022, p.264) labelled as the 'culmination point of the constitutional debate'. This would allow to more straightforwardly capture violations committed by entities operating cross-border and/or extraterritorially, to circumvent the corporate capture of enforcement and administrative agencies, and plausibly to more easily cater for the specific challenges of widespread and accelerating virtuality.

even higher degree. Resultantly, having the Constitution regulate these strands of the metaversan impact on our societies appears to be still warranted and preferable an option. Assuming that the metaverse's functioning will be subsumed under socialist principles of gratuity, free availability, and sharing aimed at promoting the common interest—as other scholars are apparently persuaded will happen[138]—is at best disingenuous, and definitely misinformed.

7 The First (Immature) Responses to these Challenges

The metaverse is not here yet, but it might be joining us within a few decades. How are Constitutions (and constitutional processes) responding, adapting, preparing to the "upcoming" challenges?

Some jurisdictions might already be having the metaverse in mind while (re)drafting their constitutional texts, e.g. via extending the right to environmental integrity up to encompassing that to enjoying a healthy environment, through semantic transfer towards all ecosystems.[139] We are pushed back to the original issue, though: the jurisdictional one. If the "ecosystem" of the metaverse is interdependent among countries, there is no exclusive sovereign jurisdiction whose Constitution can find definitive application – unless we opt for segments of a metaverse fragmented along the lines of States, as much as each jurisdiction runs separate (if interconnected) portions of Internet infrastructure. This is yet another controversial debate. The metaverse is premised upon sharing the same virtual space, but is it not true that most of us share (a great deal of) the Internet even though States assert jurisdiction on a portion of its infrastructure? When it comes to digital spheres, Constitutions so far have merely incorporated (or made explicit) a few digital rights[140] while refraining from addressing jurisdictional issues; would the same trend be confirmed with potential amendments regarding the metaverse?

Other States are not yet incorporating metaversic concepts within their constitutional design, but are, for example, experimenting with original voting mechanisms through procedures which have little in common with the long-tamed *procedure aggravate* of constitutional revision. This is quite curious, given that we are not even at a stage yet where we can affirm how access to the metaverse will work. Will it be based on free subscription with peer-to-peer validation? Will an entry-gate be coded for? Or top-down enrollment will be preferred? Expectations seem to be that its pool of users will be broad, and if a "metaversic Constitution" is to be voted for one day, that will probably be stripped of the solemnity of real-world constitutional drafting, approval, and later amendments.

---

[138] *Read e.g.* Dwivedi et al. 2022, p.9.

[139] *See* Blandino 2021.

[140] Alsharif and Hnit 2025, p.8.

8 Some Futuristic Provocations Around Metaversan Social Contracts

For what is worth, I am no big fan of the current (and yet already deflecting) hype around profit-driven metaversic projects: I believe humanity needs to fix other matters first, and the metaverse will prioritise interests and address needs that only a relatively marginal percentage of humans would want to see prioritised and addressed – that percentage not necessarily representing the most vital, forward-looking, solidaristic, constructive, and especially *sustainable* part of us. It looks more like a game for the super-wealthy than a shared vision for the future. And yet, as a consequence of all I have tried to summarise in the sections above, if we, as a society, truly long for a relatively safe and functional metaverse, the only wise strategy is to adopt global constitutional arrangements, either general *ratione materiae*, or selective (i.e. concerning solely the metaverse). Those social contracts should include legal persons, too, but as mere objects of decisions taken by and in favour of all natural-person participants. This should ensure that our constitutional liberties are not imperiled, and most crucially, that decision-making is not outsourced to private entities such as high-tech conglomerates and MNCs more generally.

International law is urged to "'get over itself" and its constant anxiety in the face of the plurality of laws and Others', metamorphosising into some sort of "global law", presided over by a Constitution or, at least, by a global constitutional thinking.[141] An overabundance of theories of global constitutionalism does exist, but the most practical path is probably that of reasoning by analogy from cyberspace (and to some extent, AI) governance. Postulating that to cater for the metaverse, constitutional law will have to combine traditional doctrines with those coined for the cyberspace[142] is only partly helpful. It is not enough to posit that the metaverse (or at least, the concept of it which is being propagandised by major market players at this stage) will deliver more comprehensive and interconnected a virtual experience compared to what the Internet has ever provided all the more so as the Internet itself will be subjected to new distributive dynamics, as soon as satellites replace submarine cables. And indeed, when it comes to the cyberspace, pseudo-constitutional fickleness had been abandoned to favour the stipulation of a "Bill of (digital) Rights" instead.[143] The feeling is that for the metaverse we will need a *sui iuris* arrangement at a higher level of doctrinal innovation, which reads beyond the "activities" and addresses the structure of (world) society to the highest possible extent.

> Are we heading, then, towards a single global social contract that deflects the parochialism of territorialised polities? That would be desirable, but the risk to avert is that private parties capture the process and turn it to their own interests and policy priorities.[144] Unfortunately, this is likely to happen, unless we stand up early enough against the idea that public agoras

---

[141] Korhonen 2023.

[142] As *e.g.* Venanzoni 2020 does.

[143] *See* Arnold-Fernández et al. 2022, pp.23–38.

[144] *See* Mattei 2024, p.24.

(such the metaverse would be) can be run by unaccountable entities despite the implicit or explicit *pro persona* underpinning of most Constitutions worldwide.[145]

Were a Constitution for the metaverse to be enacted, the question of who is going to draft it would come to the fore.[146] Why did I caution that the social contract would be stipulated with private parties? I will explain this by analogy with the offline world. When it comes to Westphalian States and their Constitutions, their legal order is based not only on some form of domestic legitimacy (or at least coercive power), but also on what we might roughly identify as "peer recognition", which is what PIL is for: a State is such only as long as two fundamental conditions are met: domestically, if a constitutional regime (yet not necessarily a full written Constitution) presides over it, and internationally, if the majority of other States accept its sovereign status. These "other States" are those which form the "international community", whose quasi-Constitution is the United Nations (UN) Charter and whose order is (theoretically) guaranteed by the UN Security Council (UNSC). Within the UNSC, the primary role is vested in the five permanent members (P5), corresponding to the major victorious States in the aftermath of the Second World War. In some ways, conceptually and of course indirectly, any Constitution of a sovereign State is drafted within the world order secured by the P5. A metaversan reality would be engineered no differently. The equivalent of the P5 in the online world are the GAMAM (Google, Amazon, Meta, Apple, and Microsoft),[147] which any metaversan Constitution would be required to deal with one way or the other; by approximation, *for the time being*, we might expect them to feature as de facto co-drafter or "referees" of any "constitutional" arrangement involving the metaverse. I have emphasised the contingency of this submission to the GAMAM as of course the relevant corporations might change, but just like with the P5 no longer corresponding to the world's balance of power (think of India, Brazil, Germany, Japan, Turkey, Indonesia, ...), the GAMAM, too, might lose momentum (recorded, in their case, in terms of e.g. market share) while still retaining bargaining power.

Whenever it is not imposed upon the citizenry, a Constitution is that solemn document which a number of people, through representation, willingly subject themselves to in order to give themselves a legal shape that can sharpen their collective identity and preside over their fate. This chapter's tone has leaned on the pessimistic strand, and yet hiding somewhere in between the shadows, there is some more promising chance that the metaverse will help populations from around all regions to constitutionalise or reconstitutionalise themselves, by interacting at such a sophisticated, realistic, and smooth manner to be enabled to choose the direction for them to take, and resist the tyranny of the neoliberal transnational élite. This is most probably an utopistic outcome, but not necessarily one to be ruled out.

---

[145] And indeed, this tension between private management/ownership and factually public function has long featured debates on social networks as well – *refer for instance to* Bassini 2022.

[146] *Check also* ETTech 2022.

[147] From a less ethnocentric perspective, however, China's BATX (Baidu, Alibaba, Tencent, and Xiaomi), Indonesia's GoTo, or other major digital conglomerates from non-Western regions should be considered just as much.

9 Concluding Note

The reader might have realised that while some discussions have been unpacked thoroughly, other points have been dispatched to the surface: this is hopefully to be excused, as the purpose of this chapter was not that of exploring one single domain of law. Rather, it was conceived as an articulated appraisal of the metaverse as a challenge to the traditional function of the Constitution as a juncture between four entities: a) the State as the overarching site of a social contract among citizens; b) all States as both "shareholders" to a global destiny and the crafters of reciprocal jurisdictional claims under the declining Westphalian order of PIL; c) state institutions with their constitutionally sanctioned dialogue and interfaces with private corporate entities; as well as d) civil society.

No one can tell whether the metaverse will technically fulfil its promises, but even in the negative, these debates will remain current for the time when XR technology actually delivers on these expectations. The overarching quandary concerns whether we need a special regime for the metaverse, which obviously depends on how technology unfolds. Forms of "digitised" citizenship are already a reality across several urban contexts, taking the shape of pandemic, algorithmic, liquid, metropolitan, and/or stateless geometries of navigating social life and interpreting the constitutional order.[148] The metaverse might implant itself onto some of these trends and catalyse them at unprecedented speeds, or deviate their path in unforeseeable directions.

If the metaverse unfolds in such an immersive manner and gathers as enthusiastic a consumer reception as its proponents forecast, then thinking *de lege ferenda* is plausibly advisable: the metaverse would alter the formal and substantive paradigms on which the modern constitutional landscape is built, to such a degree that current Constitutions would soon run out of currency. Two solutions can be envisaged at that point: a constitution for the metaverse, one and global, separate from the "offline" constitutions of all States joining; or a global Constitution which directly caters from all realities at once – online and offline, encompassing all previous dossiers plus constitutional metaversan law. This latter scenario, while at first sight futuristic and utopistic, would prove the fittest in the long run: the impact of one's metaversan life onto the real-world one (and the other way round) would end up being too interlinked for two different Constitutions to rule over them. Moreover, it seems impossible for single jurisdictions to fragment the metaverse the same way they have progressively been partitioning jurisdiction over the traditional Internet – and even then, formal boundaries have been constantly outsmarted by factual variables related to geopolitical dominance and unilateral assertions of jurisdictions by major players.[149]

If the metaverse, instead, still materialises but falls short of accomplishing the market targets envisioned by their business conceivers, then its normative impact, too, will prove of limited reach. Against such a backdrop, one could expect minor adjustments be made to Constitutions worldwide, in order to "accommodate" the

---

[148] *Refer to* Calzada 2022, p.47.

[149] *Read for instance* Mann and Daly 2020.

metaverse. This is a modest and feasible way forward, but would not make the most of the metaverse as a pretext to strive for higher, bolder, and more sustainable degrees of normative integration across regions, and for convergence towards the first embryonic exercises of a truly "global" legal—or at least "rules-based", as they say—order. Of course, States are nowhere near to ready to join such a forward-looking solution, hence the challenge is open and metaverse governance is plausibly fated to fall within endless, inconclusive readjustments along the way. A dooming alternative is that States, unable indeed to move forward in the direction they should, will function more and more as obsolete custodians of their constitutional regimes, to such a degree that the latter will lose significance and slowly confine themselves to the *ordinamenti*'s periphery. And to the margins of our societal and personal daily living, too.

Acknowledgments The author's BlueBook traineeship at the European Commission's DG CNECT back in Spring 2021 was instrumental in inspiring this research on the metaverse; in particular, he wishes to express his gratefulness to Ms. Rehana Schwinninger-Ladak for countless discussions around potential legal-policy frameworks for the most balanced development of metaversic technologies in Europe. Nonetheless, this chapter's content and stances are the author's exclusive responsibility.

References

1NY Belfer Center for Innovation and Social Impact (2022) 'Do we need a constitution for the metaverse?', A talk for the Newmark civic life series, co-presented with one shared. World and supported by craig Newmark philanthropies. Accessed on 26 Nov, 2025 from https://youtu.be/8LU1ya0dhBU

Alsharif M, Hnit H (2025) Digital human rights: legal debates and emerging foundations under the international bill of human rights. Soc Sci Humanit Open 12:102160. https://doi.org/10.1016/j.ssaho.2025.102160

Alexander O et al (2022) 'Cybersecurity, privacy and constitutional concerns: risks to know before entering the metaverse', ALM law. Accessed on 26 Nov, 2025 from https://www.law.com/legaltechnews/2022/03/29/cybersecurity-privacy-and-constitutional-concerns-risks-to-know-before-entering-the-metaverse/

Allam Z et al (2022) The metaverse as a virtual form of smart cities: opportunities and challenges for environmental, economic, and social sustainability in urban futures. Smart Cities 5(3):771–801

Anderson A and Rainie L (2022) 'The metaverse in 2040', *Pew Research Center*. Accessed on 26 Nov, 2025 from https://www.pewresearch.org/internet/2022/06/30/the-metaverse-in-2040/

Arnold-Fernández EE et al (2022) 'Toward a constitution for the metaverse: key principles for the creation process', One Shared World. Accessed on 26 Nov, 2025 from https://oneshared.world/wp-content/uploads/2022/09/Toward-a-Constitution-for-the-Metaverse-A-Thinkpiece-.pdf

Aviram H (2018) Criminal law: taking the constitution seriously? three approaches to law's competence in addressing authority and professionalism. Judges' Book 2(9):41–59

Barak A (2015) Human dignity: the constitutional value and the constitutional right. Cambridge University Press

Barfield W, Blitz MJ (2018) Research handbook on the law of virtual and augmented reality. Edward Elgar Publishing, Cheltenham

Bassini M (2019) Fundamental rights and private enforcement in the digital age. Eur Law J 25(2):182–197. https://doi.org/10.1111/eulj.12310
Bassini M (2022) Social networks as new public forums? enforcing the rule of law in the digital environment. Ital Rev Int Comp Law 1(2):311–334. https://doi.org/10.1163/27725650-01020005
Bedock C, Cappellina B (2024) Beyond digital populism: civic culture and visions of political participation among five star movement activists. Ital Polit Sci Rev 54(1):70–83. https://doi.org/10.1017/ipo.2023.25
Berger BL (2014) 'Constitutional principles in substantive criminal law'. *Osgoode Hall Law School Legal Studies Research Paper Series* 10(6), Research Paper No. 19
Berman PS (2018) Legal jurisdiction and the deterritorialization of data. Vand L Rev En Banc 71:11. https://scholarship.law.gwu.edu/cgi/viewcontent.cgi?article=2585&context=faculty_publications
Bibri SE, Allam Z (2022) The metaverse as a virtual form of data-driven smart urbanism: on post-pandemic governance through the prism of the logic of surveillance capitalism. Smart Cities 5(2):715–727. https://doi.org/10.3390/smartcities5020037
Bilionis LD (1998) Process, the constitution, and substantive criminal law. Mich Law Rev 96(5):1269–1334
Blandino P (2021) 'The new Chilean constitution and the bill on neuro rights: new perspectives in constitutional law, regulation, and in the Metaverse', *Diritti Comparati.* Accessed on 26 Nov, 2025 from https://www.diritticomparati.it/the-new-chilean-constitution-and-the-bill-on-neuro-rights-new-perspectives-in-constitutional-law-regulation-and-in-the-metaverse/
Blitz MJ (2021) The right to an artificial reality? freedom of thought and the fiction of Philip K. Dick. Mich Technol Law Rev 27(2):377–398
Böckenförde M (2022) International law and constitution-making: Sudan. In: Law DS (ed) Constitutionalism in Context. Cambridge UP, pp 157–182. https://doi.org/10.1017/9781108699068.009
Bojić L (2022) Metaverse through the prism of power and addiction: what will happen when the virtual world becomes more attractive than reality? Eur J Futures Res *10*:22. https://doi.org/10.1186/s40309-022-00208-4
Brown CML (2024) Neurorights, mental privacy, and mind reading. Neuroethics 17:34. https://doi.org/10.1007/s12152-024-09568-z
Bublitz JC (2025) Freedom of thought and digital technologies: operationalizing state obligations for social media, virtual reality, and neurotechnology. Hum Rights Rev. https://doi.org/10.1007/s12142-025-00751-0
Burbules NC (2020) Slowness as a virtue. J Phil Educ 54(5):1443–1452, https://doi.org/10.1111/1467-9752.12495
Buchholz F et al (2022) There's more than one metaverse. *i-com* 21(3):313–323
Bujić M et al (2020) "Empathy machine": How virtual reality affects human rights attitudes. Internet Res 30(5):1407–1425. https://doi.org/10.1108/INTR-07-2019-0306
Cabedo Y (2022) International race for regulating crypto-finance risks: a comprehensive regulatory framework proposal. In: Micklitz HW et al (eds) Constitutional challenges in the algorithmic society. Cambridge UP, pp 236–259
Callari TC et al (2024) An ethical framework for human-robot collaboration for the future people-centric manufacturing: a collaborative Endeavour with European subject-matter experts in ethics. Technol Soc 78:102680. https://doi.org/10.1016/j.techsoc.2024.102680
Calzada I (2022) How digital citizenship regimes are rescaling European nation-states. Space Polity 26(1):44–52. https://doi.org/10.1080/13562576.2022.2072197
Cern KM et al (2012) Whose reason or reasons speak through the constitution? introduction to the problematics. Int J Semiot Law 25(4):455–463. https://doi.org/10.1007/s11196-011-9247-4
Chen H (2022) 'Reimagining the metaverse with Chinese characteristics'. *NextTrends Asia.* Accessed on 26 Nov, 2025 from https://nextrendsasia.org/reimagining-the-metaverse-with-chinese-characteristics/

Cheong BC (2022) Avatars in the metaverse: potential legal issues and remedies. Int Cybersecur Law Rev. https://doi.org/10.1365/s43439-022-00056-9
Citron DK, Richards NM (2018) Four principles for digital expression (You Won't Believe #3!). Wash Univ Law Rev 95:1353–1387
Coccoli J (2017) The challenges of new technologies in the implementation of human rights: an analysis of some critical issues in the digital era. Peace Hum Rights Gov 1(2):223–250. https://doi.org/10.14658/pupj-phrg-2017-2-4
Cosgrove J (2023) Meta-regulation: regulatory framework for a virtual world. Infrastructure 62(3):2–14
Council of Europe and IEEE (2024) The metaverse and its impact on human rights, the rule of law and democracy. https://rm.coe.int/the-metaverse-and-its-impact-on-human-rights-the-rule-of-law-and-democ/1680b178b0
Custers B et al (2022) *Quis custodiet ipsos custodes*? data protection in the judiciary in EU and EEA member states. Int Data Priv Law 12(2):93–112. https://doi.org/10.1093/idpl/ipac002
Czarnocki J (2022) Saving EU digital constitutionalism through the proportionality principle and a transatlantic digital accord. European View 20(2):150–156
Dalla Corte L (2022) On proportionality in the data protection jurisprudence of the CJEU. Int Data Priv Law 12(4):259–275. https://doi.org/10.1093/idpl/ipac014
De Giovanni P (2023) Sustainability of the metaverse: a transition to industry 5.0. Sustainability 15(7):6079. https://doi.org/10.3390/su15076079
De Gregorio G (2022a) Digital constitutionalism across the Atlantic. Glob Const 11(2):297–324. https://doi.org/10.1017/S2045381722000016
De Gregorio G (2021) The rise of digital constitutionalism in the European Union. Int J Const Law 19(1):41–70. https://doi.org/10.1093/icon/moab001
De Gregorio G, Radu R (2022) Digital constitutionalism in the new era of internet governance. Int J Law Inf Technol 30(1):68–87. https://doi.org/10.1093/ijlit/eaac004
De Gregorio G (2022b) Digital constitutionalism in Europe: reframing rights and powers in the algorithmic society. Cambridge UP, Cambridge
De Streel A et al (2020) 'Online platforms' moderation of illegal content online: law, practices and options for reform'. A study commissioned by the IMCO committee for the policy department for economic, scientific and quality of life policies at the European parliament's directorate-general for internal policies, PE 652.718
Di Porto F (2022) 'Metaversi e aspirazioni di intervento regolatorio: quali prospettive?', a note for an informal audition on metaversic regulation at the first commission on constitutional affairs of the senate of the Italian republic. Accessed on 26 Nov, 2025 from https://www.parlamento.it/application/xmanager/projects/leg18/attachments/documento_evento_procedura_commissione/files/000/424/511/Prof.ssa_Di_Porto.pdf
Dolata M, Schwabe G (2023) What is the metaverse and who seeks to define it? mapping the site of social construction. J Inf Technol 38(3):239–266
Donini A, Novella M (2022) Il metaverso come luogo di lavoro. Configurazione e questioni regolative. Labour Law Issues 8(2):2–25
Dror-Shpoliansky D, Shany Y (2021) It's the end of the (offline) world as we know it: from human rights to digital human rights—a proposed typology. Eur J Int Law 32(4):1249–1282. https://doi.org/10.1093/ejil/chab087
Ducuing C (2020) Data as infrastructure? a study of data sharing legal regimes. Compet Regul Netw Ind 21(2):124–142. https://doi.org/10.1177/17835917198953
Dwivedi YK et al (2022) Metaverse beyond the hype: multidisciplinary perspectives on emerging challenges, opportunities, and agenda for research, practice and policy. Int J Inf Manag 66:102542. https://doi.org/10.1016/j.ijinfomgt.2022.102542
ECtHR (2019) Article 7: The "quality of law" requirements and the principle of (non-)retrospectiveness of the criminal law under Article 7 of the convention'. A report by the research and library division of the directorate of the jurisconsult of the council of Europe's European

court of human rights. Accessed on 26 Nov, 2025 from https://www.echr.coe.int/Documents/Research_report_quality_law_requirements_criminal_law_Art_7_ENG.PDF
Egliston B, Carter M (2021) Critical questions for Facebook's virtual reality: data, power and the metaverse. Internet Pol Rev 10(4):1610. https://doi.org/10.14763/2021.4.1610
ETTech (2022) 'Creating a constitutional framework for metaverse', *The Economic* Times. Accessed on 26 Nov, 2025 from https://economictimes.indiatimes.com/tech/technology/creating-a-constitutional-framework-for-metaverse/articleshow/94352294.cms
European Commission (2022a) 'State of the union: letter of intent to president Roberta Metsola and to prime minister Petr Fiala', 14 September 2022. Accessed on 26 Nov, 2025 from https://state-of-the-union.ec.europa.eu/system/files/2022-09/SOTEU_2022_Letter_of_Intent_EN_0.pdf
European Commission (2022b) Proposal for a directive of the European parliament and of the council on adapting non-contractual civil liability rules to artificial intelligence ("AI liability directive"), 28 September 2022, COM (2022) 496 final, 2022/0303 (COD), {SEC (2022) 344 final}
European Union Agency for Fundamental Rights (2018) 'Handbook on European data protection law'. ISBN 978-92-871-9849-5. Accessed on 26 Nov, 2025 from https://www.echr.coe.int/documents/handbook_data_protection_eng.pdf
Europol (2022a) '*Facing reality? Law enforcement and the challenge of deepfakes*', An Observatory Report from the Europol Innovation Lab, ISBN 978–92–95220-40-9. Accessed on 26 Nov, 2025 from https://www.europol.europa.eu/cms/sites/default/files/documents/Europol_Innovation_Lab_Facing_Reality_Law_Enforcement_And_The_Challenge_Of_Deepfakes.pdf
Europol (2022b) '*Policing in the metaverse: what law enforcement needs to know*', An Observatory Report from the Europol Innovation Lab, ISBN 978-92-95220-47-8. Accessed on 26 Nov, 2025 from https://www.europol.europa.eu/cms/sites/default/files/documents/Policing%20in%20the%20metaverse%20-%20what%20law%20enforcement%20needs%20to%20know.pdf
Falk RA (2002) Revisiting Westphalia, discovering post-Westphalia. J Ethics 6:311–352
Flew T (2022) Beyond the paradox of trust and digital platforms: populism and the reshaping of internet regulations. In: Flew T, Martin FR (eds) Digital platform regulation: global perspectives on internet governance. Palgrave, pp 281–309
Francot L, Mommers S (2017) Picking up the pace – legal slowness and the authority of the judiciary in the acceleration society (a Dutch case study). Int J Leg Prof 24(3):275–293. https://doi.org/10.1080/09695958.2016.1247711
Fuselli S (2020) Mental integrity protection in the neuro-era: Legal challenges and philosophical background. BioLaw J–Riv BioDiritto 1:413–426
Ganschow B et al (2021) Looking back from the future: perspective taking in virtual reality increases future self-continuity. Front Psychol 12:664687. https://doi.org/10.3389/fpsyg.2021.664687
Garon JM (2022) Legal implications of a ubiquitous metaverse and a web3 future. https://doi.org/10.2139/ssrn.4002551
Gillespie T et al (2020) Expanding the debate about content moderation: scholarly research agendas for the coming policy debates. Internet Pol Rev 9(4):1–29
Ginsburg T et al (2008) Commitment and diffusion: how and why national constitutions incorporate international law. Univ Ill Law Rev 1:201–237
Gleiss A et al (2023) Identifying the patterns: towards a systematic approach to digital platform regulation. J Inf Technol 38(2):108–201
Gorwa R et al (2020) Algorithmic content moderation: technical and political challenges in the automation of platform governance. Big Data Soc 7:97945. https://doi.org/10.1177/2053951719897945
Grac-Aubert V and O'Brien L (2022) 'Metaverse series #3: looking at metaverse(s) with antitrust (3D) glasses', Linklaters: Tech Insights. Accessed on 26 Nov, 2025 from https://techinsights.linklaters.com/post/102htcb/metaverse-series-3-looking-at-metaverses-with-antitrust-3d-glasses
Heidebrecht S (2025) Digital policy as a driver of integration: spillover effects and European commission empowerment. Polit Gov 13. https://doi.org/10.17645/pag.10474

Heinze A (2018) The statute of the international criminal court as a Kantian constitution. In: Bergsmo M, Buis EJ (eds) Philosophical foundations of international criminal law: correlating thinkers. Torkel Opsahl, pp 351–428
Heldt A, Dreyer S (2021) Competent third parties and content moderation on platforms: potentials of independent decision-making bodies from a governance structure perspective. J Inf Policy 11(12):266–300
Hemphill TA (2023) The 'Metaverse' and the challenge of responsible standards development. J Responsib Innov 10(1). https://doi.org/10.1080/23299460.2023.2243121
Henz P (2022) The psychological impact of the Metaverse. Discov Psychol 2:47
HLR (2016) Constitutional courts and international law: revisiting the transatlantic divide. Harv Law Rev 129(3):1362–1393
Hossain MR, Zeinali M, Papakostas N (2025) Integration of industry standards in VR training simulations. Procedia CIRP 136:924–929. https://doi.org/10.1016/j.procir.2025.08.157
Hoque R (2021) Criminal law and the constitution: the relationship revisited. Bangladesh J Law 8:45–78. https://www.biliabd.org/wp-content/uploads/2021/08/Dr.-Ridwanul-Hoque.pdf
Howe J (2022) 'The metaverse and immersive technologies – a regulatory perspective'. Official blog of the UK government's competition and markets authority. Accessed on 26 Nov, 2025 from https://competitionandmarkets.blog.gov.uk/2022/06/22/the-metaverse-and-immersive-technologies-a-regulatory-perspective/
Hung HT (2022) Keep your eyes on China's metaverse: another tool for maintaining its national security's. J Intell Confl Warf 5(2):1–31
Huq AZ (2023) Militant democracy comes to the metaverse? Emory Law J 72:1105–1141
Huq N et al (2022) 'Metaverse or metaworse? cybersecurity threats against the internet of experiences', Trend Micro Research. Accessed on 26 Nov, 2025 from https://documents.trendmicro.com/assets/white_papers/wp-metaverse-or-metaworse-cybersecurity-threats-against-the-internet-of-experiences.pdf
Hunt M (2022) 'Competition/antitrust in the metaverse', Bristows. Accessed on 26 Nov, 2025 from https://www.bristows.com/news/competition-antitrust-in-the-metaverse/
Hutson J et al (2023) Architecting the metaverse: blockchain and the financial and legal regulatory challenges of virtual real estate. J Intell Learn Syst Appl 15(1):1–23
Ienca M (2021) 'Common human rights challenges raised by different applications of neurotechnologies in the biomedical field'. A Report commissioned by the Committee on Bioethics (DH-BIO) of the Council of Europe. Accessed on 26 Nov, 2025 from https://rm.coe.int/report-final-en/1680a429f3
Ienca M, Andorno R (2017) Towards new human rights in the age of neuroscience and neurotechnology. Life Sci Soc Policy 13(5):00501. https://doi.org/10.1186/s40504-017-0050-1
Infantino M (2013) The Italian legal recipe: basic ingredients and the bustle of time. Eur J Comp Law Gov. https://doi.org/10.1163/22134514-45060012
Interesse G (2022) 'China's debut in the metaverse: trends to watch'. China Briefing. Accessed on 26 Nov, 2025 from https://www.china-briefing.com/news/metaverse-in-china-trends/
Johns F, Compton C (2022) Data jurisdictions and rival regimes of algorithmic regulation. Regul Gov 16:63–84. https://doi.org/10.1111/rego.12296
Julian S (2022) 'Le "Darkverse": Le côté obscur du métavers qui inquiète déjà les spécialistes'. *L'Express*. Accessed on 26 Nov, 2025 from https://lexpansion.lexpress.fr/high-tech/le-darkverse-le-cote-obscur-du-metavers-qui-inquiete-deja-les-specialistes_2180258.html
Kasiyanto S, Kilinc MR (2022) The legal conundrums of the metaverse. J Cent Bank Law Inst 1(2):299–322. https://doi.org/10.21098/jcli.v1i2.25
Keller DH (2022) 'The DSA's industrial model for content moderation', Verfassungsblog: on matters constitutional. Accessed on 26 Nov, 2025 from https://verfassungsblog.de/dsa-industrial-model/
Kellmeyer P (2022) 'Neurorights': a human rights–based approach for governing neurotechnologies. In: Voeneky S, Kellmeyer P, Mueller O, Burgard W (eds) The Cambridge handbook of responsible artificial intelligence: interdisciplinary perspectives. Cambridge University Press, Cambridge, pp 412–426. https://doi.org/10.1017/9781009207898.032

Kingsbury BW (2019) Infrastructure and InfraReg: on rousing the international law "Wizards of Is". Camb Int Law J 8(2):171–186. https://doi.org/10.4337/cilj.2019.02.01
Kleinfeld J (2017) Three principles of democratic criminal justice. Northwest Univ Law Rev 111(6):1455–1490
Korhonen O, Bruncevic M, Arvidsson M (2023) Subjecthood in cyberspace and the uncanny valley of international law. Nord J Int Law 92(1):138–169. https://doi.org/10.1163/15718107-bja10058
Kraft CJ, Giordano J (2017) Integrating Brain Science and Law: Neuroscientific Evidence and Legal Perspectives on Protecting Individual Liberties. Front Neurosci 11:621. https://doi.org/10.3389/2Ffnins.2017.00621
Kryvoi Y, Matos S (2021) Non-retroactivity as a general principle of law. Utrecht Law Rev 17(1):46–58. https://doi.org/10.36633/ulr.604
van Klink, B (2018) Law at the right time: a plea for slow law in hasty times. In: Temporal boundaries of law and politics. Routledge, pp 33–52. https://www.taylorfrancis.com/chapters/edit/10.4324/9781351103480-3/law-right-time-plea-slow-law-hasty-times-bart-van-klink?context=ubx&refId=02bc1fd0-f231-49f7-9033-8d68cf3d7855
Lake J (2020) Hey, you stole my avatar! virtual reality and its risks to identity protection. Emory Law J 69(4):833–879
Langvardt K (2018) Regulating online content moderation. Georget Law J 106(7):1353–1388
Leenes RE (2019) Privacy regulation in the metaverse. In: Whithworth B, de Moor A (eds) Handbook of research on socio-technical design and social networking systems. IGI Global, pp 123–136
Ligthart S et al (2022a) Persuasive technologies and the right to mental liberty: the "smart" rehabilitation of criminal offenders. In: Ienca M (ed) The Cambridge handbook of information technology, life sciences and human rights. Cambridge UP, pp 32–47. https://doi.org/10.1017/9781108775038.005
Ligthart S et al (2022b) Is virtually everything possible? the relevance of ethics and human rights for introducing extended reality in forensic psychiatry. AJOB Neurosci 13(3):144–157. https://doi.org/10.1080/21507740.2021.1898489
Madiega T et al (2022) Metaverse: opportunities, risks and policy implications. Brief Eur Parliam Res Serv PE 733:557
Mainwaring S (2020) Always in control? sovereign states in cyberspace. Eur J Int Secur 5(2):215–232
Mangada Real De Asúa E et al (2022) 'The metaverse challenges and regulatory issues', A student paper for the master in public policy and master in European affairs digital at SciencesPo Paris. Accessed on 26 Nov, 2025 from https://www.sciencespo.fr/public/sites/sciencespo.fr.public/files/Metaverse-Group-report-final-draft-June-12-1.pdf
Mann M, Daly A (2020) Geopolitics, jurisdiction and surveillance. Internet Pol Rev 9(3):1501. https://doi.org/10.14763/2020.3.1501
Martin B (2022) Privacy in a programmed platform: how the general data protection regulation applies to the metaverse. Harv J Law Technol 26(1):235–261
Martinico G et al (2019) The constitution of Italy: axiological continuity between the domestic and international levels of governance? In: Albi A, Bardutzky S (eds) National Constitutions in European and Global Governance: Democracy, Rights, the Rule of Law. Springer, pp 493–541
Masi D (2025) New digital realities and traditional problems to be solved: a metaverse to explore through digital pitfalls, sustainability issues and new regulatory perspectives. Eur Bus Law Rev 36(4):637–652. https://doi.org/10.54648/eulr2025038
Mathiyazhagan S et al (2022) 'Social work in metaverse: addressing tech policy gaps for racial and mental health equity'. *Internet Policy Review*. Accessed on 26 Nov, 2025 from https://policyreview.info/articles/news/social-work-metaverse-addressing-tech-policy-gaps-racial-and-mental-health-equity/1619
Mattei UA (2024) The legal metaverse and comparative taxonomy: a reappraisal. Am J Comp Law 20(1):1–30. https://doi.org/10.1093/ajcl/avae010
Megale L (2022) (Meta)verse as the next escaper from competition public enforcement. Mark Compet Law Rev 6(2):15–50

Moreira JLI, Vecellio Segate R (2021) The "It" arbitrator: why do corporations not act as arbitrators? J Int Dispute Settl 12(4):525–557. https://doi.org/10.1093/jnlids/idab022
Moringiello JM (2010) What virtual worlds can do for property law. Fla Law Rev 62(1):159–202
Murcia-López M, Steed A (2016) The effect of environmental features, self-avatar, and immersion on object location memory in virtual environments. Frontiers ICT 3(24):024. https://doi.org/10.3389/fict.2016.00024
Murgia M and Bradshaw T (2022) 'Metaverse "cannot escape" UK online rules, say experts: virtual worlds being created by likes of meta and Microsoft will be subject to forthcoming safety bill', *Financial Times*. Accessed on 26 Nov, 2025 from https://www.ft.com/content/fa34ddf1-03d9-4375-b38a-96f251fda98b
Murphy S et al (2021) 'Will the metaverse be a universal platform? Part II-the legal issues'. Society for computers and law. Accessed on 26 Nov, 2025 from https://www.scl.org/articles/12395-will-the-metaverse-be-a-universal-platform-part-ii-the-legal-issues
Murray, R. (2022). Trademarks, NFTs, and the law of the metaverse. Law Fac Scholar Art 781. Accessed on 26 Nov, 2025 from https://uknowledge.uky.edu/cgi/viewcontent.cgi?article=1785&context=law_facpub
Nanobashvili L (2022) If the metaverse is built, will copyright challenges come? UIC Rev Intellect Prop Law 21(1):215–251
Ndulo M (2021) International and foreign law in domestic constitutional law: a comparative examination of the practice in united states and post-conflict countries. In: Cantillo AL (ed) Constitutionalism: old dilemmas, new insights. Oxford UP, pp 373–C17.N53. https://doi.org/10.1093/oso/9780192896759.003.0018
Neuwirth RJ (2022a) Future law, the power of prediction, and the disappearance of time. Law Technol Hum 4(2):38–59
Neuwirth RJ (2022b) The EU artificial intelligence act: regulating subliminal AI systems. Routledge
Neuwirth RJ (2024) The global institutional governance of AI: a four-dimensional perspective. Int J Digit Law Gov 1(1):113–153. https://doi.org/10.1515/ijdlg-2024-0004
Nicholas CB (2020) Slowness as a virtue. J Philos Educ 54(5):1443–1452. https://doi.org/10.1111/1467-9752.12495
Nicholson A et al (2025) Trespass to the "person" in the metaverse. Int Rev Law Comput Technol:79891. https://doi.org/10.1080/13600869.2025.2479891
Nieto Martín A (2019) Saudade of the constitution: the relationship between constitutional and criminal law in the European context. New J Eur Crim Law 10(1):28–33
Olson ET (1999) The human animal: personal identity without psychology. Oxford UP
Paiva Andrade L (2019) 'NeuroReality: Um sistema para inserção, análise e gerenciamento de dados de eletroencefalografia em ambientes virtuais'. Dissertation for the Programa de Pós-Graduação em Informática at the Centro de Informática of the Universidade Federal da Paraíba in Brazil
Pałosz R (2022) How do base rules constitute a virtual world? Int J Semiot Law 35(5):1879–1901. https://doi.org/10.1007/s11196-022-09903-8
Pate RL (2022) Legal issues inside the unnatural world of metaverse. Bus Law Rev 43(5):188–193
Paz RY (2015) Kelsen's pure theory of law as "a hole in time". Monde(s) 7(1):75–94
Perrone NM (2020) Speed, law and the global economy: How economic acceleration contributes to inequality and precarity. Leiden J Int Law 33(3):557–576. https://doi.org/10.1017/S0922156520000242
Petersen N (2009) 'The reception of international law by constitutional courts through the prism of legitimacy'. 39 *preprints of the max planck institute for research on collective goods*. Accessed on 26 Nov, 2025 from https://homepage.coll.mpg.de/pdf_dat/2009_39online.pdf
Piana D (2021) Augmented democracy: more open, less free? Riv Digit Polit 1(1):37–50
Piattoni S (2010) The theory of multi-level governance: conceptual, empirical, and normative challenges, Oxford UP. https://doi.org/10.1093/acprof:oso/9780199562923.003.0012
Piscione DP, Drean J (2023) Yes, the metaverse is still happening. Harvard Business Review. Accessed on 26 Nov, 2025 from https://hbr.org/2023/05/yes-the-metaverse-is-still-happening

Properzi M (2019) Corpo vissuto ed esperienza virtuale: una prospettiva fenomenologica. Riv Int Filos Psicol 10(3):250–264

Quintais JP et al (2023) Using terms and conditions to apply fundamental rights to content moderation. German Law J 24(5):881–911

Raffield P (2000) Bodies of law: the divine architect, common law and the ancient constitution. Int J Semiot Law 13(3):333–356. https://doi.org/10.1023/A:1008989020137

Ranchordás S, Roznai Y (2020) Time, law, change. Hart

Raposo VL (2024) Beyond pixels and profiles: unveiling the legal identity of avatars in the metaverse. Interact Entertain Law Rev 7(2):97–109. https://doi.org/10.4337/ielr.2024.02.04

Roberts A et al (2022) 'Cyberspace administration of China enhances its enforcement power'. *Linklaters' Tech Insights.* Accessed on 26 Nov, 2025 from https://techinsights.linklaters.com/post/102hwq6/cyberspace-administration-of-china-enhances-its-enforcement-power

Roibu AN (2024) Protection in a virtual reality: the dire need for trademark and copyright law expansion to encompass digital content within the metaverse. Touro Law Rev 39(4), Article 14. https://digitalcommons.tourolaw.edu/cgi/viewcontent.cgi?article=3475%96context=lawreview

Roquet P et al (2023) Japan's retreat to the metaverse. Media Cult Soc 45:82001. https://doi.org/10.1177/01634437231182001

Rosenberg L et al (2023) The metaverse and conversational AI as a threat vector for targeted influence. In: IEEE annual computing and communication workshop and conference (CCWC). https://doi.org/10.1109/CCWC57344.2023.10099167

Rosenberg L (2022) The metaverse: from marketing to mind control. Future of Marketing Institute. Accessed on 26 Nov, 2025 from https://futureofmarketinginstitute.com/the-metaverse-from-marketing-to-mind-control/

Rothschild M (2013) Corporate cyber-censorship: the problems with freedom of expression online. Can J Law Technol 11(1):143–177

Sander B (2020) Freedom of expression in the age of online platforms: the promise and pitfalls of a human rights-based approach to content moderation. Fordham Int Law J 43(4):939–1006

Schmidt VA (2020) Europe's crisis of legitimacy: governing by rules and ruling by numbers in the eurozone. Oxford UP. https://doi.org/10.1093/oso/9780198797050.003.0002

Shurson J (2025) Investigative jurisdiction: the evolving limits of extraterritoriality in transnational digital investigations. Int Comp Q 74(3):675–705. https://doi.org/10.1017/S0020589325100985

Singh R (2013) 'Law as a system of values the jan grodecki lecture at the university of Leicester by sir Rabinder Singh', 24 October 2013. Accessed on 26 Nov, 2025 from https://www.judiciary.uk/wp-content/uploads/JCO/Documents/Speeches/singh-law-as-system-of-values20131031.pdf

Spahr LA (2011) Environmental self-audit privilege: the straw that breaks the back of criminal prosecutions. Fordham Environ Law Rev 7(3):635–677

Stanger AK (2022) The real cost of surveillance capitalism: digital humanism in the United States and Europe. In: Werthner H et al (eds) Perspectives on digital humanism. Springer, pp 33–40

Steffek J (2015) The output legitimacy of international organizations and the global public interest. Int Theory 7(2):263–293. https://doi.org/10.1017/S1752971915000044

Strebel M et al (2019) The importance of input and output legitimacy in democratic governance: evidence from a population-based survey experiment in four West European countries. Eur J Polit Res 58(2):488–513. https://doi.org/10.1111/1475-6765.12293

Suzor N (2010a) 'Digital constitutionalism and the role of the rule of law in the governance of virtual communities'. PhD Thesis at the Law School at the Queensland University of Technology. Accessed on 26 Nov, 2025 from https://eprints.qut.edu.au/37636/1/Nicolas_Suzor_Thesis.pdf

Suzor N (2010b) The role of the rule of law in virtual communities. Berkeley Technol Law J 25(4):1817–1886. https://doi.org/10.15779/Z381M6P

Tabassum A et al (2025) Generative AI and the metaverse: a scoping review of ethical and legal challenges. IEEE Open J Comput Soc 6:348–359. https://doi.org/10.1109/OJCS.2025.3536082

Tegmark ME (2015) 'Friendly artificial intelligence: the physics challenge'. https://doi.org/10.48550/arXiv.1409.0813

Thiel T (2023) A polarizing multiverse? Assessing Habermas' digital update of his public sphere theory. Constellations 30:69–76. https://doi.org/10.1111/1467-8675.12667

Tiwari M et al (2025) Metaverse policing: a systematic literature review of challenges and recommendations. Comput Hum Behav 166:108591. https://doi.org/10.1016/j.chb.2025.108591

Tommasi F, Degen JL, Orhan MA, Sartori R (2025) Exploring work and organizational psychology in the metaverse: a critical research agenda. Scand J Work Organ Psychol 10(1):1–12. https://doi.org/10.16993/sjwop.266

Tong E (2022) 'Opening speech by Mr Edwin Tong SC, minister for culture community and youth and second minister for law at TechLaw. Fest 2022 up your game', 20 July 2022. Accessed on 26 Nov, 2025 from https://www.mlaw.gov.sg/news/speeches/2022-07-20-opening-speech-edwin-tong-techlaw-fest-2022-up-your-game

Tronconi F, Bailo F (2025) The other side of platform politics. Law-making and online participatory democracy in the five star movement. Swiss Polit Sci Rev 31(1):14–33. https://doi.org/10.1111/spsr.12613

Van Den Meerssche D, Gordon GJ (2020) "A new normative architecture" – risk and resilience as routines of un-governance. Transnatl Leg Theory 11(3):267–299. https://doi.org/10.1080/20414005.2020.1825036

Vecellio Segate R (2019) Fragmenting cybersecurity norms through the language(s) of subalternity: India in "the East" and the global community. Columbia J Asian Law 32(2):78–138. https://doi.org/10.7916/cjal.v32i2.3371

Vecellio Segate R (2020a) Litigating trade secrets in China: An imminent pivot to cybersecurity? J Intellect Prop Law Pract 15(8):649–659. https://doi.org/10.1093/jiplp/jpaa092

Vecellio Segate R (2020b) Protecting cultural heritage by recourse to international environmental law: Chinese stances on faultless state liability. Hastings Environ Law J 27(1):153–227. Accessed on 26 Nov, 2025 from https://repository.uchastings.edu/hastings_environmental_law_journal/vol27/iss1/5/

Vecellio Segate R (2020c) Securitizing innovation to protect trade secrets between "the East" and "the West": A neo-schumpeterian public legal reading. UCLA Pac Basin Law J 37(1):59–126. https://doi.org/10.5070/P8371048804

Vecellio Segate R (2021) Cognitive bias, privacy rights, and digital evidence in international criminal proceedings: Demystifying the double-edged AI revolution. Int Crim Law Rev 21(2):242–279. https://doi.org/10.1163/15718123-bja10048

Vecellio Segate R (2022a) Horizontalizing insecurity, or securitizing privacy? Two narratives of a rule-of-law misalignment between a special administrative region and its state. Chin J Comp Law 10(1):56–89. https://doi.org/10.1093/cjcl/cxac002

Vecellio Segate R (2022b) Navigating lawyering in the age of neuroscience: Why lawyers can no longer do without emotions (nor could they ever). Nord J Hum Rights 40(1):268–283. https://doi.org/10.1080/18918131.2022.2042989

Vecellio Segate R (2022c) Shifting privacy rights from the individual to the group: A re-adaptation of algorithms regulation to address the gestaltian configuration of groups. Loyola Univ Chic J Regul Compliance 8(1):55–114. Accessed on 26 Nov, 2025 from https://www.compliancelawjournal.com/compliancelawjournal/issue_viii/MobilePagedArticle.action?articleId=1793260#articleId1793260

Vecellio Segate R (2022d) 'The distributive surveillant contract: Reforming "surveillance capitalism through taxation" into a legal teleology of global economic justice'. Talent Program PhD Thesis in International Law at the Department of Global Legal Studies (Faculty of Law) of the University of Macau. Accessed on 26 Nov, 2025 from https://library2.um.edu.mo/etheses/991010238079006306_ft.pdf

Vecellio Segate R (2022e) Resisting domestic courts' universal jurisdiction over international crimes: Comparative notes on China and Italy. In: Grzebyk PK (ed) International Crimes in National Regulations of Selected States. Wydawnictwo Instytutu Wymiaru Sprawiedliwości, pp 245–273. Accessed on 26 Nov, 2025 from https://discovery.dundee.ac.uk/ws/portalfiles/portal/96777779/GRZEBYK_ZbrodnieMiedzynarodowe_EN_www_2_3_.pdf

Vecellio Segate R (2024a) Biometric technology at the borders of citizenship: Identifying technical standards for introducer-based remote onboarding in global contexts of statelessness, nomadism, displacement, and refuge. Int J Digit Law Gov 1(2):313–360. https://doi.org/10.1515/ijdlg-2024-0010

Vecellio Segate R (2024b) Channeled beneath international law: Mapping infrastructure and regulatory capture as Israeli–American hegemonic reinforcers in Palestine. Commun Law Policy 28(4):332–366. https://doi.org/10.1080/10811680.2024.2334081

Vecellio Segate R (2024c) Drafting a cybersecurity standard for outer space missions: on critical infrastructure, China, and the indispensability of a global inclusive approach. J Asian Secur Int Aff 11(3):345–375. https://doi.org/10.1177/23477970241261432

Vecellio Segate R (2024d) The "Medical Exception" to emotion detection algorithms within the EU's forthcoming AI act: regulatory implications for therapeutical smart cobotics. In: 2024 IEEE RTSI (Research and Technologies for Society and Industry) Conference at Politecnico di Milano. https://doi.org/10.1109/RTSI61910.2024.10761570

Vecellio Segate R, Daly A (2023) Encoding the enforcement of safety standards into smart robots to harness their computing sophistication and collaborative potential: A legal risk assessment for European union policymakers. Eur J Risk Regul 15(3):665–704. https://doi.org/10.1017/err.2023.72

Venanzoni A (2020) Cyber-costituzionalismo: la società digitale tra silicolonizzazione, capitalismo delle piattaforme e reazioni costituzionali. Riv Ital Inform Dirit 2(1):5–34. https://doi.org/10.32091/RIID0016

Verardi P (2022) 'Darkverse: la parte criminale del Metaverso', *The Cryptonomist*. Accessed on 26 Nov, 2025 from https://cryptonomist.ch/2022/09/28/darkverse-parte-criminale-metaverso/

Warner DS (2022) 'The metaverse with Chinese characteristics: a discussion of the metaverse through the lens of Confucianism and Daoism'. Unpublished MA Thesis at the University of Pittsburgh. Accessed on 26 Nov, 2025 from http://d-scholarship.pitt.edu/42461/1/Warner_Final%20ETD.pdf

Wexler R (2021) Privacy as privilege: the stored communications act and internet evidence. Harv Law Rev 134(6):2721–2793

Wheeler T (2023) 'AI makes rules for the metaverse even more important'. The Brookings Institution. Accessed on 26 Nov, 2025 from https://www.brookings.edu/articles/ai-makes-rules-for-the-metaverse-even-more-important/

Wolfram S (2016) 'Computational law, symbolic discourse and the AI constitution'. Accessed on 26 Nov, 2025 from https://writings.stephenwolfram.com/2016/10/computational-law-symbolic-discourse-and-the-ai-constitution/

Woods L (2022) 'Regulating the future: the online safety bill and the metaverse' (2022) Carnegie UK. Accessed on 26 Nov, 2025 from https://carnegieuktrust.org.uk/blog-posts/regulating-the-future-the-online-safety-bill-and-the-metaverse/

Wu H, Zhang W (2023) Digital identity, privacy security, and their legal safeguards in the Metaverse. Secur Saf 2:2023011

Yarmak A (May, 2025) Trade mark dilemmas in the Metaverse: interplay between stakeholders. J Intellect Prop Law Pract 20(5):339–353. https://doi.org/10.1093/jiplp/jpae118

Yang L (2023) Recommendations for metaverse governance based on technical standards. Humanit Soc Sci Commun 10:7. https://doi.org/10.1057/s41599-023-01750-7

Zack JS (2007) The ultimate company town: wading in the digital marsh of second life. Univ Pa J Constit Law 10(1):225–255

Zalan T, Barbesino P (2023) Making the metaverse real. Digit Bus 3(2):100059

Financial Markets

NFTs And EU Financial Markets Legislation

Filippo Annunziata

Abstract The purpose of this paper is to analyse how the European Union's framework on digital finance – and, in particular, the Regulation on Markets in Crypto-Assets (MiCA) – is likely to impact markets in NFTs. Although not a dedicated regulation on NFTs per se, the MiCA Regulation is, as of today, the most relevant piece of legislation to directly address NFTs and will certainly affect their circulation and the development of the relative markets in the Union.

1 Introduction

Following the rapid spread of crypto-assets and tokens across global markets, the legal issue of how to define, classify and consequently regulate such phenomena soon arose, thereby igniting one of the most complex challenges currently in the hands of legislators and supervisors.[1] Crypto-assets are particularly sensitive for financial regulators due to the multi-faceted risks they are capable of posing, in potential, to consumers (e.g. frauds, price volatility, operational and cybersecurity risks), to the integrity of markets (i.e. due to their potential deployment in money laundering and market manipulation) and, insofar as their use becomes increasingly widespread, to the stability of financial systems.[2]

Amongst the vast number of crypto-assets being created on a regular basis, which vary immensly in terms of charateristics and purposes, non-fungible tokens

[1] See, *inter alia*, Annunziata (2020), Vondrackova (2016), Zetzsche et al. (2017), Chohan (2021), Zetzsche et al. (2020), Barsan (2017), Maume and Fromberger (2019), Rohr and Wright (2019), Henderson and Raskin (2019).

[2] Over the past few years, there have been numerous interventions by supervisory authorities to warn users of the risks associated with crypto-assets. See, e. g., ESMA (2019); EBA (2013); EBA (2019); Banca d'Italia (2018).

F. Annunziata (✉)
Milan, Italy
e-mail: filippo@filippoannunziata.eu

F. Di Porto and O. Pollicino (eds.), *Law and Politics of Virtual Worlds*, Law, Governance and Technology Series 79, https://doi.org/10.1007/978-3-032-08541-2_5

(“**NFTs**”)[3] came to prominence due to their initial, significant impact in the art market and entertainment industry as a whole, gaining notoriety for creating new forms of legitimacy and, ultimately, ownership in the digital sphere, an environment largely marked by reproduction of works with often uncertain controls over property or copyright.

From a regulatory standpoint, the phenomenon of NFTs raises new questions regarding intellectual property, ownership rights,[4] the use of distributed ledger technology (“**DLT**”) and smart contracts *vis-à-vis* the ensurance of cybersecurity. They also pose challenging questions in relation to the applicable financial and tax framework, the status of exchange platforms, disclosure and transparency standards, the applicability of consumer law and investor protection rules. Considering financial legislation, and in particular the EU regulatory landscape, the mere classification of NFTs under existing regulatory categories is problematic, mostly because of their multi-faceted nature, which traditional regulation fails to capture in a comprehensive manner.

In view of such context, the aim of this chapter is to analyse how the European Union’s framework on digital finance – and, in particular, the Regulation on Markets in Crypto-Assets (hereinafter “**MiCA**”)[5] – is likely to impact markets in NFTs. Although not a dedicated regulation on NFTs *per se*, the MiCA regime is, as of today, the most relevant piece of legislation to directly address NFTs and will certainly affect their circulation and the development of the relative markets in the Union.

---

[3] *Ex multis*, Chohan and Usman (2021), Fairfield (2022), Kong and Lin (2021), Di Bernardino et al. (2021), Guadamuz (2022), CSPLA (2022).

[4] On property law for NFTs, see Moringiello and Odinet (2021).

[5] Regulation (EU) 2023/1114 of the European Parliament and of the Council of 31 May 2023 on markets in crypto-assets, and amending Regulations (EU) No 1093/2010 and (EU) No 1095/2010 and Directives 2013/36/EU and (EU) 2019/1937 (OJ L 150, 9.6.2023, pp. 40–205).

2 The Impact of MiCA on Markets in NFTs

2.1 State of the Art of the Legislative Procedures on the Digital Finance Package

From its conception, the Digital Finance Package,[6] introduced by the European Commission on 24 September 2020, moved along two strategic lines: the so-called Digital Finance Strategy[7] and the so-called Retail Payments Strategy,[8] both of which were intended to be translated into directly applicable legislative texts in all Member States, thereby laying the ground for a fully harmonised framework on digital finance.

The main goal of the European legislator with the Digital Finance Package is that of establishing a solid common framework to support digital innovation and the digitalisation of finance, overcoming the urgency of autunomous legislative interventions carried out by the Member States individually, which result in a highly fragmented landscape prone to regulatory arbitrage. This objective has been reiterated, among many other sources, in the Communication 'Shaping Europe's Digital Future',[9] which emphasises that it is essential for Europe to seize all the advantages of the digital era and strengthen its industrial and innovation capacity within safe and ethical limits.[10]

The Digital Finance Package was composed of three legislative measures: the proposal for a Regulation on a Pilot Regime for market infrastructures operating on Distributed Ledger Technology ("**DLTR**" or "**Pilot Regime Regulation**"),[11] the Digital Operational Resilience Act ("**DORA**"),[12] and – more prominently – the

[6] See European Commission (2020).

[7] European Commission, Communication from the Commission to the European Parliament, the European Council, the Council, the European Economic and Social Committee and the Committee of the Regions on a Digital Finance Strategy for EU (COM(2020)591 final) of 24 September 2020.

[8] European Commission, Communication from the Commission to the European Parliament, the Council, the European Economic and Social Committee and the Committee of the Regions on a Retail Payments Strategy for the EU (COM/2020/592 final) of 24 September 2020.

[9] See European Commission, Communication from the Commission to the European Parliament, the Council, the European Economic and Social Committee and the Committee of the Regions Shaping Europe's digital future (COM(2020) 67) of 19 February 2020.

[10] See Noble (2021).

[11] Regulation (EU) 2022/858 of the European Parliament and of the Council of 30 May 2022 on a pilot regime for market infrastructures based on distributed ledger technology, and amending Regulations (EU) No 600/2014 and (EU) No 909/2014 and Directive 2014/65/EU (OJ L 151, 2.6.2022, pp. 1–33).

[12] Position of the European Parliament adopted at first reading on 10 November 2022 with a view to the adoption of Regulation (EU) 2022/... of the European Parliament and of the Council on digital operational resilience for the financial sector and amending Regulations (EC) No 1060/2009, (EU) No 648/2012, (EU) No 600/2014, (EU) No 909/2014 and (EU) 2016/1011, https://www.europarl.europa.eu/doceo/document/TA-9-2022-0381_EN.html#title2 (Accessed January 8, 2026).

Markets in Crypto Assets Regulation ("**MiCA**").[13] All three regulations have already been approved by EU legislators and published accordingly.

The DLTR – aproved on 30 May and published in the Official Journal of the EU on 2 June 2022, being effective as of March 2023 – creates a regulatory sandbox that allows market players to apply for licenses to operate DLT-based secondary market infrastructures under less-stringent regulatory requirements than those otherwise applicable under conventional EU capital markets legislation, thus enabling tokenised financial instruments to be traded without being hindered by the regulatory constraints applicable to traditional trading venues.[14] On the other hand, the DORA – voted and adopted by the European Parliament on 10 November 2022 – establishes a comprehensive framework on digital operational resilience for financial entities in the EU; it sets out granular provisions governing the management of risks associated with financial institutions' outsourcing of technology functions to technology providers and mandating direct regulatory oversight of critical technology providers.[15]

While both the DLTR and DORA may indirectly impact markets in NFTs – depending, of course, on the characteristics of each given business model that is developed using NFTs – they do not explicitly make reference to such tokens, reason for which they will not be contemplated in detail in the present analysis.

Focus should instead be placed on the MiCA Regulation. Following the introduction of the Commission's proposal in September 2020, opinions were shortly thereafter issued by the European Central Bank (February 2021),[16] the European Economic and Social Committee (March 2021),[17] and the European Data Protection Supervisor (June 2021).[18] The negotiations that ensued therefrom started with the European Council adopting a negotiation mandate on the proposal on 19 November 2021,[19] which was followed by the European Parliament agreeing to a position

---

[13] See Proposal for a Regulation of the European Parliament and of the Council on Markets in Crypto-Assets and amending Directive (EU) 2019/1937 (COM(2020) 593 final, https://eur-lex.europa.eu/legal-content/IT/ALL/?uri=CELEX:52020PC0593 (Accessed January 8, 2026).

[14] For a thorough analysis of the DLTR, see Zetzsche and Woxholth (2022).

[15] See Scott (2021).

[16] Opinion of the European Central Bank of 19 February 2021 on a proposal for a regulation on Markets in Crypto-assets, and amending Directive (EU) 2019/1937 (CON/2021/4) 2021/C 152/01.

[17] European Parliament Committee on Economic and Monetary Affairs, Report on the proposal for a regulation of the European Parliament and of the Council on markets in crypto-assets and amending Directive (EU) 2019/1937 (COM(2020)0593 – C9-0306/2020 – 2020/0265(COD)), A9-0052/2022. https://www.europarl.europa.eu/doceo/document/A-9-2022-0052_EN.html.

[18] Opinion of the European Data Protection Supervisor on the Proposal for a Regulation on Markets in Crypto-assets, and amending Directive (EU) 2019/1937 (OJ C 337, 23.8.2021, pp. 4–5).

[19] Council of the European Union, Proposal for a Regulation of the European Parliament and of the Council on Markets in Crypto-Assets, and amending Directive (EU) 2019/1937, 2020/0265(COD). https://www.consilium.europa.eu/media/53105/st14067-en21.pdf (Accessed January 8, 2026).

in March 2022.[20] In accordance with the ordinary legislative procedure, inter-institutional negotiations (trilogues) then started in April 2022 and a provisional agreement on the proposal was finally reached by the Commission, the Council Presidency and the Parliament on 30 June 2022.[21]

Shortly thereafter, the Council's Permanent Representatives' Committee (COREPER) meeting of 5 October 2022[22] endorsed the final compromise text with a view to agreement. The text was finally published on 31 May 2023 as Regulation (EU) 2023/1114.[23] While already in force, the Regulation shall fully apply from 30 December 2024, and is set to provide the European Union with a unique, comprehensive and directly applicable legislation on crypto-assets markets, thus making the Union the first, global integrated jurisdiction to offer a secure and groundbreaking legislative framework for these new phenomena, well ahead of other international players (the US, Switzerland, the UK, Singapore, to cite a few).

2.2 *The Regulatory Perimeter of MiCA*

2.2.1 Scope of Application

MiCA though notably broad and far-reaching, does not encompass all kinds of crypto-assets that circulate in European and global markets. In fact, the regulations has a very precise scope of application, covering only certain types of tokens and effectively excluding others from its perimeter. A clear understanding of what is covered and what is left out of its scope is essential in order to clarify up to what extent NFTs may eventually fall under its provisions, or not. In order to do so, it is necessary to break down how the EU legislator classifies existing tokens.

In general, the taxonomy adopted by MiCA follows a classification system inspired by models initially suggested by the Swiss supervisor in 2018,[24] followed almost universally across the Globe and, ultimately, also adopted by the European

[20] European Parliament legislative resolution of 24 March 2022 on the proposal for a regulation of the European Parliament and of the Council on a pilot regime for market infrastructures based on distributed ledger technology (COM(2020)0594 – C9-0305/2020-2020/0267(COD)).

[21] The press release is available at: https://www.consilium.europa.eu/en/press/press-releases/2022/06/30/digital-finance-agreement-reached-on-european-crypto-assets-regulation-mica/ (Accessed January 8, 2026).

[22] Council of the European Union, Letter to the Chair of the European Parliament Committee on Economic and Monetary Affairs, "Proposal for a Regulation of the European Parliament and of the Council on Markets in Crypto-assets, and amending Directive (EU) 2019/1937 (MiCA)", Interinstitutional file 2020/0265.

[23] Regulation (EU) 2023/1114 of the European Parliament and of the Council of 31 May 2023 on markets in crypto-assets, and amending Regulations (EU) No 1093/2010 and (EU) No 1095/2010 and Directives 2013/36/EU and (EU) 2019/1937 (OJ L 150, 9.6.2023, pp. 40–205).

[24] FINMA (2018).

Securities and Markets Authority (“**ESMA**”)[25] and the European Banking Authority (“**EBA**”).[26] Such approach has led to the systematisation of crypto-assets into three main categories: payment, security and utility tokens.

The first category concerns crypto-assets that are usually employed in payment transactions as means of payment or for the storage of value (for example, stablecoins[27] and, maybe, Bitcoin). Such type of tokens used to be commonly referred to as “crypto-currencies” but should not be confused with so-called “fiat” or “official” currencies (such as EUR, USD, etc.), that, in any case, are escluded from MiCA and are following their own paths of evolution in terms of “digitalization”.[28]

To the second category (that of “security” or “financial” tokens”) belong tokens that allow for the raising of capital by an issuer and typically provide rights in the form of ownership or entitlement to dividends, or payments of some kind.

Finally, the third category (utility tokens) covers the – quite broad – group of crypto-assets that give the right to obtain access to a good or service from the issuer and are intended neither for trading nor for investment.[29]

While this tri-partition is not without several defects, it still maintains its relevance, and is indeed followed by the EU Legislators: where it falls short, for instance, is where it fails to consider what is the treatment to be considered for “hybrid tokens”, or what rules should apply when tokens (as often is the case) change their nature once they are placed, and begin to circulate, on the market, due for instance to the ways in which they are concretely employed.[30]

---

[25] ESMA (2019).

[26] EBA (2019).

[27] See FSB (2020).

[28] For analyses on the ECB’s initiative on a central bank digital currency in the EU (so-called the “Digital Euro”), see: ECB (2020); Mooij (2021); Grünewald et al. (2021); Adalid et al. (2022). For more general analyses on CBDC, see, *ex multis,* Panetta (2018); Nabilou (2019); Bank of England (2020); Bindseil (2020); De Bonis and Ferrero (2022).

[29] Bourveau (2018).

[30] Many tokens, in fact, present a protean nature, which changes depending on how they are concretely employed. See, *ex multis*, the *Unikrn* case in the US (SEC Release No. 10841 of September 15, 2020), where Unikrn, Inc., an operator of an online eSports gaming platform, offered so-called UKG tokens to users claiming that such tokens would grant access to a variety of products and services within the platform, including placing bets online. Based on such description, it would seem that said UKG tokens would qualify as simple utility tokens. However, when analysing the factual elements of the case, the SEC found that users purchasing the tokens had a “reasonable expectation of profit” and effectively treated the tokens as a form of investment. In addition, Unikrn actually intended to have the tokens traded on the secondary market. Thus, a crypto-asset whose nature would apparently lead to its classification as a utility token in reality, because of *how* it was offered and its ultimate *purpose*, was deemed to qualify as a financial token.

However, what is important, for the purpose of this chapter, to fathom from the above classification system[31] is that only utility and payment tokens (including stablecoins) do fall under the scope of MiCA. By contrast, security tokens are intentionally carved-out from the regime and instead left to traditional capital markets legislation, at least if they fall under the notion of "financial instruments", as defined in Article 4(1) (15), MiFID II.[32]

According to MiCA, crypto-assets are defined in Article 3(1)(5) as a "*digital representation of a value or of a right that is able to be transferred and stored electronically using distributed ledger technology or similar technology*". MiCA also adopts a specific terminology to better qualify the tokens under its scope: first, *asset-referenced tokens* ("**ARTs**") refer to tokens that can be classified as stablecoins[33] and *e-money tokens* ("**EMTs**") refer to payment tokens not qualifying as ARTs.[34] The difference between ARTs and EMTs is essentially found in the value backing asset which for the first type can be the value of different fiat currencies, as well as commodities or other crypto-assets. EMTs, in turn, are denominated in unit of a fiat currency only. Where ARTs or EMTs exceed certain volumetric thresholds, they become subject to a more stringent regulatory and supervisory regime, becoming directly supervised by the ESMA or the EBA, respectively, as "significant" ARTs ("**SARTs**") and "significant" EMTs ("**SEMTs**").[35]

Crypto-assets not falling into the definitions of (S)ARTs and (S)EMTs are captured by MiCA, in the broad residual category of "*crypto-assets, other than asset-referenced tokens or e-money tokens*" (or simply, "*other crypto-assets*"), disciplined in Title II of the Regulation. Even though no specific definition is brought to ascertain the exact meaning of "other crypto-assets", Recital (18) of the Regulation clarifies that this "*the third type consists of crypto-assets other than asset-referenced tokens and e-money tokens, and covers a wide variety of crypto-assets, including utility*

[31] This tripartition does, however, leave unresolved the problem of the qualification of 'hybrid' tokens, which assemble in themselves characteristics of several categories. Without dwelving into the granularities of the discussion, it suffices to acknowledge that the issue of qualifying 'hybrid' tokens is usually solved through the criterion of prevailing function, through which the most notable feature of the token is used to determine its classification into one of the general categories.

[32] Directive 2014/65/EU of the European Parliament and of the Council of 15 May 2014 on markets in financial instruments and amending Directive 2002/92/EC and Directive 2011/61/EU (OJ L 173, 12.6.2014). The intention to exclude these tokens from the perimeter of the MiCA regime is stated in Article 2(3)(a) MiCA. Please note that Article 18(1) of the DLTR amends the definition of "financial instruments" contained in MiFID II in order to better link the different regulatory spheres. According to the new wording, which shall replace the current definition laid down in Article 4(1), point (15) MiFID II, financial instruments mean "those instruments specified in Section C of Annex I, including such instruments issued by means of distributed ledger technology", thereby explicitly including tokenized instruments within the scope of MiFID II.

[33] Article 3(1)(6) MiCA defines ART as "a type of crypto-asset that is not an electronic money token and that purports to maintain a stable value by referencing another value or right or a combination thereof, including one or more official currencies".

[34] Article 3(1)(7) MiCA defines EMT as "a type of crypto-asset that purports to maintain a stable value by referencing to the value of one official currency".

[35] See Patz and Wettlaufer (2022).

tokens". Indeed, of all the "other crypto-assets" only utility tokens have a dedicated definition under the MiCA framework, which leads to the assumption that they are likely to be the preponderant object of the "other crypto-assets" catch-all category. In this sense, a utility token is defined in Article 3(1)(9) as a "*type of crypto-asset that is only intended to provide access to a good or a service supplied by its issuer*".

From all the above, one can gather that where (S)ARTs, (S)EMTs or "other crypto-assets" are issued, offered or traded in the EU, they fall under the scope of MiCA. Security tokens, as seen, will not be left unregulated, but rather subject to traditional capital markets regulation, most notably under the MiFID II regime.[36] Utility tokens will, instead, fall under the scope of MiCA.

2.2.2 Crypto-Asset Services

In addition to regulating issuers and offerors of (S)ARTs, (S)EMTs and "other crypto-assets", MiCA also covers the so-called crypto-asset services, which include the following activities, with respect to in-scope crypto-assets:

(i) The custody and administration of crypto-assets on behalf of third parties, meaning "safekeeping or controlling, on behalf of clients, of crypto-assets or of the means of access to such crypto-assets, where applicable in the form of private cryptographic keys" (Article 3(1)(17) MiCA);
(ii) The operation of a trading platform for crypto-assets, meaning "the management of one or more multilateral systems, which bring together or facilitate the bringing together of multiple third-party purchasing and selling interests in crypto-assets, in the system and in accordance with its rules, in a way that results in a contract, either by exchanging crypto-assets for funds or by the exchange of crypto-assets for other crypto-assets" (Article 3(1)(18) MiCA);
(iii) The exchange of crypto-assets for funds, meaning "the conclusion of purchase or sale contracts concerning crypto-assets with clients for funds by using proprietary capital" (Article 3(1)(19) MiCA);
(iv) The exchange of crypto-assets for other crypto-assets, meaning "the conclusion of purchase or sale contracts concerning crypto-assets with clients for other crypto-assets by using proprietary capital" (Article 3(1)(20) MiCA);
(v) The execution of orders for crypto-assets on behalf of third parties, meaning "the conclusion of agreements, on behalf of clients, to purchase or sell one or more crypto-assets or for the subscription on behalf of clients for one or more crypto-assets, and includes the conclusion of contracts to sell crypto-assets at the moment of their offer to the public or admission to trading" (Article 3(1)(21) MiCA);
(vi) Placing of crypto-assets, meaning "the marketing, on behalf of or for the account of the offeror or a party related to the offeror, of crypto-assets to purchasers" (Article 3(1)(22) MiCA);

[36] See Maume (2022), p. 230 et seq.

(vii) Providing transfer services for crypto-assets on behalf of clients, meaning "providing services of transfer, on behalf of a natural or legal person, of crypto-assets from one distributed ledger address or account to another" (Article 3(1)(26) MiCA);

(viii) The reception and transmission of orders for crypto-assets on behalf of clients, meaning "the reception from a person of an order to purchase or sell one or more crypto-assets or to subscribe for one or more crypto-assets and the transmission of that order to a third party for execution" (Article 3(1)(23) MiCA);

(ix) Providing advice on crypto-assets, meaning "offering, giving or agreeing to give personalised recommendations to a client, either at the client's request or on the initiative of the crypto-asset service provider providing the advice, in respect of one or more transactions relating to crypto-assets or the use of crypto-asset services" (Article 3(1)(24) MiCA); and

(x) Providing portfolio management on crypto-assets, meaning "managing portfolios in accordance with mandates given by clients on a discretionary client-by-client basis where such portfolios include one or more crypto-assets" (Article 3(1)(25) MiCA).

These crypto-asset services, which largely mirror the definitions related to investment services under MiFiD II, may be provided by legal persons or other undertakings that apply for authorisation as "crypto-asset service providers" ("**CASPs**"), in accordance with the procedure and requirements laid down in Title V MiCA.

Now that the regulatory perimeter of MiCA has been by and large introduced, we shall thence focus on how precisely NFTs fit in this complex web of definitions to, subsequently, be able to ascertain how issuers and players in NFT markets could be generally impacted by the new MiCA framework.

2.3 *How do NFTs Fall Under MiCA?*

2.3.1 The Evolution of the Approaches Adopted by EU Legislators

In principle, NFTs do not seem to fall under either one of the types of tokens governed by MiCA: they are not ARTs, nor EMTs and, initially, in the first versions of the proposed Regulation, it was dubious whether they would be captured by the definition of "other crypto-assets". However, the NFT phenomenon is so articulated and has taken on such economic importance that the EU legislature has not been able to completely neglect them, and they do find some (controversial) space in the context of MiCA. The rules finally set out, however, were preceded by an apparent tug-of-war between EU legislators, which clearly had envisioned different approaches towards NFTs, and result in far-from-clear picture.

Under the Commission's original proposal of MiCA, NFTs seemed to be included in the general scope of application as "crypto-assets". However, Article 4(2)(c) provided that issuers of "*crypto-assets that are unique and non-fungible with other crypto-assets*" were exempted from publishing or registering the crypto-asset white-paper, a position that indicated an intention to provide a simplified regime for issuers of NFTs. Nonetheless, rules applicable to providers of crypto-asset services – including those related to NFTs – would in principle still be covered. This is particularly relevant with respect to requirements and obligations regarding custodianship and trading. Such approach seems to find its justification in the fact that the Commission was mostly concerned with consumer protection, market abuse, operational resilience and money laundering. For this reason, it opted to maintain CASPs providing services in connection with NFTs within the provisions of the regulation, but exempted issuers of NFTs – potentially less significant than issuers of other types of crypto-assets – from disclosure obligations. By opting to keep CASPs providing services related to NFTs subject to Title V of the regulation, such entities would be required to comply with rules of conduct, authorisation and governance that could facilitate, in the Commission's view, the mitigation and control of risks.

A different stance, however, emerged from the Council's draft, which clearly signaled an *animus* towards carving-out NFTs from the MiCA framework. To such end, a new Recital (8b) was included containing the following text:

"*This Regulation should not apply to crypto-assets that are unique and not fungible with other crypto-assets, including digital art and collectibles, whose value is attributable to each crypto-asset's unique characteristics and the utility it gives to the token holder. Similarly, it also does not apply to crypto-assets representing services or physical assets that are unique and not fungible, such as product guarantees or real estate. While these crypto-assets may be traded in marketplaces, be accumulated speculatively and, in limited cases be used as means of exchange, they are not readily interchangeable and the relative value of one crypto-asset in relation to another, each being unique, cannot be ascertained by means of comparison to an existing market or equivalent asset. Such features limit the extent to which these crypto-assets can have a financial use, thus limiting risks to users and the system and justifies the exemption. The fractional parts of an unique and non-fungible crypto-asset should not be considered unique and not fungible. The sole attribution of a unique identifier to a crypto-asset is not sufficient to classify it as a unique or not fungible. The assets or rights represented should also be unique and not fungible for the crypto-asset to be considered unique and not fungible*". Moreover, a new Article 2(2a) was introduced by the Council to unequivocally exclude NFTs from the entire regulatory scope (including, therefore, rules applicable to CASPs), establishing that "*this Regulation does not apply to crypto-assets that are unique and not fungible with other crypto-assets*".

The criteria proposed by the Council – as by the Commission – for identifying NFTs and therefore removing them from the ambit of the MiCA framework was therefore epitomized in (i) uniqueness; and (ii) non-fungibility, meaning that whenever a token presented both elements cumulatively (as well as the assets or rights it represented), they would immediately be carved-out from the regime. An exception to this standard explicitly foreseen by the Council was the case of fractional NFTs,[37] which would be deemed as lacking the features of being unique and non-fungible, therefore falling back into the framework.

Finally, the Parliament's version of the text came with yet another approach, expressed in its Recital (8a):

"This Regulation should only apply to crypto-assets that are able to be transferred among holders without the issuer's permission. It should not apply to crypto-assets that are unique and not fungible with other crypto-assets, that are not fractionable and are accepted only by the issuer, including mercant's loyalty schemes, that represent IP rights or guarantees, that certify authenticity of a unique physical assets, or that represent any other right not linked to the ones that financial instruments bear, and are not admitted to trading on a crypto-asset excange. The fractional parts of a unique and non-fungible crypto-asset should not be considered unique and non-fungible. The sole attribution of a unique identifier to a crypto-asset is not sufficient to classify it as unique or non-fungible. Similarly, this Regulation should also not apply to crypto-assets representing services, digital or physical assets that are unique, indivisable and non-fungible, such as product guarantees, personalised products or services, or real estate. However, this Regulation should apply to non-fungible tokens that grant to its holders or its issuers specific rights linked to those of financial instruments, such as profit rights or other entitlements.In those cases, the tokens should be able to be assessed and treated as security tokens, and be subject, together with the issuer, to various other requirements of Union financial servics law, such as Directive (EU) 2015/849 of the European Parliament and of the Council, Directive 2014/65/EU, Regulation (EU) 2017/1129 of the European Parliament and of the Council, Regulation (EU) No 596/2014 and Directive 2014/57/EU of the European Parliament and of the Council".

As anticipated, the Parliament's recital generally coincided with the texts proposed by the Council – and, to a lesser extent, the Commission – but it also introduced a new element concerning the nature of non-fungible tokens that "grant rights or entitlements to its issuers", establishing that in such cases the tokens *should be treated as security tokens and also submitted to EU capital markets rules.*

In addition, a new point (8b) of the Recital stemming from the Parliament's draft stated that "*For crypto-assets that are unique and not fungible with other crypto-assets, that are not fractionable and that are accepted only by the issuer, that represent IP rights or guarantees, or that certify authenticity of a unique physical assets such as a piece of art, or that represent any other right not linked to the ones that financial instruments bear, and that are not admitted to trading on a crypto-asset exchange, it is necessary to consider whether a Union-wide bespoke regime should be proposed by the Commission*". Within the Parliament's draft, point (5) of Article

[37] A fractional NFT is an NFT divided into multiple pieces, allowing for fractional ownership of the original token. The fractionalization of an NFT lowers the barrier or entry, as the fractional parts cost less than the full token.

3(1) also contained an amendment to the definition of 'utility token', which introduced *fungibility* as a marking aspect of such type of crypto-asset, thus removing any ambiguities in connection with NFTs being categorised as utility tokens.

What emerged from the Parliament's version was thus an alignment with the Commission's and the Council's proposed criteria to qualify NFTs – i.e., those of uniqueness and non-fungibility – but a divergence as to the approach with regard to a complete carve-out of such tokens from the scope of the framework – in particular from Title V on CASPs – and the legislative technique to be employed to achieve the envisaged results.

2.3.2 The Current Regime on NFTs Under MiCA

Based on the final version of the MiCA Regulation that was ultimately published, it seems that the approach towards NFTs sustained by the Council was prevalent, leading to a text which deliberately and expressely carves-out NFTs from the entire scope of application of MICA, under certain conditions.

The main confirmation of this approach comes from Recital (10), which mirrors the one proposed by the Council and reads as follows: "*This Regulation should not apply to crypto-assets that are unique and not fungible with other crypto-assets, including digital art and collectibles. The value of such unique and non-fungible crypto-assets is attributable to each crypto-asset's unique characteristics and the utility it gives to the token. Nor should this Regulation apply to crypto-assets representing services or physical assets that are unique and non-fungible, such as product guarantees or real estate. While unique and non-fungible crypto-assets might be traded on the marketplace and be accumulated speculatively, they are not readily interchangeable and the relative value of one such crypto-asset in relation to another, each being unique, cannot be ascertained by means of comparison to an existing market or equivalent asset. Such features limit the extent to which these crypto-assets can have a financial use, thus limiting risks to holders and the financial system and justifying their exclusion from the scope of this Regulation*". The recital elucidates even further the meaning of the provision contained in Article 2(3) MiCA, which is already quite categorical in its premise: "*This Regulation does not apply to crypto-assets that are unique and not fungible with other crypto-assets*".

From the recitals above, it is noticeable that the elements of uniqueness and non-fungibility remain at the core of the legal qualification of NFTs, yet such elements are curtailed, on the one side, by fractionability and, on the other, by their qualification as financial instruments. This is explained in Recital (11) MiCA: "*The fractional parts of a unique and non-fungible crypto-asset should not be considered unique and non-fungible. The issuance of crypto-assets as non-fungible tokens in a large series or collection should be considered as an indicator of their fungibility. The mere attribution of a unique identifier to a crypto-asset is not, in and of itself, sufficient to classify it as unique and non- fungible. The assets or rights represented should also be unique and non- fungible in order for the crypto-asset to be considered unique and non- fungible. The exclusion of crypto-assets that are unique and non-fungible from the scope of this Regulation is without prejudice to the qualification of such crypto-assets as financial instruments. This Regulation should also apply to crypto-assets that appear unique and non-fungible, but whose de facto features or whose features that are linked to their de facto uses, would make them either fungible or not unique. In this regard, when assessing and classifying crypto-assets, competent authorities should adopt a substance over form approach whereby the features of the crypto-asset in question determine the classification and not its designation by the issuer*".

An interesting aspect to be highlighted is the underpinning of the *"substance over form approach"* by the legislator, which makes it clear that assessing the legal nature of NFTs will not be a simple task. The ascertainment of the elements of uniqueness and non-fungibility shall not prescind from a proper evaluation of the tokens' *"de facto features or [...] features that are linked to their de facto uses"*.

Specifically concerning the qualification of NFTs as financial instruments – an issue first raised by the Parliament's document -, a Recital (14) was introduced to shed light on a new mandate to ESMA aiming to clarify the cases where crypto-assets fall under financial regulation: "*For the purpose of ensuring a clear delineation between, on the one hand, crypto-assets covered by this Regulation and, on the other hand, financial instruments, ESMA should be mandated to issue guidelines on the criteria and conditions for the qualification of crypto-assets as financial instruments. Those guidelines should also allow for a better understanding of the cases where crypto-assets that are otherwise considered unique and not fungible with other crypto-assets might qualify as financial instruments. In order to promote a common approach towards the classification of crypto-assets"* the ESAs *"should promote discussions on such classifications. Competent authorities should be able to request opinions from the ESAs on the classification of crypto-assets, including classifications proposed by offerors or persons seeking admission to trading. Offerors or persons seeking admission to trading are primarily responsible for the correct classification of crypto-assets, which might be challenged by the competent authorities, both before the date of publication of the offer and at any time thereafter. Where the classification of a crypto-asset appears to be inconsistent with this Regulation or other relevant Union legislative acts on financial services, the ESAs should make use of their powers under Regulations (EU) No 1093/2010, (EU) No 1094/2010 and (EU) No 1095/2010 in order to ensure a consistent and coherent approach to such classification*".

Aware of the challenges that may arise from leaving markets in NFTs unregulated, the legislators also agreed to review the framework in the near future as to assess whether a dedicated regulation on NFTs shall be required in order to mitigate the risks it potentially poses. Such is the content of Article 142(2)(d) MiCA, according to which: "*1. By 30 December 2024 and after consulting the EBA and ESMA, the Commission shall present a report to the European Parliament and the Council on the latest developments with respect to crypto-assets, in particular on matters that are not addressed in this Regulation, accompanied, where appropriate, by a legislative proposal. 2. The report referred to in paragraph 1 shall contain at least the following: (...) (d) an assessment of the development of markets in unique and non-fungible crypto-assets and of the appropriate regulatory treatment of such crypto-assets, including an assessment of the necessity and feasibility of regulating offerors of unique and non-fungible crypto-assets as well as providers of services related to such crypto-assets*".

In sum, the framework on markets in NFTs arising from the future adoption of MiCA will lead to the following regulatory regime:

(i) in principle, NFTs are out of the scope of MiCA provided they (and the asset or rights they represent) present cumulatively the elements of uniqueness and non-fungibility, and are not fractional NFTs;
(ii) Fractional parts of NFTs or NFTs issued in a large series or collection fall instead within the scope of MiCA;
(iii) issuers, offerors and CASPs providing services in relation to NFTs not covered by MiCA are exempted from the obligations and requirements they would otherwise be required to fulfil with regard to in-scope crypto-assets; and
(iv) NFTs qualifying as financial instruments (as shall be further clarified by the dedicated ESMA guidelines) will be subject to traditional EU capital markets regimes (especially MiFID II).

Notwithstanding the above, there remains hazy aspects to be clarified over time by stakeholders.

One of the amendments suggested by the Parliament, for example, consisting of including "fungibility" in the definition of "utility token" as a crucial element for its characterisation, was not embraced by the final version of the text. The result is that there might be room for ambiguity in the concrete assessment of the legal nature of a given token, in particular in its qualification as a utility token or an NFT – especially when both fall under the rather open category of "other crypto-assets". Another potentially contentious aspect of the Regulation is the grey zone with regard to the qualification of NFTs as financial instruments. Irrespective of the content of the ESMA guidelines, there is a possibility that such a qualification may be affected by national frameworks governing the notions of "financial instruments" and "financial products", which poses a significant threat of fragmentation and misalignment with the MiCA approach altogether.

2.3.3 NFTs and Metaverse

Due to the limits and constraints of this contribution, there is virtually no space to discuss the complex interrelations between the metaverse, the existing EU financial legislation and the MiCA. One point should, however, be considered. The use of crypto-assets in the metaverse should not change, or impact, their classification or treatment under EU law, that remains anchored in the taxonomy that we discussed. While this conclusion seems to be pretty based on common sense, there is, however, a specific perspective to be considered, i.e. the use of crypto assets, in a metaverse environment, for the purpose of settling transactions and payments. In fact, the possibility of using crypto assets in that context will also be linked to their technological features, and to the underlying protocols, resulting (potentially) in different standards.

The issue of interoperability between different platforms and technologies will, most likely, need to be addressed, together with the broader topic concerning the possible use of FIAT digital currencies (including, if and when it will be introduced the digital euro). Also in the metaverse, therefore, rules applicable to digital assets being traded, exchanged and used as a means of settlement of transaction will be differentiated on the basis of the nature of those assets, and their treatment under the different silos of EU legislation: MiFID/capital markets, MiCA, and – ultimately – the upcoming project for a digital euro and other digital official currencies across the Globe. Due to the evolving nature of the metaverse, and the fact that also crypto-assets may take up different features as they circulate on the market (see Sect. 1 above), different levels of protection for consumers will therefore apply, and will also require new supervisory approaches. For the time being, one cannot but observe the phenomenon in its evolution, without drawing hasty conclusions.

3 Final Remarks

What seems to emerge from MiCA is that the phenomenon of NFTs will be, for the foreseeable future, strictly linked to EU capital markets legislation, whether in its new form of digital finance or in the more traditional discipline of financial instruments. However, the regime is far from final and complete: in fact, fundamental aspects of the regulation are left in blank for soft law to clarify and the whole design will be revised in a rather short-term. The development of markets in NFTs will be key to orient how future legislation will be crafted and how regulators will react to the new challenges and demands that emerge from such markets.

This involves, among several other aspects, a better articulation of MiCA with the DLTR and DORA – for example, to what extent can an NFT qualifying as a financial instrument be admitted to trading in a market infrastructure operating under the DLT Pilot Regime?[38] – and the three of them with other realms of EU financial

[38] As seen, NFTs fulfilling the requirements of "uniqueness" and "non-fungibility" may – at least potentially - be traded on the market and even though they are excluded from the scope of MiCA, they may, nonetheless, qualify as financial instruments under the MiFID regime. Given that the definition of "financial instrument" in Article 4(1)(15) MIFID II comprises instruments issued by means of DLT, certain NFTs could, indeed, be qualified as such, based on their specific features and on the precise provisions of national laws implementing MiFID II. However, according to Article 3(1) DLTR, DLT financial instruments shall only be admitted to trading on a DLT market infrastructure, or be recorded on a DLT market infrastructure, if, at the moment of admission to trading or the moment of recording on a distributed ledger, the DLT financial instruments are: (i) shares, the issuer of which has a market capitalisation of less than EUR 500 million; (ii) bonds, other forms of securitised debt, including depositary receipts in respect of such securities, or money market instruments, with an issue size of less than EUR 1 billion; or (iii) units in collective investment undertakings, the market value of the assets under management of which is less than EUR 500 million. In this sense, the

legislation, including crowdfunding[39] and AI regulations.[40] As business models tend to grow more sophisticated and explore the potentialities of the new technologies that will not cease to develop, regulators will have the task to align concepts and facilitate the flourishing of a digital finance environment in the Union. Notions that already exist in EU capital markets law – such as the idea of "technological neutrality"[41] – shall be pivotal to foster innovation in a more efficient manner.

The Digital Finance Package – and MiCA, in particular – is a groundbreaking achievement by the EU and the first of its kind in global financial markets. Impactful as it is, however, it is likely to be one of the first steps of a new chapter of EU financial legislation, one that shall be enhanced progressively, guided by the evolution of markets. As for NFTs, it is too soon to tell whether they will remain unregulated, be dragged into the scope of MiCA, or be subject to a bespoke regime. Once again, the answer seems to lie on the experience of public and private stakeholders with the new framework.

References

Adalid R et al. (2022) Central bank digital currency and bank intermediation. ECB occasional paper No. 2022/293

Annunziata F (2020) Speak, if you can: what are you? An alternative approach to the qualification of tokens and initial coin offerings. Eur Co Law Rev 17:129–154

Annunziata F, De Arruda T (2022) Crowdfunding and DLTs: the imperative need for more clarity. In: Macchiavello E (ed) Regulation on European crowdfunding service providers for business: a commentary. Edward Elgar, Cheltenham, pp 565–576

Banca d'Italia (2018) Avvertenza per i consumatori sui rischi delle valute virtuali da parte delle Autorità europee. https://www.bancaditalia.it/compiti/vigilanza/avvisi-pub/avvertenza-valute-virtuali-2018/index.html

Bank of England (2020) Central bank digital currency: opportunities, challenges and design. https://www.bankofengland.co.uk/paper/2020/central-bank-digital-currency-opportunities-challenges-and-design-discussion-paper

Barsan I (2017) Legal challenges of Initial Coin Offerings. RTDF 3:54–65

Bindseil U (2020) Tiered CBDC and the financial system. ECB working paper series No. 2351

Bourveau T, George E, Ellahie A, Macciocchi D (2018) Initial coin offerings: early evidence on the role of disclosure in the unregulated crypto market. J Account Res 60(1):129–167

DLTR adopts a restrictive approach towards MiFID II instruments, significantly limiting the types of instruments eligible to the DLTR regime.Therefore, it is unclear how NFTs could be admitted to trading on a DLT market infrastructure under the DLT Pilot Regime.

[39] See, for example, Annunziata and De Arruda (2022).

[40] Regulation (EU) 2024/1689 of the European Parliament and of the Council of 13 June 2024 laying down harmonised rules on artificial intelligence and amending Regulations (EC) No 300/2008, (EU) No 167/2013, (EU) No 168/2013, (EU) 2018/858, (EU) 2018/1139 and (EU) 2019/2144 and Directives 2014/90/EU, (EU) 2016/797 and (EU) 2020/1828 (Artificial Intelligence Act).

[41] See Recital (9) MiCA. In general lines, the principle of technological neutrality establishes that legislation should neither impose, nor discriminate in favor of, the use of a particular type of technology to achieve its objectives.

Chohan UW (2021) Non-fungible tokens: blockchains, scarcity, and value. Critical Blockchain Research Initiative (CBRI) Working Papers

Conseil Superieur de la Propriete Litteraire et Artistique (CSPLA) (2022) Rapport de la mission sur les jetons non fongibles. https://www.culture.gouv.fr/Nous-connaitre/Organisation-du-ministere/Conseil-superieur-de-la-propriete-litteraire-et-artistique-CSPLA/Travaux-et-publications-du-CSPLA/Missions-du-CSPLA/Mission-du-CSPLA-sur-les-jetons-non-fongibles-JNF-ou-NFT-en-anglais. Accessed January 8, 2026

De Bonis R, Ferrero G (2022) Technological progress and institutional adaptations: the case of the Central Bank Digital Currency (CBDC), Bank of Italy occasional paper no. 690

Di Bernardino C, Penedo AC, Ellul J, Ferreira A, von Goldbeck A, Herian R, Siadat A, Siedler N-L (2021) NFT - legal token classification. EU blockchain observatory and forum NFT reports

European Banking Authority (EBA) (2019) Report with advice for the European Commission on crypto-assets. https://www.eba.europa.eu/publications-and-media/press-releases/eba-reports-crypto-assets

European Banking Authority (EBA) (2013) Warning to consumers on virtual currencies issued by the EBA (EBA/WRG/2013/01)

European Central Bank (ECB) (2020) Report on a digital euro. https://www.ecb.europa.eu/pub/pdf/other/Report_on_a_digital_euro~4d7268b458.en.pdf. Accessed January 8, 2026

European Commission (2020) Digital finance package: commission sets out new, ambitious approach to encourage responsible innovation to benefit consumers and businesses. (Press Release), 24 Setember 2020. https://ec.europa.eu/commission/presscorner/detail/en/IP_20_1684

Fairfield J (2022) Tokenized: the law of non-fungible tokens and unique digital property. Indiana Law J 97:1261–1313

Financial Stability Board (FSB) (2020) Regulation, supervision and oversight of global stablecoin arrangements. https://www.fsb.org/2020/10/regulation-supervision-and-oversight-of-global-stablecoin-arrangements/. Accessed January 8, 2026

FINMA (2018) Guidelines for enquiries regarding the regulatory framework for initial coin offerings (ICOs). https://www.finma.ch/en/~/media/finma/dokumente/dokumentencenter/myfinma/1bewilligung/fintech/wegleitung-ico.pdf?la=en. Accessed January 8, 2026

Grünewald S, Zellweger-Gutknecht C, Geva B (2021) Digital euro and ECB powers. Common Mark Law Rev 58:1029–1056

Guadamuz A (2022) Perspectives on NFTs from the EU and UK. Columbia J Law Arts 45:361–364

Henderson MT, Raskin M (2019) A regulatory classification of digital assets: toward an operational howey test for cryptocurrencies, ICOs and other digital assets. Colum Bus L 2:444–493

Kong D, Lin T (2021) Alternative investments in the fintech era: the risk and return of non-fungible token (NFT). https://ssrn.com/abstract=3914085. Accessed January 8, 2026

Maume P (2022) Financial services regulation. In: Maume P, Maute L, Fromberger M (eds) The law of crypto-assets: a handbook. Beck/Hart/Nomos, Baden-Baden

Maume P, Fromberger M (2019) Regulations of initial coin offerings: reconciling U.S. and E.U. securities laws. Chic J Int'l L 19:548–558

Mooij A (2021) European central bank digital currency: the digital Euro. what design of the digital euro is possible within the European central Bank's legal framework? BRIDGE network working paper series no 14

Moringiello J and Odinet C (2021) The property law of tokens, 74 Florida law review 607, U Iowa legal studies research paper no. 2021-44

Nabilou H (2019) Central bank digital currencies: preliminary legal observations. J Bank Regul 27:266–291

Noble E (2021) Crypto-assets, distributed ledger technologies and disintermediation in finance: Overcoming impediments to scaling. A view from the EU. In: Kaili E, Psarrakis D (eds) Disintermediation economics. The impact of blockchain on markets and policies. Palgrave, Camden, pp 193–214

Panetta F (2018) 21st century cash: central banking, technological innovation and digital currencies, suerf policy note, no. 40

Patz A, Wettlaufer J (2022) E-money tokens, stablecoins, and token payment services. In: Maume P, Maute L, Fromberger M (eds) The law of crypto-assets: a handbook. Beck/Hart/Nomos, Baden-Baden

Rohr J, Wright A (2019) Blockchain-based token sales, initial coin offerings, and the democratization of public capital markets. Hastings LJ 70:463–469

Scott H (2021) The E.U.'s digital operational resilience act: cloud services & financial companies. https://ssrn.com/abstract=3904113. Accessed January 8, 2026

Vondrackova A (2016) Regulation of Virtual currency in the European union, Charles university in Prague faculty of law research paper no. 2016/III/3

Zetzsche D, Buckley RP, Arner DW, Föhr L (2017) The ICO gold rush: it's a scam, it's a bubble, it's a super challenge for regulators. Harv Int'l L J 60:267–315

Zetzsche DA, Andreas D, Annunziata F, Arner DW, Buckley R (2020) The markets in crypto-assets regulation (MICA) and the EU digital finance strategy. Cap Mark Law J 16:203–225

Zetzsche DA, Woxholth J (2022) The DLT sandbox under the EU pilot regulation. Cap Mark Law J 17:212–236

A New Horizon for Financial Law and Policy: Non-Fungible Tokens in the Metaverse

Joseph Lee

Abstract This chapter examines the functional nature of non-fungible tokens (NFTs) in Web3 space such as the Metaverse, and provides a framework for the financial regulation of NFT transactions. The aim is to identify any paradigm shift in the understanding of (1) financial assets in private law, (2) financial services that may be provided in a more decentralised market, and (3) policies and methods of regulatory intervention. Property law is important for defining what NFTs are according to their functions and the legal objectives of certainty, justice, and innovation. Regulation will play a role in mitigating risk, proactively managing imaged risks or retroactively managing any risks that private law has not been able to address. In financial law, regulations must play an active role in ensuring financial stability, investor protection, market integrity, competition, and innovation. Technology such as 'code as law' will now play an even more pivotal role in the governance framework. Policy is determined by the development of the underlying technology, the players in the Metaverse, and by regulatory competition.

1 Introduction

This chapter examines the functional nature of non-fungible tokens (NFTs) in Web3 space such as the Metaverse, and provides a framework for the financial regulation of NFT transactions. Three aspects are investigated based on practical cases involving existing and proposed laws and regulations: (1) NFTs as a financial asset, (2) institutions providing NFT-related transaction services, and (3) the role technology intersecting with law in this digital space, using Decentralised Autonomous Organisations (DAOs) as an example. The aim is to identify any paradigm shift in the understanding of (1) financial assets in private law, (2) financial services that may be provided in a more decentralised market, and (3) policies and methods of regulatory intervention. The use of DAOs as a regulatory space for NFT transactions in the Metaverse of the future Web3 is explored.

J. Lee (✉)
University of Manchester, Manchester, UK
e-mail: Joseph-lee@Manchester.ac.uk

F. Di Porto and O. Pollicino (eds.), *Law and Politics of Virtual Worlds*, Law, Governance and Technology Series 79, https://doi.org/10.1007/978-3-032-08541-2_6

The chapter is relevant to policymakers for understanding their regulatory obligations and also to the stakeholders in the community for finding a common approach to meta-regulation.

2 The New Market Ecosystems

2.1 *Metaverse and Web3*

The Metaverse is a virtual world of the so-called Web3 space[1]—the future of internet—constructed based on blockchain technology—a type of distributed ledger technology (DLT)[2]—in which participants interact with one another in commerce,[3] public administrative work, manufacturing processes,[4] education, and medical care.[5] Web3[6] is distinguished from Web1—where users can only view contents—and Web2—where users can interact. Web3 is a space where users can create their own contents without going through traditional centralised intermediaries. Since platforms built on blockchain technology have the potential, as claimed, to democratise information, the Metaverse is said to be an information highway that enables participants to connect, co-create, and share products without the need for centralised systems, such as exchanges or centralised platforms to facilitate their transactions.[7] The Metaverse is a space known for gaming so far, but it is also a space where collaborations can move beyond current practices where access to technology such as AI,[8] to information, to finance, and to dispute resolutions may be denied because of technological, geographical, legal, and regulatory barriers.

The blockchain-enabled Metaverse can thus be seen as a digital twin to our current universe.[9] However, despite its technological power, there is still a need to use human sensibility to control the Metaverse so that our cognitive values,[10] rights, and obligations can be embedded in it.[11] Many terms are used to describe this space according to

---

[1] UK Government has announced its ambition in web3 and Metaverse https://www.gov.uk/government/publications/spring-budget-2023/spring-budget-2023-html; Japan's Web3 white paper by the Liberal Democratic Party https://note.com/akihisa_shiozaki/n/n669dee962b15.

[2] Ball (2022).

[3] UNDP #Web3for2030: How can Web3 help achieve the Sustainable Development Goals https://www.undp.org/publications/web3for2030-how-can-web3-help-achieve-sustainable-development-goals; Jung et al. (2023).

[4] Biris and Gruian (2022).

[5] Sandrone (2022), Curtis and Brolan (2023).

[6] Stackpole (2022).

[7] Cao (2022).

[8] Thien et al. (2023a).

[9] Thien et al. (2023b).

[10] Zyda (2022).

[11] Oleksy et al. (2023).

their functions and purposes: omniverse, eduverse, viveverse, and cryptoverse. I use a stronger term in my recent book published—Crypto-Republic[12]—to suggest that we need a constitutional and legal order so that our sense of purpose can be realised through a common mission.[13] This blockchain-based crypto-republic should exist to provide a more inclusive economy and society, where access to finance, justice, and a shared economy is prioritized.[14] In this way, technology can be harnessed to promote human advancement and innovation for the good of society. This call is a response to the current situation of financial inaccessibility, denial of public services, and the existence of barriers to co-creating and equitably sharing wealth. It is hoped that the crypto-republic will carry purposeful meaning through its missions (or corporate purpose), and participants will not engage in transactions in the Metaverse with a pure feeling of gaming. It is also not a place where personal data are collected while nothing substantial is returned to either individuals or the community at large—a problem known as Surveillance Capitalism,[15] in which tech-companies unilaterally claim private human experiences as raw material and translate them into behavioural data for the future commercial uses.

2.2 *What is an NFT?*

NFTs are non-fungible tokens.[16] There is no strict definition of an NFT.[17] One description calls them 'digital tokens that act like certificates of authenticity for, and in some cases represent ownership of, assets that range from expensive illustrations of apes to collectibles like celebrity autographs and physical goods like a case of rare whiskey'.[18] This description likens an NFT to a digital asset which has been defined as a 'digital representation of value or rights which may be transferred and stored electronically, using distributed ledger technology or similar technology'. Even though the EU Regulation on Market for Cryptoassets (MiCA)[19] does not include NFTs in its system of regulation, an NFT may still be legally recognised as a digital asset under national civil law.

In fact, all crypto assets are non-fungible tokens in the technical sense, as each one of them is represented by a unique series of computer codes. However, in law, a crypto asset may be treated as fungible (inter-changeable). For instance, even though

---

[12] Lee (2022b).

[13] Lee (2021). See R. Vecellio Segate's chapter in this book (discussing the emergence of a constitution for the metaverse).

[14] Lee (2022a).

[15] Zuboff and Schwandt (2019).

[16] Far et al. (2022).

[17] Girasa (2023).

[18] Lee (2021).

[19] Regulation (EU) 2023/1114 of the European Parliament and of the Council of 31 May 2023 on markets in crypto-assets (MiCA).

each is represented by a unique computer code, a security token, a money token or an exchange token, a utility token, or a governance token, may be fungible. Each belongs to the same asset class and is interchangeable just as a currency bill, such as a dollar bill. Although a dollar bill has a unique serial number, it is interchangeable with any other dollar bill by law and is therefore fungible.

So, what is the difference between an NFT and a fungible token? An NFT is intended by its creator or a participant in the market to be a unique 'object',[20] such as reflecting an artwork - a painting, a piece of music,[21] or a photograph. In the Metaverse, an NFT can represent a virtual human (i.e. an avatar), a piece of virtual land, a logo representing a brand, a store, or a programme such as an academic seminar.[22] The aim of the NFT in the Metaverse is to provide incentives to users and participants to create content[23] by giving them power over the content through ownership or other forms of control.[24] There has been much debate about whether legal ownership can be created in NFTs.[25] Can it be property in law?[26] Can a set of computer codes (digital files) be considered property in law?[27] How can a set of computer codes—merely information—constitute a property in law?[28] The legal debate highlights the complexity of identifying existing legal tools for creating ownership of a virtual 'thing'.[29] This has prompted the Law Commission of England and Wales to propose an additional category for digital assets to the existing categories of physical property and chosen action (a right).[30]

As the Law Commission also suggests that a functional approach should be used, it is important to recognise the intention of NFT users in the Metaverse as well as the missions and goals of the Metaverse. The broad objective of the Metaverse is to create a democratised blockchain-based information system through which participants can collaborate and share benefits equitably. In this sense, denying creators access to a share of what they have produced would go against the purpose of designing the space. If the proprietary legal concept is not suitable for accommodating the mission and goal, lawmakers should develop appropriate tools. The Law Commission is currently

---

[20] See UK Treasury early plan for NFTs, but later abandoned 'UK government drops plans for NFT made by Royal Mint' (2022) https://www.theguardian.com/technology/2023/mar/28/uk-government-nft-royal-mint-rishi-sunak-cryptocurrencies.

[21] Turchet (2023).

[22] Belk (2022).

[23] Criddle and Gabert-Doyon(2022).

[24] Wang and Lau (2023).

[25] Doaa and Fatma (2021).

[26] First Chinese court decision recognises NFT as virtual property see Chan and Mok (2022), Caswell and Furtado (2021), Windsor (2022); also see Stevens (2023).

[27] Michels and Millard (2022).

[28] Lee and Van de Looverbosch (2022).

[29] Legal Statement on the Status of Cryptoassets and Smart Contracts by the UK Jurisdiction Taskforce of the LawTech Delivery Panel (the UKJT).

[30] Law Commission, Digital Assets: Consultation Paper (2022) Law Com No 256 https://s3-eu-west-2.amazonaws.com/lawcom-prod-storage-11jsxou24uy7q/uploads/2022/07/Digital-Assets-Consultation-Paper-Law-Commission-1.pdf.

tackling this problem. New tools should be introduced not only in private law but also in public, criminal, corporate and financial law, and reporting and accounting regimes.[31] In addition, technology can play an important role through fintech, regtech, suptech, and corptech (such as DAOs) as tools in helping to achieve the Metaverse's goals.[32]

2.3 *How is Crypto Finance Relevant?*

Crypto assets are defined as digital representations of value or contractual rights created, transferred, and stored on a distributed ledger technology (DLT) network (e.g. blockchain) and authenticated through cryptography.[33] 'Crypto liabilities' are defined as obligations arising from the issuance of crypto assets, resulting in a present obligation for the issuing entity to transfer or grant access to an economic resource in digital or non-digital form.[34]

Crypto finance is relevant to the Metaverse in three major ways. Firstly, crypto assets can be used as a payment method for transacting goods, services, and data in the Metaverse.[35] Secondly, goods, services, and data can be represented by crypto assets through tokenisation using technical and legal means. And thirdly, service providers who maintain the market in the Metaverse include some financial intermediaries such as payment systems, settlement and custodian services,[36] brokering and order routing services, promotion[37] and advertising services, transaction validation, and mining services. Each of these aspects presents its own risks, including systematic, market, and legal.

---

[31] OECD (2022a).

[32] Lee and Darbellay (2022).

[33] Digital assets: Non-fungible Tokens. UK Finance https://www.ukfinance.org.uk/policy-and-guidance/reports-and-publications/digital-assets-non-fungible-tokens.

[34] In 2019, the UK LawTech Panel issued an authoritative legal statement, which stated that crypto assets are property and associated smart contracts are legally enforceable.

[35] Vidal-Tomás (2023).

[36] ESMA (2022), Julius Bär (2022), Financial Express (2023).

[37] See also the recent reform proposal on promotion in the financial services in the UK, The Financial Services and Markets Act 2000 (Financial Promotion) (Amendment) Order 2023, https://www.legislation.gov.uk/ukdsi/2023/9780348246490/pdfs/ukdsi_9780348246490_en.pdf.

3 NFTs as a Financial Asset and Institutions Providing NFT-Related Transaction Services

3.1 Is a NFT a Financial Asset?

A number of court cases show an inclination to give crypto assets property status through which they are capable of being owned, transferred, pledged, and loaned. Private law and especially property law have several objectives: creating legal certainty for transacting crypto assets, realising the concept of justice to give confidence to the community, and further creating a space for innovation whereby the law is a medium for parties to use these assets for their own commercial or other purposes. Private law and property law, while taking these policy objectives into account, may not be sufficient to deal with additional policy objectives, such as maintaining financial stability, protecting market integrity against specific manipulative methods, and creating a space for innovation.[38] Regulations may be required to fill this gap.

There can be many layers of interaction within private law, either common law rules developed by judges or statutory laws enacted by the parliament, and regulations and guidelines developed by regulators or industries. The development of private law may be slow and thus affect other areas of property law. Regulation can be developed to provide a remedial response for a specific purpose,[39] such as money laundering and investor protection without overarching property law principles being created for the parties to transact. Therefore, regulations can map a market structure for private law to discern how legal certainty, delivery of justice, and innovation, including legal innovation, can be factored into the property law formula for a particular crypto asset.[40]

This is the approach we have seen in the EU's MiCA where the property law question, that is, whether Bitcoin is considered a property, is left to each member's national law. MiCA does not specify whether Bitcoin or other stable coins are properties, or what kind of property they are. Similarly, many transnational agencies such as the Financial Action Task Force (FATF) focus on the 'assets' that may be used to launder money, even though they may not be classified as assets under a particular national law. The more specific question of the nature of money is also a contentious issue. What is legal tender is also contested, and how it should be applied to crypto assets has raised policy questions.

Under common law, property law requires several elements, such as control, possession, the capability of being disposed of, and the capability of being against a third party (exclusive use of it). English trust law has been further developed to allow joint and common ownership, with the creation of a separation between legal and beneficial ownership. Tort law has developed the doctrine of the tort of conversion to compensate owners against third parties who have used the property. Trust law

---

[38] Such as a sandbox regime.

[39] HMRC (2023).

[40] Lee (2022b).

also creates tracing rules so that the true owner can recover the property when it is disposed of in a transaction chain. Contract law has been developed to allow parties to negotiate when, under what conditions, and by which methods property can be transferred. Agency law was developed to supplement trust law and allow for the creation of an accountability relationship regarding property.[41] Company law was created to resolve the common property issue, where a legal personality was created to which the property could be transferred and managed. The company holds the property itself, and capital providers or shareholders rely on the decision-making process to administer and influence the disposition of the property. Securities held by shareholders do not have a direct legal relationship with a company's property. In this regard, the securities issued by a company are not, in law, reflective of the property of the company. The depreciation of property value is not directly linked to the value of securities.

In the securities market, holders are not necessarily the ultimate owners of the property; securities can be intangible, and these securities are not necessarily linked to any tangible asset. However, securities can be owned and controlled physically or virtually. Financial market infrastructure providers develop technology to facilitate the transfer of assets among participants by combining property, trust, contract and agency law, along with regulations to achieve functionally intended results.

The amount of property under property law may depend on whether the market has the capability to store, control, possess, and dispose effectively. Data may also be treated as property that can be owned, transferred, held in trust, or pledged. The English Law Commission has thus proposed a third category of property in addition to physical assets, and chooses its actions.[42]

In this regard, whether an NFT is a property depends on (1) the NFT's function, (2) whether the market has the capability to process it and (3) whether there is regulatory support to map out the market infrastructure. An NFT's formulation in property law depends on how it can achieve legal certainty, deliver justice, and create space for innovation.

3.2 *What are the Regulatory Issues?*

Although there are legal concerns about crypto assets, regulations can be implemented to mitigate some of the problems.[43] Defining the legal nature of crypto assets will play a vital part in providing commercial certainty in civil law and societal trust by, for example, punishing bad behaviour, and regulation can complement and supplement the legal rules in civil law. Regulations have been implemented in the areas of taxes, anti-money laundering, consumer and investor protection in financial

---

[41] See Tulip Trading Limited v Wladimir van der Laan and Ors [2023] EWCA Civ 83 https://caselaw.nationalarchives.gov.uk/ewca/civ/2023/83.

[42] Law Commission (2022).

[43] FSB (2022).

services, entity regulation for market integrity, and market stability. These regulations have specific aims and are enforced by designated agencies such as the UK Financial Conduct Authority, the UK Prudential Market Authority,[44] the Inland Revenue and the National Crime Agency. Each agency has its own mandate and regulatory objectives.

A significant development at the EU level as been the introduction of MiCA which provides regulatory frameworks for crypto service providers in financial services. The approach is regulatory even though the legal nature of crypto assets is left to member states. While member states are still developing their national rules on crypto assets, the EU is not being prevented from creating rules to regulate the organisation and conduct of the crypto services provided, on the grounds of market protection. This is an example of how international standards can be set up despite differences in national law. The same transnational approach has also been adopted in areas such as anti-money laundering frameworks, competition laws, and banking regulations. This transnational approach facilitates cross-border activities and addresses the risks of interconnectedness across the market. In an interconnected market, jurisdictional issues determine which law applies, which court or dispute resolution mechanism can hear a case, and which public agencies have oversight and enforcement responsibility. National civil law may play a role here, either as an enabler or an obstacle. In private international law, where a mutual transactional framework does not exist, the jurisdiction issue presents a major legal and regulatory risk.

3.3 *Anti-money Laundering Regime*

At the international level, the FATF has issued several guidelines for national agencies to comply with.[45]These guidelines contain substantial standards for crypto asset service providers (CASPS) in terms of registration, approval, and regulation. Nevertheless, this has been challenging in terms of definitions, methods of regulation, and enforcement. For example, would a natural person dealing with NFTs qualify as a CASP? Should a person or entity dealing with NFTs register with, or be regulated by the authority? How should regulatory agencies enforce rules for registration failures?[46] The legal question regarding the nature of NFTs is crucial here since if financial regulators are to control persons or entities dealing with financial instruments, clarity on whether an NFT amounts to a financial instrument is essential. Although some financial regulators, including those under MiCA, are clear that an

[44] Bank of England (2022) If a blockchain became more critical to the financial system, how should it be governed? https://www.bankofengland.co.uk/bank-overground/2022/if-a-blockchain-became-more-critical-to-the-financial-system-how-should-it-be-governed?sf173934642=1.

[45] FATF Updated Guidance for a Risk-Based Approach to Virtual Assets and Virtual Asset Service Providers (2022); EU's AML Directive (EU) 2018/843 (the Fifth AML Directive).

[46] Money Laundering, Terrorist Financing and Transfer of Funds (Information on the Payer) Regulations 2017 https://www.legislation.gov.uk/uksi/2017/692/contents/made.

NFT is not a financial instrument, fractionalised NFTs may amount to a financial instrument or contract.[47]

However, for the purpose of protecting the market integrity against anti-money laundering, an NFT may come under the regime as recommended by the FATF. FATF's Guidance in October 2021 states that NFTs that are unique and used in practice as collectibles are not virtual assets for the purpose of the FATF Standards. However, jurisdictions should apply FATF Standards on virtual assets to NFTs in cases where they perform the same function as virtual assets and are used for payment (medium of exchange) or investment purposes.[48] Given the rapid development of NFT markets both in their functions and forms, it is important that the FATF as well as other law enforcement agencies should continue monitoring this issue to close legal loopholes.[49] If the NFT in question is not a regulated asset, no disclosure would be required and this can encourage the use of NFTs to launder money for illicit and legal purposes.[50] There is no rule on whether or not financial institutions can purchase NFTs, and NFTs are not considered risky assets in terms of the prudential treatment for financial stability. However, NFT exchanges such as OpenSea are not regulated by the financial authorities and may pose a risk to market integrity. As far as the Travel Rule for anti-money laundering is concerned, it only applies to transactions between exchanges and not within an exchange.[51] However, an exchange may also facilitate cross-border transactions which may not be subject to the internal risk management regime of a particular jurisdiction.[52]

---

[47] CrytpoVantage (2024) What are fractionalised NFTs? https://www.cryptovantage.com/non-fungible-tokens/what-are-fractionalized-nfts/.

[48] FATF Updated Guidance for a Risk-Based Approach to Virtual Assets and Virtual Asset Service Providers (2024). https://www.fatf-gafi.org/content/dam/fatf-gafi/recommendations/2024-Targeted-Update-VA-VASP.pdf.coredownload.inline.pdf.

[49] US Department of Treasury (2022) Study of the Facilitation of Money Laundering and Terror Finance Through the Trade in Works of Art/ https://home.treasury.gov/system/files/136/Treasury_Study_WoA.pdf.

[50] Federal Department of Justice and Police (DFJP) Swizerland (2024) National Risk Assessment (NRA)Risk of money laundering and the financing of terrorism through crypto assets https://www.newsd.admin.ch/newsd/message/attachments/86329.pdf.

[51] FATF (2022) Targeted Update on Implementation of FATF's Standards on VAs and VASPs.

[52] UK Wire Transfer Regulation; Money Laundering, Terrorist Financing and Transfer of Funds (Information on the Payer) Regulations 2017 (MLR 2017); interVASP Messaging Standards http://34.64.107.172/~vasp/wp-content/uploads/2020/05/IVMS101-interVASP-data-model-standard-issue-1-FINAL.pdf.

3.4 Conduct Rules and Prudential Rules

Business conduct and prudential rules are the two major pillars of financial regulatory frameworks. Business conduct rules are aimed at protecting investors and market integrity,[53] whereas prudential rules maintaining financial stability.[54]

Financial institutions must ensure that they have adequate knowledge of the NFT markets –when become regulated markets—to invest in this area and, for example, must be in compliance with the requirements for the senior management, such as the senior managers regime in the UK.[55] If NFTs were to be offered to clients, they would require systems and processes to ensure fair dealing, and if they engage in trading both for their clients and as proprietary traders, they would also need to ensure that the traders comply with the market abuse regime.[56]

For business conduct rules, financial institutions, such as asset management firms,[57] offering NFTs to clients need to ensure that investors are being treated fairly.[58] This means that financial institutions must use reasonable care and skills to investigate and select suitable NFTs and NFT-related products for their clients.[59] They need to ensure that they adhere to the best execution rules[60] and obtain the best price possible for their clients.[61] The fees charged to their clients must be disclosed and prices and research fees shown separately.[62] They must not receive commission from sellers.[63] In addition, they need to ensure the safety of the NFTs when custody services are provided,[64] or to ensure that appropriate custody services are chosen.[65] There is also an obligation to explain to clients the nature of NFTs and their associated risks.[66] In their role as asset managers, they must comply with AML rules, such as the travel rule, and they must ensure that NFTs are not used for illegal and illicit purposes.[67]

---

[53] FCA Conduct Rules https://www.fca.org.uk/firms/senior-managers-and-certification-regime/conduct-rules.

[54] PRA Prudential Regulation https://www.bankofengland.co.uk/prudential-regulation.

[55] HM Treasury (2022).

[56] HM Treasury Consultation paper. P54

[57] HM Treasury Consultation paper. P66.

[58] HM Treasury Consultation paper. P45.

[59] UK Government (2024).

[60] FCA COBS 11.2A Best execution – MiFID provisions.

[61] Best Execution Rules under MiFiDII https://www.esma.europa.eu/sites/default/files/library/2015/11/07_320.pdf.

[62] FCA COBS 12.2 Investment research and non-independent research.

[63] COBS 6.1A Adviser charging and remuneration.

[64] PwC (2021) Crypto-custody https://www.pwc.com/gx/en/financial-services/pdf/pwc-crypto-custody-short-flyer.pdf. Financial Times (2023) SEC pushes for tougher custody rules on assets including crypto https://www.ft.com/content/72a9f784-5144-4ff0-8914-f52620a81a41.

[65] CASS 2.4 Custodian agreement.

[66] CASS 2.4 Custodian agreement.

[67] FATF Targeted Update on Implementation of FATF's Standards on VAs and VASPs (2022).

If NFTs are treated as financial products, then these regulatory frameworks apply. But if they are not, there are two possibilities. Firstly, financial institutions would be less willing to engage in the NFT market because of the high financial, regulatory, and reputational risks. This would lead to traditional financial institutions (TradFi) and centralised financial institutions (CeFi), such as exchanges, broker-dealers, custodians, and payment services, losing opportunities in this space and allowing decentralised finance providers (DeFi)[68] to develop without TradFi and CeFi. And secondly, CeFi might continue to engage in this space without proper accountability because NFTs would be outside the regulatory framework that prohibits financial institutions from dealing in NFTs. Since dealing in NFTs is not included in the institutional accounts and reports, it is likely that regulatory oversight would be substantially reduced.

In such an IT-intensive financial environment, activities can occur virtually, without the limitations of physical borders, and clients are able to purchase NFTs from virtual financial institutions outside the reach of financial regulators. Regulators are then limited to issuing 'warnings' to investors and have no way of ensuring sound development in this internet finance. This has prompted the UK Government to introduce a financial promotions regime for the crypto-assets, if NFTs are to be treated as the qualifying crypto-assets, to protect the consumers.[69]

3.5 Market Integrity

Apart from the anti-money-laundering rule, the NFT market is prone to manipulation.[70] For instance, Yuga[71] is currently facing a class-action lawsuit which alleges it is partnering with celebrities to 'artificially inflate and distort prices' of NFTs.[72] Both issuers and traders may engage in manipulative behaviour using tactics similar to the conventional market manipulation seen in securities markets, such as spreading false information,[73] pump-and-dump,[74] and insider dealing.[75] In addition, there are new

[68] OECD (2022b).

[69] The Financial Promotions Regime.

[70] United States v. Chastain, 22-CR-305 (JMF), (S.D.N.Y. Apr. 18, 2023); Gandal et al. (2018).

[71] Reuters (2023) Yuga Labs' win in Bored Apes NFT counterfeiting case upheld by US appeals courthttps://www.reuters.com/legal/litigation/yuga-labs-win-bored-apes-nft-counterfeiting-case-upheld-by-us-appeals-court-2023-10-31/.

[72] US Department of Justice (2022) Former employee of NFT marketplace charged in first ever digital asset insider trading scheme, https://www.justice.gov/usao-sdny/pr/former-employee-nft-marketplace-charged-first-ever-digital-asset-insider-trading-scheme.

[73] Digital Assets: An expanding arena for insider trading and market manipulation https://www.jdsupra.com/legalnews/digital-assets-an-expanding-arena-for-1287685/.

[74] Digital Assets: An expanding arena for insider trading and market manipulation https://www.jdsupra.com/legalnews/digital-assets-an-expanding-arena-for-1287685/.

[75] United States v. Chastain, 22-CR-305 (JMF), (S.D.N.Y. Apr. 18, 2023).

types of NFT manipulation equivalent to 'mining' on the blockchain.[76] 'Miners' in the cryptocurrency market can exploit a time-lag to conduct front-running activities,[77] and although NFTs differ in their operation from fungible cryptocurrencies such as Bitcoin, when NFTs are traded as a liquid asset, there is a chance that traders may engage in front running. Furthermore, non-conventional traders in the NFT market may use other social media platforms to engage in herding.[78] This may not be easily captured by the existing law, as seen in the GameStop trading saga where social trading by small retail traders created a short-squeeze effect on trade flows, which increased the cost of short sellers.[79] In the swarm trading space of the NFT market,[80] regulating market manipulation through social trading is difficult.

3.6 Investor and Consumer Protection

If NFTs are to be treated as an asset class capable of being promoted to investors and traded in the market,[81] protection of investors and consumers is essential to ensure confidence. Those who issue NFTs must disclose information about them, such as the rights, obligations, and functionalities attached to them. Additional information about a particular type of NFT may also need to be disclosed. If, for example, it is a digital representation of an artwork, the issuer will need to disclose the author, owner, history, and creation of the artwork to the market. And if the NFTs represent a basket of assets, issuers will need to disclose the valuation methods: cost-based, market-to-market, or realised value.[82]

How are NFTs promoted in the blockchain ecosystem? Although certain information about them must be disclosed, the initial token offering (ITO) process should also be made transparent,[83] hence an ITO framework is necessary for an NFT market. Many artwork sales are not subject to regulatory frameworks. As a framework for IPO, the ITO process can help the market grow and develop with enhanced market confidence. Notably, the sale of an artwork is different from the sale of a financial product, and their promotion differs. If an artwork is to be sold and promoted to the clients of a financial institution, such as an asset management company, it will

---

[76] Auer et al. (2022).

[77] Above.

[78] Oh (2023).

[79] Pedersen (2021).

[80] Macey (2021).

[81] UK Treasury Proposed Financial Promotions Regime.

[82] IFRS Holdings of Cryptocurrencies https://www.ifrs.org/content/dam/ifrs/supporting-implementation/agenda-decisions/2019/holdings-of-cryptocurrencies-june-2019.pdf; ICAEW, Digital assets: what are the accounting issues? https://www.icaew.com/insights/viewpoints-on-the-news/2022/aug-2022/digital-assets-what-are-the-accounting-issues.

[83] Lee and Geidel (2021); Deloitte, Corporates using NFTs How NFTs might fit your business and what to watch for https://www2.deloitte.com/content/dam/Deloitte/us/Documents/audit/us-corporates-using-nfts-how-nfts-might-fit-your-business-pov.pdf

need to comply with rules to ensure investor and consumer protection specific to that industry. Regulatory compliance will be a benefit to the digital art industry, but if the industry wants to have access to the capital pool of traditional financial institutions, it will need to be subject to their protective rules.

It may be that the so-called DeFi institutions would like to be beyond TradFi regulation and to offer NFTs to a specific group of people for purposes other than investment. These people—the collectors—may not be classified as investors, consumers or as collaborators in a community who use NFTs to connect with each other, deliver goals, and reinforce commitments. Here, the process of obtaining and transferring an NFT may be different from that in the investment world in which the primary purpose of holding an asset is future returns.

3.7 Prudential Regulation

Prudential regulation deals with the systemic risks that financial institutions may be exposed to.[84] Regulators may use stress testing to gauge risk and impose further rules or regulatory measures such as capital requirements on financial institutions.[85] Crypto assets have also been considered by transnational regulators, such as the Bank for International Settlements (BIS),[86] and rules were drafted to deal with the risks posed by such assets. Crypto assets without stabilisation mechanisms, such as Bitcoin, have been treated as the riskiest assets, and the corresponding measures imposed require any financial institution that holds them to have increased regulatory capital.[87] However, crypto assets that have some stabilisation mechanism, such as stablecoins that are classified along with more stable assets such as USD, do not require the same level of regulatory capital. Hence, regulatory capital can function as a *de facto* ban, containment, and regulation of crypto asset transactions in the market.

---

84 ECB Banking Supervision (2023).

85 Financial Stability Oversight Council (2022).

86 Basel Committee on Banking Supervision (2022).

87 ECB (2023).

4 A Collaborative Regulatory Space—Is DAO a Solution?

4.1 DAO as RegTech

As financial markets become virtualised from assets to interaction, IT infrastructure will play a significant regulatory role.[88] Reporting can be digitised, analytics used for risk management, and digital tools used for sanctions.[89] However, regulators may not have the resources or capacity to ensure market safety.[90] Crypto services providers' operation within the strictures of data protection, cyber security, and human rights laws means that there are limitations on what regulators can do. There should be a collaborative space in which stakeholders have incentives to maintain systems and processes for the benefit of the community.[91] For instance, in the Ethereum space 'proof-of-work' operates as a consensus regulatory system.[92] Even though 'proof-of-stake' has been suggested as the next step,[93] 'proof-of-work' system remains an essential regulatory system in the Ethereum space, that ensures the authenticity of transactions. Some of these regulatory functions are performed by a more centralised system in the TradFi space to ensure safe and smooth transactions.

Platforms, smart contracts, analytics, automation tools, and artificial intelligence are used in DAOs where stakeholders contribute to the 'common good' of the platform.[94] In a DAO community, the NFTs created are certified, and transactions validated by a mutually agreed mechanism. Virtual firms may act as both 'regulators' and 'participants'. Breaches invite sanctions based on agreements. Using a DAO has the potential to enable a regulatory framework from the process of making rules to manage risk, execute sanctions, and offer restitution. This procedure is not new as the methods are already being used in the financial regulation through so-called meta-regulation[95] whereby regulatory functions are devolved to increase effectiveness. Despite this, there are shortcomings, such as regulatory capture, regulatory abuse of majority powers, and neglect of minority interests.[96]

Some NFTs have been sold to and managed by DAOs, in which stakeholders or token holders share the risks and benefits derived from the DAOs. The fundamental

---

88 FCA & Bank of England (2023).

89 See FCA (2024).

90 Baldwin et al. (2011).

91 Jędrzejczyk and Marzantowicz (2019); The Digital Regulation Cooperation Forum, https://www.gov.uk/government/collections/the-digital-regulation-cooperation-forum.

92 Introduction to Ethereum governance https://ethereum.org/en/governance/.

93 Proof-of-stake (POS) https://ethereum.org/en/developers/docs/consensus-mechanisms/pos/.

94 Law Commission (2023) 'Decentralised autonomous organisations (DAOs) Call for evidence' https://www.lawcom.gov.uk/project/decentralised-autonomous-organisations-daos/; World Economic Forum (2022) Who will govern the metaverse? https://www.weforum.org/agenda/2022/05/metaverse-governance/.

95 Baldwin above; Rouknyn (2022).

96 Chap. 11, J Lee Crypto-Finance.

idea of a DAO is 'sharing' through DAO tokens which can be used for decision-making and profit allocation. In DAOs, smart contracts with predetermined rules play an important governance role, like contracts in a partnership, deeds in a trust, or the constitution and shareholder agreements of a company. In a regulated industry such as the financial services market, regulation plays a far greater role than it does in private contracts or in collective constitutions. Embedding regulations in a DAO through smart contracts is a novel aspect of technology and law.[97]

4.2 Technology

In technology, unlike in a private contract or a collective constitution, the purpose of regulation is often multifaceted; the nature of the regulation is beyond private sphere, and has multiple modes.[98] The technology must reflect and implement these regulatory features. If it does not, a new regulatory ethos may enter the DAO space, making the regulation of a private contract similar to that of a collective constitution. While regulation dynamically aligns purpose and risks, constant updates are required. Three types of regulation can operate in a DAO consent model. First, token holders who can decide on the governance of the DAO can elect a person, committee, or entity to conduct the regulatory function. Second, regulators can join the DAOs in order to perform their regulatory functions. Third, token holders can make decisions on an *ad hoc* basis, which involves more frequent updates of the DAO's protocols. Regardless of the mode chosen, the technology used must reflect the aims of the regulation and ensure the enforcement with the intended consequences, such as sanctions.

The most common technological difficulty is the presence of bugs in software protocols which can be exploited by malicious hackers.[99] It may be difficult to instantaneously detect defective regulations and enforcement. There can be a mismatch between the intended regulation (real regulation) and the actual regulation (defective regulation). Malicious hackers can explore such vulnerabilities, so the software must be thoroughly checked by legal and regulatory experts and technologists to ensure that whatever regulation is implemented achieves the intended effects. Auditing the software will need to ensure that the algorithms developed,[100] the data used for developing algorithms, and the oracle services used are accurate and reliable.

---

[97] BIS Innovation Hub work on suptech and regtech https://www.bis.org/about/bisih/topics/suptech_regtech.htm; Brownsword (2022).

[98] Chap. 11, J LEE.

[99] Cryptopedia What Was The DAO? https://www.gemini.com/cryptopedia/the-dao-hack-makerdao.

[100] Hedera What Is a Smart Contract Audit? https://hedera.com/learning/smart-contracts/smart-contract-audit.

4.3 Law

As mentioned previously, private law is required to provide legal certainty, regulations to mitigate risks, and other public laws to address external issues. Even though software may encode private rules in transactions, such as the use of smart contracts, there are gaps (as there are in normal contracts) which may need mechanisms such as courts or other dispute resolutions to reduce disparity. This may mean that the laws for DAOs must be more certain to avoid the need to resort to other dispute resolution mechanisms, and this demands flexibility in innovation. Courts and other dispute resolution mechanisms have played an important role in providing both legal certainty and flexibility to accommodate innovation. If laws are written into a code that have the effect of depriving a trusted third party such as the courts, from legal and real opportunities to develop the law, innovation may be negatively impacted.[101] Optimising this balance is a challenging task: on the one hand, the legal framework must be certain and attractive for users in order to reduce transaction costs, but at the same time it should be able to drive innovation, and this may involve removing barriers or elements that can increase transaction costs. In addition, the law needs to be sufficiently capable of innovation to capture reality and be future-proof.

Regulators also need to review the frameworks of rule-making (state or self-regulation), the mode of regulation (soft law or hard law), the principles- or rules-based regulation, enforcement tools (public censure, fines, or imprisonment), and the regulatory policies that determine how rules may be suspended or whether enforcement should be implemented. For example, how can a no-action letter be implemented?[102] When enforcement actions need to be coordinated with other similar agencies, they may need to be realised in the new DAO space. For instance, the tax authorities, the law enforcement agencies, the financial regulators and the courts may need to adjudicate disputes. There may be regulatory equivalents that use this technology. Regulatory agencies must identify risks and use optional means to address them in the light of the regulatory objectives, and suitable powers conferred. In a collaborative DAO space, regulators must be confident that the technology is appropriate to the context in which the DAO operates. Regulators' attention should focus on several points. First, whether the underlying asset invokes their regulatory power. Second, whether individuals, entities, or protocols fall within their regulatory scope. Third, whether the interactions of these individuals, entities, or protocols are subject to regulatory oversight. Finally, whether certain elements call for regulatory intervention in a specific form or market space.

---

[101] Law Commission (2021) Smart Legal Contracts: Advice to Government https://s3-eu-west-2.amazonaws.com/lawcom-prod-storage-11jsxou24uy7q/uploads/2021/11/Smart-legal-contracts-accessible.pdf; Sako and Parnham (2021).

[102] ESMA issues No Action Letter on the new ESG disclosure requirements under the Benchmarks Regulation https://www.esma.europa.eu/press-news/esma-news/esma-issues-no-action-letter-new-esg-disclosure-requirements-under-benchmarks.

In DAOs, certain elements are automated through non-human activity.[103] Traditional methods of asserting personal jurisdiction must be revised and subject matter jurisdiction needs to be revisited.[104] Furthermore, regulatory capabilities will need to be reassessed, in the light of the resources available, the technological knowledge, the internal risks and liabilities, and the agenda of the regulation agencies. It is possible that regulators will be part of the DAO space and thus themselves become stakeholders which may compromise their independence and integrity. Moreover, a lack of regulatory resources and technological knowledge may expose regulators to reputational damage and liability. The relationship between regulatory agencies and those regulated needs to be redefined.[105] A new digital jurisprudence that helps pave the way for law, regulation, and code as law, with the resulting new institutions, such as a digital notary, digital reporting, and a digital court, is needed.[106]

5 Conclusion

The Metaverse is an important space for creativity and collaboration in which NFTs can act to link participants. There are different types of NFTs, and their functionalities are important in determining their success. The private sector will continue to be an important intermediary tool for parties to determine their relationships and ensure the smooth operation of transactions and certainty of the consequences. Property law is important for defining what NFTs are according to their functions and the legal objectives of certainty, justice, and innovation. Regulation will play a role in mitigating risk, proactively managing imaged risks or retroactively managing any risks that private law has not been able to address. In financial law, regulations must play an active role in ensuring financial stability, investor protection, market integrity, competition, and innovation. Technology such as 'code as law' will now play an even more pivotal role in the governance framework. In short, the financial law on NFTs in the Metaverse is shaped by private law, regulation, and technology. Policy is determined by the development of the underlying technology, the players in the Metaverse, and by regulatory competition.

References

Baldwin R, Martin C, Lodge M (2011) Self-regulation, meta-regulation, and regulatory networks understanding regulation: theory, strategy, and practice, 2nd edn. Oxford Academic, Oxford. https://doi.org/10.1093/acprof:osobl/9780199576081.003.0008

---

[103] Ethereum 'Decentralized autonomous organizations (DAOs)' https://ethereum.org/en/dao/.

[104] Schillig (2022).

[105] Regulatory effectiveness in the era of digitisation https://www.oecd.org/gov/regulatory-policy/Regulatory-effectiveness-in-the-era-of-digitalisation.pdf; Eggers et al. (2018).

[106] Johnstone (2022).

Ball M (2022) The metaverse : and how it will revolutionize everything, 1st edn. Liveright Publishing Corporation, New York
Basel Committee on Banking Supervision (2022) Prudential treatment of cryptoasset exposures. https://www.bis.org/bcbs/publ/d545.pdf. Last accessed May 29, 2025.
Belk R et al (2022) Money, possessions, and ownership in the metaverse: NFTs, cryptocurrencies, Web3 and wild markets. J Bus Res 153:198–205. https://doi.org/10.1016/j.jbusres.2022.08.031
Biris C, Gruian DT (2022) How metaverse will influence industrial innovation. Int J Adv Stat IT&C Econ Life Sci 12(2):53–56
Brownsword R (2022) Technology, governance and respect for the law: pictures at an exhibition. Routledge, Abington, p 210
Cao L (2022) Decentralized AI: edge intelligence and smart blockchain, metaverse, Web3, and DeSci. IEEE Intell Syst 37(3):6–19. https://doi.org/10.1109/MIS.2022.3181504
Caswell J, Furtado L (2021) What Is an NFT? Probate Prop 35(2):10–15
Chan B, Mok S (2022) In the news: NFTs deemed property. China Law & Practice
Criddle C, Gabert-Doyon J (2022) NFT creators diversify into real-world assets to generate new revenues. Financial Times. https://www.ft.com/content/69da37d1-11de-430f-8a86-ea51bd2ae82b. Last accessed May 29, 2025.
Curtis C, Brolan C (2023) Health care in the metaverse. Med J Aust 218(1):46–46. https://doi.org/10.5694/mja2.51793
Doaa A, Fatma E (2021) Prospects of investment in digital art: case of Ethereum and non-fungible token (NFT). Econ Law 3(2):20–30. https://doi.org/10.37708/el.swu.v3i2.3
ECB (2023) Crypto-assets: a new standard for banks. https://www.bankingsupervision.europa.eu/press/publications/newsletter/2023/html/ssm.nl230215_1.en.html. Last accessed May 29, 2025.
ECB Banking Supervision (2023) Crypto-assets: a new standard for banks. https://www.bankingsupervision.europa.eu/press/publications/newsletter/2023/html/ssm.nl230215_1.en.html. Last accessed May 29, 2025.
Eggers W, Turkely M, Pankaj K (2018) The future of regulation: principles for regulating emerging technologies. https://www2.deloitte.com/content/dam/insights/us/articles/4538_Future-of-regulation/DI_Future-of-regulation.pdf. Last accessed May 29, 2025.
ESMA (2022) Report on DLT pilot regime. https://www.esma.europa.eu/press-news/esma-news/esma-publishes-report-dlt-pilot-regime. Last accessed May 29, 2025.
Far S et al (2022) A review of non-fungible tokens applications in the real-world and Metaverse. Procedia Comput Sci 214:755–762. https://doi.org/10.1016/j.procs.2022.11.238
FATF (2022) Updated guidance for a risk-based approach to virtual assets and virtual asset service providers; EU's AML Directive (EU) 2018/843 (the Fifth AML Directive)
FCA (2024) Digital regulation cooperation forum. https://www.fca.org.uk/about/how-we-operate/who-work-with/drcf. Last accessed May 29, 2025.
FCA & Bank of England (2023) Digital regulatory reporting. https://www.fca.org.uk/innovation/regtech/digital-regulatory-reporting. Last accessed May 29, 2025.
Financial Express (2023) Cryptocurrency firms struggle to find banking partners after US bank collapses- where to next? Singapore? Switzerland? Hong Kong? https://www-financialexpress-com.cdn.ampproject.org/c/s/www.financialexpress.com/business/blockchain/cryptocurrency-firms-struggle-to-find-banking-partners-after-us-bank-collapses-where-to-next-singapore-switzerland-hong-kong/3028866/lite/. Last accessed May 29, 2025.
Financial Stability Oversight Council (2022) Report on digital asset financial stability risks and regulation https://home.treasury.gov/system/files/261/FSOC-Digital-Assets-Report-2022.pdf
FSB (2022) Regulation, supervision and oversight of crypto-asset activities and markets: consultative report. https://www.fsb.org/2022/10/regulation-supervision-and-oversight-of-crypto-asset-activities-and-markets-consultative-report/. Last accessed May 29, 2025.
Gandal N, Hamrick J, Moore T, Oberman T (2018) Price manipulation in the bitcoin ecosystem. J Monet Econ 95:86–96
Girasa R (2023) Regulation of cryptocurrencies and blockchain technologies: national and international perspectives, 2nd edn. Palgrave Macmillan, Cham

HM Treasury (2022) Future financial services regulatory regime for cryptoassets consultation and call for evidence. https://assets.publishing.service.gov.uk/government/uploads/system/uploads/attachment_data/file/1133404/TR_Privacy_edits_Future_financial_services_regulatory_regime_for_cryptoassets_vP.pdf. Last accessed May 29, 2025.
HMRC (2023) Consultation paper 'future financial services regulatory regime for cryptoassets'. https://www.gov.uk/government/consultations/future-financial-services-regulatory-regime-for-cryptoassets. Last accessed May 29, 2025.
Jędrzejczyk M, Marzantowicz K (2019) Blockchain, smart contracts and DAO'. https://www.wyoleg.gov/InterimCommittee/2019/S3-20190506DAOLegalPerspectives.pdf. Last accessed May 29, 2025.
Johnstone S (2022) Regulating for blockchain ecosystem development means getting past the stumbling block of regulatory incrementalism. Stanford Journal of Blockchain Law & Policy. https://stanford-jblp.pubpub.org/pub/regulating-for-blockchain-ecosystem-development (https://stanford-jblp.pubpub.org/pub/regulating-for-blockchain-ecosystem-development/release/2). Last accessed May 29, 2025.
Julius Bär (2022) Security for digital assets. https://www.juliusbaer.com/en/business-navigator/security-for-digital-assets/. Last accessed May 29, 2025.
Jung T, Dieck M, Loureiro S (2023) Extended reality and metaverse: immersive technology in times of crisis. Springer, Cham
Law Commission (2022) Digital assets: consultation paper. Law com no 256. https://s3-eu-west-2.amazonaws.com/lawcom-prod-storage-11jsxou24uy7q/uploads/2022/07/Digital-Assets-Consultation-Paper-Law-Commission-1.pdf. Last accessed May 29, 2025.
Lee J (2021) Cryptoassets, developments and the regulatory Perimeter. In: Chiu I, Deipenbrock G (eds) Routledge handbook on fintech and law—regulatory, supervisory, policy and other legal challenges. Routledge, Abingdon
Lee J (2022a) Crypto finance, law and regulation: governing an emerging ecosystem. Routledge, Abingdon
Lee J (2022b) Chapter 3, crypto finance, law and regulation: governing an emerging ecosystem. Routledge, Abingdon
Lee J, Darbellay A (eds) (2022) Data governance in AI, FinTech and RegTech: law and regulation in the financial sector. Edward Elgar, Cheltenham
Lee J, Geidel D (2021) Mapping an investor protection framework for the security token offering market: a comparative analysis of UK and German law. Taiwan Law Rev 316:73–105
Lee J, Van de Looverbosch M (2022) Property and data: a confused relationship. In: Lee J, Dabellay A (eds) Data governance in AI, FinTech and RegTech: law and regulation in the financial sector. Edward Elgar, Cheltenham
Macey J (2021) Securities regulation as class warfare. Columbia Bus Law Rev. https://doi.org/10.2139/ssrn.3789706
Michels J, Millard C (2022) The new things: property rights in digital files. Camb Law J 81(2):323–355
OECD (2022a) Crypto-asset reporting framework and amendments to the common reporting standard. https://www.oecd.org/tax/exchange-of-tax-information/crypto-asset-reporting-framework-and-amendments-to-the-common-reporting-standard.htm. Last accessed May 29, 2025.
OECD (2022b) Why decentralised finance (DeFi) matters and the policy Implications. https://www.oecd.org/daf/fin/financial-markets/Why-Decentralised-Finance-DeFi-Matters-and-the-Policy-Implications.pdf. Last accessed May 29, 2025.
Oh S (2023) Market manipulation in NFT markets. Munich personal RePEc archive. https://mpra.ub.uni-muenchen.de/116704/1/MPRA_paper_116704.pdf. Last accessed May 29, 2025.
Oleksy T et al (2023) Migration to the metaverse and its predictors: attachment to virtual places and metaverse-related threat. Comput Hum Behav 141:107642. https://doi.org/10.1016/j.chb.2022.107642

Pedersen L (2021) Game On: Social networks and markets. NYU Stern Sch Bus. https://doi.org/10.2139/ssrn.3794616. Last accessed May 29, 2025.
Rouknyn T (2022) Decentralized finance: information frictions and public policies approaching the regulation and supervision of decentralized finance. https://finance.ec.europa.eu/system/files/2022-10/finance-events-221021-report_en.pdf. Last accessed May 29, 2025.
Sako M & Parnham R (2021) Technology and innovation in legal services: final report for the solicitors regulation authority. https://www.sra.org.uk/globalassets/documents/sra/research/full-report-technology-and-innovation-in-legal-services.pdf?version=4a1bfe. Last accessed May 29, 2025.
Sandrone S (2022) Medical education in the metaverse. Nat Med 28(12):2456–2457
Schillig M (2022) Decentralized autonomous organizations (DAOs) under English law. King's Coll Lond Law Sch Res Pap. https://doi.org/10.2139/ssrn.4221221
Stackpole T (2022) What is Web3. Harvard business review https://hbr.org/2022/05/what-is-web3. Last accessed May 29, 2025.
Stevens R (2023) Crypto is not property. Law Q Rev 139(4):615–628
Thien HT et al (2023a) Artificial intelligence for the metaverse: a survey. Eng Appl Artif Intell 117:105581. https://doi.org/10.1016/j.engappai.2022.105581
Thien HT et al (2023b) Blockchain for the metaverse: a review. Futur Gener Comput Syst 143:401–419. https://doi.org/10.1016/j.future.2023.02.008
Turchet L (2023) Musical metaverse: vision, opportunities, and challenges. Pers Ubiquit Comput 27:1811–1827. https://doi.org/10.1007/s00779-023-01708-1
UK Government (2024) Policy paper Factsheet: cryptoassets technical. https://www.gov.uk/government/publications/economic-crime-and-corporate-transparency-bill-2022-factsheets/fact-sheet-cryptoassets-technical. Last accessed May 29, 2025.
Vidal-Tomás D (2023) The Illusion of the metaverse and meta-economy. Int Rev Financ Anal 86:102560. https://doi.org/10.1016/j.irfa.2023.102560
Wang M, Lau N (2023) NFT digital twins: a digitalization strategy to preserve and sustain miao silver craftsmanship in the Metaverse era. Heritage 6(103):1921–1941. https://doi.org/10.3390/heritage6020103
Windsor K (2022) When is a collectible not a 'collectible'? NFTs and internal revenue code section 408(m)(2). Pract Tax Lawyer 36(3):17–21
Zuboff S, Schwandt K (2019) The age of surveillance capitalism: the fight for a human future at the new frontier of power. Profile Books, London
Zyda M (2022) Building a human-intelligent metaverse. Computer 55(9):120–128. https://doi.org/10.1109/MC.2022.3182035

The New EU Framework for Crypto-Assets: Recent Developments and Main Challenges Ahead

Paolo Ciocca and Irene Tagliamonte

Abstract This paper analyses the Markets in Crypto-Assets Regulation (MiCAR) as the EU's pioneering framework for the crypto-asset market. It examines the challenges of classifying emerging assets such as NFTs and distinguishing them from traditional financial instruments, stressing the tension between economic substance and legal form. The analysis explores MiCAR's approach to accountability in disintermediated ecosystems, with a focus on the allocation of responsibility to identifiable actors. It also reviews the provisions on market integrity, drawing parallels with the Market Abuse Regulation (MAR), and highlights the importance of technological capacity and international coordination for effective supervision. The paper concludes that MiCAR is a crucial, albeit still improvable, step toward safer digital finance, but global convergence remains highly desirable for the evolution of Web3 and the metaverse.

1 Introduction

The global capitalization of crypto-asset markets, after peaking at over €2.7 trillion in 2024, experienced a correction in early 2025, dropping to around USD 2.8 trillion by March, before rebounding to approximately USD 3.4 trillion (€3.1 trillion) by late June 2025.[1] Bitcoin continues to lead, representing roughly 61%–64% of total market cap. Additionally, ESMA's analysis stresses persistent market concentration: as of end-2023, the top ten exchanges processed around 90% of trading volume.[2] Moreover, crypto-asset volatility is a growing risk driver in EU financial

[1] ECB (2025).
[2] ESMA (2024).

P. Ciocca · I. Tagliamonte (✉)
CONSOB, Rome, Italy
e-mail: i.tagliamonte@consob.it

P. Ciocca
e-mail: cioccap@gmail.com

F. Di Porto and O. Pollicino (eds.), *Law and Politics of Virtual Worlds*, Law, Governance and Technology Series 79, https://doi.org/10.1007/978-3-032-08541-2_7

markets, given their speculative nature and co-movement with equities.[3] Although the market remains smaller than equity and bond markets globally, its rapid growth, concentration and sustained volatility underscore the importance of robust regulatory frameworks and international coordination.[4]

The process of asset tokenization on decentralized blockchain platform led to a substantive increase in the number and type of crypto assets, e.g. cryptocurrencies, stablecoins, and other fungible and non-fungible tokens (NFTs).

Decentralized finance (DeFi) has developed far beyond the digital payments sector and now covers a variety of asset classes which serve different purposes. DeFi activities mirror those of conventional capital markets from an economic standpoint. Financial services may be provided using smart contracts, and technical protocols perform several tasks previously handled by traditional intermediaries.[5] As highlighted by the International Organization of Securities Commissions (IOSCO), in 2021–2022 various products and services were launched, encouraging new institutional investors to approach DeFi. Retail participation in DeFi is also increasing due to the development of intuitive interfaces and aggressive marketing campaigns through social media, sponsorship, and celebrity endorsements.[6]

The boom of NFTs has opened new developments: NFTs may allow building bridges between the on-chain and the off-chain, potentially integrating finance with the metaverse. However, notwithstanding the transformative nature of NFTs (and crypto-assets in general), the crypto-market has been exploited mainly for speculative purposes around highly volatile tokens, often tradable on centralized crypto-asset trading platforms.

Markets in crypto assets continued to display significant volatility. Following the collapse of TerraUSD (UST) – an algorithmic stablecoin - in May 2022, key protocols such as Bitcoin and Ethereum lost roughly half their value since November 2021. The bankruptcy of FTX and other centralized crypto trading platforms with a highly complex and opaque business model demonstrated contagion risks due to vulnerabilities and confidence effects.[7] This episode was followed by stress at crypto banks like Silvergate and Signature, highlighting transmission channels to traditional finance. Since then, crypto has experienced renewed interlinkages with traditional markets.[8] In April 2025, ESMA warned that even though crypto remains relatively

---

[3] ESMA TRV (2025).

[4] Crypto-asset prices boomed following the US election, with the new administration's pro-crypto stance fuelling optimism in the market. These developments prompted ESMA to renew its warning to investors on the highly speculative nature of many crypto-assets, see ESMA TRV (2025).

[5] Auer et al. (2023).

[6] IOSCO (2022), p. 27.

[7] See the Opening Statement of Steffen Kern, Head of Risk Analysis and Chief Economist, European Securities and Markets Authority (ESMA) at the Economic and Monetary Affairs Committee European Parliament made on 30 November 2022, available at: https://www.esma.europa.eu/sites/default/files/library/public_statement_to_econ_sk.pdf.

[8] ESMA (2024, 2025).

small in terms of direct exposure, "*turmoil even in small markets can originate or catalyse broader stability issues*" in the EU financial system.[9]

The Financial Stability Board (FSB) has also acknowledged these risks. Its public consultation and subsequent final report report highlights the urgent need for an effective and comprehensive regulatory framework for crypto-assets activities, promoting international consistency and responsible innovation.[10]

Still, there is a long way to go before global policy coordination in the crypto sphere is achieved. International efforts are ongoing, and policy recommendations from securities authorities were issued at the end of 2023.[11] However, the current fragmented approach to crypto regulation creates risks and undermines a global level playing field.[12]

2 Crypto-Market Agency Costs: The EU Regulatory Response

At the regional level, the European Union appears to be a front-runner in the current blockchain regulatory race, as it comes from the recent establishment of new frameworks for the DLT-based markets. The legislative process on the Markets in Crypto-Assets Regulation (MiCAR) has been recently finalized and Regulation (EU) 2023/1114 of the European Parliament and of the Council of 31 May 2023 on markets in crypto-assets is now in force.[13] The initiative is part of the European Commission *Digital Finance Package,*[14] designed to "*support innovation and fair competition, while ensuring a high level of protection of retail holders and market integrity in*

---

[9] https://www.esma.europa.eu/sites/default/files/2025-04/ESMA50-43599798-27866_Natasha_Cazenave_s_opening_statement_at_ECON_hearing_on_cryptoassets_and_financial_stability__8_April_2025.pdf. Accessed on 18 February 2026.

[10] FSB (2022, 2023).

[11] On 7 July, 2022 securities regulators within IOSCO published their Crypto-Asset Roadmap for 2022–2023 that sets out the regulatory policy agenda and work program for the sector, https://www.iosco.org/news/pdf/IOSCONEWS649.pdf. A final Report containing policy recommendations on crypto was issued in November 2023./

[12] See FSB Chart at: https://www.fsb.org/2024/10/g20-crypto-asset-policy-implementation-roadmap-status-report/. Accessed on 18 February 2026.

[13] MiCAR is applicable as of 30 December 2024, except for Title III and Title IV relating to stablecoin issuers (ARTs and EMTs) which are applicable as of 30 June 2024. MiCAR also provides for a subsequent (maximum) 18-month transitional period for crypto asset service providers that ends in July 2026. By this time, all entities providing crypto asset services must be wholly compliant with the EU regulations. Member States may decide not to apply the transitional regime or reduce its duration. MiCAR 1 text is available at https://eur-lex.europa.eu/legal-content/EN/TXT/?uri=CELEX:32023R1114.

[14] MiCAR goes hand in hand with the EU Regulation (EU) 2022/2554 of the European Parliament and of the Council of 14 December 2022 on digital operational resilience for the financial sector (DORA) and the EU DLT Pilot Regime, i.e.: Regulation (EU) 2022/858 of 30 May 2022, entered in force in December 2021 and applicable as of 23 March, 2023 to DLT trading and settlement systems for bonds, shares, and units of investment funds. The DLT pilot regime introduces a regulatory

crypto-asset markets"[15] and support Europe's global leadership in digital finance. According to the EC Blockchain Strategy, DLT and crypto markets are an opportunity to accelerate financial inclusion, competition, and growth. The common rules will be directly applicable to the whole region (full harmonization), and market participants will be granted passporting rights to scale up activities across the Member States.

The measures are grounded on the principles of "*same activity, same risk, same regulation*", "*proportionality*" and "*technological neutrality*". The aim is to build a sound "*ever-green*" framework to regulate new ways of performing financial activities in digitally distributed ecosystems without imposing the use of a particular type of DLT.

The ultimate purpose is to foster the growth of a healthy and robust EU blockchain ecosystem. A well-functioning DLT may reduce certain capital markets' coordination, monitoring and agency costs through consensus protocols, smart contracts, and transparency Transactions and on-chain processes may be carried out automatically without interference (e.g., conflicts of interest, opportunistic conduct) and are verifiable on a decentralized basis in unprecedented ways. With *permissionless blockchain* checks can be carried out by the public (the "crowd") so that the role (and costs) of "gatekeepers" may even become redundant. Additionally, DLT has the potential to simplify processes, disintermediating and automating exchanges, reducing counterparty risks and facilitating asset servicing.[16] There are also benefits arising from modularity and programmability that allow for advanced planning and control of the lifecycle of an on-chain product or service and enable new open finance models and integration with AI and IoT. Blockchain may allow for the adoption of more efficient processes for compliance through on-chain mechanisms.[17]

On the other hand, the redundancy of distributed ecosystems and the multitude of actors operating in anonymity may increase information asymmetry and create centers of hidden power.[18] The high number of participants in the ecosystem, often performing different roles simultaneously, increases coordination costs, inducing free riding, rational apathy and control concentration. This latter phenomenon is not immediately perceptible to all users.[19] The transparency of protocols and smart contracts, which theoretically should prevent most frauds and attacks, may have no substantive effect since end users typically lack the expertise and time to check. The

---

sandbox to adapt existing rules on securities market infrastructures to the new digital environment. It applies only to the aforementioned *security* tokens, not to native cryptocurrencies of a *blockchain,* nor to the generality of other crypto-assets. In a nutshell, it will open up to the possibility of: (i) granting natural persons access to market infrastructures, in compliance with certain minimum requirements, (ii) giving competent authorities direct and real-time access to transaction data; (iii) combining *trading* and *post-trading* on the same platform, or in any case implementing mechanisms for the efficiency of securities settlement, (iii) store security tokens or the means of access to them at the market itself.

[15] See MiCAR recital no. 6.

[16] ECB (2021).

[17] Auer (2019).

[18] Aramonte et al. (2021).

[19] FSB (2022), OECD (2022).

danger is that "less sophisticated" participants (i.e., those for whom monitoring cost is too high) will pay the price, while trust moves from humans to machines.[20]

Crypto-assets are vulnerable to conventional scams, frauds, and manipulative practices (e.g., whitewashing, rug pulls, pump and dump, etc.). Additionally, new forms of crypto-market abuses may arise from the different roles that blockchain participants simultaneously play (e.g., new forms of conflict of interest) and/or from the multiple services offered by providers (e.g., wallet provider, trading platform, issuer, and exchange).[21] The risk of information-based market abuse is exacerbated by gamification,[22] bots and social media, including fin-influencers, alongside a general lack of technical expertise by the majority of investors.[23] Challenges are similar to those of the traditional financial sector but deepened by the absence of clear accountability rules coupled with pseudonymity, which makes it difficult to trace wallets to owners.

Overall, blockchain and DeFi do not eliminate the asymmetries that traditionally characterize capital markets, such as the ability to evaluate projects seeking financial resources from the public. A thorough and dynamic assessment requires access to reliable information. Here, access to past trade records held in a distributed ledger is insufficient to address information asymmetry, correctly set prices or eliminate counterparty risks linked to a "promise" of future (market) returns.

From a systemic point of view, contagion and risks may arise from the widespread use of leverage (with ensuing pro-cyclical effects), fragile stablecoins used for on-chain payments, interconnectedness arising from the DLT modular architecture, smart contract composibility,[24] and increasing crypto market links with traditional finance and the real economy.[25]

Finally, open source, verifiable and decentralized blockchain or DeFi protocols are often employed just as settlement layers, while centralized crypto service providers typically act as agents maintaining custody of user assets, matching buy and sell orders, and maintaining the order and trading books on their platforms via internal records (maintained off-chain). Crypto service providers and new forms of intermediation may well act in the ecosystem, implying the same principal-agent problems and need for human trust present in traditional markets.[26]

---

[20] Deutsche Bundesbank (2021).

[21] Examples in this respect are manipulations based on flask loans, oracle manipulations, or the exploitation of inside information by validators in so-called sandwich trading, with mining pools extracting value at the detriment of everyday blockchain users, see Auer et al. (2022).

[22] A multitude of Defi gaming or gambling protocols rely on financial building blocks, and many core Defi financial services and related DApps incorporate gamification elements to increase user adoption.

[23] Chainalysis (2022).

[24] Smart contracts typically are designed to be composable, i.e., they may interact and be used in combination with other smart contracts, see *ex multis* IOSCO (2023), pp. 39–40.

[25] See *ex multis*, FSB (2022); Aramonte et al. (2021).

[26] OECD, *Institutionalisation* (2022), underlying that currently observed Defi protocols usually have centralized characteristics (see specifically p. 10).

Against this background, MiCAR introduces an all-encompassing bespoke regime for primary and secondary crypto markets to address new risks stemming from the decentralized nature of DLT systems, along with the typical types of financial risks.

The new regime provides a white paper compulsory disclosure for comprehensive and precise information on the fundraising campaign. Service providers are subject to mandatory authorization and application of prudential, governance, and conduct rules. MiCAR captures actors and activities currently outside the perimeter of capital markets regulation. It does so in a fashion heavily inspired by the traditional financial sector, employing the prospectus and MiFID regimes as models. Rules on market integrity relating to insider trading and market manipulation are also established along the Market Abuse Regulation.

3 What to Regulate: The Definition of Crypto-Assets

Achieving a satisfactory level of convergence on classification issues around the MiCAR scope of application will be a significant challenge across the Union.

In principle, MiCAR applies to products and activities displaying financial risks and market failures. Nevertheless, the blurring boundaries between finance and technology in the crypto sector and the multiple concurrent functions that crypto-assets and crypto-actors usually play make it very difficult to draw a clear line between what should be in and what should be out of regulation. Furthermore, different legal qualifications triggering the application of different sets of rules on crypto assets could encourage circumvention and escape from more rigorous and expensive sector-specific legislation.

MiCAR addresses this challenge by providing a broad and all-encompassing notion of crypto-assets[27] and a list of crypto-services, coupled with a few exclusions and exemptions.[28] Defining these exclusions and exemptions was one of the main battlegrounds during the political negotiation.

[27] "Crypto-asset" means a digital representation of a value or a right that may be transferred and stored electronically using distributed ledger technology or similar technology. MiCAR identifies three categories of crypto-assets, e-money-token, asset-referenced tokens, and other crypto-assets, including utility tokens. This paper focuses only on the latter without expanding on stablecoins, capital requirements, banking and payment systems, and anti-money laundering.

[28] Expressly, a series of crypto assets are excluded from the scope of MiCAR public offering rules (Title II) as they serve non-financial purposes. The exclusion applies to digital assets that cannot be transferred to other holders, like loyalty schemes, and to crypto-assets offered for free or automatically created as a reward in the context of a consensus mechanism or when a utility token represents the purchase of an existing good or service within a limited network of merchants. Such exceptions do not include crypto-assets representing stored goods that are not meant to be collected by the purchaser following the purchase. The limited network exemption does not apply to crypto-assets typically designed for a network of service providers continuously growing. When the offer or offers exceed a certain threshold, the competent authority evaluates the limited network exemption each time an offer is made (offers made after an offer that benefited from an exemption do not automatically benefit from such exemption). These exemptions cease to apply when the offeror or another person on his behalf communicates its intention of seeking admission to trading

The outcome has been that MiCAR does not apply to crypto-assets that are unique and not fungible with other crypto-assets (i.e. NFTs).[29] The rationale is expressed in MiCAR recitals. While NFTs may be traded in marketplaces, accumulated speculatively, and sometimes also used as means of exchange, they are still not readily interchangeable: the value of one crypto-asset relative to another, each being unique, cannot be ascertained using comparison to an existing market or equivalent asset. Such features limit the extent to which these crypto-assets can have a financial use and increase the risks to users and the system. Consistently, MiCAR recitals explain that the fractional parts of a unique and non-fungible crypto-asset should not be considered unique and not fungible and the sole attribution of a unique identifier to a crypto-asset is not sufficient to classify it as a unique or not fungible: the assets or rights represented should also be unique and not fungible.[30]

Still, MiCAR lacks a clear-cut legal definition of NFTs, despite the significant role that NFTs may play, for example, should the metaverse become a successful experiment, and their current primarily speculative nature. Leaving the definition of such a legal boundary to a recital is undoubtedly not ideal. MiCAR's application to such tokens will depend on their case-by-case qualification by market participants and competent national authorities. This could give rise to uncertainties, regulatory loopholes, and market fragmentation to the detriment of adequate financial supervision.[31] The challenge for regulators will be to ensure that the economic substance of the asset prevails over its legal form, to leave no room for regulatory circumvention and "fake labels".

At the same time, it is crucial to establish when crypto-assets and NFTs should qualify as a MiFID "*financial instrument*" such as shares, bonds, investment funds, and derivatives. Financial instruments are excluded from MiCAR scope of application, as they are subject to the relevant existing legislation (MiFID II,[32] Prospectus

in any communication or the exempted crypto-assets are admitted to trading on a trading platform. See art. 4 of MiCAR.

[29] Out-of-scope NFTs include crypto-assets that represent IP rights or product guarantees that certify the authenticity of a unique physical asset, such as a piece of art or real estate, or that represent any other services or physical assets that are unique and not fungible.

[30] See recitals 10 and 11 of MiCAR. Also, according to recitals 9, 11 and 14 of MiCAR, NFTs may trigger the MiFID definition of financial instruments and be subject to ordinary sectoral rules, see *infra*.

[31] In Italy, for instance, NFTs could still meet the national definition of financial product, which may trigger the application of prospectus regulation and distance marketing-related prior authorization requirements.

[32] Directive 2014/65/EU of the European Parliament and of the Council of 15 May 2014 on markets in financial instruments and amending Directive 2002/92/EC and Directive 2011/61/EU (recast).

Regulation,[33] MAR,[34] etc.). Such classification is not a trivial task,[35] given that the notion of financial instruments has been provided by Directive: national transpositions may differ across Member States and are linked to non-harmonized national civil and corporate laws. Once again, this lack of fully-fledged EU-wide definitions may give rise to regulatory arbitrage.[36]

To foster convergence across the Member States, MiCAR grants competent authorities the ability to request the European Banking Authority (EBA), the European Securities and Markets Authority (ESMA), or the European Insurance and Occupational Pensions Authority (EIOPA) an opinion on the classification proposed; also, ESMA issued guidelines on the classification of a crypto-asset as a financial instrument.[37] However, opinions and guidelines are non-binding soft-law measures, which may prove insufficient to achieve a level playing field.

The topic is particularly pressing for host countries which, like Italy, tend to import financial products and services from other Member States and are granted limited powers to protect local investors. Again, the prevalence of economic substance over legal form should be the overarching principle guiding the interpreters.

4 Whom to Regulate: Accountability in Disintermediated and Distributed Ecosystems

MiCAR sets a mandatory white paper regime with disclosure and prior notification requirements. The rules are fine-tuned to the peculiarities of the crypto markets, where project developers usually offer tokens to finance projects not yet in operation or "software ideas" at their infancy. Financial resources may be collected in a disintermediated fashion, with no identifiable issuer or financial service provider involved.

[33] Regulation (EU) 2017/1129 of the European Parliament and of the Council of 14 June 2017 on the prospectus to be published when securities are offered to the public or admitted to trading on a regulated market, and repealing Directive 2003/71/EC.

[34] Regulation (EU) No 596/2014 of the European Parliament and of the Council of 16 April 2014 on market abuse (market abuse regulation) and repealing Directive 2003/6/EC of the European Parliament and of the Council and Commission Directives 2003/124/EC, 2003/125/EC and 2004/72/EC.

[35] See F. Annunziata's chapter in this book.

[36] The responsibility for the classification of the crypto-asset is on the offeror or person asking for admission to trading. Still, competent authorities may challenge the classification, both before the date of publication of a white paper and at any moment afterward. See recital 11 of MiCAR recitals also recognize that when assessing and classifying crypto-assets, competent authorities should adopt a substance-over-form approach, under which the features of the asset in question should determine the qualification, not its designation by the issuer.

[37] See ESMA (2024). Information on ESMA policy initiatives on MiCA are available at: https://www.esma.europa.eu/esmas-activities/digital-finance-and-innovation/markets-crypto-assets-regulation-mica. Accessed on 18 February 2026.

These dynamics have shaped both the form and content of the white paper as well as the allocation of responsibilities among the various actors. Conduct obligations are imposed on the offeror and the person seeking admission to trading[38]: these must be identified and accountable, i.e. liable towards crypto holders and potential holders. The identities of the project development team must be disclosed in the white paper, along with the conditions under which the crypto-asset rights and obligations may be modified. This is a substantial positive change compared to *status quo*, where most DeFi projects are developed and controlled by anonymous teams, and little or no information is disclosed to investors on governance arrangements.[39]

As to crypto-services subject to prior authorization, MiCAR includes not only exchanges and investment-type activities but also transfer and custody services, including holding of the crypto-assets or means of access to such crypto-assets. Custody of financial instruments in MiFID is an ancillary activity; in MiCAR, it is recognized as a core service reserved for authorized entities to better protect crypto holders. This regulatory development will help overcome the currently prevailing practice of commingling retail clients' assets in omnibus wallets controlled by the crypto-service provider.

As in MiFID, MiCAR provides rules on conflicts of interest, provision of services, trade transparency, and asset segregation, although with a principle-based and proportional approach. Crypto-service providers are mandated to act in the best interest of their clients and be accountable for their actions towards them.[40]

MiCAR acknowledges that hardware or software providers of non-custodial wallets do not fall within its scope of application and that crypto service providers do not include validators, nodes, or miners that may be part of confirming a transaction and updating the state of the underlying blockchain. Therefore, providers of un-hosted wallets and actors in the DLT infrastructure are out of scope[41]: this

[38] Offerors and persons seeking admission to trading are required to be legal persons and act honestly, fairly, and professionally. They shall communicate with holders and potential holders of crypto-assets in a fair, clear, and truthful manner and identify, prevent, manage and disclose conflicts of interest. They maintain all of their systems and security access protocols in conformity with the appropriate Union standards. ESMA, in close cooperation with EBA, shall develop guidelines to specify those Union standards (see Article 14 of MiCAR).

[39] IOSCO (2023), pp. 9–10.

[40] Final MiCAR provisions move away from the strict liability rule initially proposed by the European Commission for custodians. Specifically, the crypto-custodian shall be liable for losses resulting from an incident attributable to the provision of the relevant service or the service provider's operation. The liability shall be capped at the market value of the crypto-asset lost when the loss occurred, see art. 67(8) MiCAR. This is to say that participation in the crypto-market implies that users of a distributed ledger accept the risks inherent to that DLT, like hacks and bugs or other malfunctions, insofar as they are outside the service provider's sphere of control. MiCAR goes far in explicating that events not attributable to the service provider include any event for which the crypto-asset service provider could demonstrate that it occurred independently of the provision of the relevant service or operations of the crypto-asset service provider, such as a problem inherent in the operation of the distributed ledger that the crypto-asset service provider does not control. Strengthening financial education appears therefore crucial for the average investor to become aware of these new risks.

[41] See recital 83 of MiCAR.

suggests that MiCAR is meant to focus on financial sector dynamics and related market failures.

Still, it is fair to maintain that MiCAR will expand the perimeter of EU financial regulation to a substantial part of the current crypto universe. From a policy perspective, this development should be welcomed, as an essential step to building confidence in a potentially disintermediated and distributed financial ecosystem. However, the way these rules intertwine with decentralized governance is not clear.

Crypto markets recall a plurality of actors within a complex ecosystem composed of networks organized in several layers and with different degrees of decentralization.[42] Governance rules may vary significantly across layers and ecosystems; roles may be (more or less) distributed through various mechanisms, such as through decentralized autonomous organizations (DAOs) and governance tokens. MiCAR is silent on these phenomena.

Specifically, MiCAR appears to have little or no say on dynamics going beyond the hierarchical principal-agent model. Decentralized governance where the decision-making process ultimately relies on users (e.g., because they are entitled to fork) rather than single actors or a group of actors controlling the protocol, appears to be out of scope. MiCAR focuses on trust points and does not tackle pure peer-to-peer transactions or governance around a community of users.[43]

In this context, a significant regulatory challenge ahead is ensuring a mutual understanding of how to distinguish what is genuinely decentralized from what is partially centralized or controlled directly or indirectly by persons or undertakings, thus falling within MiCAR scope.

As a matter of fact, MiCAR does not provide regulatory criteria to distinguish between the two.

Still, competent authorities may intervene by inhibiting non-authorized activities[44] when DeFi protocols rely on centralization in one or more areas (and most, if not all currently do so). Protocols may even have a hidden centralized authority, being decentralized in name only.[45] When any MiCAR activity is carried out professionally by persons or undertakings through automated interfaces or smart contracts,

---

[42] World Economic Forum (2021).

[43] The point is made in MiCAR recital 22. Where crypto-asset services are provided in a *fully decentralized* manner without any intermediary or crypto-assets that have no identifiable issuer, they do not fall within the scope of this Regulation. The same recital specifies upfront that MiCAR applies to natural, legal persons and undertakings and the activities and services performed, provided, or controlled, *directly or indirectly*, by them, including when *part* of such activity or services is performed in a decentralized way. It is interesting to note that a similar approach used to be endorsed by the US authorities as regards the qualification of crypto-asset, particularly in discriminating when it should be treated as a security or a commodity. US SEC Chair G. Gensler (2022).

[44] On top of the typical pre-cautionary and enforcement powers provided in existing sectoral legislation, MiCAR grants competent authorities with new banning powers to block or remove contents from websites, apps, and interfaces over the Internet, see art. 94 of MiCAR. One challenge for competent authorities will be to build a solid and legally grounded case to act swiftly, where necessary, in a purportedly decentralized environment.

[45] IOSCO (2023).

the activity requires prior authorization as a crypto-service provider. Therefore, standards should be defined to detect who exercises effective control of the protocols and make them accountable.

In this vein, MiCAR would address DeFi to the extent that trust points may be identified. Nevertheless, legal clarity on such boundaries is not yet sufficiently achieved.

For instance, it is far from straightforward when a DAO should be considered a centralized entity/undertaking or a decentralized smart contract where a dispersed community of users makes relevant decisions. Such a legal qualification may well be influenced by national private law, which is not harmonized in the EU.

Also, the ability to exercise authority over a protocol may be due not only to the (formal) ownership distribution of governance tokens (which is not easy to track where multiple pseudonymous wallets are used) but also to the actual ability to control the administrative keys and codes from a technological standpoint (e.g., it should be verified whether the code is run automatically and cannot be stopped by only one entity). This new concept of "technological control" currently lacks any explicit legal definition. MiCAR does not solve this ambiguity nor provide explicit standards to guide the interpreters in navigating this complexity.

Therefore, it is easy to predict that regulatory circumvention by tech-washing or DeFi-washing may threaten crypto-market credibility and confidence in the future of DeFi. Specifically, there is a risk of service providers escaping regulation towards (purportedly) more decentralized and difficult-to-regulate platforms. The current fragmented and ever-developing regulatory patchwork may contribute to DeFi continuing to operate with minimal checks and deficits in compliance. These flaws may affect confidence in the entire blockchain ecosystem and compromise the potential of creating an integrative virtual world, the "metaverse" in a decentralized setting.

5 Market Integrity

Compared to the original EC proposal, the last version of MiCAR mirrors more closely the scope and content of the MAR regime to avoid more lenient rules with crypto-asset transactions.[46] As in the context of a traditional market, there will be significant challenges around coordinating cross-border investigation in a highly fragmented marketplace and double jeopardy risks.

On top of more conventional frauds (like exit scams and rug pulls orchestrated by developers and influencers who promote a project and disappear with the funds), new forms of market abuse emerge in the DLT context: manipulative conducts – e.g.

[46] The discipline shall apply to any persons (including in third countries) concerning crypto-assets admitted to trading on an EU trading platform (or for which a request for admission to trading on such a trading platform has been made), regardless of whether or not the transaction or behavior occurred on the platform or elsewhere. This widens the scope of the prohibition and the powers of competent authorities to intervene across jurisdictions.

attacking oracles or the validation process, miners or validators profiting of their ability to re-order or censor transactions submitted to the blockchain – may seriously threaten the credibility of the crypto-market price formation process.[47]

MiCAR recognizes the relevance of such new conduct and, for instance, prohibits insider dealing by any person having access to inside information due to their role in the DLT or similar technology. Also, the massive use of bots and web-based aggressive promotional campaigns in building network effects and influencing market sentiment could be new means of propagating fraud, false information, and price manipulation. As in MAR, the prohibition of market manipulation applies to the false or misleading dissemination of information through the media, including the internet, or any other means.

Nevertheless, challenges may be faced in adapting the definition of inside information in the context of crypto markets. This holds particularly where the price formation mechanism does not rely on the issuer's traditional economic fundamentals (as in conventional capital markets), but on "trust" in the proper functioning of the underlying technology, on the quality of the services and products offered on top of it and the expectation of network effects. MiCAR endorses a principle-based approach to address these challenges, leaving room for interpretative maneuver, and attaches disclosure responsibilities to the offerors and persons requesting admission to trading, since an issuer may be lacking.

In addition, MiCAR is key in contributing to market integrity by imposing prevention and detection measures at trading platforms and service providers. In this respect, similarly to MAR, MiCAR requires any person professionally arranging or executing transactions in crypto-assets to have in place effective systems, procedures, and arrangements to prevent and detect market abuse and report without delay to the competent authority any reasonably suspicious orders/transactions or any other issues related to the DLT mechanism (e.g. the consensus mechanism). To some extent, this obligation of suspicious transaction reporting could help facilitate, among others, the detection of market manipulation conduct including front-running and sandwich trades or other illegal exploitations.

Overall, competent authorities will be granted the same supervisory and enforcement powers available in traditional securities markets, overcoming the current supervisory vacuum.

The main challenge will be to develop data-based and proactive approaches supporting the detection of the new emerging abusive conduct and tracing the effective beneficial owners behind multiple wallets. Technology (RegTech and SupTech) will play a key role in monitoring social media and accessing real-time trading data from the ledger.[48] On-chain supervision can be implemented through the participation of the authorities in relevant infrastructure nodes.[49] Not only AI will be of help. The endgame for competent authorities is fostering embedded compliance through

[47] So-called *Miner (or Maximum) Extractable Value* or *Maximum Extractable Value* ("MEV"), see Auer et al. (2022). See also ESMA (2025).

[48] World Bank (2021).

[49] Auer (2019).

appropriate protocol design.[50] At the same time, risk mitigants may be developed by the participants in the crypto ecosystem themselves by coding functionalities when designing their protocols. Strengthening the dialogue with the vast variety of market participants is a key requisite.

6 Conclusions

MiCAR is a cornerstone of crypto-market regulation in addressing market failures and fostering investor protection, market integrity, and financial stability in a highly speculative sector currently out of public supervision.

The legislative style is close to the conventional one, meaning that regulation is directed to entry points according to a mixture of a (sectorial) activity and entity-based approach. Regulation remains faithful to technological neutrality but opens to new monitoring and enforcement approaches that should consider the specific digital environment in which crypto markets develop. These yet-to-be-developed approaches will require significant regional and global coordination efforts, given the growing interconnectedness and contagion risks across the crypto and traditional markets.

Blockchain establishes new means for coordination based on financial incentives and tokenomics[51]: here technology and finance are increasingly merging. Poor incentives may lead to interest misalignments and weak business models with unintended and unpredicted consequences across the ecosystem. Thus, market integrity becomes crucial: depending on the DLT consensus protocol and governance architecture, crypto-market prices and their formation process may affect the good functioning of the underlying distributed ledger technology.

Earlier adoption of MiCAR has become urgent in the aftermath of the recent crypto-asset market failures and downturns, which are showing increased market concentration and risks; prompt legislative action should be considered the number one priority for a safe and sustainable digital finance.

Nonetheless, given the significant and fast developments in the crypto-markets, one should wonder whether a novel policy approach needs to be discussed in parallel

---

[50] Direct access to DLT trade information may be also effective support to real-time efficient market monitoring thus reducing the need for firms to collect, verify and deliver data. New forms of embedded supervision will be experimented with under the EU pilot regime on market infrastructure (see Regulation (EU) 2022/858 of the European Parliament and of the Council of 30 May 2022 on a pilot regime for market infrastructures based on distributed ledger technology) and may eventually emerge across the EU also as regards crypto public blockchains.

[51] Tokenomics means the economics of the tokens in circulation, i.e.: the mechanisms for the supply and distribution of the tokens, and their utility (business case); the concept is closely linked to the incentive structures designed to reward good behaviours in blockchain ecosystems (ensuring the good functioning of the system). Poor tokenomics design is often the reason behind the failure of some of the biggest ecosystem projects, e.g., the collapse of Luna and TerraUSD in early 2022, see Biancotti (2022), pp.. 13–14.

at the global level in view to foster, for instance, interoperability, international standards, protocol compliance by design, and on-chain supervision.[52]

MiCAR provides several review clauses to reconsider the current "agnostic approach" vis-à-vis decentralized finance. In the future, such reviews may lead to adapting regulations to the advent of decentralized protocols that enable financial services without traditional intermediaries. Regulation could move beyond addressing just market failures and agency costs and be more focused on protocols and systemic outcomes. One example of a novel approach is the proposed EU AI Regulation, which looks at the technology on a risk-based basis to prevent danger to fundamental rights.[53] In the future, this approach could become a model in neighboring areas.

Naturally, policy initiatives at the regional level are not enough for markets and technologies that operate on a global scale. The need to coordinate internationally is today stronger than ever, particularly with other major financial centers like the U.S., which holds technological and financial leadership. Policy reflections in the U.S. are ongoing broadly in the same areas as in the EU, albeit more slowly.[54] Moreover, the U.S. Securities and Exchange Commission (SEC), while investing substantial resources in the dialogue with the crypto world, focused on enforcement actions.[55] In doing so, the U.S. SEC endorsed the principle of the prevalence of substance over form, which should be inspirational for the European Union.[56] The recent political landscape has reopened the debate on regulatory clarity and competitiveness,[57] with Congress showing renewed interest in establishing a federal framework for crypto-assets.

By moving trust from man to machine, new technologies give rise to biases different from those known by classical economic theory. On the other hand, DLT may allow the creation and management of common and public goods in a more decentralized fashion, incentivizing the spreading of power and control from providers (agents) to users (principals) and opening up to innovation, financial inclusion, and competition. These features could be crucial for the success of Web3 and an open metaverse truly serving users' needs and creating value.

Unprecedented interdisciplinarity is required to understand this fast-evolving environment proactively. There is a need for stronger collaboration between different branches of science that traditionally do not communicate with each other. National and international hubs and sandboxes should put authorities and experts from

---

[52] Auer (2019), OECD (2022).

[53] See European Commission (2021).

[54] FACT SHEET: White House Release, https://www.whitehouse.gov/briefing-room/statements-releases/2022/09/16/fact-sheet-white-house-releases-first-ever-comprehensive-framework-for-responsible-development-of-digital-assets/. Accessed on 18 February 2026.

[55] https://www.sec.gov/spotlight/cybersecurity-enforcement-actions. Accessed on 18 February 2026.

[56] The White House framework recommends regulators, like the Securities and Exchange Commission (SEC) and Commodity Futures Trading Commission (CFTC), to continue coordinating efforts to enforce the law in the industry and to share data on consumer complaints.

[57] See US SEC Chairman Speech (Atkins 2025).

different fields of knowledge around the same table and include experiments on NFTs and the metaverse, promising significant social and economic changes, and bringing about new social and business models of "*competitive collaboration*".

Suitable global solutions to such policy challenges should be pursued through multilateralism and multi-stakeholder approaches involving different parties (e.g., different types of regulators, service providers, and users) from other jurisdictions. It is difficult to say whether the existing financial architecture fits this purpose given current geopolitical tensions, so coordination across smaller groups of countries could prove more practical in the near future.

References

Aramonte S, Huang W, Schrimpf A (2021) DeFi risks and the decentralization illusion, BIS quarterly review

Atkins P (2025) Keynote address at the crypto task force roundtable on tokenization, speech. https://www.sec.gov/newsroom/speeches-statements/atkins-remarks-crypto-roundtable-tokenization-051225-keynote-address-crypto-task-force-roundtable-tokenization. Accessed on 12 May 2025

Auer R (2019) Embedded supervision: how to build regulation into decentralised finance. BIS working paper n. 811 (revised in 2022)

Auer R, Frost J, Vidal Pator JM (2022) Miners as intermediaries: extractable value and market manipulation in crypto and DeFi, BIS bulletin no. 58

Auer R, Haslhofer B, Kitzler S, Saggese P, Victor F (2023) The technology of decentralized finance (DeFi), BIS working papers no 1066

Biancotti C (2022) What's next for crypto? Bank of Italy occasional paper no. 711. https://www.bancaditalia.it/pubblicazioni/qef/2022-0711/QEF_711_22.pdf

Chainalysis (2022) Crypto crime report. https://go.chainalysis.com/2022-Crypto-Crime-Report.html. Accessed on 18 February 2026

Deutsche Bundesbank (2021) Crypto tokens and decentralised financial applications, monthly report, July 2021. https://www.bundesbank.de/resource/blob/873132/74fc658db07569219ff74f4e4e55c36f/mL/2021-07-kryptotoken-data.pdf. Accessed on 18 February 2026

ECB (2021) The use of DLT in post-trade processes, advisory groups on market infrastructures for securities and collateral and for payments. https://www.ecb.europa.eu/pub/pdf/other/ecb.20210412_useofdltposttradeprocesses~958e3af1c8.en.pdf. Accessed on 18 February 2026

ECB (2025) Introductory statement in three charts, June 2025. https://www.ecb.europa.eu/press/key/date/2025/html/ecb.sp250623_annex~d4b29a7252.en.pdf?utm_source=chatgpt.com. Accessed on 18 February 2026

ESMA (2024) Report on trends, risks and vulnerabilities, crypto assets: market structures and EU relevance, April 2024. https://www.esma.europa.eu/sites/default/files/2024-04/ESMA50-524821-3153_risk_article_crypto_assets_market_structures_and_eu_relevance.pdf. Accessed on 18 February 2026

ESMA (2025) Report on trends, risks and vulnerabilities, maximal extractable value implications for crypto markets, July 2025, https://www.esma.europa.eu/sites/default/files/2025-07/ESMA50-481369926-29744_Maximal_Extractable_Value_Implications_for_crypto_markets.pdf. Accessed on 18 February 2026

ESMA TRV (2025) Report on trends, risks and vulnerabilities, no. 1

European Commission (2021) Regulatory framework proposal on artificial intelligence. https://digital-strategy.ec.europa.eu/en/policies/regulatory-framework-ai. Accessed on 18 February 2026

FSB (2022) Statement on international regulation and supervision of crypto-asset activities. https://www.fsb.org/2022/07/fsb-issues-statement-on-the-international-regulation-and-supervision-of-crypto-asset-activities/. Accessed on 18 February 2026

FSB (2023) Global regulatory framework for crypto-asset activities. https://www.fsb.org/2023/07/fsb-finalises-global-regulatory-framework-for-crypto-asset-activities/. Accessed on 18 February 2026

Gensler G (2022) Kennedy and crypto, speech. https://www.sec.gov/news/speech/gensler-sec-speaks-090822. Accessed on 18 February 2026

IOSCO (2022) Decentralised finance report, OR0122. https://www.iosco.org/library/pubdocs/pdf/IOSCOPD699.pdf. Accessed on 18 February 2026

IOSCO (2023) Policy recommendations for crypto and digital asset markets, final report, November 2023, https://www.iosco.org/library/pubdocs/pdf/IOSCOPD747.pdf. Accessed on 18 February 2026

OECD (2022) Why decentralised finance (DeFi) matters and policy implications. https://www.oecd.org/daf/fin/financial-markets/Why-Decentralised-Finance-DeFi-Matters-andthe-Policy-Implications.pdf. Accessed on 18 February 2026

World Bank (2021) World bank technical note, the next wave of suptech innovation suptech solutions for market conduct supervisio. https://documents1.worldbank.org/curated/en/735871616428497205/pdf/The-Next-Wave-of-Suptech-Innovation-Suptech-Solutions-for-Market-Conduct-Supervision.pdf. Accessed on 18 February 2026

World Economic Forum (2021) Decentralized finance (DeFi) policy-maker toolkit, white paper. https://www3.weforum.org/docs/WEF_DeFi_Policy_Maker_Toolkit_2021.pdf. Accessed on 18 February 2026

Intellectual Property

NFTs: Copyright Profiles—and Beyond

Giovanni Cavani and Gustavo Ghidini

Abstract The 'world' of NFTs (Non-Fungible Tokens) is booming. But not so much because of any particular artistic added value—NFTs do not present any specificity that could derogate from the basic regulatory principles of copyright. Rather, because they have become a new form of investment, in which tokens are transformed into a kind of atypical 'security', the object of a new (and unregulated) market. The increasing simplicity of the technical means by which an NFT can be created and then placed on the blockchain allows an ever-widening array of 'investors' to access this new market: from simple collectors, to authors of 'digital art' seeking notoriety, to charities seeking funds. Unfortunately, the NFT market, precisely because of its substantial anonymity and the requirement that price be paid in cryptocurrencies, also facilitates money laundering operations. While in the first case the blockchain is used by people and for legitimate and proper purposes, in the second case NFTs turn into a vehicle for illegal transactions that current criminal legislation is not yet apt to effectively counter.

1 Introduction

The exponential development, not only in the field of art, of Non Fungible Tokens NFTs—a technologically blockchain—based expression of Digital Rights Management DRMs—has translated into a pervasive (and in some respects alarming: below, § 10) form of parallel art market vis-à-vis the traditional one(s).[1]

[1] It is estimated that the global NFT market is currently worth around three billion dollars, but could reach over 13 billion within five years. Although these figures are estimated and approximate, they nevertheless show a certainly significant trend.

G. Cavani (✉)
Modena and Reggio Emilia University, Modena, Italy
e-mail: giovanni.cavani@studiocavani.com

G. Ghidini
LUISS University, Rome, Italy
e-mail: ghidini@ghidini-associati.it

F. Di Porto and O. Pollicino (eds.), *Law and Politics of Virtual Worlds*, Law, Governance and Technology Series 79, https://doi.org/10.1007/978-3-032-08541-2_8

2 NFTs and Intellectual Property: Setting the Scene

Speaking of art, the basic issue to be addressed relates to IP: which *specific* features do NFTs present as concerns copyright regime?

The answer is: quite a few, if any.

Let's examine why.

3 The Mere Act to "Tokenize" Something, is Not Creative

First: the fact of putting an artistic/expressive content into an NFT—or 'tokenizing' it[2]—does not per se represent anything creative and protectable under copyright law. In fact, as far as we know (and understand, given the strong technicality of the subject!), the inclusion of a content (video, audio, written, etc.) on the *blockchain,* after its (necessary) dematerialisation and digitisation, is a purely technical operation. In particular, once an image (or a video, or a music file) has been created digitally (e.g. a photograph of an object) and a '*wallet*' (i.e. a sort of bank account opened on the *blockchain*) has been opened, it is then sufficient to access one of the platforms found on the *web* through which the previously created image can be transformed into NFT, and thus placed on the *blockchain.* These are all operations that, in themselves, do not seem to have anything creative about them.

Therefore: if what is entered into an NFT is (no longer, or was not *ex ante*), protected/protectable by copyright, it does not become so as a result of its mere entry on the blockchain.[3]

On the other hand, it cannot be ruled out that the digitization required 'upstream' for the realization of an NFT is not limited to mere technical operations, but involves a *more or less* creative processing activity.

This applies, for example and in particular, to the digital photographic reproduction of what is intended to be included in the NFT; reproduction that, depending on the photographer's contribution, may constitute a creative work protected under Article 2.7 of the Italian Copyright Act (Act 22 april 1941 n. 633) or a simple photograph subject to the related right under Article 87 of the Italian Copyright Act.[4]

The protection that may be granted to the result of the digitization activity, which is necessary for the inclusion of a work (or object) in an NFT, precedes and is in any

---

[2] However, most of the time the content of an NFT (the image of a work, a video, a piece of music, etc.) is not embedded directly in it. Usually the NFT consists of an encrypted code (URL) that refers to a digital file in which the image, video, audio or other object is located. On this point Frye (2022). However, there are also NFTs in which the work is uploaded in its entirety onto the *blockchain.* In that case, one speaks of '*blockchain native works'* referred to as '*onchain works'*. See on this point. Guadamuz (2021).

[3] For a detailed description of the steps to "tokenize" a digital content see Guadamuz (2021), *op. cit*, p. 1369 ff.

[4] In this sense Cavani (2022).

case independent of the inclusion in the *blockchain.* That is to say, the creation of an NFT is not in itself the acquisition of a copyright on the NFT itself.

Therefore, if the *content* of the NFT is not itself protected by copyright, its eventual '*hacking*' and subsequent commercialisation do not constitute an infringement of a copyright. as must be said in the opposite case.

4 A NFT is Classifiable as a Legal Asset

However, it is worth pointing out that, since the electronic file on which the NFT is written is still classifiable as a legal asset,[5] it is in any case the subject of a property right owned by its 'creator'; and this, of course, regardless of who is the owner of any rights on the physical asset 'encapsulated' in the NFT.[6]

That is why anyone who takes possession of another person's NFT by '*hacking'*—or any other computer technique that enables the theft of electronic files—is liable not only for a criminal offence,[7] but also for a civil offence, on account of the infringement of another person's property right.[8]

5 The Content of a NFT can be Protected by Copyright

Of course, that content can be *as such,* before and independently of its insertion in the *blockchain.* In this case, of course, the insertion of the work in a NFT must first be authorized by the owner of the copyright on the work itself, and if this has not been done, such unauthorised tokenization must be deemed to constitute copyright infringement.[9]

On the other hand, the inclusion of a (still) protected work on the blockchain cannot be ruled out as (also) infringing the author's moral right. This is more tenable in the absence of the author's authorisation of the insertion on the blockchain, since such a way of using the work can easily conflict with the author's moral interest in a correct perception of his work. But even if such an insertion has been expressly authorised, the infringement of the moral right cannot be ruled out if such a transfer

---

[5] And in particular as a movable thing. In this sense, Court of Cassation no. 11959 of 10 April 2020.

[6] On the concept of NFT ownership see Steiner (2022).

[7] Both for unauthorised access to a computer system (Article 615 ter of the Italian Criminal Code) and for theft of the file in which the NFT is contained. The question of whether computer files qualify as "movable property" according to an evolutionary interpretation of the notion set out in Article 624 of the Italian Criminal Code and whether their misappropriation therefore qualifies as theft within the meaning of the same article, is the subject of a wide-ranging criminal law debate, in which the above-mentioned Court of Cassation no. 11959 of 13 April 2020 recently intervened in the affirmative, for some comments see: Bruna (2020), Pagella (2021), Pisani (2020).

[8] On this point G.Cavani, op. cit. § 3.3.

[9] See, on the matter, Bednarski et al. (2021)

on the blockchain results in a modification, alteration, or mutilation of the work, which is detrimental to the author's interests.

6 The "Tokenization" of a Copyrighted Work Does Not Extend its Protection Under Copyright Law

On the other hand, the use of the *blockchain* does not affect the conditions and limits of copyright protection of the 'tokenized' content/object. This, starting with the term of protection, which as always starts running with the mere creation of the work. Also, the 'tokenization' of a work already in the public domain does not 'resurrect' a protection that has already expired. Neither the inclusion of a still copyright-protected work in an NFT allows for a temporal extension of the protection.

In sum, an intellectual copyrighted work 'encapsulated' in a NFT remains protected to an extent not differently from the 'traditional' copyrightable works.

As a corollary, the purchaser of a NFT does not acquire any right of economic exploitation of the expressive work as such, but only of its digital "medium", not unlike the purchaser of a painting or a book[10]—this, in default of, and to the extent that, the contrary is expressly provided for in the *smart contract* accompanying the circulation of the NFT itself. Therefore, the "owner" of an NFT may not, in particular, reproduce the work in any other medium (digital or physical); or display and/or disseminate the work outside a personal and domestic context, for example in an exhibition open to the public;[11] nor is he allowed to modify or process the work in order to create a new and different NFT.

7 A NFT can be Transferred by Means of a Smart Contract

A further corollary. As happens for any physical support of an expressive content, the ownership of a NFT can be transferred. And the *smart contract* can well grant (at the expense of the subsequent sellers, and in favour of the original creator), a percentage of the increase of the price of the work due to the effect of the resales of the NFT: a sort of *droit de suite*, of a contractual nature. For these reasons, the circulation of digital works by means of NFT and blockchain can be of significant

[10] The principle that the transfer of ownership of a NFT does not involve the transfer of copyright in the work contained therein is also underscored by Guadamuz (2021), op cit., §3.1, On the topic of whether and what rights the owner of an NFT has over the "*digital resources*" associated with the NFT, see Steiner (2022)

[11] However, in the event that the owner of the rights to the work has allowed it to be included in a NFT intended to be placed on a public or hybrid *blockchain*, it must be considered that all those who have free access to these types of *blockchains have* been authorised to view, read, or listen to it, depending on the nature of the file; unlike in the case of a private (so-called *permissioned*) *blockchain* to which access is only allowed to authorised persons.

economic importance in promoting digital art in particular, which tends not to involve 'physical' original works. Just for the sake of completeness, it should also be pointed out that the remuneration mechanism described above is also triggered if the content of an NFT circulating on the *blockchain* is a work that is no longer protected by copyright, or even if it is an object that is not even abstractly protectable. It is in fact evident that digital works of art, precisely because they are by definition destined for circulation in a digital environment (the hypothesis that they are transferred onto a physical medium and as such circulated being marginal), can only be economically exploited if they are 'locked up' by means of their insertion in a NFT. Circulation on the web, as is well known, can also be controlled by means of the affixing, by those who put the work on the Internet, of special computer keys (the technical protection measures, DRM: *Digital Right Management*) that prevent, for example, its reproduction or reading, unless they accept the conditions under which this operation can be done and pay the required fee. However, the digital work protected by DRM is still, even if not easily, 'hackable', albeit with the criminal consequences provided for by Article 171 ter of the Italian Copyright Law; whereas the risk of 'breaking into' a *blockchain* is technically almost impossible since this would require the simultaneous validation of the break-in itself by 51% of the countless nodes of the chain. *The "if...then"* automatism of the *smart contract* implies that if ("*if*") a buyer accesses the *blockchain* to purchase the NFT, then ("*then*") he automatically accepts the *smart contract* containing the NFT and the exchange occurs between the transfer of the NFT to the buyer and the payment of the consideration requested by the seller, inclusive of the *royalty* due to the person who placed the NFT on the *blockchain*. All this is regulated and managed, precisely automatically—and thus in a *self-executing* manner, with no possibility of default—by the software that manages the *smart contract*.[12]

This can be achieved through algorithms that regulate access to, and use of, NFTs. *The "if...then"* automatism of the *smart contract* implies that if ("*if*") a buyer accesses the *blockchain* to purchase the NFT, then ("*then*") he automatically accepts the *smart contract* containing the NFT and the exchange occurs between the transfer of the NFT to the buyer and the payment of the consideration requested by the seller, inclusive of the *royalty* due to the person who placed the NFT on the *blockchain*. All this is regulated and managed, precisely automatically—and thus in a *self-executing* manner, with no possibility of default—by the software that manages the *smart contract*.

[12] On the adoption of technical protection measures (DRM: Digital Right Management) see, among many others, Arezzo (2008), Arezzo and Maziotti (2011), Lavagnini (2019).

8 The Possible Use of a Blockchain in the Field of Copyright Management

The insertion in a *blockchain* certifies who is the author of the expressive content, and its subsequent buyers: an effect is in principle equivalent to the registration that authors of traditional intellectual/expressive works perform in the registers of the *collecting societies* (like SIAE in Italy,[13] GEMA in Germany,[14] etc.). Of course, the *smart contract* that accompanies the insertion can provide for an automated management of existing copyrights on the work and the allocation of revenues for its use (functions, too, typically performed by *collecting societies*). And this even on a global scale, with obvious benefits in terms of lower transaction costs for authors.[15]

9 The Consequences of the "Immutability" of the Blockchain in Case of Copyright Infringement

A difference, however, with traditional copyrightable works can be envisaged as concerns *infringement*. Anyone who appropriates someone else's expressive work still protected by copyright and puts it on the *blockchain* is obviously violating the author's rights. However, in the case of NFTs, the 'immutability' of the *token*, once entered on the *blockchain*, can lead to a gap between virtual and material reality. In practice, once the true ownership of the *tokenized* work has been judicially assessed, the 'impermeability', in principle, of the *blockchain* makes it impossible to specifically enforce a judicial order of 'cancellation' of the NFT itself. Thus, in default of a spontaneous execution of said order by the person who has placed the NFT on the *blockchain,* the only remedy available consists of a penalty for non-compliance with the order. We note that the degree of 'impermeability' of the *blockchain* changes depending on whether it is a so called 'public' blockchain—one in which any change requires the consent of the majority of the nodes of which the chain is composed—or a so called 'private', or 'hybrid', blockchain—one entrusted to the control of a manager technically enabled to intervene on the *blockchain*).

[13] Società Italiana degli Autori ed. Editori, https://www.siae.it/it/. Accessed June 18, 2025.

[14] https://www.gema.de/en. Accessed June 18, 2025.

[15] On the potential, but also the limitations, of using *blockchain* in the field of copyright management see the interesting considerations of Flink and Moscon (2019).

10 A *Mauvaise Pensée* About the Possible Use of NFT as Money Laundering

Let's now briefly submit a *mauvaise pensée* hinted at (we said: "alarming") in the opening sentence of this essay.

As well known, transactions involving NFTs typically (though not necessarily: see below in this paragraph) involve the payment of a fee in *cryptocurrencies.* Equally known, the latter allow for large margins of anonymity and non-traceability of the person making the payment. Hence, one of the major risks inherent in the very mechanism of *blockchain* is that it may be used to launder, or self-launder, money of illicit origin. An indeed real danger since, in fact, the controls provided for by money laundering regulations are of uncertain application in the context of such currencies (below, shortly, in this paragraph). This remark may well explain some of the frequent abnormal increases of the price of NFTs, even vis-à-vis quite modest, to say the least, expressive contents.

Of course, as a long experience confirms, even the traditional markets of art, antiques, collectors' items etc. are often opaque, concealing 'black money' and laundering operations. But, on the one hand, the degree of traceability ensured by the market of traditional operators, especially the large auction houses, tends to be sensibly higher than that which characterises blockchain-based markets, and its operators. On the other hand, as hinted, in the current stage of national and international law, the control mechanisms, while theoretically effective, result much less so in their practical implementation. The Bank of Italy has confirmed significant shortcomings in the application of anti-money laundering regulations to cryptocurrencies and has banned the German online operator N26 from engaging in Italy in 'new customer transactions' and offering new products and services to existing customers, in cryptocurrencies (Bitcoin etc.).[16]

Our perplexities are supported, i.a., by the recent report by the US Treasury Department «*Study of the facilitation of money laundering and terror finance through the trade in works of art*»[17].

On the European side, the Council, in announcing the agreement reached on the European Regulation on Crypto-Activities (MiCA), recently announced[18] that NFTs will be excluded from its scope and that "within 18 months, the European Commission will have to execute a comprehensive assessment and, if it will deem it necessary, a specific, proportionate and horizontal legislative proposal to create a regime for NFTs and address the emerging risks of this new market."

---

[16] See the news on https://www.corriere.it/economia/finanza/22_marzo_30/n26-bankitalia-blocca-operazioni-nuovi-clienti-criptovalute-carenze-nell-antiriciclaggio-096cbc70-afe7-11ec-9789-5da5d2d36231.shtml. Accessed June 18, 2025.

[17] See the news on https://www.money.it/Gli-NFT-possono-favorire-riciclaggio-denaro. Accessed June 18, 2025

[18] See the news on https://www.consilium.europa.eu/it/press/press-releases/2022/06/30/digital-finance-agreement-reached-on-european-crypto-assets-regulation-mica/. Accessed June 18, 2025.

Of course, the NFT market is mostly attended by respectable' people! Just think to authors of digital works in search of visibility for themselves or relatives former authors of traditional works of art, or persons interested in increasing the value of manuscripts or other items of private collection, etc. Now, if inexperienced in *blockchain* and cryptocurrencies, these righteous persons risk, due to the volatility of this market (NFT + cryptocurrencies), to become unconscious victims of fraudulent manipulations.

For them, then, the only significant form of self-protection consists in tying the NFT with a *smart contract* regulating the circulation thereof. For example, providing that access to the NFT only allows the vision of its content and not also its re-sale. Or, if the re-sale is permitted, limiting this faculty to those who 'qualify' themselves, coming out of anonymity. And also providing that the payment for access or subsequent purchases be made in 'real' money, through bank transfers and similar instruments. Or, if the use of virtual money is inevitable, imposing a condition of traceability on whoever makes the payment.

References

Arezzo E (2008) Technological protection measures, software and interoperability in the digital era, in IDA 340 ff

Arezzo E, Maziotti M (2011) Commentary on art. 102 quater et seq. In: Galli C, Gambino A (eds) Code commentato della proprietà industriale e intellettuale. Utet, Torino

Bednarski M, Witkam A, Vtolijk R (2021) NFTs: new legal challenges on the horizon. https://www.stibbe.com/publications-and-insights/nfts-new-legal-challenges-on-the-horizon. Last accessed June 2, 2025.

Bruna D (2020) Computer data and embezzlement: note to Cassazione Penale, sec. II, 10.04.2020, no. 11959. https://www.devita.law/dati-informatici-e-appropriazione-indebita-nota-a-cassazione-penale-sez-ii-10-aprile-2020-n-11959/. Last accessed June 2, 2025.

Cavani G (2022) Non fungible tokens (NFT): what interference with copyright? in AIDA, § 3.2

Finck M, Moscon V (2019) Copyright law on blockchains: between new forms of rights administration and digital rights management 2.0. IIC 50:77–108

Frye BL (2022) Are cryptopunks copyrightable? Pepperdine Law Rev 105:119

Guadamuz A (2021) The treachery of images: non-fungible tokens and copyright. J Intellect Prop Law Pract 16: 1369 ff

Lavagnini (2019) Commentary on articles 100–102 quinquies. In: Ubertazzi LC (ed) Commentario breve. UTET, Italy

Pagella M (2021) La Cassazione sulla riconducibilità dei file al concetto di "cosa mobile" oggetto di appropriazione indebita: un caso di analogia in malam partem? https://www.sistemapenale.it/it/scheda/cassazione-11959-2020-appropriazione-indebita-file-cosa-mobile#_ftn1. Last accessed June 2, 2025.

Pisani N (2020) La nozione di "cosa mobile" agli effetti penali e i file informatici: il significato letterale come argine all'applicazione analogica delle norme penali, in Dir pen proc 651 ss

Steiner, AD (2022) The paper it's printed on: NFTs, ownership and conceptual art. https://papers.ssrn.com/sol3/papers.cfm?abstract_id=3997352. Last accessed June 2, 2025.

The Uncanny Token

Brian L. Frye

Abstract *Art is a funny thing. Everybody knows it when they see it, but nobody sees the same thing. Anyway, the art market is the market for art as an investment. But what are art collectors buying when they buy an artwork in the art market? The obvious answer is that they're buying authentic objects. But it's wrong. In fact, they're buying an entry on an artist's catalogue raisonné, and the object is merely a physical token that represents ownership of a ledger entry.*

The NFT market is identical. It merely does away with the need for a physical token and allows the art market to transact directly in ledger entries. That's why NFTs are "uncanny tokens." They make us uncomfortable because they show us that the conventional art market was always a market for ledger entries, but we couldn't see it, because objects got in the way.

> *Let us not mince words. The marvelous is always beautiful, anything marvelous is beautiful, in fact only the marvelous is beautiful.*[1]

1 Introduction

Art is a good that consumers don't understand. Consumers know what they like and like what they know. Everyone thinks they like art, except for those who think they dislike art. But most people don't actually care about art. In fact, they can't even see it.

---

[1] André Breton, *Nadja* (1928).

B. L. Frye (✉)
University of Kentucky J. David Rosenberg College of Law, Lexington, KY, USA
e-mail: brianlfrye@gmail.com

F. Di Porto and O. Pollicino (eds.), *Law and Politics of Virtual Worlds*, Law, Governance and Technology Series 79, https://doi.org/10.1007/978-3-032-08541-2_9

Consumers like things they understand. So consumers usually don't like art, because they don't understand it. But that can change, when art becomes a brand. Consumers like brands, because everyone knows what they mean. Prices also help, because consumers understand prices.[2] The higher the price, the better the art.

The art market is strange. For some reason, eggheads and billionaires agree that dirty canvases and lumpy rocks are worth millions of dollars because they were created by name brand artists. This makes no sense. They're just decorations. It's cheap and easy to make a copy that's identical to the original.

Not so fast. When art collectors buy artworks, what are they buying? The obvious answer is that they're buying objects. But that's obviously wrong. What they're really buying is an investment in an artist's career. Artworks are valuable in the art market only because they represent ownership of an entry on an artist's catalogue raisonneé. When art collectors buy artworks, what they're really buying is ledger entries. The artwork is just a physical token that represents ownership of a ledger entry.

Along came "non-fungible tokens" or "NFTs." Some people love them, more people hate them, but no one understands them. Don't worry, they're actually easy to understand.[3] But you might not like what they teach you about art and creativity.

In a nutshell, an NFT is a blockchain entry that represents something other than a cryptocurrency transaction. A blockchain is a collection of cryptographic ledger entries. Those ledger entries can represent anything, but they usually represent cryptocurrency transactions. Entries on the Bitcoin blockchain usually represent Bitcoin transactions, and entries on the Ethereum blockchain usually represent Ether transactions.

NFTs represent something else, anything else. But usually, NFTs represent "ownership" of an artwork, typically a digital image.[4] A lot of people seem to think NFTs are weird and nonsensical, because NFT owners don't actually own anything other than their NFT. I don't get it. The art market and the NFT market are identical. Art collectors were never buying objects, they were buying ledger entries.[5] The NFT market just enables them to buy and sell ledger entries without having to bother with physical tokens. What a relief.

Why do people hate NFTs? Because they are "uncanny." Freud observed that the uncanny makes the familiar seem unfamiliar, by showing what is supposed to be hidden. Or rather, the uncanny forces us to recognize that the familiar was always unfamiliar, because we chose not to understand the truth of it. The art market seems familiar only because it uses objects to obscure its economic reality. The NFT market is uncanny because it dispenses with the physical tokens that make the art market seem familiar, and thereby reveals an unspeakable truth.

What does it reveal? The art market has always been a securities market, and the NFT market is also a securities market, in exactly the same way. When you buy an artwork in the art market, you aren't really buying an object, you're buying

---

[2] *See*, *e.g.*, Hayek (1945).

[3] See generally Frye (2022a).

[4] See generally Frye (2022b).

[5] See Frye (forthcoming).

a fractional interest in an artist's career, represented by an object. In other words, artworks are just physical tokens that represent ownership of a ledger entry. NFTs are the same, they just eliminate the physical tokens and enable collectors to trade ledger entries directly. The art market is implicitly a securities market, but the NFT market makes it explicit. That's why NFTs make people upset. They say the quiet part out loud.

Understandably, many people find the NFT market repellant. We love art and tolerate the art market because we love art. The NFT market dispenses with all of the things people think they're supposed to love about art, or at least most of them. No more objects, no more craft, no more galleries, no more museums. An NFT represents the price of an artwork, nothing more and nothing less. The thrill is gone when you turn the magic ticket into a claim check.

But the venality of the NFT market is also its promise. Nothing has changed. We just opened our eyes. The art market has always promised access to the capital markets, but only to a precious few. For better or worse, the NFT market opens the floodgates.

2 The Artist, the Artwork, and the Art Market

What is art? Who knows. It depends who you ask. Everyone's got an opinion about what's art and what isn't, but they rarely agree. The only universal definition is that art is something made by an artist. While it seems circular, at least it has the advantage of being true. Of course, no one agrees about who is an artist, either.

As a great philosopher once said, "Art is anything you can get away with."[6] As Marcel Duchamp observed, "Art may be bad, good or indifferent, but, whatever adjective is used, we must call it art, and bad art is still art in the same way that a bad emotion is still an emotion."[7] It's art all the way down, the only real question is whether people like it.

While defining art is a fool's errand, defining the art market is easy. The art market is the market for art purchased as an investment. People buy art for two reasons: decoration and investment. When you buy art for decoration, you're buying an object. Its value depends on whether other people also want it for decoration. But when you buy art as an investment, you're buying a share in an artist's career. Its value depends on whether the artist becomes famous.

Obviously, art is often both decoration and investment. But it's important to distinguish between the two. In the decoration market, artwork is a consumption good, so its value depends on the demand for similar goods. In the art market, artwork is an investment in an artist's career, so its value depends on the artist's success.[8]

---

[6] Attributed to Andy Warhol, plagiarizing Marshall McLuhan.

[7] Marcel Duchamp, *The Creative Act* (1957).

[8] See Frye (forthcoming).

3 The Art Market

Superficially, the art market looks like a market for objects. Artists create objects, art galleries sell objects, art collectors buy objects, and art museums collect objects. It's objects all the way down. An artwork is a painting, sculpture, drawing, print, or photograph. Of course, it gets complicated on the margins, when it comes to artworks in the form of videos, digital images, and concepts. Where's the object? Everyone just pretends it still exists. Artists sell a certificate of authenticity and everyone pretends the certificate represents ownership of an object. Collectors don't love it, but at least it kind of works.

Objects are essential to the art market, because objects are how the art market creates scarcity.[9] Artworks are typically original works of authorship protected by copyright. But the art market is largely indifferent to copyright, because it creates scarcity via authenticity. The art market only values authentic works of authorship, so it doesn't really care about copying. If anything, the art market encourages copying, because the more people talk about an artwork, the more valuable it becomes.

None of that is true. The art market isn't a market for objects. The art market has never been a market for objects. The art market has always been a securities market. When artists sell artworks to art collectors, what they're really selling is an investment in their career. Each artwork represents a share in the artist's commercial goodwill or "clout." Of course, some artworks represent larger shares than others. But the art market doesn't really care about objects. It cares about what those objects represent.

I'll put it another way. The art market is really a market for ledger entries. Every artwork attributed to an artist appears on the artist's catalogue raisonnée, in whatever form it exists. An artwork is valuable only because it represents ownership of an entry on an artist's catalogue raisonnée. Or rather, an artwork is valuable only because it is a physical token that represents ownership of a ledger entry.

Let me emphasize, the art market doesn't value objects. It values what those objects represent. Specifically, it values ledger entries. Without the ledger entry, what we call artworks are just dirty pieces of canvas, lumpy rocks, and used paper. They are physical tokens, magically made desirable and valuable by virtue of their connection to a ledger entry. Walter Benjamin famously observed that artworks are valuable because of the aura of authenticity that attaches to art objects.[10] He was almost right. It isn't the object that's valuable, only the ledger entry that it represents. The ledger entry is where the magic happens. Without the ledger entry, an art object is just another object. An authentic Picasso painting is immensely valuable, but if the object turns out not to be authentic, it immediately becomes worthless. The object hasn't changed, only its connection to the ledger entry. But the ledger entry is all the art market cares about.

In other words, the economic reality of the art market isn't really a market for objects. The art market is a securities market, merely masquerading as a market for

[9] See generally Adler (2018).

[10] Benjamin (1935).

objects.[11] The art market doesn't really value artworks, it values what they represent, which is an investment in an artist's career. Or rather, in securities law terms, the art market is a "scheme whereby a person invests his money in a common enterprise and is led to expect profits solely from the efforts of the promoter or a third party."[12] When art collectors buy artworks, what they are buying is an interest in an artist's career, and they expect to profit from their investment because they expect those artists to pursue artistic fame.

The only thing that prevents us from seeing the economic reality of the art market as a securities market is the comically transparent fiction that it is a market for objects. Conceptual art should already have disabused us of that misconception.[13] The fact that the art market is perfectly happy to value artworks that don't consist of an object should have made it obvious that the art market was never really a market for objects. The art market is a market for objects only insofar as a financial instrument is a virtual object. The art market values objects the same way a stock exchange values shares in a company.[14]

Or rather, the thing that really prevents us from seeing the economic reality of the art market as a securities market is that the art market has become familiar, so familiar that we can't see how strange it is anymore. Somehow, we have come to accept that a dirty canvas or lumpy rock can be worth millions of dollars, so long as the art market accepts its attribution to a famous artist, but is worth nothing without the attribution. It is transparently absurd to pretend that is a description of a market for objects, rather than a market for attribution. But we have spent so many years pretending that the art market values objects that we can maintain the pretense, no matter how absurd. It's a familiar pretense, and one we find comforting, because it absolves us from wrestling with what the economic reality of the art market tells us about what we actually value and why.

NFTs are interesting for many reasons. But one of the reasons they're interesting is that they make it impossible to maintain the illusion that the art market is a market for objects, rather than a market for clout. The NFT market is just a cryptographic version of the art market. Put it on the blockchain! But the NFT market makes it explicit that the art market doesn't care about objects, because there are no objects to care about.[15]

You won't believe what happened next.

[11] See generally Holm (1981).

[12] 328 U.S. 293, 298–99 (1946)

[13] See,.e.g., Rub (2020) and Frye (2021).

[14] See Schwartz (2019) (discussing the possibility of "celebrity stock markets").

[15] See Frye (2022).

4 What is an NFT?

An NFT is a blockchain entry that represents something other than a cryptocurrency transaction, anything other than a cryptocurrency transaction. Different blockchains can record different kinds of data, so the potential content of an NFT depends on the design of the blockchain on which the NFT is recorded. For example, the Bitcoin blockchain has a relatively simple design, so creating Bitcoin NFTs is challenging. By contrast, the Ethereum blockchain is far more flexible, so creating Ethereum NFTs is relatively easy. Many blockchains can record any kind of data, so NFTs on those blockchains can consist of just about any kind of data.

While an NFT can represent literally anything, most NFTs represent "ownership" of an artwork, usually a digital image. Typically, NFT artists create a digital image and then create one or more NFTs that represent "ownership" of the image. Some NFTs consist of all of the data associated with an artwork.[16] But recording data on a blockchain is costly, so most NFTs consist of as little data as possible. For example, NFTs that represent ownership of a digital image usually consist of nothing more than a URL pointing to a copy of the image.

When artists sell NFTs to collectors, what are the artists selling and what are the collectors receiving? Well, it depends. An NFT doesn't necessarily consist of any more than the right to say what the NFT represents and the right to transfer the NFT to someone else. An NFT is a ledger entry that represents "ownership" of an artwork, to the extent that the NFT market recognizes the NFT as representing ownership of the artwork. Nothing more, nothing less.

NFTs don't necessarily convey any other rights, although they can, if the NFT creator makes NFT ownership convey additional rights and has the capacity to convey those rights. For example, some NFT creators give NFT owners a copyright license to use the digital image associated with their NFT or a trademark license to use the brand associated with the NFT collection. But other NFT creators choose to place the digital images associated with their NFTs in the public domain, typically by adopting the Creative Commons CC0 public domain tool.[17] For example, all of the images associated with the popular Nouns NFT collection are in the public domain.[18]

It's unclear whether the copyright owner of a digital image can use an NFT to transfer copyright ownership. Under the Copyright Act, a transfer of copyright ownership requires a signed writing.[19] While courts are likely to find that transferring an NFT can satisfy the signed writing requirement, it remains uncertain at the

[16] See, e.g., the digital artworks created by 0xDEAFBEEF, which exist entirely on-chain, at https://www.deafbeef.com/

[17] See Frye (2022d).

[18] See, e.g., The Nifty Revolution, *Top 10 CC0 NFT projects*, Aug. 15, 2022, at https://medium.com/@NiftyRevolution/top-10-cc0-nft-projects-c70f0f9b8813

[19] 17 U.S.C. § 204(a) ("A transfer of copyright ownership, other than by operation of law, is not valid unless an instrument of conveyance, or a note or memorandum of the transfer, is in writing and signed by the owner of the rights conveyed or such owner's duly authorized agent.").

moment.[20] In any case, using an NFT to transfer copyright ownership in the digital image associated with the NFT is undesirable, because nothing would connect the copyright to the NFT. In other words, the NFT owner could separate the NFT from the copyright and transfer them separately. NFT creators who convey a copyright interest in their NFTs typically want ownership of the copyright interest to follow the NFT. Accordingly, those NFT creators typically grant a copyright license to whoever owns the NFT.[21]

There is considerable disagreement about NFT collectors about whether "owning" the "intellectual property" associated with their NFTs is important and valuable. The scare quotes are intended to underscore the incoherence of the conversation. Presumably, when NFT collectors refer to the "intellectual property" in their NFTs, they primarily mean the copyright in the images associated with their NFTs, and perhaps secondarily the trademarks associated with the NFT collection.[22] Either way, some NFT owners insist owning the "intellectual property" is essential, others think NFTs are more valuable without it, and the overwhelming majority don't care one way or the other, so long as the NFT market keeps on pumping.[23]

I don't get it. Art collectors don't care about owning the copyright in the artworks they own, let alone the trademark in the artist's brand. They don't need or want to own either. All they need to own is the right to sell the artwork.

The economic reality of the NFT market is identical to the art market, so it should work the same way. Why would NFT collectors want to own the copyright in the digital image associated with their NFT or the trademark in the NFT collection's brand? What they care about is the market price of their NFT. Of course, the value of their NFT depends on the value of the brand it represents. But the value of the brand depends on the NFT creator, not the NFT collectors. If the NFT creator commits to growing the brand, the NFTs might increase in value, as more people want to own them. If the NFT creator "rugs," or stops promoting and endorsing their NFTs, then they will almost certainly become worthless. What NFT collectors are buying is the belief that the NFT creator will succeed in building a brand.[24]

I think the problem is that NFT collectors are still struggling to figure out what they bought and why they bought it. NFTs are a market in search of a product. It shouldn't be a surprise when collectors latch on to whatever familiar product is on hand. Everyone "knows" that "intellectual property" is important and valuable, even if they don't really understand what it is, how it works, or why they would want to own it. So it makes perfect sense that some NFT collectors would fixate on "intellectual property," even if they don't really need it.

[20] Cf. Free Holdings Inc. v. Kevin McCoy, et al., No. 1:2022cv00881 (S.D.N.Y. March 17, 2023) (holding that ownership of a blockchain entry formerly associated with an artwork didn't necessarily convey ownership of the artwork).

[21] See, e.g., Board Ape Yacht Club, Terms and Conditions. https://boredapeyachtclub.com/#/terms

[22] See, e.g., Frye (2023).

[23] See, e.g., Frye (2022d).

[24] See generally Frye (forthcoming).

5 NFTs & Their Discontents

Scholars are intellectual landlords.[25] They never saw an idea they didn't want to own. Legal scholars are no exception. If anything, we are even more committed to intellectual landlordism than our peers, as exemplified by our citation practices. Typically, every sentence of a law review article is annotated, ideally with a string of citations. Legal scholars routinely bemoan onerous and pointless citations, especially when they are asked to provide citations for their "original" ideas. But they inevitably complain when someone fails to provide them with a citation they think they deserve. Legal scholarship is a seamless web of citations, let the circle remain unbroken.

Anyway, legal scholars in particular are in the business of using old ideas to describe new things. NFTs are no exception. While NFTs have been around for awhile, legal scholars didn't really notice them until 2021, when Christie's sold an NFT of Mike "Beeple" Winkelmann's artwork *Everydays: The First 5000 Days* for $69 million.[26] That's a new thing worth describing! Especially if you can stake an ownership claim in it.

Unsurprisingly, most legal scholars writing about NFTs characterized them as digital objects. After all, the NFT market looks an awful lot like the art market, which everyone assumes is a market for objects, so surely the NFT market is a market for objects as well. Some scholars helpfully explained how existing property law doctrines would be likely to address NFTs.[27] Others argued that NFTs represent a new form of intellectual property.[28] And still others insisted that NFTs are a form of digital personal property.[29]

Obviously, I don't think property is a helpful framework for understanding the economic realities of the NFT market. Are NFTs a form of property? Of course, just like any other kind of security is a form of property. When you buy a security, you own something, or rather you own certain rights, most importantly the right to sell your security to someone else. But property law doesn't tell us much about securities regulation, other than who owns the securities at issue.

I'm more interested in another question. Why are so many people so angry that NFTs and the NFT market exist in the first place? It's quite strange. People complain that NFTs are stupid, because when you buy an NFT you don't really own anything. Of course, that's silly. When you buy a share in a company, you don't really own anything either, except the right to sell it to someone else. But that's all the ownership you care about. When you buy a share in a company, you are primarily buying the

---

[25] See, e.g., Frye and Marx (2022).

[26] See Mike "Beeple" Winkelmann, Everydays: The First 5000 Days (2021), at https://onlineonly.christies.com/s/beeple-first-5000-days/beeple-b-1981-1/112924

[27] See, e.g., Moringinello & Odinet (2022, 2023). These articles are especially interesting and important, because NFT technology seems likely to have many different uses, many of which may still be unanticipated. Moringinello and Odinet provide an immensely helpful framework for thinking about those potential uses.

[28] Lee (2023).

[29] See Fairfield (2022).

right to sell it to someone else, although it may come along with additional rights, like the right to make a symbolic vote in favor of whoever is nominated to the board of directors. Likewise, when you buy an NFT, you are buying the right to sell it to someone else. Sure, it doesn't seem like much. So what? If the market says it's enough, you can't argue with the market.

There's more. Many people think NFTs are bad, because they devalue art. Apparently, art means objects, which are the only thing that can be authentic, and NFTs are objectionable because they eliminate the art object and leave only the artwork. Or maybe NFTs are bad because they financialize art by reducing it to a price. I will confess, I think those are all points in favor of NFTs and the NFT market.[30] The art market has always been a financial market. But nothing says art has to care about money. If NFTs and the NFT market can encourage us to separate the meaning and price of art, all the better.

I think NFT discourse reveals something interesting and important about our understanding of art and the art market. We think we understand art and the art market. But we don't. NFTs and the NFT market show us that we don't. Even better, they suggest possibilities we couldn't see, because conventional wisdom got in the way (see Fig. 1).[31]

6 The Uncanny & the Marvelous

NFTs are interesting and important because they are profoundly uncanny. NFTs and the NFT market take everything we thought we understood about art and the art market and turn it upside down. We thought art meant authentic objects and that the art market was a market for authentic objects. But NFTs and the NFT market show us that the art market was always a market for clout and art objects were always just physical tokens that represented ownership of clout.

I will put it bluntly. NFTs are interesting and powerful because they are "uncanny tokens." No one thinks they understand art, but everyone thinks they understand what art is and how the art market works. They couldn't be more wrong. People understand art better than they understand the art market, because they don't understand the art market at all.

In 1919, Sigmund Freud famously described an "aesthetic" experience he called the "uncanny."[32] He observed that the uncanny "undoubtedly belongs to all that is terrible—to all that arouses dread and creeping horror." He observed that the term "implies some intrinsic quality which justifies the use of a special name," and asked "what this peculiar quality is which allows us to distinguish as 'uncanny' certain

[30] See Frye (2022c).

[31] https://picryl.com/collections/the-world-turned-upside-down-or-no-news-and-strange-news.

[32] Sigmund Freud, The "Uncanny" (1919). Freud used the German word *unheimlich*, which is usually translated as "uncanny." The German word *heimlich* means "homelike" in the sense of "private" or "familiar." *Unheimlich* means unfamiliar, in a peculiarly unsettling way.

Fig. 1. The world turned upside down, or, no news, and strange news. (J. Kendrew 1820)

things within the boundaries of what is 'fearful.'" His answer was "the "uncanny" is that class of the terrifying which leads back to something long known to us, once very familiar." The familiar and the uncanny are literal opposites.[33] And yet not everything unfamiliar is uncanny. Something more is needed.

Freud defined the "uncanny" as "something which ought to have been kept concealed but which has nevertheless come to light."[34] In other words, the "uncanny" consists of the experience of a familiar phenomenon made strange by repression. "We can understand why linguistic usage has extended the Familiar into its opposite, the Uncanny, for this uncanny is in reality nothing new or alien, but something which is familiar and old - established in the mind and which has become alienated from it only through the process of repression."[35]

Hal Foster used the concept of "the uncanny" to describe the premise of surrealism. While his psychoanalytic reading of surrealism isn't particularly interesting, his observation that the rhetorical power of surrealism depended on its use of the uncanny is quite interesting indeed. According to Foster, "the uncanny" is "a concern

[33] Freud used the German words *heimlich* and *unheimlich,* which literally mean "homely" and "unhomely," but are conventionally translated as "familiar" and "uncanny."

[34] Sigmund Freud, The "Uncanny" (1919). Freud used the German word *unheimlich,* which literally means "unhomely," but is conventionally translated as "uncanny."

[35] Sigmund Freud, The "Uncanny" (1919).

with events in which repressed material returns in ways that disrupt unitary identity, aesthetic norms, and social order."[36] As Foster observed, surrealism relied on the uncanny by blurring the real and imaginary, authentic and artificial, object and symbol.

The concept of the "uncanny" and the "return of the repressed" were a stock theme of 90 s postmodernist scholarship. But it doesn't seem to have stuck. Or maybe everyone repressed it. In any case, NFTs and the NFT market are uncanny in just the way Freud and Foster described, and prompted exactly the reaction he predicted.

Why are NFTs and the NFT market uncanny? Because they make something we thought was familiar seem unfamiliar. LOL. Obviously, it's because they show us that something we thought was familiar was unfamiliar all along. We thought we understood the art market. But we were just deluding ourselves. We pretended it was a market for objects, when we should have known it was a market in clout.

7 The Return of the Repressed

As I now beheld the robe, it seemed to me suddenly to become a mirror-image of myself:

myself entire I saw in it, and it entire I saw in myself, that we were two in separateness, and yet again one in the sameness of our forms.[37]

Freud described the uncanny as a "simulacrum" or double. This double becomes the conscience, the familiar of the ego criticizing itself. The uncanny makes us uncomfortable precisely because it forces us to see that which we wish to unsee. The uncanny is the return of the repressed, the truth making an unwelcome appearance.

NFTs and the NFT market are uncanny because they show us the truth about art and the art market and we don't like it. But we should. Sometimes a token is only a token. But NFTs are unusually symbolic. They aren't just digital objects, but ledger entries that represent fractional ownership of an artistic enterprise. An NFT is the doppelganger of the artwork it represents.

The art market recuperates the uncanniness of art by lashing it to authenticity. It makes the ledger entry disappear, by merging it with a physical token and thereby rendering it familiar. We pretend the object is intrinsically valuable, and thereby deny the magic of ledger entry that transforms it into a token. Conceptual art dematerialized art only to reify itself. The authentic object dissolved into the authentic certificate.

NFTs are the return of the repressed because they represent the art market in a new, starker form. We have repressed our knowledge that the art market is just a securities market in which art collectors speculate on the future popularity of artists. NFTs strip away the art market's aesthetic veneer and display its economic logic.

[36] Hal Foster, Compulsive Beauty xvii (1993).

[37] The Hymn of the Pearl (Hans Jonas trans. 1958).

Good. We should be honest about why we value art and how the art market works. NFTs and the NFT market force us to be honest. It's awkward and a little embarrassing. But I think it will ultimately be good for artists and the art market. After all, we're in the business of selling things. NFTs and the NFT market are all about selling art. But they're also about making it more efficient, and making sure it benefits artists, rather than intermediaries.

Why do people dislike NFTs and the NFT market? Because they are so crass. They make it obvious that artists are economic actors responding to economic incentives. Of course they are. And that's fine. The interesting and important question is how we structure those incentives. Everything is changing, but it doesn't have to stay the same.

References

Adler A (2018) Why art does not need copyright. Geo Wash L Rev 86:313

Benjamin W (1935) Art in the age of mechanical reproduction. Schocken Books, New York

Fairfield J (2022) Tokenized: The law of non-fungible tokens and unique digital property. Ind Law J 97:1261

Frye BL (2021) SEC no-action letter request. Creighton Law Rev. 54:537

Frye BL (2022a) After copyright: Pwning NFTs in a clout economy. Colum JL Arts 45:341

Frye BL (2022b) How to sell NFTs without really trying. Harv J Sports Entertain Law 13:113

Frye BL (2022c) NFTs & the death of art. In: Hecker S, Karol PJ (eds) Posthumous art, law and the art market. Routledge, New York, NY

Frye BL (2022d) NFT marks. Amsterdam Law & Technology Institute Forum, Amsterdam

Frye BL (2022e) Karl Marx, literary landlord. 25 Va J Law Technol 279, 214–224

Frye BL (2023) Tokenized brands. 9 St Thomas J Complex Litig 31

Frye BL (forthcoming) The value of art. In: The cultural history of collecting. Bloomsbury, London, New York

Hayek FA (1945) The use of knowledge in society. Am Econ Rev 35:519–530

Holm M (1981) The art investment contract: application of securities law to art purchases. Fordham Urban Law J 9:385

Lee E (2023) NFTs as decentralized intellectual property. Univ Ill Law Rev 2023:1049

Moringinello JM, Odinet CK (2022) The property law of tokens. Fla Law Rev 74:607–670

Moringinello JM, Odinet CK (2023) Blockchain real estate and NFTs. Wm & Mary L Rev 64:1131

Rub GA (2020) Owning nothingness: Between the legal and the social norms of the art world. BYU L Rev 2019:1147

Schwartz VL (2019) The celebrity stock market. UC Davis Law Review 52:2033

NFTs and IP: Easier Said Than Understood

Stefania Ercolani

Abstract After 2022, the hype of NFTs and virtual worlds has slowed down; it is time to reflect thoroughly how Intellectual Property interacts with the NFTs and blockchain technology. In this context, particular attention should be paid to the protection of digital art, of entertainment and of fashion brands in the framework of Metaverse.

This analysis outlines risks and opportunities generated by the exploitation of IP matters in the virtual environment, which requires a the preliminary exercise to define what is intended for NFTs and their role in the circulation and trading of copyright works. Information transparency is critical as far as it concerns the legal relationship between an NFT and the copyright in the digital content, where the transaction normally concerns a license or a certificate, but not the ownership or the assignment of copyright. The risk for the NFT purchaser can also be amplified by the volatility of cryptocurrencies, that are normally used in NFT transactions.

Moreover, national fragmentation adds uncertainty to the actual legal enforceability of smart contracts.

Technologies can and must help to build up a transparent market where transactions are legally correct and safe, starting with metadata and content identification tools that are reliable, shared and interoperable. Transparency and interoperability are indispensable to pave the way for the mass use of blockchain and the acceptance of the Metaverse beyond the dimension of sophisticated videogames.

S. Ercolani (✉)
Rome, Italy
e-mail: stef.ercolani@gmail.com

Alai Italia (Associazione Letteraria e Artistica Internazionale), Roma, Italy

Alai Italia, Rome, Italy

F. Di Porto and O. Pollicino (eds.), *Law and Politics of Virtual Worlds*, Law, Governance and Technology Series 79, https://doi.org/10.1007/978-3-032-08541-2_10

1 Where are we Starting From

On June 24, 2022, googling "what is an NFT", 320 million results were available in 0,63 s. Limiting the search to the last year, the result is 47,700,000. The information sources vary hugely, from news to marketplaces, from tech magazines to ads for any kind of products. According to statistical surveys, since the beginning of 2021, NFTs have captured a global audience, with Asia in the leading position,[1] contributing to the popularity of blockchain technology far more than cryptocurrencies, while more recently, in part for a more reasonable consideration of the NFT short-term effects on IP, the attention of experts and stakeholders has been diverted to the emergence of generative AI and its impact on the market of creative productions.

Mass media speak about NFTs mainly because of the exorbitant prices they have reached in special digital art auctions[2] or in the marketing of digital collectibles,[3] and also because their circulation is supposed to expand widely in the Metaverse. From Spring 2022, the NFT market has decreased dramatically,[4] only partially in line with the oscillations in the value of cryptocurrencies that are used in NFT transactions. It should be noted also that the aggregated data do not reflect the differences among the various NFT offers, and the relevant markets. Missing a reliable mass of data due to a short period since their introduction, a trend clear enough to attempt a forecast is not discernible. Discernible enough is, on the contrary, the interest of venture capital that fuels the development of NFT in expectation of Web3 and the Metaverse.

The rocket increase of NFT sales and the uncertainties about their real value have raised a number of questions relevant to the IP rights in the digital object represented by or referred to in an NFT. For a number of reasons, it is doubtful that standard consumers are aware of what they are buying, in particular when dealing with copyright content NFTs. A frequently mentioned case of confusion about NFTs is the purchase for 3 million $ by SpiceDAO[5] of the script Bible of Dune by Jodoroswski, that had been initially auctioned for 40.000$. SpiceDAO intended to "free"

---

[1] "NFT Transaction Activity Stabilizing in 2022 After Explosive Growth in 2021", Chainanalisys, https://blog.chainalysis.com/reports/chainalysis-web3-report-preview-nfts/. accessed December 2022.

[2] After introducing non-fungible tokens (NFTs) onto the global auction stage with the sale of Beeple's *Everydays: The First 5000 Days* for $69 million, in September 2022, Christie's auction house launched Christie's 3.0, a fully on-chain auction platform dedicated to digital art.

[3] Examples from the Washington Post are: $69 million for a JPEG file by the digital artist Beeple; $10.5 million for a pixelated image that resembled the Joker character in Batman; and $5.4 million for a token of Edward Snowden's face made out of court documents, https://www.washingtonpost.com/technology/2022/05/25/nft-value-drop/. accessed December 2022.

[4] https://www.bloomberg.com/news/articles/2022-06-29/nfts-have-fallen-off-the-cliff-as-sales-sink-to-lowest-in-year#xj4y7vzkg. accessed December 2022.

[5] "Essentially, a DAO is a group of people pursuing a shared goal, using a blockchain to make decisions in a transparent and efficient way. You can think of a DAO like a cooperative group that's bound together by a set of bylaws, and those bylaws are hard-coded on the blockchain",. From *Everything you need to know about DAOs. A primer on how DAOs are working to collectively shape the new creative economy*, published 28 April 2021. accessed December 2022. https://foundation.app/blog/everything-you-need-to-know-about-daos.

Jodorowsky's work, issuing NFTs taken from it and making the text and illustrations available to the public, as well as encouraging the creation of derivative works of any kind; in reality, the ownership of the Dune NFT – exactly as it happens when one buys a book – did not include or imply any intellectual property assignment (brand, characters, copyrights, etc.), which apparently Spice DAO failed to understand.

A few examples can help to understand some basic legal implications of NFT transactions in certain IP-intensive sectors (e.g. artistic and literary property, fashion and trademarks, entertainment) that are crucial for the NFT perspective in the Web3 developments.

2 What is Actually Embedded Into an NFT

Under the headline "what is an NFT" on a very popular crypto-art NFT marketplace Niftygateway.com one could read[6]:

> *A non-fungible token (NFT) is a digital certificate of ownership built on blockchain technology, that contains the provenance, the history, and all activities surrounding a digital asset. It is on the blockchain - meaning the activities can be viewed by the public and it is immutable - it cannot be forged.*

While, according to Wikipedia (accessed 30 November 2025):

> *"An NFT is a unit of data, stored on a type of digital ledger called a blockchain, which can be sold and traded. The NFT can be associated with a particular digital or physical asset such as images, art, music, and sport highlights and may confer licensing rights to use the asset for a specified purpose. An NFT (and, if applicable, the associated license to use, copy, or display the underlying asset) can be traded and sold on digital markets. The extralegal nature of NFT trading usually results in an informal exchange of ownership over the asset that has no legal basis for enforcement, and so often confers little more than use as a status symbol."*

The two definitions show almost plastically that a critical approach is absolutely necessary when discussing the intellectual property aspects, that can differ widely depending on the digital or physical asset the traded NFT is associated with and on the possible combination between NFTs and the conditions automatically applied by means of a "smart contract". The NFT definitions in other marketplaces do not really help to reconcile the confusion between an NFT and the associated IP protected asset.[7]

The Wikipedia definition highlights that the NFT is intended to affect the perception of cultural products, countering the commoditization effects of the digital technology by reinstating particular digital assets as status symbol. The scarcity created

[6] https://www.niftygateway.com/what-is-an-nft. accessed December 2022.

[7] Robyn Conti, *What Is An NFT? Non-Fungible Tokens Explained, May 10, 2024, "An NFT is a digital asset that can come in the form of art, music, in-game items, videos, and more. They are bought and sold online, frequently with cryptocurrency, and they are generally encoded with the same underlying software as many cryptos."*.

by the unicity of the NFT confers iconic value to an otherwise universally accessible digital object[8] and such scarcity can be translated into commercial value, or, at least, into a marketing tool.

The only information the mentioned definitions have in common is that an NFT is on the Blockchain. It is true that, in principle, the registrations on the blockchain are immutable, but this is no guarantee that the information on the digital asset the NFT is associated with is truthful, reliable and complete. The NFT may be a digital certificate of ownership, but could also be only a license or even a mere right to access. It does not certify, however, the chain of the right transfers of the asset.

It is often overlooked that the protected item is not usually incorporated in the NFT in the blockchain, and the token is simply a digital code in the blockchain, with no IP attached to it, for example where it points to a digital item off-chain, stored in Amazon Cloud or in any Cloud service of the kind. Most frequently, in fact, the buyer of the NFT buys the code and not the digital asset accessible through the NFT. The smart contract incorporated in the token defines the characteristics of the access, that depends on the kind of rights, if any, the buyer acquires. Very rarely these rights include the assignment of intellectual property rights, neither on an exclusive nor on a non-exclusive basis.

An interesting example of contractual terms attached to NFTs offered to individual users, could be the conditions of the NFT football card collectibles of Sorare, a European company that, for the purposes of its videogame, concludes license agreements with football teams or football collective organization to issue the NFTs of individual players. The definition of Collectible in the contract published on Sorare website clarifies[9] the function attributed to the NFT: "*Collectibles are unique digital trading cards featuring a professional athlete with a non-fungible token ("**NFT**") using Blockchain Technology and issued by Sorare. The NFT ensures the scarcity and authenticity of the Collectible and the transparency of the Services....*". By purchasing the NFT and entering the game, the user is granted "*on a non-exclusive basis, a worldwide license to use, display and transfer the Third-Party Collectible Elements associated with the Collectibles incorporated into the NFTs that you legitimately own for the period that you own the relevant NFT(s), for personal and non-commercial purposes only.*" Further specific license restrictions are provided in the terms and conditions that the user accepts, while the same user is requested[10] "*to grant and/or agree to grant to Sorare the transferable, sub-licensable, free of charge, global right to exclusively use, copy, distribute, adapt, creative derivative works, reproduce, distribute, modify, translate, and otherwise exploit, any content*" ... "*by any present or future process and by any means of distribution on the Website, social networks, or media (such as TikTok, Facebook, Twitter, Instagram, Reddit, Youtube, etc.) or platforms (such as*

[8] By Li Jin and Katie Parrot, *The Web 3 Renaissance: A Golden Age for Content* Published 2021 https://every.mirror.xyz/y_WLA-Tk3VF5uPqHi-glDLVVfHxLUbjXakRI7SMISas. accessed Decembere 2022.

[9] Para. 6 Sorare Terms and Conditions, effective 16 May 2024, https://sorare.com/terms_and_conditions. accessed December 2024.

[10] Para 12 Sorare Terms and Conditions, effective 16 May 2024. accessed December 2024.

YouTube), e-banners and promotional emails or newsletter and on Sorare intranet or in its internal documentation, whether in whole or in part, and whether as provided or as modified, for commercial or promotional purposes".

The mere comparison between what the user acquires (a license for personal, non-commercial purposes) and what the user grants to the platform marketing the NFT (an exclusive license covering any type of exploitation through present or future technology and media) underlines the narrowly limited rights attached to the NFT; a more general overview justifies the conclusion that "The vast majority of NFTs convey zero intellectual property ownership of their underlying content (artwork, media, etc.).[11]

The multifaceted offer of music NFTs shows that the token can be useful to create multiform opportunities for independent artists as well as for entertainment companies. Currently, the main music NFT projects are aimed at building up a fan community through private sales of premium tickets for future concerts or access to opportunities like community songwriting sessions, in order to strengthen the connection between the artist and his or her fanbase Community building is also the focus of newly created Music DAOs.[12] In the music sector, DAOs are a tool to exploit the potential of blockchain for micromanagement of royalties for the exploitation of rights in single recordings, that can be realized through DAO crowdfunding, where the share due to the participants is represented by an NFT.

Other music projects merge the experiences in different artistic fields using NFTs to transform, for example, a digital pack of 4 songs into a unique collectible digital asset, to be auctioned and possibly traded.[13] Many other music project are essentially collaborative, involving the community and the artist/s, in order to produce dynamic digital assets including music and original unique digital covers.

In music as well as in other sectors, the creators' aim to limit or eliminate the layers of intermediation existing in the exploitation of copyright is pursued in many ways thanks to the blockchain; communities organized as a DAO (Decentralized Autonomous Organization), whose benefits refer to transparency, efficiency, autonomy, anonymity, seem among the most adaptable and promising tools for this purposes.

---

[11] A report published in August 2022 describes the IP licenses attached to 25 NFT projects and the relationship between NFTs and underlying IP digital asset. https://www.galaxy.com/research/insights/a-survey-of-nft-licenses-facts-and-fictions/. accessed December 2022.

[12] According to the collaborative research study accessible at https://www.waterandmusic.com/the-state-of-music-daos/, "the way music DAOs conceptualize themselves is decidedly different from that of the more technically-oriented, maximalist crypto community and focuses on social collaborative values, shared by artists and fans." accessed December 2024.

[13] From the website: https://campchaos-frontend.vercel.app/,." What the purchaser acquires is described as follows: "Opening a pack is much like receiving your own personal EP created by Chaos - with 4 songs, and entirely unique cover artwork for each." The original rightowners (Members of the Collective) allow: "The Members further authorize Chaos to grant owners of NFTs from the Album a license to download, access, and use the Art associated with their NFT(s) for non-commercial purposes, and to market and sell their NFT(s). The Members may later decide to offer additional rights to NFT owners." accessed December 2022.

3 Risky Business for Adventurous Buyers

When the interests at stake are so huge, the efforts to penetrate the impregnable blockchain distributed ledger increase too, with inevitable risks for more or less informed investors, on the one hand, and rights holders, on the other hand. The lack of a clear regulatory framework and oversight is a big challenge for the Web 3 ecosystem to become the normal stage for interactions and transactions on the web.[14]

Among the risks deriving from information asymmetry, the overestimation of the total value of the NFT trading is a common occurrence, where crypto-bubbles can be created, for example through wash-trading,[15] when the same person operates, through different crypto wallets, as buyer and seller in the same transaction, increasing the nominal value and inflating the number of NFT transactions.

There are also phenomena similar to traditional piracy, when the work associated to the NFT is an imitation or a real plagiarism of an original work, put up for sale as a "certified" asset in the distributed blockchain ledger. The NFT is in fact associated with a digital or a material asset but this does not guarantee that it is minted by the legitime rightowner.

The FAQ published by Creative Commons[16] specify: "*Notably, however, the NFT buyer does not automatically acquire the copyright to the linked work unless they also have a separate legal agreement explicitly assigning copyright. Similar to owning a numbered print of a piece of art, the owner of an NFT controls what happens to the particular token they own. Without a separate assignment, they do not hold the rights to the work underlying the token nor do they control others' ability to copy or remix the work—those rights remain exclusively held by the rightsholder of the underlying work.*"[17] A very disappointing fact is that frequently the rightholder of the underlying work is not aware that the NFT is minted and marketed.

It may be extremely complicated to check if the chain for the transfer of right in the object is correct and uninterrupted and the improvised buyer may acquire an NFT "certifying" a false ownership and therefore valueless. The advantages of blockchain technology in data preservation, meaning that the recording of the transaction in each digital wallet for a certain NFT is immutable and transparent, are based on the assumption that the information is correct. If it is not, tracing the digital wallet (a string of numbers and letters) to its owner is not warranted. Anonymity is an obstacle when a buyer is seeking for remedies against fraudulent sellers of NFTs, and also when

---

[14] https://www.forbes.com/sites/bernardmarr/2022/07/13/web3-and-the-future-of-music/?sh=36ebb1612a29. accessed December 2022.

[15] https://www.reuters.com/technology/unreal-demand-irregular-sales-worth-billions-fire-up-wild-nft-market-2022-02-07/. accessed December 2022.

[16] In the section *FAQ: CC and NFTs* at https://creativecommons.org/cc-and-nfts/ it is also specified "We are aware that some NFTs are created without the consent of the creators whose works are minted, some make misleading or false promises about the value of the tokens or what is being sold to potential investors, and some direct funds toward the NFT issuer through other deceptive means; many other unethical uses also exist, and CC does not support those activities even where CC licenses or legal tools are used." accessed December 2022.

[17] https://creativecommons.org/cc-and-nfts/, last updated Sept. 9, 2022. accessed December 2022.

rightowners want to enforce the licence terms in subsequent transactions involving their NFTs.

In addition to the cases of misappropriation or plagiarism, any transaction happening online can be subject to phishing scams. An example is the NFTs auction of the CryptoBatz collection of 9666 NFTs created by Ozzy Osbourne and Sutter Systems.[18] A few days after the NFT auction announcement, the server moved from "cryptobatznft" to simply "cryptobatz" and scammers took over the former server of Discord (the marketplace carrying out the auction) and were able to defraud supporters of hundreds of dollars draining cryptocurrency from their wallets.

OpenSea, one of the major NFT marketplaces, tweeted in January '22 that 80% of the NFTs minted on its platform were "plagiarized works, fake collections and spam." According to CNN (February 19, 2022),[19] "Reports of scams, counterfeits and wash trading have become commonplace".

The platform Hitpiece ceased activity after RIAA, the trade Association of record producers, as well as several artists, initiated legal actions claiming their music was auctioned off as NFTs without the rightowner's knowledge or permission.[20] The risk of mass infringement and scam networks being set up around music-centric NFTs is a major obstacle to the music business's projects in NFT used for administration purposes or for fandom communities.

Furthermore, NFT trading is currently carried out in cryptocurrency and the link between NFTs and cryptocurrency adds one more aleatory feature to the trade, very close to a betting exercise, since the exchange rate between cryptocurrencies and regular currencies are extremely volatile and the cryptocurrency circulation such as Ethereum and Bitcoin is limited to certain environments for now; in general, a cryptocurrency is not easily negotiable or accepted in the real world.

Finally, in all cases where the content – music, video, art, collectible or other – is saved in the cloud separately from the token that certifies it, it is possible that, for technical reasons or by human intervention, the digital asset is accidentally lost, as it can happen, for example, in the case of definitive loss of the access credentials.

4 Technology, Law, Contract Mix & Shake

A basic distinction must be drawn between NFTs incorporating the copyright content and NFTs associated to copyright content. Not least for technological complexities (including energy consumption needed for minting), the copyright work is not normally embedded (or, digitally reproduced) in the NFT. When the NFT contains

---

[18] Ozzy Osbourne's NFT project shared a scam link, and followers lost thousands of dollars - The Verge, accessed December 2022.

[19] https://edition.cnn.com/2022/02/13/tech/nft-marketplace-plagiarism/index.html. accessed December 2022.

[20] Eamonn Forde, *Greatest Hit: RIAA Targets Hit Piece Over NFT Infringements,* https://www.forbes.com/sites/eamonnforde/2022/02/07/greatest-hit-riaa-targets-hitpiece-over-nft-infringements/. accessed December 2022.

the digital reproduction of the work, the existing rules on the reproduction right apply and complexities can affect detecting and monitoring the NFT minting and circulation, even when the embedded smart contracts could provide automatically applicable rules.

In the real world, a consumer's purchase of an authenticated work of art, of a collectible or a recording does not include the acquisition of copyright, but only the right to use it for private purposes and personal enjoyment. The same would happen in the trade of the NFT incorporating the object, unless a smart contract regulating the sale does provide something different and provided that the terms of the smart contract are also enforceable or, at the least, admissible. It is worth reminding, in fact, that wherever the NFT certified object is located, whether in the blockchain or off-chain, the ownership of the inherent intellectual property rights can be transferred and the transfer must be proven according to the rules in force in the real world.

Most common and, above all, more problematic are the NFTs associated through a link to a digital work or its copy, stored off-chain. The legal analysis should focus on three aspects at least.

The first aspect refers to the copyright restricted acts involving the digital asset; the initial act is the storage of the copyright object by means of a cloud service since the upload of the digital work and its storage do imply an act of reproduction and are therefore subject to the copyright law. The first step is therefore the determination of the person liable for this act, presumably the legal or natural person who decides when and how to store the object and for which purposes. More complex is the determination of the applicable law/s because of copyright territoriality principle, while Jurisdiction can depend on the location of the server where the digital object is stored or, more likely, on the hosting provider i.e., the storage platform (that can differ from the marketplace offering the NFT to the public) and on where the access to the stored digital object occurs.

Secondly, how are the acts following the storage qualified? In the straightforward, although rare, case where the object is embedded in the NFT in the blockchain, then the crucial problem is the qualification of the so called purchase of the NFT. In fact, the transaction on the blockchain does normally consist in a licence, most frequently restricted to personal non-commercial use, which means that no ownership transfer occurs and, evidently, no exhaustion takes place, contrary to what happens for the sale of physical media that incorporate copyright works.

Even more doubtful is the copyright qualification of the link that ensures the access to the digital object to the owner of the NFT; evidently, the implications of this qualification are of paramount importance for copyright owners. The first question is whether the mere link between the NFT and the stored digital object can be a communication to the public or, more in general, an exploitation act covered by the copyright law.[21] For the NFT to be subject to copyright, it must be determined if creating and selling the link between the NFT recorded in the distributed ledger and the protected work can be deemed an act of exploitation. And what if the access to

[21] The oscillating case law of the CJEU on linking does not seem applicable here.

the digital object is exclusively reserved to the NFT owner and no actual or potential public is involved?

Then, another issue is the distinction between the NFT and the asset: we have the not so rare occasions where the NFT is mined by someone who does not have the necessary right/s in the digital object linked to the NFT. By illegally reproducing the digital object and linking it to an NFT without authorization, the miner infringes copyright, but the mechanism of NFT makes it quite complicated to stop the infringement when the NFT is traded. The copyright enforcement is impossible without the active cooperation of the marketplace but the precedents are not encouraging. It is not clear also how and where the owner of the infringed right can obtain damages.

Third aspect: the negotiation of the actual terms implemented by the smart contract in the NFT and their validity under copyright and, possibly, under consumer Law.

Let's take the most common examples of digital copyright assets that are represented by or associated to an NFT: a collectible or a work of visual art or a special recording of a song. Thanks to the technological features of the blockchain, the NFT is considered to be an authentication tool, witnessing that the owner of NFT has at least a right of access to the collectible or the work of art and allowing normally the owner of the NFT to trade the NFT itself while the inherent copyrights remain in the linked digital object.

As mentioned, the object linked to that code is normally off-chain, possibly in a custodian hosting platform. In other words, the subject of the trade is the code in the blockchain (rather than the digital object itself) including a license or a sublicence when third-party elements are present for certain rights. The possibly licensed rights are normally non-exclusive and have a strictly defined scope, usually aimed at personal usage.

The role of the smart contracts in the future NFT economy should be considered closely, since it presents layers of uncertainty under civil law too, in particular to the legal requirements of the agreement between the parties.[22] This is not a minor issue since the smart contracts on the blockchain are seen by tech specialists as a tool for the copyright holders to monitor the circulation of their works and possibly require automatically a royalty at each transfer or usage. NFTs would be or could become the tool for certain categories of rightowners to receive a remuneration for each exploitation mediated by the NFT, however granular it is. Potentially, blockchain technology would constitute the basis of a digital copyright infrastructure and NFTs would be the tools for rights micro-management.

It is also foreseeable that, when NFTs become actual consumer goods,[23] not limited to crypto-enthusiasts, and their usage becomes commonplace for certain

[22] Enzo Maria Incutti, *NFT: profili civilistici e questioni aperte*, report in the Seminar at Rome University la Sapienza, October 19, 2022, promoted by ALAI Italia and Juridical Observatory on Digital Innovation unpublished.

[23] The Uniform Commercial Code defines NFTs as digital goods in the recently approved new article 12, that deals with transfers of interests in a catch-all class of digital assets branded "controllable electronic records" (CERs).

types of transactions, the automatic application of smart contracts[24] will be disputed in those jurisdictions where special requirements are provided for the validity of copyright transfers.[25] At present, the companies auctioning or marketing NFTs seem, in fact, to rely on the strict clauses in their Terms and Conditions, rather than merely on the automatic code implementing the license and the related restrictions.

In more general terms, however, especially when the NFT investment is substantial, a number of questions that now remain without answer, need to be solved, for example it is not clear what would be the destiny of NFTs and the associated (under license) copyright asset in inheritance.[26]

5 The Importance of Metadata

Anything that can be digitized can be turned into an NFT and the unique combination confers the scarcity and therefore the value to the digital object, while it keeps being universally accessible. Most non-fungible tokens are a metadata file that has been encoded and associated to a digital object; the copyright data (when the object is protected) are meant to be immutable when registered in the blockchain; as mentioned, this advantage can convert into a problem when data are false or incorrect, but the problem "garbage-in, garbage-out"[27] can be solved only acquiring data at the source, which is all but easy in the case of right transfers, absent any formality obligation for copyright attribution and where adequate standardization and authoritativeness of identifiers are practically non-existent.

---

[24] Art. 8-ter, para 2 of the Italian Decree Law 14 December 2018, no. 135, converted by Law no. 12 of 11 February 2019 (the so-called Simplification Law) contains a definition of smart contract in paragraph 2, here translated:. [smart contract is a computer program that operates on distributed ledger-based technologies and whose execution automatically binds two or more parties according to the effects predefined by them. Smart contracts satisfy the requirement of written form subject to computer identification of the interested parties, through a process compliant with the requirements set by the Agency for digital Italy ….]

[25] Italian Copyright Law prescribes the written form *ad probationem* for all transfers of rights and the possible equivalence of smart contract with a written agreement is not tested.

[26] Talk of Marco Spolidoro at the meeting *The Future of Copyright* in memory of L.C. Ubertazzi *NFT: from the metaverse to catching dummies.* The author highlights that the use of platforms and blockchain has the main purpose of making rare something that is not rare, in a way expensive even in environmental terms, https://ipkitten.blogspot.com/2022/09/the-future-of-copyright-in-memory-of_30.html. accessed December 2022.

[27] https://hackernoon.com/lying-to-the-blockchain-applying-the-garbage-in-garbage-out-problem-to-decentralized-networks-g52i3e66?source=rss&ref=morioh.com&utm_source=morioh.com. accessed December 2022.

The European Commission expects[28] that blockchain technology helps achieving "more transparency and better data management, notably with regard to copyright and an improved identification of rights owners". One of the main obstacles to pursue this goal is highlighted by the European Study published in 2022 about the creative sectors and their use of new technologies, such as blockchain and artificial intelligence (AI), from a copyright perspective.[29]

The certification and administration of intellectual property rights by means of NFTs or through a blockchain is not in sight yet, also for reasons not inherent to the technology, first of all the scarce availability of reliable, authoritative metadata on intellectual works and subject matters.

There are no doubts that, technically, blockchain technology could support copyright transactions and even microtransactions associated, for example, to the views of a film or to the streams of a music performance online, offering a blockchain based DRM system (DRMdigital rights management).[30] However, this presupposes at least two elements of different nature: first, a company that has a business model based on blockchain (assuming that energy sustainability is achieved) and a critical mass of consumers willing to use that service. It is envisaged that this sort of business models will spread in the Metaverse while several tech companies offer their advice and services to develop metaverse NFT marketplaces.[31]

Secondly, the availability of univocal, authoritative and shared identifiers associated to the digital object, that allow the correct attribution to the rightowners whenever a smart contract is implemented in a transaction involving the object. In most cases, different rights subsist in the same object (e.g. rights belonging to the author, to the producer, to the performers, or to the broadcaster, etc.) and therefore, more than one identifier should be available and correctly embedded in the object; evidently, cross referencing among different metadata in the same object is also needed.

---

[28] Section 4. Easier access to and sharing of IP-protected assets, in the Communication From The Commission To The European Parliament, The Council, The European Economic And Social Committee And The Committee Of The Regions - Making the most of the EU's innovative potential An intellectual property action plan to support the EU's recovery and resilience, COM(2020) 760 final, 25.11.2020.

Currently NFTs are outside the EU Regulation on crypto-asset e crypto-asset service provider, since they are not considered financial instruments because of their non-fungibility. This position may result shortsighted, if the usage of fractional NFTs becomes common. Currently we have examples of initiatives to support investments in works of art, where the NFT is fractioned in equal tokens representing shares (that are fungible); see: https://fractional.art/

[29] European Commission, Directorate-General for Communications Networks, Content and Technology, *Study on copyright and new technologies: copyright data management and artificial intelligence*, Publications Office of the European Union, 2022, **https://data.europa.eu/doi/10.2759/570559**.

[30] US Copyright Office, Non Fungible Tokens and Intellectual Property, A Report to Congress, March 2024, page 42, https://www.copyright.gov/policy/nft-study/Joint-USPTO-USCO-Report-on-NFTs-and-Intellectual-Property.pdf. accessed December 2024.

[31] https://medium.com/javarevisited/metaverse-nft-marketplace-development-f5c9c40dfab4. accessed May 2024.

According to the analysis carried out in the mentioned European Study, the difficulties depending on metadata refer to the still existing numerous cases of imperfect metadata attached to content, or conflicts between metadata coming from different sources; the frequent intentional deletion of metadata from content[32]; the persistent lack of interoperability and proper standardization, and the immature cross referencing capabilities.

Moreover, despite its features as a secure distributed ledger, pros and cons of blockchain for copyright data management may vary among industries,[33] not least because the immutable character of the blocks is not easily adaptable to the complexities of copyright transfers and licensing fragmentation.

It is realistic, therefore, that in the short term, NFTs can be used as experimental tools for copyright management[34] for specific initiatives and niche markets, while the current multiple intermediaries, such as agents, publishers, collective management organizations and, in most general terms, content distributors will continue to carry out their respective services for some time. It is possible that some of the intermediaries opt for innovative strategies and transform their business models to provide the services and the know-how necessary for an effective copyright administration infrastructure within the same period of time necessary to actually setting up the Metaverse.

6 NFTs and Brands

While tech and videogame companies set up projects for their own metaverses, aiming at reserving a space in the future globally interconnected virtual world, many famous brands have decided to register their trademarks in the merchandise category that can grant their protection also in the VR environment. The aim of this protection can differ, since some luxury brands wish to avoid the dilution of their fame based on highly sophisticated, perfectly accurate products, and therefore are intentioned to prohibit the use of their trademark on virtual goods, while other fashion companies plan to create their own digital assets, including NFTs, and put them on sale through specialized marketplaces or even through their own auctions or VR initiatives.

An example of the first type is the French luxury group Hermés, that has filed proceedings in the USA against an American artist, Mason Rothschild, for his

[32] https://www.cmswire.com/digital-asset-management/embedded-metadata-debate-to-stripor-not-to-strip/. accessed December 2022.

[33] French Ministry of Culture, Mission Report – Towards more effectiveness of copyright law on online content sharing platforms: Overview of content recognition tools and possible ways forward, French Ministry of Culture, Paris, 2020.

[34] In cooperation with Algorand, the Italian Society of Authors and Publishers (SIAE) has announced a project, through which 4 million NFTs have been minted registering as digital assets the data of SIAE members' works https://www.siae.it/it/iniziative-e-news/siae-rappresenta-i-diritti-degli-autori-con-asset-digitali-creati-pi%C3%B9-di-4000000. accessed December 2022.

digital art depicting “MetaBirkins”, based on Hermés well-known Birkin bags,[35] marketing them on OpenSea. The conflict here is also conceptual since it concerns the qualification of the virtual objects themselves, i.e. art opposed to trademark.[36]

The second type is Nike, that has filed proceedings against StockX for selling NFT receipts of limited-edition Nike sneakers and including an image of the sneakers themselves.[37] Nike has opened the Nikeland space on Roblox, a videogame platform where the users’ Avatars can use its virtual products. Other projects among the many that allude to the Metaverse, are Afterworld by Balenciaga or also Adidas – Prada: Re-Source.[38]

Many fashion companies have taken their first steps in this direction, in order to counter parasitic initiatives and to launch their own projects. Famous brands, such as Gucci and Prada, have filed applications in the US for the application of their trademarks to virtual products, while brands such as Puma, Crocs, Kerastase, Kiehl and others have applied for registration of their trademarks in the “downloadable virtual goods” sector pursuant to EUIPO Guidelines.[39]

European Union Intellectual Property Office (EUIPO) published a “practical approach for classification purposes” in June 2022, that indicates Class 9 for the trademark registration of virtual downloadable goods (where a key aspect of virtual goods is to emulate core concepts of real-world goods), such as computer programs featuring footwear and clothing for use online and in online virtual worlds; digital art; downloadable music authenticated by NFTs (e.g. labels, covers, etc.). Class 35 is indicated for online virtual environment for trading virtual art and virtual art tokens, while Class 41 is indicated for entertainment services, namely, providing virtual

[35] In Hermes Int’l et al. v. Rothschild, Case No. 1:22-cv-00384 Case 1:22-cv-00384 (SDNY), the District Court of New York denied the motion to dismiss Hermès’s claims, observing that “Like the physical Birkin handbag itself, MetaBirkins are extremely valuable commodities,” and that “the NFTs have sold for over a million dollars collectively.” Moreover, “consumers and media outlets have expressed actual confusion as to whether Hermès is affiliated with Rothschild’s line of NFTs, with many believing it to be the product of a partnership between the two.” Judge Rakoff’s opinion’s is accessible at: https://cases.justia.com/federal/district-courts/new-york/nysdce/1:2022cv00384/573363/61/0.pdf?ts=1665062744.
accessed December 2024.

[36] A precedent concerning trademarks in a videogame is the case AM General LLC v Activision Blizzard, Inc. et al., (Case 1:17-cv-08644-GBD-JLC) https://case-law.vlex.com/vid/am-gen-llc-v-885458377. accessed December 2024.

[37] Nike, Inc. v. StockX LLC, Case No. 1:22-cv-00983, pending 7 Oct. 2024

[38] https://www.pradagroup.com/en/news-media/news-section/adidas-prada-re-source.html an interactive platform where user-generated and creator-owned art are uploaded and finally 3000 community-sourced artworks are minted as NFTs and compiled as tiles in a single mass-patchwork NFT designed by renowned creative coder and digital artist, Zach Lieberman. The final NFT is auctioned on Superrare marketplace, accessible on https://www.adidas.com/prada-nft/canvas. accessed December 2024.

[39] https://guidelines.euipo.europa.eu/2058843/2065747/trade-mark-guidelines/6-25-downloada ble-goods-and-virtual-goods. accessed December 2022.

environments in which users can interact for recreational, leisure or entertainment purposes.[40]

Global luxury brands are also preparing to defend their reputation when Virtual Reality platforms spread in China.[41]

7 The Liability of NFT Marketplaces

Fashion, videogaming, entertainment, education, and e-learning are likely, as are IP intensive industries in general, to benefit from the Metaverse due to its features, but the benefits depend on the rules allowing those industries to exploit, enforce and respect IP rights.

NFT marketplaces are not numerous (yet), but they can be extremely complicated to surf; rights holders are unlikely to be able to keep them monitored, although the technologies for automated content recognition (ACR)[42] that certain marketplaces like e-Bay or Amazon are implementing seem promising and could be developed for wider adoption. Automated content recognition and automated removal systems such as You Tube's Content ID and Meta's Rights Manager, may be applied in future also to detect fraudulent NFTs. While the interest for NFTs increases, also the level of security must be enhanced by ex-ante measures, because once the sale of the illegally minted NFT is done (a matter of days or even hours), the blockchain guarantees anonymity of the seller.

Digital assets certified by NFT traded by specialized marketplaces can infringe IP right in several manners and the potential for damages is known both in relation to copyright works and to trademarks. Some NFT marketplaces have an IP take-down system similar to that seen on social media platforms and online marketplaces selling physical goods, and their terms of service explicitly forbid infringing another party's intellectual property rights, be that copyright, trademarks or publicity rights (where applicable). The legal uncertainties surrounding NFTs are exemplified by the mentioned MetaBirkin case, where Hermes has submitted to OpenSea a specific take-down request and according to online reports, the MetaBirkins were removed. In 2023 the judge has issued a permanent injunction against Mason Rothschild from further infringing on Hermès' trademarks.Despite the decision, a U.S. district judge in the

[40] Webinar of 25 September 2022 "Trade marks and designs in the metaverse: legal aspects/EUIPO practice"; https://euipo.europa.eu/knowledge/course/view.php?id=4763. accessed December 2024.

[41] https://www.worldipreview.com/article/the-metaverse-nfts-and-ip-issues-in-china. acccessed December 2024.

[42] The project on ACR and its implementations, started in 2019 by the EUIPO European Observatory on Infringements of Intellectual Property Rights, has been developed in two phases: at the end of phase 1, in November 2020, EUIPO published the study "Automated Content Recognition: Existing technologies and their impact on IP"; on September 22, 2022 the EUIPO published a discussion paper entitled "Automated Content Recognition: IP Enforcement and management use cases".

Southern District of New York accessed May 2024[43] has ruled that the "MetaBirkin" NFTs can be displayed in a Spiritmuseum exhibition in Stockholm, provided that it is promintly highlighted and clearly visible to museum visitors that the NFT is in no way sponsored by and a Court[44] has deemed that it was originally intentionally designed to confuse the public.

NFT marketplaces make it clear that they do not ascertain the truthfulness and legitimacy of NFT certificates. It is regrettable that no copyright information on auctioned items is shown on listings in popular NFT marketplaces like OpenSea, self-defined peer-to-peer web3 service. On the contrary, OpenSea's terms and conditions, for example, state that: "... you bear responsibility for verifying the legitimacy, authenticity, and legality of NFTs that you purchase from third-party sellers".[45] On the other hand, the liability for the content offered to the public is fully attributed to the seller "You represent and warrant that you have, or have obtained, all rights, licenses, consents, permissions, power and/or authority necessary to grant the rights granted herein for any content that you create, submit, post, promote, or display on or through the Service. You represent and warrant that such content does not contain material subject to copyright, trademark, publicity rights, or other intellectual property rights, unless you have necessary permission or are otherwise legally entitled to post the material and to grant OpenSea the license described above, and that the content does not violate any laws."[46] This clauses echo clearly the intent of the marketplaces to act as hosting service provider.

As to copyright, it should be noted that art. 17 of the Directive on Copyright in the Digital Single Market concerns specifically Online Content Sharing Service Providers and does not apply to marketplaces, which means that rightholders must devote their effort to police the circulation of infringing NFTs, while the marketplaces themselves have very limited liability and no obligation to monitor their platform. The marketplace is supposed to carry out an intermediary activity as hosting service provider and is subject therefore to the rules applicable in the EU to e-commerce intermediaries,[47] but the Digital Services Act operates a distinction between hosting services and online platforms, and marketplaces will qualify as platforms. As to Marketplaces established in the US in October 2022, they remain subject to the

---

[43] Rosemary Faltenberg, *Judge Allows for 'MetaBirkin' NFTs to Be Exhibited in Stockholm Museum*, May 1, 2024, https://wwd.com/fashion-news/fashion-scoops/hermes-metabirkin-nfts-judge-lawsuit-stockholm-museum-1236350032/. accessed December 2024.

[44] June 23, 2023, *Hermès International, et al. v Rothschild, S.D.N.Y.*, No. 1:22-cv-00384, https://law.justia.com/cases/federal/district-courts/new-york/nysdce/1:2022cv00384/573363/140/. accessed December 2024.

[45] Section 5 – OpenSea Terms of Service, October 2022.

[46] Section 7 – OpenSea Terms of Service, October 2022.

[47] Directive 31/2000/EU (ECD), article 14. A Study of the European Commission, Directorate-General for Communications Networks, Content and Technology addresses the question of what are the kinds of services that could invoke Article 14 ECD and develops an updated typology of hosting intermediaries for policy experts. Hoboken, J., Quintais, J., Poort, J., et al., *Hosting intermediary services and illegal content online: an analysis of the scope of article 14 ECD in light of developments in the online service landscape: final report*, Publications Office, 2019, https://data.europa.eu/doi/10.2759/284542. accessed December 2024.

Digital Millennium Copyright Act of 1998, according to which platforms have no monitoring obligations and must cooperate in the enforcement of copyright limited to notice and take-down requests of the rightowners.

8 The Long and Winding Road to the Metaverse

Brands are today the most immediate "point of attachment" between NFTs and the future Metaverse that, however, is not in place but in prototypical fragments.

A precedent for the Metaverse could be the "Second Life" platform, operating since 2003. It has been launched as a graphic environment where the users would be acting through an Avatar; they could buy digital real estate and objects to use on the platform. Second Life offers some of the features that should become commonplace in the Metaverse, but lacks the strong interactivity and hyperrealistic features of the most sophisticated videogames. Its current version is associated to Tilia market-place,[48] specialized in "gaming, VR & virtual world Companies", where digital tokens (including branded accessories and so-called skins[49] for the personal Avatar) are traded and the relevant payments are regulated through the user's personal wallet.

As anticipated, the Metaverse may be where the NFTs enter the mass market definitively.

The most advanced experiments for what is supposed to be the Metaverse[50] are today visible in the videogame environment and many companies, not just Meta, are working on metaverse projects, confident that the necessary global open infrastructure will be ready and accessible in a foreseeable future.

Taking again the above mentioned Sorare as an example, currently the company operates as a walled garden and, despite its reference to Web3, its NFT collectibles can be traded on Sorare's own market place and cannot be transferred to a third party service or marketplace but obtaining Sorare's consent and paying the relevant gas fees. This kind of rules is in contradiction with the seamless freedom that virtual reality is supposed to allow to the Metaverse users.

Avatars equipped with crypto wallets and willing to spend cryptocurrency, are NFT's potential customers of signed products, to be used in the virtual world, where social media, content providers, e-commerce platforms coexist and interact at various levels, raising sensible issues in terms of personality rights, privacy and publicity.

---

[48] https://www.tilia.io/

[49] According to Wikipedia, the term skin is "used to refer to cosmetic options for a player's character and other in-game items, which can range from different color schemes, to more elaborate designs and costumes. Skins are often awarded as unlockable content for completing specific in-game goals or milestones." and are "deemed a virtual good as part of monetization strategies, especially within free-to-play games and those otherwise treated as a service."

[50] The perspectives of music in the Metaverse are analysed in the collaborative study *Meeting in the musical metaverse: Expectations vs. reality,* published in July 2022, accessible on https://www.waterandmusic.com/meeting-in-the-musical-metaverse/.

In order for the current virtual reality platforms to become the immersive mass experience promised by the Metaverse, there are several developments that are just starting and need time to mature[51]; a crucial one is that the various "metaverses" that we find in press articles today become not just interoperable but pacifically integrated, not least for commercial transactions and NFT trading. An adequately developed infrastructure, sufficient to process simultaneously trillions of data globally, is needed to ensure the user's seamless experience.

If Web 2.0 poses already tricky legal questions as to personal data processing and right exploitation, the promised global virtual reality universe may easily be a much worse nightmare for legal compliance and security.[52] Furthermore, image and publicity rights in the metaverse may play out just as they do in other scenarios, meaning the metaverse may be less of a free zone than one might think.

The Metaverse development will meet extremely complex technical, commercial and legal issues; among them not secondary are the issues relevant to User's data portability across platforms, meaning the ability for an individual to bring and utilize her data (including Avatar, wallet and NFT) from one metaverse environment into another, especially if – according to the promises – this ability will not require manual bridging or transferring of data from one platform format to another.

What is interesting here, however, is to see how the early experiences in NFTs may be transferred into the Metaverse. As IP is concerned, the transfer will present the some critical aspects as to right ownership and enforcement and will raise additional problems.

The major fashion brands and luxury companies are getting ready to transfer their history and identity across the metaverse, creating a continuity of reputation and social status across environments through the extension of their trademark registrations in virtual goods. In the case of brand protection there is also a component of consumer's protection that may help to prevent the parasitic exploitation or unfair competition.

---

[51] In more general terms, according to Anutosh Banerjee, Robert Byrne, Ian De Bode, and Matt Higginson, *Web 3 Beyond the Hype,* published 26 September 2021, accessible at https://www.mckinsey.com/industries/financial-services/our-insights/web3-beyond-the-hype.

"transaction cost is also a factor, making some of the technology protocols too expensive to use at present. For example, fees paid to complete and record a transaction on the Ethereum blockchain (so-called gas fees) could be prohibitive for users in large parts of the world, while cheaper and faster alternatives do not typically have the same level of resilience or operational uptime that is needed for mainstream adoption. Smart-contract resilience is unproven, with new exploits of weaknesses in new code or "logic hacks" happening weekly, and the accuracy of "oracles"—that is, information feeds that are used in decisioning by smart contracts—continues to be a work in progress. Web3 infrastructure needs to continue to evolve to become more robust—many critical services are often too centralized or too sensitive to failure. Finally, given their environmental footprint, proof-of-work blockchains could present specific adoption challenges for users, corporations, and regulators at a time of growing attention to environmental, social, and governance issues, although the footprint of proof-of-work blockchains is continuously evolving, and there is ongoing work to reduce it."

[52] Out of the scope of this analysis are patents, but it is worth nothing that Disney has obtained a patent in the U.S. for a "virtual-world simulator." Meta has also filed a large number of patent applications relating to the context of virtual worlds.

As to copyright, the closest comparable environment is Internet videogaming, nowadays used as a sort of proto-Metaverse to experiment Virtual Reality.

Videogame platforms, such as Twitch or Roblox, offer already opportunity for live concerts and live connections between the public and the artists. In all cases where virtual reality is an extension of experiences and activities involving copyright content in ways substantially similar to the real world, also the applicable rules (exclusive rights and acts that need the authorization of the rightholder, as well as licensing schemes and enforcement) should follow the existing consolidated schemes. For example there are no doubts that live concerts held on Roblox or Twitch (that have become a common experience during the pandemic) are covered by the exclusive right of communication to the public for authors and performers. In the case of performing artists, the Metaverse could become also an unexplored land where to defend their image and their publicity rights.

Waiting to see how the Metaverse will actually be, we can assume, based on the videogaming experiences we know, that the activities the Avatars carry out there should involve at least the communication and provision of rights where they concern IP-protected works and subject matters, meaning that an authorization or a license (and a remuneration) should be paid to the right owners; said protected works can range from visual art hanging on the wall of a virtual dining room, to music in background in a bar or in a virtual disco, to a drama performed in a virtual theatre, and so on.

As far as Metaverse activities replicate uses that are covered by exclusive rights in the real world, the copyright protection is applicable also in this future virtual universe, since an analogy with on demand services is more than likely. This observation can lead to two different conclusions: the legal framework for copyright remains valid, while some adjustments may be needed, at least concerning the enforcement means and sanctions The main liability for content appearing in the reality environment is on the persons acting there; in the previous example, the owner of the disco for the music performed there or the seller of the art hanging on the wall or the organizer of the virtual theatre show. It impossible, at the present stage, to say whether this transfer from physical to virtual reality is feasible or desirable. It may also happen that the transformation of the Internet into the Metaverse leads to a global market failure for the enforcement of exclusive rights and therefore impose a change of paradigm.

The exclusive rights, implying authorizations and negotiated fees, may need to be replaced by standardized practices based on the implementation of equitable remuneration (and maybe some forms of opting-out). If the Metaverse is really going to be an immersive fully comprehensive reality, a global copyright remuneration system might become, in the long run, a necessary part of the of the services offered by the companies managing the Metaverse.

It is even too easy to forecast that the problems due to the introduction of online content sharing services in the last two decades are going to multiply and amplify in the Metaverse, whichever decentralized form it will actually assume, especially when enforcement should involve multiple jurisdiction. It is also impossible to evaluate which solution may be advisable for copyright to survive in the virtual universe.

The crucial issue will be the liability regime of the platforms, be it in a conservative scenario of exclusive rights or in the change-of-paradigm of a global remuneration as a Metaverse service. In all cases the liability regime and the ID data management are and will be crucial; what happens with NFTs and with their marketplaces offers food thought to the IP world.

Bibliography

Accordi Rickards M, Romanini M, Malagò T, Bizzoco A (2022) L'industria culturale dei videogiochi, Fondazione Simbola https://www.symbola.net/approfondimento/lindustria-culturale-dei-videogiochi/

Cavani G (2022) Non fungible tokens (NFT): Quali interferenze con il diritto d'autore?, AIDA Annali Italiani del Diritto d'Autore. della Cultura e dello Spettacolo Giuffré:494–502

Cavani G, Ercolani S (2023) Mondi virtuali e sfide reali Proprietà intellettuale (PI) e metaverso. Riv Dirit Ind 3:154–193

Guadamuz A (2021) Non-fungible tokens (NFTs) and copyright, WIPO Magazine, December 2021

Fabiana DP, Andrea S (2025) Metaverso. Mercato e regole. 2025, Passigli Ed

EUIPO (2024) Impact of technology deep dive report ii, impact of the metaverse on infringement and enforcement of intellectual property, EUIPO. Luxembourg

EUIPO (2020) Automated content recognition: Existing technologies and their impact on IP, EUIPO. Luxembourg

European Commission (2020) Communication To The European Parliament, The Council, The European Economic And Social Committee And The Committee Of The Regions - Making the most of the EU's innovative potential An intellectual property action plan to support the EU's recovery and resilience, COM (2020) 760 final, 25.11.2020

European Union (2025) Outcome document - global multistakeholder high level conference on governance of web 4.0 and virtual worlds. https://digital-strategy.ec.europa.eu/en/policies/event-web-4-governance

Matthieu N, Laura A, Flavio DG et al (2021) Mapping the NFT revolution: market trends, trade networks, and visual features. Sci Rep 11:20902. https://doi.org/10.1038/s41598-021-00053-8

Numa N, Gustavo G, João T (2024) At the frontier of the metaverse: NFTs, artistic expression, and digital immersions. Metaverse 5(1):2449

Ramos A (2022) The metaverse, NFTs and IP rights: to regulate or not to regulate? WIPO Magazine, June 2022

Stephanie R, Costantino M (2023) NFTs: digital collectibles or IP investment opportunity? IAEL

Spolidoro MS (2022) Dal metaverso ad Acchiappacitrulli? Riflessioni in tema di NFT, AIDA. Annali Italiani Del Diritto d'Autore, della Cultura e dello Spettacolo:518–551

Westenfeld A (2022) The saga of the dune crypto bros and their very pricey mistake is at its end, 28 July 2022, https://www.esquire.com/entertainment/books/a38815538/dune-crypto-nft-sale-mistake-explained/. Accessed May 2024

Yun CO, Yun TS (2024) Expanding metaverse market: New opportunities and challenges for the content industry. Metaverse 5(2)

Zhang L (2024) Editorial: Navigating the convergence of AI and the Metaverse. Metaverse 5(2)

Contract Law

Smart Contracts, NFT Trading and Weaker Party Protection

Andrea Stazi

Abstract "Smart contracts" are characterised by the self-execution of contractual clauses without the need for human intervention, and generally excluding the possibility of interrupting such execution or modifying the content. Non-Fungible Tokens are digital assets that might signify ownership of other physical or digital assets. NFTs and related minting, selling and purchasing are publicly verifiable. They are available for trading and exchanging, are persistently stored and cannot be manipulated. The peculiarities of smart contracts and NFT trading give rise to interesting use cases and opportunities, but also to operational issues and legal challenges. Among them, the protection of weaker parties is particularly relevant.

1 "Smart Contracts" and Their Characteristics

"Smart contracts"[1] automate contractual relationship through the self-execution of the contractual clauses without the need for human intervention, and generally excluding the possibility of interrupting such execution or modifying the content, with the exception of the options of multi-signature or self-destruct.[2]

[1] Regarding the definition of "smart contracts", see also: Stazi (2021, p. 105 ff.); Zeno-Zencovich (2021); De Caria (2019); Herian (2018, p. 16 ff.); Cong and He (2018, p. 11). From the technical point of view, smart contracts are computer programs that run on distributed ledger technologies, first of all the blockchain. These technologies provide the ecosystem within which the idea of smart contracts proposed by Nick Szabo in the nineties of the last century can be realised, which at the time still seemed substantially utopian; see: Szabo (1994, 1996, 1997), who argued that the objectives of such contracts would be to fulfil contractual obligations such as payment terms, privileges, confidentiality and even enforcement, and to minimise both harmful and accidental exceptions and the need for trusted intermediaries.

[2] Multi-signature, or "multisig", verification technology allows you to stop running a smart contract until several parties have signed the transaction with their private keys. These can include not only the parts of the smart contract, but also an external third party, a so-called arbiter. See: Werbach

A. Stazi (✉)
San Raffaele Roma University, Rome, Italy
e-mail: andrea.stazi@uniroma5.it

F. Di Porto and O. Pollicino (eds.), *Law and Politics of Virtual Worlds*, Law, Governance and Technology Series 79, https://doi.org/10.1007/978-3-032-08541-2_11

In some cases, the smart contracts represent the implementation of a previous contractual agreement in the legal sense, the clauses of which are formalised in the computer code. So, the contracting parties have the advantage of structuring their relationships and performances in a more efficient and self-executing way, regardless of the ambiguity of natural language.[3]

In other cases, smart contracts introduce new coded relationships that are both defined and automatically applied by the computer code, but are not linked to any underlying contractual right or obligation.[4]

On the other hand, regardless of the technical necessity, there may be a legal need to draw up a smart contract in writing, in order to make its clauses legally binding and applicable at the judicial level.[5]

However, a smart contract is not always immutable. First, the blockchain could be "forked" by the majority of users. Second, the computer code of smart contracts can contain several functions that allow for a certain range of flexibility.[6]

Again, registering smart contracts on a blockchain platform usually comes at a cost.[7] This in fact excludes the provision of detailed and complex clauses in smart contracts, as vice versa happens in practice especially in common law but increasingly also at an international level.[8]

In a technical sense, smart contracts can be defined as computer protocols that execute themselves by applying the lines of the computer code for which they were programmed, stored on a distributed register.[9]

---

and Cornell (2017, p. 345). Furthermore, the code of most smart contracts contains a so-called "kill switch". Solidity, the language used to write smart contracts on the Ethereum blockchain, allows an operation called "self-destruction", which removes the smart contract code from the blockchain; see: Eenmaa-Dimitrieva and Schmidt-Kessen (2019, pp. 84–85).

[3] Thus, for example, a smart contract can be created as a mechanism for a crowdfunding campaign (see e.g.: https://dev.to/envoy_/create-a-crowdfund-smart-contract-using-solidity-3dkf). The creation of smart contract models, in practice, could lead to a reduction in the role of lawyers in the moment of contract formation, especially with respect to those that can be easily modelled; on this point; see: Corrales et al. (2019).

[4] In this regard, see among others: Chamber of Digital Commerce - Smart Contracts Alliance (2018) p. 10 ff.

[5] See: De Filippi and Wright (2015), p. 11, who found that, while at the beginning smart contracts were mainly developed to automatically execute derivatives, options, futures and swaps, later they began to be used to facilitate the sale of goods on the network between unrelated persons without the need for a centralised organisation. The Authors cite in this sense the example of OpenBazaar, an open source service aimed at creating a decentralised global market in which people can buy and sell products directly, without intermediation costs or centralised control (https://openbazaar.org).

[6] Like the multi-signature or self-destruct examples mentioned above, but also functions like "call", which accepts an arbitrary number of arguments of any type, "enums", a way to create a user-defined type, "self-destruct", and also variable functions that allow the smart contract to process external inputs. In this regard, see: Juels, Marino (2016).

[7] Named, for example, "gas" on the Ethereum platform; see: https://ethereum.stackexchange.com/questions/3/what-is-meant-by-the-term-gas.

[8] On this point, see: Jaccard (2017), p. 7.

[9] See: De Filippi and Wright (2018), p. 33 ff; Buterin (2013).

Eventually, if through them an economic function recognized by the legal system in which they are intended to carry out their effects is pursued, they allow the drafting and possible automation of the agreements between the parties - according to an "if/then" logic - as truly "contractual" in the legal sense.[10]

A smart contract program is executed by a network of so-called miners, who, once consensus has been reached on the outcome of the execution, update the status of the contract on the blockchain accordingly. In this way, users can send or receive money, data, etc. through a contract.[11]

Based on the capabilities of the blockchain, therefore, the smart contracts operate autonomously, in a transparent, anti-tampering and tendentially immutable way.[12]

Although most of the data comes from the blockchain or other databases connected to it, some smart contracts, for their execution, may have to acquire data from outside the blockchain. This creates the need to make use of reliable external sources, so-called oracles, which represent interfaces between contracts and the outside world.[13]

Reliable oracles that support and can satisfy a wide range of data requests are of paramount importance to many smart contracts.[14] On the other hand, this phenomenon requires the guarantee that the oracle is reliable and actually a third party, and that there is no interference or security threats during the acquisition of data from the same.[15]

2 Use Cases and Opportunities

The use cases of smart contracts are numerous. They can be used, at least in theory, in all cases in which economic activities are correlated to the internet and some events can be digitally verified.[16]

In addition to the financial and insurance sectors, where digital bargaining already plays a central role, the use of smart contracts is developing in sectors such as agri-food, energy, entertainment, etc.[17]

---

[10] See eg: Idelberger (2016). One may also see: Gambino and Stazi (2021).

[11] See: Jaccard (2017), p. 5 ff; Juels, Kosba, Shi (2016).

[12] In this regard, see: De Filippi and Wright (2018), p. 72, one may also see: Stazi (2021), p. 71.

[13] A case of smart contracts activated by external inputs is, for example, that of the insurance policies proposed by AXA and Etherisc, insurance companies which offer policies that compensate travellers who suffer flight delays or cancellations. Flight information is acquired automatically and in real time by an oracle company indicated in the contract and the compensation is paid automatically.

[14] In this sense, see: Sokolov (2018), p. 10.

[15] See, among others: Mik (2017), p. 292 ff.

[16] In this regard, see: Governatori et al. (2018), p. 377 ff.

[17] See: Chamber of Digital Commerce – Smart Contracts Alliance (2016); Unsworth (2019). One may also see: Stazi and Jovine (2022).

Contracts that concern access to digital content, and are therefore easily translatable into software, represent privileged use cases of smart contracts.[18] By virtue of the growing interconnection of devices, sensors, etc. through the Internet of Things, then, this phenomenon affects ever wider areas.[19]

Devices and other material properties can be registered on a blockchain and, using smart contracts, transformed into "smart properties", thus allowing the control of material properties on the network, even through other machines.

A blockchain can store the relationship between internet-enabled machines at any time and smart contracts can allocate the corresponding rights and obligations of connected devices.

Different relationships and credentials can also be encoded in the blockchain regarding certain cryptographically activated resources, such as key blocks or smartphones, to ensure that only certain subjects or nodes can have access to the functionality of the property.[20]

The above mentioned peculiarities of smart contracts may give the contracting parties several significant advantages over traditional contracts. The parties can rely on contractual promises that are stored in the smart contract, i.e. the transaction protocol automatically executed without recourse to judicial intervention, and do not have to trust the counterparty.

This allows them to take calculated risks, even in areas where the parties are not directly opposed to each other, but which are often characterised by anonymity and application risks, as is usually the case in electronic commerce and international contracts.[21]

Consumers/users, in particular, could benefit from these advantages in a relevant way, since they usually face difficulties and costs for which they neglect to assert their rights in court.[22]

Furthermore, smart contracts involve the possibility of reducing transaction costs, performing some functions currently performed by intermediaries such as eBay, Amazon, PayPal, etc.[23] The smart contracts allow the parties to incorporate the commercial practice in their agreement, bypassing the need for explicit but redundant negotiation.[24]

Automatic application or compensation has the potential to reduce the amount of disputes, increasing certainty and reducing performance monitoring costs.[25]

[18] This would allow the generalised implementation of a so-called metered internet, where stocks are tied to micro-payments through related smart contracts. Since cryptocurrencies and smart contracts greatly reduce transaction costs, in particular, they allow artists, musicians, authors, etc. to automatically collect royalties inherent to the copyrights on their works every time they are viewed or used. See: De Filippi and Wright (2015), p. 29 ff; Wallach (2014).

[19] In this regard see, among others: Wendehorst (2016).

[20] On this point, see again: De Filippi and Wright (2015), p. 14 ff.

[21] See: Ryan (2017).

[22] In this regard, see: Borgogno (2019a), p. 8 ff.

[23] See: Borgogno (2019b-2), p. 13 ff.; Sokolov (2018), p. 11; Mik (2017), p. 277.

[24] On this point, see: Sklaroff (2017), p. 282 ff.

[25] See: Werbach, Cornell (2017), p. 318 and 352 ff.

In general, therefore, smart contracts give rise to a further reduction of human intervention and formalisation of the contract.[26]

Compared to traditional contracts, again, smart contracts increase the speed with which contractual relationships can be executed. Because smart contracts are not dependent on paper and related procedural steps and can be performed in real time, they simultaneously enable cost savings and faster execution than paper contracts.[27]

Finally, smart contracts offer an alternative to one of the most characteristic aspects of contractual drafting: the intrinsic ambiguity of natural language,[28] with the relative flexibility in terms of contractual performance.[29]

The ambiguity and editorial shortcomings can also be used by the parties who intend to free themselves from contractual conditions that they no longer want to honour.[30] Compared to this phenomenon, smart contracts provide a different binding option by incorporating legal provisions into the computer code.[31]

3 Operational Issues and Legal Challenges

On the other hand, smart contracts also present a number of new issues and challenges for trade law and practice.

A first question that can arise is that of the identification of the other contracting party, when the blockchain allows anonymous, or rather pseudonymous transactions,[32] such as in the case in which transactions are registered by referring to an IP address or a cryptocurrency wallet.[33]

The codification of the clauses in computer language could lead to a limitation of the possible contents of the smart contracts, linked to the possibilities of automation of the contractual prose according to the if/then logic.[34]

Connected to this is the risk that the computer code, drawn up by IT technicians, incorrectly reports the provisions of the contractual agreement between the parties, or that it may operate differently from what was planned, with the related issue

[26] In this perspective, see: Savelyev (2017), p. 120 ff.

[27] In this regard, see: De Filippi and Wright (2015), p. 25.

[28] See, among others: Raskin (2017), p. 324; Farnsworth (1967).

[29] In this regard, see: Gergen (1992), p. 1006; Hadfield (1984).

[30] In this sense, see: Burnham et al. (2009).

[31] Thus: De Filippi and Wright (2015), p. 25.

[32] Pseudonymity means the possibility that, although a person is not identifiable with his real name, such identification can still take place through the acquisition of further information about her, such as a pseudonym, an IP address, a current account, etc.; on the subject, see: Article 29 Data Protection Working Party (2014), p. 20 ff.

[33] On this point, see: European Bank for Reconstruction and Development, Clifford Chance (2018), p. 22 ff.

[34] See: Cardozo Blockchain Project (2018), p. 365 ff.

of attributing liability. Furthermore, there is the risk of misunderstanding of smart contracts by the parties and the legal operators.[35]

In practice, the connection between the text in computer code and a contractual text drawn up in natural language is increasingly widespread. The texts may have the same content, so-called split contracting, or may be the specification and/or execution of the other, so-called hybrid agreement.[36]

From the point of view of execution, contrary to traditional contracts,[37] in which the parties can decide whether or not to fulfil their obligations, smart contract cannot be violated.[38]

In a system governed by self-imposed smart contracts and other technical agreements, there would be less need for judicial intervention, since the computer code through which the rules were defined is the same tool through which they are applied.[39]

In this perspective, another problematic issue concerns the need to intervene on a smart contract in the event that an injunction issued by the judicial authority must be executed.

In general, given the impossibility of interrupting the execution of a smart contract - excluding the above-mentioned exceptions-the realisation of such a result may take place in the hypothesis of using a private blockchain that provides mechanisms for blocking the execution under the responsibility of certain nodes.[40]

4 Protection of Weaker Parties

For the relationships between professionals and weaker contracting parties, smart contracts, on the one hand, have the potential to facilitate the protection of the latter, as they can automate it by eliminating the possibility for professionals to rely on their inertia and the relative failure to activate their rights.[41]

---

[35] Regarding these profiles, see: Giancaspro (2017), p. 830 ff; Mik (2017), p. 281 ff. One may also see: Stazi (2021), p. 75 ff.

[36] On this point, see: European Bank for Reconstruction and Development, Clifford Chance (2018), p. 17 ff; De Filippi and Wright (2018), p. 76 ff; Allen (2018).

[37] Beale et al. (2019), p. 3 ff.

[38] Unless of course the parties could terminate the contract if they decide they do not want to remain tied to it.

[39] From the merger of law and computer code it follows, therefore, that the only way to violate the law is to effectively break the code.

[40] On this point, see: Giuliano (2019).

[41] See: Borgogno (2019a), p. 892 ff, and ID. (2019–2), p. 8 ff., who notes that in this way consumers should not spend resources to ascertain whether they are entitled to compensation, or to incur often excessive expenses with respect to the injury suffered resulting from the dispute resolution procedure. This, highlighting how instead consumers so far have not adequately asserted the rights recognized by the legal systems, especially in the European context, because they are either unaware of it or have difficulty in enforcing it, also due to the amount of information they receive. So, even

On the other hand, smart contracts also pose relevant legal questions because of their rigidity and complexity.[42]

Although doubts have been expressed regarding the compatibility between the general structure of smart contracts and consumer protection,[43] the regulation in force to protect them must be deemed applicable, where the requirements for its applicability are met.[44]

Under EU contract law, in particular, standard terms are subject to restrictions which may also apply to smart contracts. Some scholars have argued that consumer legislation in principle applies to smart contracts, but have expressed doubts about the applicability of directive 93/13/EEC on Unfair Contract Terms, as it would imply an unfair contractual clause in text form that would not exist in the case of an algorithm.[45]

This objection is not acceptable because the Unfair Contract Terms Directive and subsequent EU rules to protect consumers require for their application a text document, and because it would be counterproductive if the protection afforded therein could easily be circumvented by converting unfair terms etc. in the computer code of a smart contract.[46]

Other scholars raised the question of the applicability of the same Unfair Terms Directive with reference to the fact that not the entire content of the smart contract could be pre-formulated but some terms could be negotiated individually.[47]

As is known, in contracts with consumers a clause is considered abusive if, despite the requirement of good faith, it causes a significant imbalance in the rights and obligations deriving from the contract to the detriment of the consumer.

However, the fact that certain aspects of a clause or a specific clause have been individually negotiated does not exclude the application of the regulation on unfair

---

if the standardised contracts between businesses and consumers usually contain many mandatory terms in favour of the latter, in practice they are often difficult to exercise given the costs and complexity or criticality of the remedies envisaged. The Author also appropriately specifies how, in order to assess when consumer rights can be adequately optimised through smart contracts, a preliminary assessment of the fulfilment of three conditions is required. First, only consumer rights that are not based on ambiguous or abstract terms can be translated into computer code. Second, they must be independent of relational expectations between the parties. Finally, they must be activated on a large scale and in an identical or at least standardised form. For an example that supplements these conditions, therefore, the Author cites the rights of passengers, also mentioning the need for coordination with external information sources. In a similar perspective, see also: Fairfield (2014), p. 36 ff. Regarding the issues of individual and collective consumer protection in Europe and the United States, see among others: Di Porto and Zuppetta (2020); Geradin (2015); Ben-Shahar and Schneider (2014), and IIDD (2011); Bar-Gill and Ben-Shahar (2013).

[42] In this regard, see: Durovic and Janssen (2019), p. 768 ff; De Filippi and Wright (2015), p. 26.

[43] In this perspective, see: Savelyev (2017), p. 20.

[44] Thus: Durovic and Janssen (2019), p. 769; see also: Buchleitner and Rabl (2017), p. 12 ff.

[45] In this regard, see: Söbbing (2018), p. 46.

[46] In this sense, see: Durovic and Janssen (2019), p. 769.

[47] See: Kaulartz and Heckmann (2016), p. 622, who also concludes for the applicability of the provisions of the Directive.

terms to the rest of the contract, if a global evaluation of the same indicates that it is still a pre-formulated standard contract.[48]

Such regulation must be deemed fully applicable also in the cases in which the clauses of the smart contracts act as standard contractual terms, or the contracts themselves have been unilaterally prepared by one of the contracting parties.

For both cases, the professional has the burden of proving that a standardised clause, or the entire contract prepared by her, have been the subject of individual negotiations with the consumer.[49]

Vice versa where, as it occurs frequently in commercial practice, the use of modules–possibly also prepared by platforms for smart contracts,[50] which have been assembled and customised according to their needs by the contracting parties themselves or by their respective consultants – can be deemed to be outside the scope of the aforementioned regulation on unfair terms.

The directive 2011/83/EU on consumer rights, then, provides for various rights and related information obligations,[51] for the exercise and respect of which, on the one hand, it is necessary to use a text written in natural language.[52]

On the other hand, it must be taken into account that, at least in current practice, a party for a multitude of contracts does usually not draw up contractual forms in advance, but they are prepared by the suppliers of platforms for smart contracts.

Therefore, the professional must verify that the information required by the consumer regulation is provided or adapt the smart contract and/or provide the missing information.[53]

If smart contracts are not individually negotiated, their clauses will be subject to the obligation of good faith and to the prohibition of giving rise to significant imbalances in the rights and obligations of the parties provided for in the Unfair Terms Directive.[54]

---

[48] See: Directive 93/13/EEC, art. 3, par. 1–2. In this regard, see: Möslein (2019), p. 15.

[49] This can be done by producing representative documents of the negotiation signed by them with electronic signatures, or even emails exchanged before the conclusion of the contract if their compliance with the facts represented is not denied. See again: Durovic, Janssen (2019), p. 769.

[50] In this perspective, one may see more specifically: Stazi (2021), p. 126 ff.

[51] Extended beyond contracts negotiated away from business premises and remotely. In this regard, see art. 5 ff. of Directive 2011/83/EU; see: Finocchiaro and Bomprezzi (2020), p. 124–7; Srivastava (2017); Helberger et al (2013).

[52] Through the so-called split contracting or hybrid agreement approaches mentioned above, or possibly through the provision *ad hoc* in natural language of the information required by the aforementioned regulation.

[53] On this point, see: Möslein (2019), p. 15.

[54] See: Kaulartz and Heckmann (2016), p. 622. Similar considerations can be made, *mutatis mutandis*, regarding the provisions of EU Regulation 2019/1150 on promoting fairness and transparency for business users of online intermediation services, with the related obligations placed on operators that provide them with transparency on distribution channels and related affiliate programs, as well as ownership, control of intellectual property rights and the parameters that determine positioning.

A provision of particular importance for smart contracts is the one in letter q) of the Annex of the Directive,[55] as, due to their self-executive nature, they could limit consumers' right to take actions or appeals or to exercise legal remedies.[56]

Similarly, depending on the specific method in which the computer code is drawn up, further hypotheses listed in the Annex itself may also be highlighted, including those of i) the exclusion or limitation of the consumer's legal rights against the professional or another party, ii) the provision of a definitive commitment of the consumer while the performance of the professional's services is subject to a condition that depends solely on her will, iii) the obligation of the consumer to fulfil her obligations even in the event of a non-fulfillment of the professional,[57] etc.

The provisions of art. 5 of the Unfair Terms Directive and art. 7–8 of the Consumer Rights Directive, then, require that the pre-formulated terms must always be drafted in simple and understandable language and the professional must provide the consumer with the mandatory information in an appropriate manner to the means of distance communication used.

If on the one hand the parties are in principle free to choose any language for the stipulation of the contract, including computer language, in the context of relations between professionals and consumers autonomy in this sense is in fact considerably limited by the aforementioned rules, as it is difficult to maintain that the computer code is a simple and understandable language for consumers.

This, therefore, implies an obligation for professionals to provide consumers with translations of the computer code that are clear and understandable for them, that is usually in natural language.[58]

With regard to the right of withdrawal, to be exercised within fourteen working days,[59] in the smart contract it can actually be implemented by programming the same so that its execution remains suspended within the first fourteen days of the conclusion of the contract.

At the end of this period, the smart contract will check whether or not the condition for exercising the withdrawal exists, and if not, it will give rise to automatic execution.

In this context, the withdrawal becomes a pre-set option within the smart contract, which is provided on the web interface through which the contract with the consumer is concluded and it takes place automatically and without the need for actions aimed at its exercise.[60]

Finally, recent additional regulations relevant for smart contracts at EU level are represented by the directives 2019/770 and 2019/771, respectively on contracts for

---

[55] Which, pursuant to art. 3, par. 3 of the Directive, contains an indicative and non-exhaustive list of clauses that can be declared unfair.

[56] In this sense, see again: Möslein (2019), p. 15.

[57] See: Annex to Directive 93/13/EEC, respectively lett. b), c), o).

[58] In this sense, see again: Durovic and Janssen (2019), p. 770; Söbbing (2018), p. 46; Kaulartz, Heckmann (2016), p. 622.

[59] Under art. 9 ff. of Directive 2011/83/EU.

[60] Therefore, it will no longer be necessary to send any registered letter, email or fax.

the supply of digital content and services and for the sale of goods in which such content is incorporated or interconnected and services.

Such Directives provide that the digital content or service or the supporting goods must correspond to the description, quantity and quality provided for in the contract, presenting the functionality, compatibility, interoperability and other characteristics provided for by the contract, and be adequate for the purposes for which similar digital content or services would normally be used.

This, taking into account any EU and national law and existing technical standards, or in the absence of them the industry specific codes of conduct applicable to the sector.[61]

These provisions, therefore, subject the terms of smart contracts to a correspondence check with respect to what was agreed and of adequacy to the use of the content or service provided, characteristics that must be evaluated, unlike the regulation on unfair terms, not only with respect to legal parameters but also to best market practices.[62]

Lastly, the "Omnibus" Directive 2019/2161 amended some of the Directives mentioned so far and introduced enhanced enforcement measures for consumer protection and greater transparency requirements, imposed further obligations for B2C contracts, and incorporated the definition of digital goods and services - including "free services" offered in exchange for personal data instead of money - in the relevant provisions of the above mentioned Directives.[63]

In the case of smart contracts, the increased transparency obligations for traders, including information obligations for online marketplaces regarding the identification of sellers and the algorithms used for ranking search results, could be difficult to meet in practice.

In fact, smart contracts can be concluded and executed directly between parties that may be unknown, without an intermediary platform, automatically entering into a contract and potentially executing it without even worrying about who the counterparty is.

5 Non-Fungible Tokens and Their Peculiarities

Non-fungible tokens, or NFTs, are digital assets that signify ownership of other digital or physical assets.

---

[61] See: Directive (EU) 2019/770, articles 7, lett. a) and art. 8, par. 1, lett. a); directive (EU) 2019/771, art. 6, lett. a) and art. 7, par. 1, lett. to).

[62] With respect to the 2019/770 and 2019/771 directives, see: Beale (2021), p. 96 ff; Möslein (2019), p. 15–16; Giliker (2017), p. 110 ff.

[63] Regarding which, see: Lodder and Morais Carvalho (2022), p. 537 ff; Cauffman (2019), p. 469 ff.

Through blockchain technology, NFTs record ownership and authenticity and enable the owner of the good or asset to transfer ownership to a buyer, while maintaining a record of the transfer on the blockchain.[64]

An NFT is, in fact, a unique cryptographic key contained within a digital token that verifies the corresponding content file as genuine and establishes a record of ownership as it is transferred on a blockchain, which allows it to be transferred without risk of fraud.[65]

By using NFTs, a creator can easily prove the existence and ownership of physical or digital assets such as for example food and drink, fashion, arts and collectibles, music, images, videos, event tickets, gaming, virtual real estate, etc.

The creator can trade NFTs through smart contracts, and also earn royalties each time of a successful trade on any NFT market or by peer-to-peer exchanging.[66]

Although NFTs are being impactful on the current decentralised markets and are bringing promising business opportunities, the NFT technologies are still in the very early stage, and their use and trade gives rise to some potential challenges which must be carefully tackled.[67]

To transfer NFTs, the owner must prove to be in possession of the corresponding private key and send the assets to another address with a correct digital signature. This simple operation is usually performed using a cryptocurrency wallet and is represented as sending a transaction through smart contracts. Typically, NFTs are traded on online NFT marketplaces for a fixed price or auctioned amount.[68]

Being created and traded on distributed ledgers, NFTs and related minting, selling and purchasing are publicly verifiable. They are available for trading and exchanging, are persistently stored and cannot be manipulated.[69]

---

[64] See, among others: US Congressional Research Service (2022), p. 2; Idelberger and Mezei (2022), p, 1 ff; Trevisi et al (2022), p. 332 ff; Chohan (2021); Chugani, Levine (2021).

[65] More specifically, NFTs are created through the "tokenization" process called minting. Through it, it is possible to convey in the blockchain not only the information or documentation relating to the asset or reference work, but also its fingerprint via the hash code.

[66] See: Wang, et al. (2021), p. 2, who highlights how full-history tradability, deep liquidity, and convenient interoperability enable NFTs to become a promising solution for the protection of intellectual property.

[67] See: Trevisi et al (2022), p. 335 ff; Wang et al (2021), p. 2–3, who mention some initial successful use cases: CryptoPunks, one of the first NFT on Ethereum, created more than 10,000 collectible punks. CryptoKitties hit the market in 2017 with the gamification of the breeding mechanics. Participants fiercely competed at high prices to auction the rare cats, and the highest price reached more than 999 ETH (about 3 M USD). Through NBA Top Shot, thousands of NBA fans from all over the world have collected over 7.6 million digital short videos of top shot moments. Bored Apes collection features profile pictures of cartoon apes that are generated by an algorithm. Owners of a Bored Ape NFT are granted access to a private online club, exclusive in-person events, and intellectual property rights for the image. One year after launch the sales of the Bored Ape Yacht Club NFT collection totaled over US$1 billion. Regarding how NFT trading challenge traditional marketing, see: Hofstetter et al (2022), p. 705 ff.

[68] An NFT marketplace is an online platform for the sale and exchange of NFTs, similar to cryptocurrency exchanges. See: US Congressional Research Service (2022), p. 7; Wang et al (2021), p. 4–5. Usually, these platforms also act as a secondary market; see: Trevisi et al (2022), p. 336.

[69] So-called tamper resistance. See: Wang et al (2021), p. 8–9.

6 NFT Trading and Weaker Party Protection

NFT trading can give rise to multiple risks. For example, scammers may create fake marketplace platforms to collect credit card and other financial information, or impersonate famous artists to sell NFTs.

When an NFT trading, via a blockchain-based smart contract, involve a business-to-consumer transaction,[70] the regulation of contractual guarantees and consumer protection is applicable.[71]

However, transactions via blockchain are facilitated through a cryptocurrency wallet address which may not be associated with the wallet owner's real identity. So in practice, as already highlighted above regarding smart contracts, it may not always be possible to determine whether someone is acting in a professional capacity.

On the other hand, anonymity can sometimes be overcome, and therefore also the question on whether you are dealing with a professional or a consumer, for example using verified accounts and verified cryptocurrency wallet addresses, or – specifically for NFTs–tracing back the underlying artwork to its individual physical owner or creator etc. through the references to the goods or artwork provided in the NFT, or looking at the quantity of NFT transactions tied to a particular wallet address.[72]

In the European Union, in particular, even before the contract is concluded, the professional seller must be transparent about the properties of NFT and the underlying goods. The Unfair Commercial Practices Directive 2005/29/EC, in fact, prohibits professionals from adopting commercial practices that distort the decision-making process of consumers.[73]

In the contractual relationship, the whole set of Directives mentioned above regarding smart contracts, that is the Unfair Terms Directive,[74] the Consumer Rights Directive with related information duties,[75] the Digital Content and Sale of Goods Directives,[76] and the Omnibus Directive,[77] are applicable to NFT trading between professionals and consumers.

Regarding the right of withdrawal, instead, NFT trading can be considered to fall within the exception from the right of withdrawal provided by art. 16(b) of the

[70] While it is irrelevant whether the NFT transfer is exclusively performed via a smart contract or whether a real-world contract is also concluded.

[71] See: US Congressional Research Service (2022), p. 12–13; Koolen (2022), p. 2 ff.

[72] In this regard, see: Koolen (2022), p. 2.

[73] According to the Directive, commercial practices are prohibited if they qualify as misleading or aggressive. In particular, misleading actions, such as misrepresenting the nature and the characteristics of the sold goods (art. 6) or misleading omissions, such as leaving out material information from the product description (art. 7) may render the contract null and void. In the United States, under Title 15, Section 45, of the U.S. Code, the Federal Trade Commission has authority over unfair or deceptive acts or practices, including deceptive advertisements.

[74] Directive 93/13/EEC.

[75] See: directive 2011/83/EU, art. 5–8.

[76] Directives (EU) 2019/770 and 2019/771.

[77] Directive (EU) 2019/2161.

Consumer Rights Directive, given that "the price is dependent on fluctuations in the financial market which cannot be controlled by the trader and which may occur within the withdrawal period".[78]

As per the conformity requirements provided by the Directives on Digital Content and Sale of Goods,[79] then, in case of complaint about an NFT[80] the professional seller will have to bring that and/or related content or goods into conformity, which for some hypotheses may be difficult to implement given the tendential immutability of the blockchain.

In the same perspective, the increased transparency obligations provided by the Omnibus Directive, including information obligations for online marketplaces regarding the identification of sellers and the algorithms used for ranking search results, could be difficult to meet in practice for NFT traders.

7 Conclusion

In conclusion, although the regulations for the protection of weaker parties in smart contracts and NFT trading are in principle applicable, in fact their implementation can prove to be complex, given the formalised and deterministic nature of the computer code and the anonymity and tendential immutability allowed by the blockchain.[81]

Even in a decentralised environment, then, together with the promotion of user consciousness and accountability of online intermediaries,[82] it seems appropriate to start wondering if some sort of responsibility to modulate smart contracting and NFT trading ex ante should be placed on smart contract development companies and NFT marketplaces.[83]

Are smart contract development companies and NFT marketplaces interfaces which provide the tools for trading through blockchain? Or do we need a "playing field" for web3 in line with the guarantees and protections currently provided for the web2 online platforms and marketplaces?

Smart contracts and NFTs are gaining more and more relevance, showing the many opportunities but also the limits of decentralisation.

---

[78] On this point, see again: Koolen (2022), p. 3.

[79] See: directive (EU) 2019/770, art. 7–8, and directive (EU) 2019/771, art. 6–7.

[80] Regarding which non-conformity could occur, for example, when NFTs include URLs which point towards altered or removed content, or NFTs include content that is not free from third-party IP rights, or the seller decreases the rarity of the NFT by flooding the market with other collectibles within the same NFT collection following the conclusion of the sale, or NFTs are linked to an obsolete standard that compromises its core features. In this regard, see again: Koolen (2022), p. 3.

[81] See: Cutts (2019); De Filippi and Wright (2015), p. 26. One may also see: Stazi (2021), p. 127 ff.

[82] Regarding the promotion of user e-consciousness and accountability of online intermediaries in emerging digital markets, see: Kim and Plotka (2022), p. 3 ff.

[83] In this perspective, regarding NFT trading, see: Koolen (2022), p. 4.

Thus, the time has come for thinking about legal solutions, which also consider the use of technology as an aid to legal guarantees and protections.

References

Allen JG (2018) Wrapped and stacked: 'Smart contracts' and the interaction of natural and formal languages. Eur Rev Contract Law 14:307–343

Article 29 data protection Oworking party (2014) Opinion 05/2014 on anonymisation techniques, WP 216. https://ec.europa.eu/justice/article-29/documentation/opinion-recommendation/index_en.htm. Last accessed January 30, 2025.

Bar-Gill O, Ben-Shahar O (2013) Regulatory techniques in consumer protection: A critique of European consumer contract law. Common Mark Law Rev 50:109–125

Beale H (2021) Digital content directive and rules for contracts on continuous supply. Jipitec – J Intellect Prop Inf Technol E-Commer Law 12:96–110

Beale H, Fauvarque-Cosson B, Rutgers J, Vogenauer S (2019) Cases, materials and text on contract law, 3rd edn. Hart, Oxford

Ben-Shahar O, Schneider CE (2011) The failure of mandated disclosure. Univ Pa Law Rev 159:647–749

Ben-Shahar O, Schneider CE (2014) More than you wanted to know. The failure of mandated disclosure. Princeton University Press, Princeton

Borgogno O (2019a) Smart contracts as the (new) Power of the Powerless? The stakes for consumers. Eur Rev Priv Law 26:885–902

Borgogno O (2019b-2) Usefulness and dangers of smart contracts in consumer and commercial transactions. In: Di Matteo LA, Cannarsa M, Poncibò C, The Cambridge handbook of smart contracts, blockchain technology and digital platforms. Cambridge University Press, Cambridge. https://papers.ssrn.com/sol3/papers.cfm?abstract_id=3350128

Buchleitner C, Rabl T (2017) Blockchain und smart contracts. Revolution oder alter Wein im digitalen Schlauch? Ecolex 2017:4–14

Burnham SJ et al (2009) Transactional skills training: contract drafting-beyond the basics. Trans: Tenn J Bus Law 2009:253–296

Zeno-Zencovich (2021) "Smart contracts", "granular norms" and non discrimination. In: Busch C, De Franceschi A (eds) Algorithmic regulation and personalized law. Beck, Munich, pp 264–278

Buterin V (2013) Ethereum white paper: A next-generation smart contract and decentralized application platform. https://ethereum.org/en/whitepaper. Last accessed January 30, 2025.

Cardozo Blockchain Project (2018) Research report #2: "Smart Contracts" & legal enforceability. https://larc.cardozo.yu.edu/blockchain-project-reports/2

Cauffman C (2019) New EU rules on business-to-consumer and platform-to-business relationships. Maastricht J Eur Comp Law 26:469–479

Chamber of Digital Commerce – Smart Contracts Alliance (2016) Smart contracts: 12 use cases for business & beyond a technology, legal & regulatory introduction. http://www.digitalchamber.org/smartcontracts.html. Last accessed January 30, 2025.

Chamber of Digital Commerce – Smart Contracts Alliance (2018) Smart contracts: is the law ready?. https://digitalchamber.s3.amazonaws.com/Smart-Contracts-Whitepaper-WEB.pdf. Last accessed January 30, 2025.

Chohan UW, (2021) Non-Fungible Tokens: Blockchains, Scarcity, and Value. Critical Blockchain Research Initiative (CBRI) Working Papers https://papers.ssrn.com/sol3/papers.cfm?abstract_id=3822743

Chugani S, Levine T (2021) The notorious NFT: Consumer protection issues raised by non-fungible tokens (NFTs). https://content.next.westlaw.com/practical-law/document/I0d808b9b97b311ebbea4f0dc9fb69570/The-Notorious-NFT-Consumer-Protection-Issues-Raised-by-NonFungible-Tokens-NFTs. Last accessed January 30, 2025.

Cong LW, He Z (2018) Blockchain disruption and smart contracts. NBER working papers 24399. https://papers.ssrn.com/sol3/papers.cfm?abstract_id=2985764
Corrales M, Fenwich M, Haapio H (eds) (2019) legal tech, smart contracts and blockchain. Perspectives in law, business and innovation. Springer, Berlin
Cutts T (2019) Smart contracts and consumers, LSE legal studies working paper No. 1/2019. https://papers.ssrn.com/sol3/papers.cfm?abstract_id=3354272
De Caria R (2019) The legal meaning of smart contracts. Eur Rev Priv Law 26:731–751
De Filippi P, Wright A (2015) Decentralized blockchain technology and the rise of lex cryptographia. https://papers.ssrn.com/sol3/papers.cfm?abstract_id=2580664. Last accessed January 30, 2025.
De Filippi P, Wright A (2018) Blockchain and the law: The rule of code. Harvard University Press, Cambridge
Di Porto F, Zuppetta M (2020) Co-regulating algorithmic disclosure for digital platforms. Polic Soc 40:1–22
Durovic M, Janssen A (2019) The formation of blockchain-based smart contracts in the light of contract law. Eur Rev Priv Law 6:753–771
Eenmaa-Dimitrieva H, Schmidt-Kessen MJ (2019) Creating markets in no-trust environments: The law and economics of smart contracts. Comput Law Secur Rev 35:69–88
European Bank For Reconstruction and Development, Clifford Chance (2018) Smart contracts: Legal framework and proposed guidelines for lawmakers. https://www.ebrd.com. Last accessed January 30, 2025.
Fairfield JAT (2014) Smart contracts, bitcoin bots and consumer protection. Wash Lee Law Rev Online 71:36–50
Farnsworth EA (1967) "Meaning" in the law of contracts. Yale Law J 76:939–965
Finocchiaro G, Bomprezzi C (2020) A legal analysis of the use of blockchain technology for the formation of smart legal contracts. MediaLaws:111–135
Gambino AM, Stazi A (2021) Contract automation from telematic agreements to smart contracts. Ital Law J 7:97–115
Geradin D (2015) Collective redress for antitrust damages in the European union: Is this a reality now? George Mason Law Rev 22:1079–1101
Gergen MP (1992) The use of open terms in contract. Columbia Law Rev 92:997–1081
Giancaspro M (2017) Is a 'smart contract' really a smart idea? Comput Law Secur Rev 33:825–835
Giliker P (2017) Regulating Contracts for the supply of digital content: The EU and UK response. In: Synodinou T et al (eds) EU internet law: Regulation and enforcement. Springer, Berlin, pp 101–124
Giuliano M (2019) The blockchain and smart contracts in the innovation of law in the third millennium. https://medium.com/studiogedg/blockchain-and-smart-contracts-in-the-innovation-of-law-in-the-third-millennium-conclusion-7d2face9e256. Last accessed January 30, 2025.
Governatori G, Idelberger F, Milosevic Z, Riveret R, Sartor G, Xu X (2018) On legal contracts, imperative and declarative smart contracts, and blockchain systems. Artif Intell Law 26:377–409
Hadfield GK (1984) Judicial Competence and the Interpretation of Incomplete Contracts. J Leg Stud 23:159–184
Helberger N et al (2013) Digital content contract for consumers. J Consum Policy 36:37–57
Herian R (2018) Legal recognition of blockchain registries and smart contracts. https://www.eublockchainforum.eu/knowledge. Last accessed January 30, 2025.
Hofstetter R et al (2022) Crypto-marketing: how non-fungible tokens (NFTs) challenge traditional marketing. Mark Lett 33:705–711
Idelberger F et al (2016) Evaluation of logic-based smart contracts for blockchain systems. In: Alferes JJ et al (eds) Rule technologies. research, tools, and applications. 10th international symposium ruleML, stony brook, Springer, Cham, NY, USA, p 167
Idelberger F, Mezei P (2022) Non-fungible tokens. Internet Policy Rev J Internet Regul 11:1–9
Jaccard GOB (2017) Smart contracts and the role of law. In: Jusletter IT. https://papers.ssrn.com/sol3/papers.cfm?abstract_id=3099885

Kaulartz M, Heckmann J (2016) Smart Contracts - Anwendung der Blockchain-Technologie. Comput Recht 32:618–624

Kim HE, Plotka MB (2022) Decentralisation and digital transformation: user e-consciousness and accountability of intermediators https://papers.ssrn.com/sol3/papers.cfm?abstract_id=4256243. Last accessed January 30, 2025.

Koolen C (2022) "Apes gone", but what about consumer protection? Applying EU consumer law to the transfer of NFTs. https://law.kuleuven.be/ccm/blog/?p=289. Last accessed January 30, 2025.

Lodder AR, Morais Carvalho J (2022) Online platforms: Towards an information tsunami with new requirements on moderation, ranking, and traceability. Eur Bus Law Rev 33:537–556

Mik E (2017) Smart contracts: Terminology, technical limitations and real world complexity. Law Innov Technol 9:269–300

Möslein F (2019) legal boundaries of blockchain technologies: Smart contracts as self-help? In: De Franceschi A et al (eds) Digital revolution - new challenges for law. Beck, Munich, pp 313–326

Raskin M (2017) The law and legality of smart contracts. Georget Law Technol Rev 1:305–341

Ryan P (2017) Smart contract relations in e-commerce: Legal implications of exchanges conducted on the blockchain. Technol Innov Manag Rev 7:14–21

Savelyev A (2017) Contract law 2.0: 'Smart' contracts as the beginning of the end of classic contract law. Inf Commun Technol Law 26:116–134

Sklaroff JM (2017) Smart contracts and the cost of inflexibility. Univ Pa Law Rev 166:263–304

Söbbing T (2018) Smart contracts und blockchain-technologie. IT-Rechts-Berater, pp 43–46

Sokolov M (2018) Smart legal contract as a future of contracts enforcement. https://papers.ssrn.com/sol3/papers.cfm?abstract_id=3208292. Last accessed January 30, 2025.

Srivastava A (2017) The new EU consumer rights directive: An empirical study on compliance issues by e-tailers. J Bus Law:282–309

Stazi A (2021) Smart contracts and comparative law - a western perspective. Springer, Berlin

Stazi A, Jovine R (2022) Food traceability in Europe, the us and China: Comparative law and technological regulation. BioLaw J:399–425

Szabo N (1994) Smart contracts. http://www.fon.hum.uva.nl/rob/Courses/InformationInSpeech/CDROM/Literature/LOTwinterschool2006/szabo.best.vwh.net/smart.contracts.html. Last accessed January 30, 2025.

Szabo N (1996) Smart contracts: Building blocks for digital markets. https://www.fon.hum.uva.nl/rob/Courses/InformationInSpeech/CDROM/Literature/LOTwinterschool2006/szabo.best.vwh.net/smart_contracts_2.html. Last accessed January 30, 2025.

Szabo N (1997) Formalizing and securing relationships on public networks. http://firstmonday.org/ojs/index.php/fm/article/view/548/469. Last accessed January 30, 2025.

Trevisi C, Moro Visconti R, Cesaretti A (2022) Non-fungible tokens (NFT): Business models, legal aspects, and market valuation. MediaLaws:332–356

Unsworth R (2019) Smart contract this! an assessment of the contractual landscape and the herculean challenges it currently presents for "self-executing" contracts. In: Corrales M, Fenwich M, Haapio H (eds) (2019) legal tech, smart contracts and blockchain. Perspectives in law, business and innovation. Springer, Berlin, pp 17–61

US Congressional Research Service (2022) Non-fungible tokens (NFTs). https://crsreports.congress.gov/product/pdf/R/R47189. Last accessed January 30, 2025.

Wallach DA (2014) Bitcoin for rockstars: How cryptocurrency can revolutionize the music industry. https://www.wired.com/2014/12/bitcoin-for-rockstars. Last accessed January 30, 2025.

Wang Q, Li R, Qi W, Chen S (2021) Non-fungible token (NFT): Overview, evaluation. Oppor Chall arXiv 2015:07447. Last accessed January 30, 2025.

Wendehorst C (2016) Consumer contracts and the internet of things. In: Schulze R, Staudenmayer D (eds) Digital revolution: challenges for contract law in practice. Hart-Nomos, Baden-Baden, pp 189–224

Werbach K, Cornell N (2017), Contracts Ex Machina, 67 Duke Law Journal, 313–382

Non-Fungible Tokens (NFTs), Smart Contracts and Contracts: The Need for Legal and Technology Assurances

Joshua Ellul and Ioannis Revolidis

Abstract Non-Fungible Tokens are often referred to as a technological manner to keep track of 'ownership' of various digital or physical assets. However, the reality is that, 'ownership' is defined by the law of the land, and NFTs are seen to be challenging what such ownership really means. NFTs, thus are, not only a complex technological 'ownership' solution but, a more complex techno-legal one that also raises many questions – especially in light of technological failure. Herein we pose that technology assurances should be considered to mitigate problems where possible, and other legal assurances can kick in where the technology cannot close such gaps.

In this paper we first introduce NFTs including their technical and legal complexities and their relation to smart and legal contracts. We thereafter provide an overview of the technology, an analysis of their potential as legal contracts and then make the case for the need for legal and technology assurances.

J. Ellul (✉) · I. Revolidis
Department of Computer Science, and Centre for DLT, University of Malta, Msida, Malta
e-mail: joshua.ellul@um.edu.mt

Department of Media, Communications and Technology Law, and Centre for DLT, University of Malta, Msida, Malta

I. Revolidis
e-mail: ioannis.revolidis@um.edu.mt

F. Di Porto and O. Pollicino (eds.), *Law and Politics of Virtual Worlds*, Law, Governance and Technology Series 79, https://doi.org/10.1007/978-3-032-08541-2_12

1 Introduction

Despite the fact that Non-Fungible Tokens (NFTs) have been dominating blockchain-related discussions,[1] especially during their heyday in 2022[2] issues related to NFT (smart) contracts have, for the most part, attracted little attention. Most materials on NFTs focus on issues of current immediate interest, such as rough descriptions of the technology, market capitalization, the volume of NFT projects, investment-related problems and legal questions,[3] intellectual property issues[4] and hacks. While the importance of such resources shall not be underestimated, as they provide a wealth of different informational pieces allowing for one to internalize the NFT mosaic, there is still room for a systematic techno-legal analysis.

From a technical stand-point, an NFT is often seen to be, discussed and treated as a digital token, an object one can hold within their digital wallet – yet in actual fact this view is just a representation that the various software, web sites and decentralised applications (dApps) provide to users. NFTs are ultimately smart contracts (or other forms of on-chain code), and given that they are smart contracts which could possibly imply a form of a legal contract, we should ask the question whether NFTs are contracts and the implications of them being so.

Legal certainty with respect to NFTs and associated privileges or rights is a grey area in most (if not all) jurisdictions – and some forms of certainty must be provided. To highlight the need for legal certainty, consider a deed-like NFT that according to the creator allows for the NFT holder to make claim to an associated physical art painting (potentially of high value). The NFT is sold to a purchaser under this premise, and the art piece is delivered to the purchaser as well. Later, the art piece is stolen from the purchaser – and somehow the purchaser becomes knowledgeable of who the thief is. If the purchaser were to take the thief to court to claim back the art piece, would the fact that the purchaser still holds the NFT provide any proof towards their claim of ownership of the physical art piece? Legal clarity with regards to what 'ownership' means with regards to NFTs and any associated digital or physical assets is crucial, especially in relation to the effect such legal ownership would have on contracts.

In this paper we provide an overview of various techno-legal components and perspectives of NFTs and contracts to allow the reader to understand the complexities involved. We then explore whether NFTs are contracts (and/or when they are contracts) and discuss legal implications and solutions towards closing techno-regulatory gaps between NFTs and contracts. We now follow with historical context, and technical background in Section 2, followed by analysis on the need for legal

[1] for the non-technical.

[2] See for example, the collection of articles and posts compiled by https://decrypt.co/news/nft, or https://www.coindesk.com/tag/nfts/, while for the reasons that might fuel the huge attention that NFTs have drawn see the analysis of Pinto-Gutierrez et al. (2022). Last Accessed: 29th November 2025.

[3] See for example Goforth (2021).

[4] See for example Guadamuz (2021) and Bodo et al. (2022).

assurances in Section 3 and technology assurances in Section 4, and then conclude in Section 5.

2 Background

We now provide background information and related work to allow the reader to appreciate the rest of this paper. We start by providing historical and economical context in Section 2.1. Then, in Section 2.2 we provide an overview and introduction of the technology underlying NFTs which, beyond being crucial to understand legal and regulatory implications, is often misunderstood or misrepresented.

2.1 A Brief Overview of the Recent NFT Sector

To better understand NFTs, it might be important to put them within a historic and economic context. While the technological and legal ramifications of NFTs are, undoubtedly, the most pressing issues that merit scientific analysis, it is the history and development of NFTs that allows a better conceptualization of the phenomenon. This conceptualization will in turn inform the analysis of the technical and legal issues related to NFTs.

In that regard, it must be stressed that NFTs represent a unique and individual chapter within the ecosystem of blockchain-based digital products that have entered the market and attracted considerable attention from enthusiasts and skeptics alike.

Cryptocurrencies (Bitcoin and altcoins) represent the first generation of blockchain-based assets. Based, mostly, on the original Bitcoin white paper published by the mysterious Satoshi Nakamoto,[5] who provided a solution to solve the 'double spend' problem in a decentralized architecture, which also minimises the potential for direct transaction recourse or intervention (given the lack of ability of centralised actors to intervene).[6] Nakamoto also expressed the ambition to create a form of digital currency that would set internet transactions free from traditional currencies or web2.0 monetisation models, which rely heavily on the processing of user personal information.[7] Cryptocurrencies have been followed by the development of tokens.

Unlike cryptocurrencies, which were originally designed in order to provide an alternative method of financing digital interactions, tokens are digital representations of rights. They are not meant to display the functional characteristics of money, but they serve as digital certificates that entitle their holder to some kind of privilege,

---

[5] Available Last Accessed: 29th November 2025 at https://bitcoin.org/bitcoin.pdf

[6] For a very illuminating explanation see Werbach (2018).

[7] For an interesting historical analysis of digital money, especially cryptocurrencies, their philosophy and the motivation of the groups involved in their creation see Grabowski (2019) pp. 19–35.

right, good, or service (or even a combination of them).[8] They come in a wide variety of shapes and forms because the potential rights they represent are equally diverse. The rights represented by tokens are usually fungible, namely, they refer to abstract privileges that can be exercised irrespective of the identity and other characteristics of the token and are not unique to the token. They also usually entitle their holder to exercise the rights they represent only against their original issuer, limiting, therefore, their circulation to the network of the issuer. In addition, tokens offer ample room for the development of new forms of financing blockchain-based projects, as quite quickly on in 2017, blockchain start-ups started issuing tokens via so-called initial coin offerings (ICOs), namely the blockchain equivalent to initial public offerings (IPOs).[9] Typically, blockchain start-ups issue tokens that represent a promise for future profit or some kind of good, service, or privilege, in order to attract investors. Acquiring capital at an early stage of the development of the project, against the promise (expressed in a token) to profit from the project or receive a privilege, good, or service at a future point has been a convenient way to finance cryptoprojects since 2017, albeit more recently ICOs have encountered problems and limitations of their own.[10]

As mentioned above, NFTs constitute a separate type of blockchain-based asset, one that could be clearly distinguished from cryptocurrencies and other tokens. It is, of course, true that even their name (Non-Fungible Tokens) reveals their relationship with other kinds of tokens. However, an intended functional characteristic of NFTs sets them apart from both cryptocurrencies and other categories of tokens: non-fungibility. Unlike other tokens, NFTs are not intended to display the functional characteristics of money and, therefore, should not be classified as cryptocurrencies. At the same time, unlike other tokens, NFTs do not constitute any kind of fungible units, as their existence is characterized by digital uniqueness. In fact, the basic premise of NFTs is that they can redefine the way we relate to digital assets, since they can, by virtue of the inherent values of blockchain technology, grant digital assets the traits of uniqueness and scarcity. In other words, while in other tokens the identity of the token is irrelevant to the exercise of the rights stemming from it, as they all fall within the same cluster of tokens and rights, NFTs are distinguished exactly because each individual token comes with inherent unique characteristics that set it apart from its counterparts.

NFTs have captivated the attention of crypto-enthusiasts and crypto-sceptics alike for the past two years. For crypto-enthusiasts NFTs represent a genuine paradigm change in the area of creating, transferring, and controlling digital assets and pave the way for the future of the internet.[11] For crypto-sceptics they are nothing but a new

[8] On tokens, see Treiblmaier (2021).

[9] On ICOs see Howell (2020).

[10] See, for example, the SEC v. LBRY litigation drama, https://www.sec.gov/litigation/litreleases/2022/lr25573.htm.

[11] See, for example, Tzanidis Th., NFT's: A digital revolution that embodies the Metaverse, https://www.linkedin.com/pulse/nfts-digital-revolution-embodies-metaverse-theofilos-tzanidis/. Last Accessed: 29th November 2025.

mania that is destined to fade away after causing considerable economic chaos.[12] The truth, as is maybe always the case when there are such polarised reactions vis-a-vis a new digital product, lies somewhere in the middle: NFTs represent an interesting alternative to the centralized architectures that are currently dominating the digital asset industry, albeit an alternative that comes with its own limitations, both from a legal and from a technological point of view. These limitations require some reflection, in order to cognitively map their potential and their risks and ponder on possible solutions.

2.2 What are NFTs, Really?

Whilst an NFT is often thought to be a digital image or some other form of digital collectible, really an NFT is nothing more than code – typically encoded within a smart contract, or some other unit of code written for a specific supported blockchain. Functionality of the NFT is fully-defined and based upon the logic written into the smart contract code that implements the respective NFT. As their name implies, NFT smart contracts should provide an implementation of a token that is non-fungible, which also must support the concept of possession and transfer.

For ease of demonstration, consider a digital collectible NFT. The fact that a particular NFT makes reference to a digital image or other digital object, does not mean that that digital object is the NFT. Typically the digital images and other collectibles exist independent of the NFT itself – and in some cases, the collectible can be created/recreated by following instructions (which may be encoded into a smart contract or elsewhere). Really, a typical digital collectible NFT is comprised of and facilitated through the following components:

1. **The NFT** which is uniquely identifiable and allows for ‘someone’ to ‘own’ it. The NFT is implemented in a smart contract which is stored and executed on a blockchain.
2. **Metadata** which defines the NFT’s features, attributes and any associations it has to other resources (such as an image). The metadata may be stored on either centralised or decentralised storage.
3. **The digital collectible/s** which may include image/s, video/s and/or other forms of data or media that are the underlying assets which may be stored on either centralised or decentralised storage – and may not necessarily be the same storage used for the metadata.
4. **The dApp** which, whilst is executed within a user’s browser, is retrieved (most typically) from a centralised server.

---

[12] See, for example, the substantiated criticism of Hawkings J., NFTs, an overblown speculative bubble inflated by pop culture and crypto mania, https://theconversation.com/nfts-an-overblown-speculative-bubble-inflated-by-pop-culture-and-crypto-mania-174462. Last Accessed: 29th November 2025.

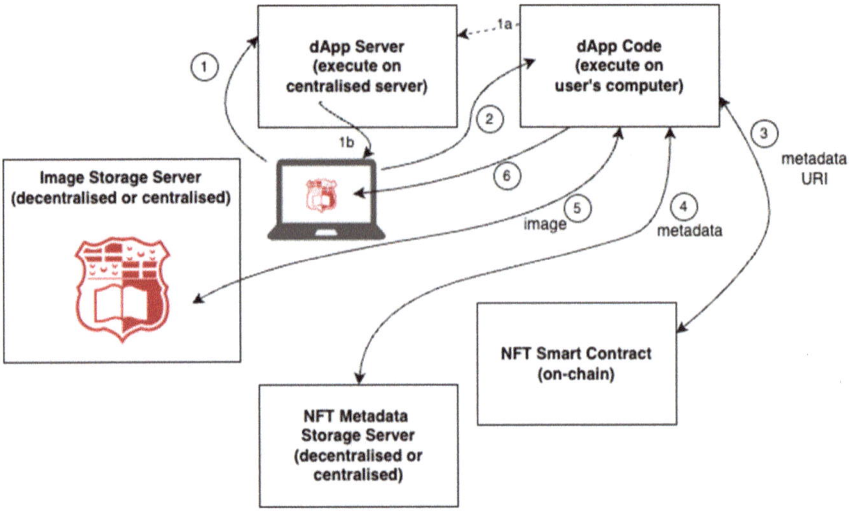

Fig. 1. An overview of various components making up an NFT dApp demonstrating the execution path towards viewing a referenced image

5. **The dApp Server** which: (i) provides a known URL that allows for users to interact with the dApp; and when requested (ii) sends the dApp code to the user's browser.

The components are depicted in Fig. 1, along with the steps required to be followed to access the digital collectible (from the software under-the-hood) which are further discussed below.

Walking through this typical digital collectable use-case, let's assume the dApp in question allows an NFT digital collectable 'owner' to view images associated with the NFTs that are associated to them. A user would first enter the website's URL that provides access to the dApp (Step 1). At this point, the website (dApp server) would package all the dApp code (Step 1a) and send the code back to the user's browser (Step 1b). The user's browser would then start executing the dApp's code received (Step 2). The dApp code would then instruct the browser to: (i) retrieve back from the smart contract URIs of metadata associated with NFTs owned by the user (Step 3); (ii) retrieve back the metadata files (for each NFT owned by the user) by querying the URIs retrieved (Step 4) which may be retrieved from either centralised or decentralised storage; (iii) retrieve back the images (for each NFT) which the metadata files make reference to (Step 5) which may be retrieved from either centralised or decentralised storage; and then finally (iv) display the images in the browser (Step 6).

There exists many different ways in which such tokens can be implemented and the above is but the typical way in which digital collectibles are typically implemented (just like any other type of token or smart contract). Whilst such flexibility when it comes to code implementation allows for creators to define their tokens and processes as required, different ways of implementing NFTs including different software interfaces allowing for the differing components to communicate according to need implies that all the different software platforms that would need to interact with such NFTs would need to be aware and allow for integration with the myriad of different possibilities of implementing code and interfacing the different components. As is done in other software (and non-software) processes, standardised interfaces and specifications are proposed and supported so as to minimise component incompatibilities and requirements to support different interfaces. The ERC-721[13] is the most popular NFT standard used for implementing NFTs in smart contracts on Ethereum[14] and other compatible blockchains. Similar and also completely different standards have emerged for other blockchains as well. It should be highlighted that, access to NFT functionality is defined in code, which may or may not follow a particular standard, which may or may not be supported by other software components – though most typically NFTs on specific platforms are tending towards the emergent standard for the platform.

From the breakdown of components provided it should be clear that, the NFT smart contract code implementation does not allow for users to interact with the 'NFT' in isolation and is dependent on other system components – of which some may be controlled or maintained by a centralized service providers. Indeed, another point requiring highlighting is that: whilst the NFT smart contract code and functionality is guaranteed to be accessible to the 'owner' since it is on-chain, other NFT features or rights may be provided through off-chain code for which there is no guarantee that such digital artefacts or functionality will be accessible (e.g. if a centralised storage server's storage is corrupted, or if for some reason a file was deleted from a decentralised storage service).

Indeed there are many other use-cases beyond art and collectibles for NFTs including for video games and the metaverse,[15] tickets,[16] healthcare[17] amongst others – yet the scope of this section was to help the reader appreciate the complexities of NFTs in general to appreciate arguments put forward in the following sections.

3 NFTs and Contract Law: The Need for Legal Assurances

NFTs are market and technology creatures. Nevertheless, the market and technology forces (most importantly blockchain technologies) behind NFTs do not invalidate a legal analysis. On the contrary. NFTs do not exist outside or independently of the law. Exactly because they try to promote a new philosophy as regards digital assets, they need concrete legal assurances which will reinforce stakeholder trust. In this section,

[13] https://eips.ethereum.org/EIPS/eip-721. Last Accessed: 29th November 2025.

[14] https://ethereum.org

[15] See for example Gonserkewitz et al. (2022).

[16] See for example Valeonti et al. (2021).

[17] See for example Musamih et al. (2022).

we will explore NFT legal assurances from the area of contract law. Section 3.1 will explain why NFT (smart) contracts play a pivotal role in the entire NFT ecosystem. Section 3.2 will introduce some basic parameters of the relationship between NFT (smart) contracts and contract law and Section 3.3 will explore how EU contract law may accommodate NFT (smart) contracts. Section 3.4 will conclude with final thoughts on legal assurances.

3.1 Why (smart) NFT Contracts Matter

NFTs have been developed impulsively by technological and market forces that have not necessarily taken into account existing regulatory choices.[18] This should not come as a surprise, nor should it necessarily create skepticism toward NFTs. Technological and market progress come, quite often, without regard for pre-existing rules and business models, or sometimes they even occur despite those. Disruption, in other words, goes beyond existing architectures. That does not necessarily make it unwelcome, even if disruptive solutions might not, especially at their very early stages, fit perfectly within the incumbent technological, market, and legal institutions.

NFTs are undeniably a disruptive business model. They aim to introduce a new ethos in our relationship with digital assets.[19] This relationship is currently characterized by the access model. In a nutshell, via a combination of technological, legal, and market choices, individual internet users are not currently allowed to exert control over digital assets. On the contrary, digital assets are controlled by powerful centralized intermediaries that seemingly provide unlimited access to them. This arrangement comes with a number of advantages.[20] For example, it provides intellectual property holders with security as regards the exploitation of their IP portfolios. Indeed, digital asset and content services provided by centralized intermediaries come with several digital rights management safeguards that severely discourage the uncontrollable dissemination of the protected asset. In addition, individual users enjoy a high level of convenience, as they don't have to worry about the storage, availability, functionality, and accessibility of the digital assets since all these activities are undertaken by the platform. On the other hand, the current digital asset arrangement, by virtue of which users give up control of their assets to centralized intermediaries, comes with important drawbacks.[21] Centralized intermediaries have obtained a disproportionately high influence over the entire operation of digital activities. In addition, the ultimate dependence of users on centralized intermediaries leaves them completely powerless and exposed to all kinds of misuse and foul play on the end of

[18] For a similar opinion in that regard see Cornelius (2021).

[19] See Fortnow and Terry (2021) p. 47–57.

[20] For a very positive appraisal of the access model see Rifkin (2001) p. 81–124.

[21] For a very critical account of the existing access model see Perzanowski and Schultz (2016) p. 151–166.

intermediaries, as, in reality, users are restricted to a tentative access right that can be taken away at any moment.

It is exactly in this background that NFTs try to introduce a different level of interaction with digital assets. Like the blockchain technology that lies in their background, NFTs aim to empower the individual user, by affording higher levels of control over digital assets. We have provided a technological overview of NFTs in the previous section, and, therefore, we refer there for the details. The real takeaway of this section is that, unlike existing centralized architectures, NFTs come with the ambition to do away with centralized intermediaries and minimize their influence over the process of creating, disseminating, and enjoying digital assets. To achieve this, NFTs enable the exercise of rights over a digital asset via the NFT token. As we have also highlighted in the previous section, the NFT is completely independent of any underlying digital assets, even though the two may share a certain kind of association between them. This means that whether the user is entitled to exercise any power over an underlying digital asset does not depend on the ecosystem or the decision-making power of a centralized service provider, but, predominantly, by exerting control over the independent token, with which the underlying asset is associated. It is, in other words, the independent record-keeping function of the blockchain that establishes and verifies the right of the user to exercise powers over the underlying asset and not an intermediary service provider that retains exclusive control over it. At the same time, the individual user holding the NFT token is also entitled to decide whether to transfer the token to somebody else, again without any necessity of a centralized platform that would authorize or perform such an action.

The fact that NFTs have been developed despite pre-existing legal norms or market arrangements, increases the importance of contract law. In order to achieve their desired outcome, namely independent control over digital assets without the critical involvement of centralized intermediaries, NFTs employ a network of (smart) contractual arrangements between a multitude of stakeholders such as blockchain infrastructure participants (e.g. miners, nodes), creators of NFTs, dApp providers, NFT platforms and blockchain users interested to acquire NFTs.

In addition, the observation that NFTs are based on a (smart) contractual architecture rather than statutory legal norms, confirms the assumption that the success of the NFT business model depends more on the will of the blockchain communities (e.g. how many and which blockchain platforms, users or stakeholders will honour the (smart) contractual arrangement supporting the NFT ecosystem) and less on legal concepts such as "ownership'" or "property" (it is a different question whether this is an ideal arrangement). Because they lack, at the moment, institutional and systematic regulation as regards their legal nature and legal effects, NFTs do not create any rights that can be exercised against everybody, that is to say, rights with an *erga omnes* effect. They are rather supported by a network of individual (smart) contractual arrangements that are, first and foremost, binding for the parties involved in them. Whether such individual (smart) contractual arrangements will obtain any meaning for third parties, is a matter that depends on the willingness of such third parties to respect any NFT-related claims presented to them. Simply put, NFT (smart) contracts are the building block of a new (digital) social contract as regards our relationship with digital assets. Nonetheless, the individual NFT (smart) contractual arrangements are still in need of legal assurances and default contract law rules. In fact, the exact nature of rights and obligations stemming from the NFT (smart) contractual arrangements, as well as the extent to which involved parties can be forced to respect the NFT (smart) contractual architecture (especially in view of the fact that the code can fail in many different ways) heavily depend upon default contract law rules.[22] It is the main subject of the next section to explore the relationship between existing EU contract law rules and individual (smart) contractual NFT arrangements.

3.2 NFT smart Contracts: Some Important Preliminary Observations

It is important to note at the outset that NFT smart contractual arrangements are, by definition, international in their nature. Indeed, the majority (if not all) of the NFT stakeholders will be domiciled or established in different countries. This observation reveals two important parameters of the analysis: (i) private international law is of critical importance; and (ii) the potential involvement of different applicable contract laws might lead to legal discrepancies, as different national contract laws might react differently to the (smart) contractual arrangements of each individual NFT architecture.

As regards the first parameter, namely the importance of private international law, it needs to be stressed that the technological arrangements achieved within blockchain ecosystems do not render the quest for the law applicable meaningless. More precisely, claims about some kind of *"alegality"* of blockchain-based products[23] and about an absolute primacy of private contractual arrangements vis-a-vis pre-existing contract law rules[24] must be dismissed as rather inaccurate, since the interrelation of (contract) law and NFTs is much more complicated and, most importantly, it is not necessarily an antagonistic one.[25] NFT (smart) contractual arrangements do not exist independently from applicable contract law regulations, nor can the code replace the necessity for recourse to legal provisions in order to deal with gaps in the deployment of NFT relationships, problems of NFT (smart) contract interpretation, or ambiguities as regards the exact width, depth, and meaning of the assigned rights.

In that sense, the identification of the applicable contract law to NFTs is not an unnecessary mental exercise, nor should it be substituted by mere reference to the code of the smart contract ecosystem that powers the NFT architecture. Private law-making and private justice need not, in other words, replace basic statutory choices, nor would something like that be desirable: notions such as that of fairness, good

---

[22] On the value of default legal rules compare Kaal (2021) p. 16–18.

[23] As advertised by De Filippi et al. (2022).

[24] In that spirit Becker (2022).

[25] For a similar approach Herian (2018) p. 237. In the same spirit, Schrepel (2021) p. 14–16.

faith, protection of the will of the parties, abuse resistance, protection of the socioeconomically weaker party (to name but a few widely accepted contract law principles), are not the shackles that enslave private ingenuity. They are rather basic guarantees that provide the necessary level playing field within which NFT stakeholders can legitimately pursue their individual rights and interests.

In that spirit, one might claim that EU Private International Law is flexible enough in order to win the hearts and minds of NFT stakeholders. If, for example, one looks at the basic rule of art. 3 of the Rome I Regulation, the designation of the law applicable is primarily left to the parties. If freedom is what NFT stakeholders are looking for, then art. 3 is offering them a strong guarantee that their contractual freedom will be expressed within a legal framework of their choice. In addition, in cases where NFT stakeholders will not express a clear choice of applicable law, the default choice of law rules provided in art. 4 of the Rome I Regulation could be interpreted in a way that would accommodate the particular characteristics of NFT smart contracts. It is, of course, true that this might not always be an easy task. But the Rome I Regulation has already been challenged by digital contract applications before and has survived the test of time and change.[26] One could, with some degree of probability, support the same for smart NFT contracts.[27]

As regards the second parameter, namely the fact that smart NFT contracts might be regulated by different applicable laws, it must be noted that the legal character of smart contracts has not been substantially challenged in different legal traditions,[28] so long as smart contracts *"create, embody or execute contractual rights and obligations"*.[29] The fact that NFT smart contracts might express the will of the parties in the form of code or the fact that NFT smart contracts might reinforce, again by employing code, the execution of NFT stakeholder rights and obligations, shall not necessarily put into question the existence of a legally binding agreement between the different transacting stakeholders.[30] In fact, EU Law might even provide strong arguments that support this assumption. According to art. 9 of the Electronic Commerce Directive: "*Member States shall ensure that their legal system allows contracts to be concluded by electronic means. Member States shall in particular ensure that the legal requirements applicable to the contractual process neither create obstacles for the use of electronic contracts nor result in such contracts being deprived of*

[26] The CJEU, for example, has been able to translate the mandates of the Rome I Regulation in digital commercial transactions as evidenced in Case C-191/15 Verein für Konsumenteninformation v Amazon EU Sàrl [2016] ECLI:EU:C:2016:612.

[27] See for a similar approach Rühl G., The Law Applicable to Smart Contracts, or Much Ado About Nothing?, https://blogs.law.ox.ac.uk/business-law-blog/blog/2019/01/law-applicable-smart-contracts-or-much-ado-about-nothing

[28] See, for example, as regards UK law Durovic M., Janssen A., Formation of Smart Contracts under Contract Law, in Di Matteo L., Cannarsa M., Poncibó C.(eds.), Smart Contracts, Blockchain Technology and Digital Platforms, 2020, p. 61, esp. p. 66–72, while for German law see Möslein Fl., Rechtsgeschäftslehre und Smart Contracts in Braegelmann T., Kaulartz M.(eds.), Rechtshandbuch Smart Contracts, 2019, p. 181–207.

[29] As neatly put by Mik (2019) p. 7.

[30] See in the same spirit Werbach and Cornell (2017) esp. p. 338–343.

legal effectiveness and validity on account of their having been made by electronic means". This provision could also be applied to smart contracts, as they also constitute electronic contracts. In that sense, the use of pure code in order to express the will of the parties or guarantee the enforcement of their obligations shall not become an excuse for skepticism or discrimination vis-a-vis NFT smart contracts, as art. 9 of the Electronic Commerce Directive guarantees full legal parity between electronic and non-electronic contracts.

The fact that the application of different contract laws might result in different solutions as regards issues related to NFT smart contractual arrangements could be registered as a problem of legal certainty and it might even turn out to be one. Indeed, different contract laws might answer certain fundamental questions such as the conclusion or the validity of a smart NFT contract, the delivery of party obligations, and remedies against non-compliance in somewhat different ways. Such differences must be carefully considered by contracting NFT parties before entering such contracts. Nevertheless, such national contract law discrepancies shall not be exaggerated. On the one hand, NFT stakeholders can minimize the uncertainty as regards the law applicable, by making an express choice of law.[31] On the other hand, even if NFT stakeholders do not explicitly choose a governing law, it is important to note that national contract laws have undergone various processes of international and regional harmonisation. These harmonisation efforts can provide a solid foundation for the analysis of cases involving digital assets.[32] In that sense, while the application of different national contract laws comes with a certain degree of uncertainty, such uncertainty could be mitigated.

3.3 Smart NFT Contracts and EU Contract Law

As explained in the previous subsections, contract law is an important instrument for the realization of the ambition of NFT projects, namely the creation of a more decentralized regime as regards digital assets. Contract law can offer an extra layer of security and certainty as regards the rights and obligations of the involved stakeholders, fill in the gaps of any unregulated contractual issues between the parties (as the smart contract code might not cover any eventuality), and, generally, provide a framework of interpretation for the entire relationship. For this to happen, nonetheless, one will have to identify the contractual nature and perform a legal characterization of the individual (smart) contracts.

---

[31] In fact, some NFT stakeholders are already doing so. See, for example, clause number 17 in the terms and conditions of the OpenSea NFT platform https://opensea.io/tos. Last Accessed: 29th November 2025.

[32] See, for example, Osbourne v Persons Unknown,[2023] EWHC 39 (KB) from England, or anesh s/o Rajkumar v Unknown Person("CHEFPIERRE") [2022] SGHC 264 from Singapore. Such decisions demonstrate that accommodating digital assets, particularly NFTs, within civil law might be challenging, but it is not impossible.

In order to conceptualize the contractual relationships developed within an NFT ecosystem, one will have to identify the different stakeholders and the different relationships that develop between them. NFTs are complex contractual arrangements between different stakeholders that do not necessarily directly enter contractual relationships with one another. To achieve the intended goal, namely the identification of the legal nature of NFT smart contract arrangements under EU law, it might be meaningful to separate the life cycle of an NFT into different stages and, subsequently, to analyze the different relationships developed during each individual stage. For the sake of the current analysis, we will split the life cycle of an NFT into three different stages: (i) minting; (ii) placing into the market; and (iii) peer-to-peer transfers. We will subsequently explore the development of (smart) contractual relationships within each individual stage.

3.3.1 Minting an NFT. Relationships and contracts

The very first activity in the life cycle of an NFT is that of the minting process. Simply put the minting process results in the creation of the NFT digital certificate that tokenizes the existence of somebody's right to exercise a certain degree of control over an underlying digital asset (the blockchain offers no legal guarantees, nonetheless, that such a right exists. It merely documents the claim of a person that they do have such a right). During this minting process relationships develop between the NFT creator (i.e. the person that mints the NFT for the first time), a (most usually) centralized platform that supports the minting process, and the blockchain ecosystem.

NFTs can be minted in different blockchains: Ethereum, Polygon, and Solana are just some of the most popular blockchains for the creation and deployment of NFTs. Whether the NFT certificate will be associated with an underlying asset that is stored "on-chain" or "off-chain" depends on the will of the creator – though typically such underlying assets are not stored on-chain due to storage limitations and associated costs. Some NFT projects prefer to store both the NFT certificate and the underlying asset "on-chain", while other NFT projects prefer "off-chain" decentralized storage for the underlying asset (such as IPFS)[33] or even "off-chain" centralized storage.[34]

The different stakeholders involved in the minting process fulfill different roles. For its part, the NFT creator is the one that kickstarts the minting process, by making use of the minting tools of the dApp provider and by setting in motion the immutable logging of the NFT certificate on the blockchain. The dApp provider, which is usually a centralized entity completely independent from the blockchain ecosystem, provides the necessary tools that enable the minting of the NFT. Typical marketplace platforms do so, of course, against remuneration provided by the NFT creator. The blockchain ecosystem for its part documents the genesis and existence of the NFT certificate

[33] https://www.nfi.edu/bored-ape-nft/. Last Accessed: 29th November 2025.

[34] https://blog.chromia.com/chromia-fixes-this-centralized-nft-metadata-and-images/. Last Accessed: 29th November 2025.

and also guarantees the monitoring and recording of any subsequent transaction on this NFT.

There are, therefore, at least two different sets of relationships during the minting process: (i) the relationship between the NFT creator and the dApp provider offering the minting tools; and (ii) the relationship between the NFT creator and the blockchain ecosystem. For the purposes of the current analysis, we will focus on the relationship between the NFT creator and the blockchain ecosystem where the NFT is created.

Minting an NFT means that a blockchain will have to register the genesis of the NFT on the digital ledger. From that point on, the blockchain ecosystem will associate the NFT creator with an underlying asset by virtue of holding the NFT and will also guarantee the ability of the creator to end this association by transferring the NFT certificate to somebody else. In reality, when the minting process is completed, the blockchain ecosystem undertakes, against remuneration paid by the creator of the NFT certificate usually in the form of the so-called "gas fees", the obligation to guarantee that the original data recorded on the blockchain via the minting process will not be susceptible to changes and also that the code included in the smart contract of the NFT will be executed as programmed. The code of the NFT usually includes two important elements: (i) the association of the NFT creator with an underlying asset; and (ii) the ability of the NFT creator to transfer the NFT certificate to another user. Translated in transactional terms, the above means that the blockchain ecosystem will uptake the NFT certificate in its public ledger, it will guarantee the execution of the NFT code as programmed by the creator, and ensure the immutability of the arrangement. In other words, when the NFT creator mints an NFT, the blockchain ecosystem (where the NFT is minted) will undertake the responsibility to publicly associate the creator with an underlying asset in an immutable manner and will also guarantee that the creator can end this association by transferring the certificate to another user, who will hence be associated with the asset instead.

It is important to be stressed that the right of the NFT creator (or any subsequent holder) to be publicly associated with an underlying digital asset is a contractual claim that can be exercised against the blockchain ecosystem. Third parties do not have any obligation to respect this association. It must also be stressed that the blockchain ecosystem cannot provide any guarantee as regards the correctness of the information it records about the NFT, for example, it cannot confirm whether the creator of the NFT is indeed entitled (from a legal point of view) to be associated with the underlying asset or whether they have the authority, from a legal point of view, to transfer this association to somebody else.

If one were to summarize the transaction between the creator of the NFT and the blockchain ecosystem during the minting stage, one would note that, in essence, the blockchain ecosystem assumes, against remuneration paid by the NFT creator, the obligation to perform certain activities (registering the NFT certificate on their ledger, testifying to the association of the holder of the NFT certificate with an underlying asset, executing the NFT smart contract as programmed, providing immutability to the NFT arrangement). In that sense, it might not be untenable to suggest that the legal relationship between the NFT creator and the blockchain ecosystem is a contract for the provision of services pursuant to relevant CJEU case law.[35]

3.3.2 Putting an NFT into the Market. Relationships and Contracts

The process of putting an NFT into the market is usually intermediated by centralized NFT marketplaces. OpenSea[36] is one of the most famous of them, but there are several others.[37]

NFT marketplaces create individual and independent relationships with the NFT creators and the persons interested to acquire NFTs.

As regards the NFT creators, NFT marketplaces list their NFTs, help them promote them and they, generally, aim to attract the interest of third parties. NFT Marketplaces usually deploy smart contracts to perform their services, apply pre-defined terms and conditions[38] and require the creators to abide by a set of rules in order to allow them to list NFTs on their digital premises. In return, creators pay fees during the minting process, maintenance fees for the period of the listing of their artwork, and also a fixed commission fee for every NFT they sell via the marketplace. The functional characteristics of this relationship will probably again trigger the application of rules on the provision of services, as NFT marketplaces carry out marketing activities against remuneration.

The relationship between NFT marketplaces and persons interested to acquire NFTs is also displaying characteristics of a contract for the provision of services. Indeed, the NFT marketplace allows users to identify the NFTs of their liking and also offers them a user interface (including smart contracts) to acquire them. While persons interested to acquire NFTs do not appear to be paying any fees directly to the marketplace, marketplaces collect and process user personal data and also retain the right to share it with third parties.[39] This arrangement is reminiscent of the typical web2.0 personal data monetization model. In that sense, even though it appears as if there is no direct remuneration, one could, with some degree of certainty, assume that NFT marketplaces monetize the personal data collected by interested NFT enthusiasts and, therefore, they receive remuneration for their services in that form. In addition, one should note that persons interested to acquire NFTs would usually do so for reasons that are outside their trade or profession. In that case, the EU consumer acquis will definitely come into play and NFT marketplaces will have to comply

[35] See most prominently the decision of the CJEU in C-533/2007, Falco Privatstiftung, Thomas Rabitsch v Gisela Weller-Lindhorst, ECLI:EU:C:2009: 257, par. 29.

[36] https://opensea.io/. Last Accessed: 29th November 2025.

[37] Such as Rarible, https://rarible.com/, Super Rare, https://superrare.com/, Foundation, https://foundation.app/. Last Accessed: 29th November 2025.

[38] See, for example, the publisher terms of Nifty Gateway, https://www.niftygateway.com/termsofuse/. Last Accessed: 29th November 2025.

[39] See, for example, the privacy policy of OpenSea https://opensea.io/privacy, or the privacy policy of Nifty Gateway, https://www.niftygateway.com/privacypolicy. Last Accessed: 29th November 2025.

with secondary EU consumer law, especially with the Unfair Terms Directive,[40] the Consumer Rights Directive,[41] and the Electronic Commerce Directive.[42]

3.3.3 Peer-to-peer NFT Transfers. Relationships and Contracts

Regarding, finally, the relationship between the NFT creator and the person interested in acquiring the NFT, it must be highlighted that it is a peer-to-peer arrangement, by virtue of which the creator of the NFT transfers their digital NFT certificate to the interested acquirer.

The legal discussion as regards this transaction is usually heavily charged by the question of whether an NFT constitutes property in a legal sense.[43] While the discussion on the legal nature of NFTs is a very attractive and hotly debated topic, we will not provide a detailed analysis here, as this would go well beyond the scope of the current contribution.

Having said that, the question remains what would be the legal nature of the transaction between an NFT creator and the person interested to acquire the NFT.

There are two general parameters that will usually apply in the majority of cases, irrespective of whether NFTs constitute property or not:

(i) the NFT creator will only be able to transfer the rights they originally created during the minting process. As explained above, an NFT certificate entails a claim vis-a-vis the blockchain ecosystem of being associated with a digital asset and also a claim of having the power to transfer this association to somebody else; in that sense, a peer-to-peer NFT transaction will display strong elements of an assignment contract since, by transferring the NFT certificate, the NFT creator is now assigning the right to be associated with an underlying digital asset and the right to transfer this association to the new acquirer.

(ii) Persons interested in acquiring NFTs might qualify as consumers, as the acquisition of NFTs will often occur for purposes outside of one's trade or profession. If the NFT creator is engaging in NFT transactions professionally, they would obtain

---

[40] Council Directive 93/13/EEC of 5 April 1993 on unfair terms in consumer contracts, OJ L 95, 21.4.1993, p. 29–34.

[41] Directive 2011/83/EU of the European Parliament and of the Council of 25 October 2011 on consumer rights, amending Council Directive 93/13/EEC and Directive 1999/44/EC of the European Parliament and of the Council and repealing Council Directive 85/577/EEC and Directive 97/7/EC of the European Parliament and of the Council, OJ L 304, 22.11.2011, p. 64–88.

[42] Directive 2000/31/EC of the European Parliament and of the Council of 8 June 2000 on certain legal aspects of information society services, in particular electronic commerce, in the Internal Market (Directive on electronic commerce) OJ L 178, 17.7.2000, p. 1–16.

[43] This discussion has recently been fueled by decisions of Courts in the UK and Singapore, which have recognized the common law status of property in NFTs. See, for example, the UK High Court decision in Lavinia Deborah Osbourne and 1) Persons Unknown, 2) Ozone, [2022] EWHC 1021 (Comm) and the decision of the High Court of Singapore in Janesh s/o Rajkumar and Unknown Person [2022] SGHC 264. It must be stressed, nonetheless, that these cases were decided based on certain common law particularities. Therefore, their analysis is relevant for other jurisdictions only to the extent that regulatory similarities exist.

the status of a trader. In that case, EU consumer law acquis will govern the legal relationship, and the (smart) contracts supporting the NFT arrangement will have to comply with it, as the transaction will be a B2C one. Conversely, if the NFT creator does not engage in NFT transactions professionally, there will be no need to apply EU consumer law, as the transaction will occur between nominally equal counterparties (C2C transaction).

3.4 Some Final Thoughts on Legal Assurances

The analysis performed above demonstrated that the success of the NFT ecosystem depends on a harmonious symbiosis between code and the law. While traditional legal institutions like those of "ownership" or "property" might need some time before embracing the new developments, market forces in combination with contractual freedom have been trying to close this gap. NFTs are an interesting digital experiment that aims to redefine our relationship with digital assets. The ever-evolving ingenuity of private market forces is harnessing the power of the code in order to create new digital universes. Default contract law rules are an important companion in this effort, as it is ultimately up to them to decide whether the aspirations of NFT stakeholders will meet reality. They guarantee the rights and obligations of the parties (independently from any technical assurances provided by the smart contract code), they regulate any issues left unregulated by the parties and they offer a general framework for the exercise of the freedom of NFT stakeholders. By thinking about NFT smart contracts in terms of contract law we have not tried to minimize the flexibility or autonomy of NFT projects, but we have tried to uncover a possible default legal regime that will support their ambition and creativity. In summarizing our sketch of a possible general framework of operation for NFTs within the EU Common Digital Market we conclude that: (i) NFT (smart) contracts will, quite often, merit the legal characterization of contracts for the provision of services and that transfers of NFT certificates would probably qualify as assignment agreements under EU law; and (ii) certain NFT constellations will trigger the application of EU consumer law. It is within this legal framework that NFT stakeholders will have to develop their smart contractual arrangements.

4 The Need for NFT Technology Assurances

Above we discussed the need for legal assurances, and whilst legal assurances ultimately can provide recourse, ideally further assurances can be provided: (i) to lower the need for recourse to legal remedies – after all the law also prefers prevention over intervention to lower the needs to resort to legal solutions; and (ii) given the often unidentifiable nature of parties involved, to allow the mitigation of risks associated with the inability of traditional law enforcement mechanisms to effectively

```
contract NFT {
  ...
  function initWallet(initOwner) {
     require(owner == 0, "The owner has already been set!");
     owner = initOwner;
  }
  ...
}
```

Fig. 2. The above pseudo-code illustrates a bug that would allow anyone to claim ownership of any wallet in black, while the red line of code would fix the bug.

address situations where the identification of the involved stakeholders is difficult. Now, here we discuss such assurances that can be provided through or relating to the technology.

Now, NFTs are smart contracts, code – and code can have bugs. Yet smart contracts unlike code used in traditional systems cannot be changed once deployed. In this section, we'll first demonstrate a simple bug and contextualize the impact bugs could have on NFTs in Section 4.1, and then in Section 4.2 discuss techno-regulatory solutions to minimize such negative consequences and provide measures for recourse.

4.1 A Simple Bug and Potential Impact of Bugs on NFTs

The parity bug,[44] which due to a single missing line of code, allowed anyone to claim ownership of any wallet.[45] Pseudo-code illustrating the bug is provided in Fig. 2. The line of code in red was missing and would have prevented the bug from happening. The red line of code checks to see if the owner of the wallet has already been set up – if it has then an error is raised, otherwise the code continues allowing for the owner of the wallet to be set with the initial owner's address on the next line. The code demonstrates that even simple code can lead to bugs that could potentially lead to large amounts of theft or losses.

Let's look at the deed-like NFT art piece use-case introduced in Section 1 again. Now, let's also assume that legal certainty within the particular jurisdiction exists and for the specific NFT, it is the NFT token holder who has legal rights to the physical painting. If the NFT's smart contract had a bug in it, similar to that of the parity bug discussed in Section 4.1, then anyone could exploit the bug and become the holder of the NFT. If legal rights to claim the physical art would be solely dependent upon who the NFT holder was, then could an NFT thief make a legal claim to that physical art piece is theirs and 'rightfully' have the art piece handed over to them?

[44] https://ilyasergey.net/papers/maian-draft.pdf. Last Accessed: 29th November 2025.

[45] or rather all wallets.

4.2 A Simple Bug and Potential Impact of Bugs on NFTs

Whether an NFT is classified as a legal contract or not, given that code once written can never be changed, it is vital that sufficient technology assurances are in place to safeguard correct behaviour (i.e. technical implementation behaviour that matches the legal contractual expectations) – and when technology assurances in place are not good enough, legal forms of recourse may kick-in.

We do not go into the discussion of within which contexts such assurances should be mandated (or not), or when different paths to recourse should be provided, and neither within which shape or form of regulation they would best be specified – which may include hard or soft laws, regulatory guidelines, standards, market/self-regulation or other. Yet, we now provide an overview of assurance and regulatory tools that could be considered depending upon the exact context within which NFTs are used (e.g. for digital art; securities; as utility tokens for decentralised digital services, centralised digital services or centralised non-digital real-world services; soul-bound tokens for credentials; or others).

4.2.1 Certainty on 'Code vs Law'

'Code is Law', a statement that many in the blockchain space use to imply that what is written in smart contract code is the 'final say'. This argument is based on the fact that: (i) smart contracts are transparent and available for 'all' to read/verify (or to delegate this task to someone else); (ii) smart contract code cannot be changed, even if a fix is required; and (iii) code is objective. If there happens to be some unwanted behaviour in the code (potentially due to a bug, or due to a party not understanding the code) within this 'code is law' framework, the response would be that the code executed exactly as it was written in the smart contract, and it is the fault of any party that misunderstood that smart contract. When operating within such a framework, assurances to ensure that code is as correct as possible is crucial.

Many often attribute this view to Lessig's work on 'Code is Law'.[46] Yet, the type of code Lessig was referring to, and how it relates to law differs:

> *But notice the important difference. In real space, the law means you can be penalized for violating the "high/low" rule. In Second Life, you simply can't violate the 15-meter rule. The rule is part of the code. The code controls how you are in Second Life. There isn't a choice about obeying the rule or not, any more than there's a choice about obeying gravity. So code is law here. That code/law enforces its control directly. But obviously, this code (like law) changes. The key is to recognize that this change in the code is (unlike the laws of nature) crafted to reflect choices and values of the coders.*

Above, Lessig discusses how code becomes law within the boundaries of a specific system, however, that doesn't mean to say that the laws within the system are beyond the laws of the land in the real-world. Furthermore, the above refers to code that

[46] Lessig (2009)

'(like law) changes' – which is not the case for smart contract code, which becomes immutable once deployed. If this is the view that one subscribes to, technology assurances are also just as crucial since, although the laws of the land will prevail, and legal recourse may be sought, if one loses an NFT (potentially an expensive one) due to a software bug (or other reason) the law may be unable to return back the NFT to the particular party (e.g. if there was no way in code to transfer back the NFT).

Furthermore, irrespective of whether one subscribes to either views above, or that another description of what the smart contract does should determine what is binding, the reality is that it is the legal system that ultimately will decide what is law. In light of potential software bugs, the potential to misunderstand smart contracts, or the potential to have conflicting descriptions of what the smart contract is meant to do, legal certainty should be provided with respect to what would ultimately be seen as 'law' (within specific contexts and where possible of course). In Malta, such ambiguity was made clear for smart contracts certified[47] with the Malta Digital Innovation Authority.[48] Any such certified NFT would require that an English description of the NFT is provided which describes the expected behaviour, and thereafter it is the 'English description [that] will be deemed to prevail over the implementation' where any discrepancies emerge.

4.2.2 NFT System Correctness

As discussed in Section 2.2 the term NFT is often used to describe more than just digital tokens implemented within smart contracts by also including any physical or digital artefacts which the NFT references, when in fact the NFT itself is really confined within the implementation of the smart contract. Again, access to view or interact with associated digital artefacts is often controlled from a centralised server which typically sends dApp code to requesting users' browser for execution. This implies that the entity governing the centralised server could change the dApp code as required. The dApp is the typical way an average user would interact with their NFT and associated artefacts or additional services – and if the dApp code was (to become) buggy this could mean that many (average) users would be deprived of making use of rights associated with their NFT since either they would be unlikely to know how to interact directly with the underlying smart contract, or also some rights are implemented as centralised functionality. Therefore, ensuring code correctness (as much as possible) for both on-chain and off-chain code facilitating interaction with the NFT and related assets and rights is crucial.

Software techniques and tooling could be used to facilitate higher levels of guarantees with respect to correctness throughout the NFT software life-cycle including:

---

[47] as Innovative Technology Arrangements – the umbrella term defined in the Innovative Technology Arrangements and Services Act (2018) used to encompass technology offerings that can be certified with the Malta Digital Innovation Authority.

[48] See Ellul et al. (2020).

(i) making use of tried and tested software libraries and standards[49]; (ii) utilising frameworks that raise the level of programming abstraction away from low level internals[50]; (iii) testing[51] at development time; (iv) verifying that logic matches expected behaviour prior to deployment[52] and whilst code is executing live[53]; and (v) security[54] and code audits.[55]

4.2.3 Infrastructure Guarantees and Monitoring

As illustrated in Fig. 1 an NFT dApp, which allows users to interact with their NFT, involves a number of different software components that are stored and executed on different platforms including centralised dApp server code, dApp code that is executed on users' computers, NFT smart contract code on a blockchain, and then typically metadata and associated digital artefacts that could be stored on any type of platform that may be centralised or decentralised. It is crucial that not only the the code providing access to users is correct (as possible), yet the infrastructure hosting and executing the code must also be operational in order to allow for users to enjoy their any rights associated with the NFT.

As part of EU's digital finance package a Digital Operational Resilience Act was proposed that would require service providers to put in place suitable ICT risk management frameworks especially with respect to potential cyber-threats.[56] It is not yet clear to what extent this will be imposed on different NFT service providers given that they do not currently explicitly fall within the ambit of EU's proposed Markets in Crypto-Assets (MiCA) framework.[57] However, inclusion/exclusion of a crypto-asset based upon whether it is implemented in an NFT smart-contract (rather than some other means that may not be classified as an NFT) may not be the ideal manner of determining a crypto-asset's inclusion/exclusion. Furthermore, as put by Herian et al.[58]:

> *The mere assignment of a unique identifier to a crypto asset should thus not be sufficient to classify it as unique or non-fungible.*

Whilst, infrastructure resilience is of utmost importance to allow for individuals to enjoy their rights to NFTs in their possession, in the event that some error, hack or any fault occurs, it would be ideal that all information relevant to the event is

[49] https://eips.ethereum.org/EIPS/eip-721. Last Accessed: 29th November 2025.

[50] See for example Chirtoaca et al. (2020).

[51] See for example Barboni et al. (2022).

[52] See for example Ahrendt et al. (2019).

[53] See for example Ellul and Pace (2018).

[54] See for example Ramos et al. (2022).

[55] See for example Ellul et al. (2020).

[56] See for example Ramos et al. (2022).

[57] See Jansson et al. (2022b).

[58] See Herian et al. (2021).

accessible for any post-mortem exercise that could support fixing the problem or to support seeking any potential recourse possible. A 'Forensic Node' was proposed by Ellul et al. (2020), which requires that not only such monitoring infrastructure is in place, but also that an appointed 'Technical Administrator' is in place to be able to act when required (e.g. when authorities or enforcement require them to do so).

4.2.4 Un/Identifiable Parties and Tech-Guarantees

Beyond ensuring that the technology is fit for purpose, the NFT market has seen countless victims fall to scams.[59] This is primarily due to the ability to operate in a highly anonymous manner. Whilst licensed activities can help minimise such cases, this remains a problem for those activities that do not require any form of oversight – as all the laws and contractual agreements in the world may be able to do nothing if a counter-party can not be identified to be held responsible when required.

The above highlights the need for other forms of assurances that can provide users with peace of mind. Such technology assurances could include: (i) NFT-project registries that undertake due diligence and KYC on projects and individuals involved; (ii) rating and reputation systems; and (iii) guarantee/insurance schemes. Such assurances could be operated either by centralised entities or by decentralised autonomous organisations (DAOs). Indeed, such solutions involve introducing new points of trust, yet such trusted parties could help fill a void that may not have been possible to fill otherwise. When it comes to centralised entities providing such trust-solutions, indeed many of the same concerns remain – e.g. 'Can I trust the opinion/guarantee of this entity?'. Yet for well-known entities, e.g. known reputable insurance companies, this may be a solution. When it comes to DAOs providing such solutions, trust can be built through different through code guarantees (e.g. funds can only be spent according to the rules of associated smart contracts), the community involved (e.g. if the community is made up of individuals that are involved/invested in the specific project and 'skin in the game'), and potentially through the law for jurisdictions that may grant legal personality to DAOs.[60] Indeed, defining such a legal framework raises many questions for which immediate answers are not available and would need to be investigated. Various recommendations have been made to investigate such a framework through regulatory and evidence based sandboxes.[61]

4.2.5 Un/Identifiable Parties and Tech-Guarantees

The decentralised technology sector is rapidly challenging, and undoubtedly, ensuring that a particular legal and regulatory framework is suitable cannot be seen until evidence of its appropriateness is seen in practice. This is due to many unknown

[59] See for example Kshetri (2022).

[60] See for example Ganado et al. (2020).

[61] See for example Arribas et al. (2020); Jansson et al. (2022b).

and moving parts including constantly evolving technology, ideological and social governance models, acceptance by various stakeholders, and the effects it has on involved parties, the market and society in general. Furthermore, until such frameworks are designed and implemented, extensive time is passing whilst leaving operators, investors and stakeholders with legal uncertainty and potential lack of protection to the market.

It is therefore ideal, that rather than wait for well-defined frameworks to be designed for which ultimately their success is uncertain, is to use a regulatory sandbox[62] based approach to: (i) build evidence towards how such a framework should be designed; and (ii) provide immediate certainty and protection (with respect to the current state of the sandbox). In line with this direction the EU had announced that it would be launching a pan-European regulatory sandbox.[63]

5 Conclusions

NFTs are bringing forth a new paradigm allowing individuals to be more in control of digital assets in their possession, and whilst the technology has a lot of potential to change many sectors, extensive ambiguity exists regarding what exactly NFTs are and their relationship to the real and legal world. In this paper, we tried to shed some light on how NFTs actually work. We have also attempted to disambiguate the technical complexities surrounding NFTs, as well as their relationship to contract law. While we concluded that contract law could be an important tool for achieving a certain degree of legal certainty and for acquiring some form of recourse shall something go wrong, we have also discussed the need for additional techno-regulatory assurancces. Such tcchno-rcgulatory assuranccs can support thc cffort to mitigatc certain risks that traditional legal remedies might not be able to resolve in a fully satisfactory manner, mostly in view of the fact that certain blockchain characteristics might make law enforcement untenable (e.g. the inability to identify the responsible party might neutralize the effectiveness of existing legal remedies). We have also provided an overview of the technical solutions proposed. The key takeaway is the following: NFTs are complex technical and legal creatures and exactly because of their complexity, neither technical nor legal solutions will be able to support them in isolation. It is rather a mutualistic symbiosis of technical, legal, and techno-regulatory solutions that will allow NFTs to maximize their potential.

References

[62] See for example Jansson et al. (2022a).

[63] https://digital-strategy.ec.europa.eu/en/policies/regulatory-framework-blockchain. Last Accessed: 29th November 2025.

Ahrendt W, Bubel R, Ellul J et al (2019) Verification of smart contract business logic. In: Hojjat H, Massink M (eds) Fundamentals of software engineering. Springer International Publishing, Cham, pp 228–243

Arribas I, Arroyo D, Reshef Kera D (2020) Sandbox for minimal viable governance of blockchain services and daos: claudia. In: International congress on blockchain and applications. Springer, Cham, Switzerland, pp 24–30

Barboni M, Morichetta A, Polini A (2022) Smart contract testing: Challenges and opportunities. In: 2022 IEEE/ACM 5th international workshop on emerging trends in software engineering for blockchain (WETSEB). Institute of Elecrtical and Electronics Engineers/Association for Computing Machinery, New York, pp 21–24

Becker K (2022) Blockchain matters—Lex cryptographia and the displacement of legal symbolics and imaginaries. Law Critique 33:113–130

Bodo B, Giannopoulou A, Mezei P, Quintais JP (2022) The rise of NFTs: These aren't the droids you're looking for. Eur Intellect Prop Rev 44:268–283

Chirtoaca D, Ellul J, Azzopardi G (2020) A framework for creating deployable smart contracts for non-fungible tokens on the ethereum blockchain. In: 2020 IEEE international conference on decentralized applications and infrastructures (DAPPS). Institute of Elecrtical and Electronics Engineers, Oxford, UK, pp 100–105

Cornelius K (2021) Betraying blockchain: Accountability, transparency and document standards for non-fungible tokens (nfts). Information 12:358

De Filippi P, Mannan M, Reijers W (2022) The alegality of blockchain technology. Polic Soc 41:358–372

Joshua Ellul, Jonathan Galea, Max Ganado, Stephen Mccarthy, Gordon J. Pace (2020) Regulating blockchain, DLT and smart contracts: A technology regulator's perspective. ERA forum, Volume 21, No.2. Springer, Berlin, pp 209–220

Ellul J, Pace GJ (2018) Runtime verification of ethereum smart contracts. In: 2018 14th european dependable computing conference (EDCC). Institute of Elecrtical and Electronics Engineers, Iasi, Romania, pp 158–163

Fortnow M, Terry Q (2021) The NFT handbook: How to create, sell and buy non-fungible tokens. John Wiley & Sons, Incorporated, New Jersey

Ganado Max, Ellul Josha, Pace Gordon J., et al (2020) Mapping the Future of Legal Personality. MIT Computational Law Report

Goforth CR (2021) How nifty! But are NFTs securities, commodities, or something else? UMKC L Rev 90:775

Gonserkewitz P, Karger E, Jagals M (2022) Non-fungible tokens: Use cases of NFTs and future research agenda. Risk Gov Control: Financ Mark Insti tutions 12:8–18

Grabowski M (2019) Cryptocurrencies: A primer on digital money. Routledge, Oxfordshire, England

Guadamuz A (2021) The treachery of images: Non-fungible tokens and copyright. J Intellect Prop Law Pract 16:1367–1385

Herian R (2018) Regulating blockchain: Critical perspectives in law and technology. Routledge, Oxfordshire, England

Robert Herian, Claudia Di Bernardino, Andres Chomczyk Penedo, Joshua Ellul, Agata Ferreira, Axel von Goldbeck, Alireza Siadat (2021). NFT–legal token classification. Repot. EU Blockchain Observatory & Forum. Brussels. https://blockchain-observatory.ec.europa.eu/publications/nft-legal-token-classification_en. Last accessed: November 2025

Howell ST, Niessner M, Yermack D (2020) Initial coin offerings: Financing growth with cryptocurrency token sales. Rev Financ Stud 33:3925–3974

Jansson T, Siadat A, von GA et al (2022a) Regulating for the Future: EU Regulatory Sandbox Proposal Report. International Association for Trusted Blockchain Applications. Brussels. https://www.researchgate.net/publication/360945350. Last accessed: November 2025

Jansson T, Siadat A, Goldbeck A von et al (2022b) Regulating for the future: Policy notes on non-fungible tokens. Report. International Association for Trusted Blockchain Applications. Brussels. https://www.researchgate.net/publication/360945035. Last accessed: November 2025
Kaal WA (2021) Blockchain-based corporate governance. Stanf J Blockchain Law Policy 4:19–10
Kshetri N (2022) Scams, frauds, and crimes in the nonfungible token market. Computer 55:60–64
Lessig L (2008) Code: And other laws of cyberspace, version 2.0. Basic Books, New York City
Mik E (2019) Smart contracts: A requiem. J Contract Law 36(1)
Musamih A, Salah K, Jayaraman R et al (2022) NFTs in healthcare: Vision, opportunities, and challenges. IEEE Consum Electron Mag 12:21–32
Perzanowski A, Schultz J (2016) The end of ownership: Personal property in the digital economy. MIT Press, Cambridge, Massachusetts
Pinto-Gutiérrez C, Gaitán S, Jaramillo D, Velasquez S (2022) The NFT hype: What draws attention to non-fungible tokens? Mathematics 10:335
Ramos S, Melon L, Ellul J (2022) Exploring blockchains cyber security techno-regulatory gap. An application to crypto-asset regulation in the EU. Report presented at 10th graduate conference in law and technology, sciences po, Paris. https://papers.ssrn.com/sol3/papers.cfm?abstract_id=4148678. Last accessed: November 2025
Rifkin J (2001) The age of access: The new culture of hypercapitalism where all of life is a paid-for experience. Penguin, New York
Schrepel T (2021) Smart contracts and the digital single market through the lens of a "law+ technology" approach. European Commission Brussels
Treiblmaier H (2021) Beyond blockchain: How tokens trigger the internet of value and what marketing researchers need to know about them. J Mark Commun 29(3):238
Valeonti F, Bikakis A, Terras M et al (2021) Crypto collectibles, museum funding and OpenGLAM: Challenges, opportunities and the potential of non-fungible tokens (NFTs). Appl Sci 11:9931
Werbach K (2018) The blockchain and the new architecture of trust. MIT Press, Cambridge, Massachusetts
Werbach K, Cornell N (2017) Contracts ex machina. Duke Law J 67:313–382

Competition Law

Virtual Worlds and Competition Issues: Same Problem, Same Solution

Jacques Moscianese and Fabrizio Di Benedetto

Abstract The paper tries to figure out the possible competitive outcomes in the field of metaverse, taking stocks of previous experiences in the digital economy. Competition among Virtual Worlds could either take the form of a market where each Virtual World constitutes a separate relevant market (due to lock-in effects), or results in a market that tips, so where a monopolist prevails. To avoid such outcomes, interoperability is key. In this regard, the article offers some examples to demonstrate the importance of interoperability rules to ensure competition, considering interoperability standards adopted by other industries (such as the financial one). In conclusion, the paper foresees the "inevitability" of interoperability in the metaverse due to the possible application of the Digital Markets Act to Virtual Worlds.

1 Introduction

The battle for the metaverse has already started. Many players of the digital sector have entered or are planning to enter in the metaverse market as a new frontier of social networking,[1] and – in general – as a new way to provide services online.

[1] Cfr. Meta, Microsoft, Decentraland, NVIDIA, Unity, Sandbox, Roblox.

This paper only contains the views of the authors and does not represent the view of their organizations. The authors wish to thank Elisabetta Victoria Peraldo (Institutional Special Projects and Policies, Intesa Sanpaolo) for her valuable comments. The present paper is based on Di Benedetto and Moscianese (2022).

J. Moscianese · F. Di Benedetto (✉)
Intesa Sanpaolo, Milan, Italy
e-mail: fabrizio.dibenedetto@intesasanpaolo.com

J. Moscianese
e-mail: jacques.moscianese@intesasanpaolo.com

J. Moscianese
ESSEC Business School Paris, Cergy, France

F. Di Porto and O. Pollicino (eds.), *Law and Politics of Virtual Worlds*, Law, Governance and Technology Series 79, https://doi.org/10.1007/978-3-032-08541-2_13

Looking the metaverse from a competition law perspective is like looking into a crystal ball.

Well, let's look inside it. The crystal ball essentially contains two pictures that represent the possible outcomes of metaverse's evolution in the next years. The first one is a payment card; the second one is the search bar of a search engine.

The payment card basically means that one of the possible evolutions of metaverse could be similar to what happened in the past to payment cards: the introduction of payment schemes (*i.e.*, rules to ensure interoperability) made it possible for consumers to use a card issued by their bank also at Automatic Teller Machines (ATM) and Points Of Sale (POS) of other banks. Schemes allowed the coexistence of different service providers for card issuing and acquiring, ensuring at the same time interoperability and competition among them.[2] Without schemes, each consumer would be locked-in, having – for example – the possibility to withdraw money only at his/her bank's ATMs.

The search bar of a search engine represents the other possible evolution (at least the other one that we see) of metaverse. Search engine market, indeed, is basically dominated by one single operator (at least in Western countries), because the market tipped.[3] One player took it all, essentially creating a monopoly equilibrium.

The aim of this paper is to analyze these two alternative evolutions of the metaverse market, trying to learn the lessons of the past, using – as points of reference – the European case-law and European antitrust enforcement practice. Hence the chapter proceeds as follows: para. 2 will confront the two possible competitive outcomes in metaverse markets (the coexistence of a plurality of Virtual Worlds versus the emergence of a single dominant Virtual World), according to precedent experience in digital and technological markets; then, para. 3 will focus on the importance of interoperability rules to ensure full competition between Virtual Worlds; para. 4 will provide some examples of the utmost relevance of interoperability in competition terms, with reference to a traditional market (the banking one); in conclusion, para. 5 will highlight the inevitability of interoperability between Virtual Worlds due to the entry into force of the so-called Digital Markets Act.

2 Plurality of Virtual Worlds *vs* a Tipping Market with a Dominant Metaverse

Currently there are some providers of Virtual Worlds around the world: not only incumbents of the social networking (such as Meta), or traditional companies active in the provision of Operating Systems (OS) for personal computers (such as Microsoft), but also new incomers like Decentraland, just to name one of them.

---

[2] *Infra*, paragraph 4.

[3] The reference here is obviously to Google. In this regard, see Petit and Moreno Belloso (2021).

Thus, we start our analysis of the competitive landscape considering the existence of a plurality of Virtual Worlds in competition among them to attract both business users and end users (*infra*, users).

In terms of "product", today Virtual Worlds seem to be a kind of evolution of social networking, rather than being now the evolution of the internet. Indeed, the internet basically is the global interconnection among telecommunication networks that was made possible by the common adoption of standard network protocols. Thus, while the internet is more similar to a standard (*i.e.*, a scheme of rules that has some similarities with those linked to payment cards), at the moment, Virtual Worlds look like digital virtual places (like social networks) where users with their avatars can socialize and interact with a more immersive experience.

If Virtual Worlds' plurality is here to stay, competition among Virtual Worlds will remain, at least in the first phase, when users decide to enter a specific Virtual World, instead of another one. However, that is not enough to ensure full competition. Indeed, real competition exists only when users can move across Virtual Worlds without limits. In fact, users could be induced not to move between one Virtual Worlds to the next, due to a lack of interoperability between them. In the long run (*i.e.*, when Virtual Worlds will be sufficiently developed and adopted by users), this would lead each Virtual World to constitute a separate market with respect to its own customers, which would be bound to the so-called single homing.[4] In this case, each Virtual World would have a strong market power over its commercial counterparts, who would be discouraged to change Virtual World platform.

That would have an impact on all the services offered on every Virtual World. Indeed, it cannot be excluded that in response to a small, permanent price increase (or quality decrease) of services offered on one Virtual World by its provider users will not or will insufficiently move towards another Virtual World because of the lock-in effect.[5]

Such a theory of harm is not new in the field of competition law, especially in those cases where a single operator basically constitutes a distinct product or service market. That was already argued – although in speculative terms – by the European Commission in the *Nintendo case* in 2003,[6] where the European Commission stated that "although N64 (a Nintendo console) compatible game cartridges were sold at slightly higher prices than, for instance, games compatible with Sony's Playstation, this did not prevent the N64 from achieving the fastest sales rate in game history after its launch, indicating that the relative higher price level for N64 game cartridges had little, if any, influence on consumers' willingness to purchase the N64 console".[7]

---

[4] When a user, instead of using multiple providers (so-called multi-homing), decides or is forced, by the market power of one of them, to use a single provider.

[5] When users find it very hard or impossible to move from one provider to another, for example due to high switching costs.

[6] Commission decision 2003/675/EC of 30 October 2002 relating to a proceeding pursuant to Article 81 of the EC Treaty and Article 53 of the EEA Agreement (COMP/35.587 PO Video Games, COMP/35.706 PO Nintendo Distribution and COMP/36.321 Omega — Nintendo), OJ L 255, 8.10.2003, pp. 33–100.

[7] *Ibidem*, para. 50.

According to the European Commission that basically meant that "game cartridges compatible with a particular game console belong to a different market than those compatible with another".[8] In other words, once a consumer had chosen his/her favorite console, the consumer was basically locked-in with regard to his/her possibility to choose game cartridges, because only those compatible with the chosen console constituted the only possible alternatives.

The same could happen now with Virtual Worlds: a lock-in between platform and services, very similar to that between console and game cartridges. Obviously to the benefit of the owner of the platform.

However, instead of a coexistence of different Virtual World, it could happen that one Virtual World among the others will emerge as the dominant one until the market tips and a monopolistic equilibrium consolidates.

That happened to Google[9] in the search engine market in 2017, where the European Commission found that a very large portion of internet users did not switch to other search engines for different reasons, including a loyalty-effect of Google's brand on consumers' behavior. Indeed, "because of the strength of the Google brand, users trust in the relevance of search results provided by Google. Consequently, as supported by internal Google document and two third party studies, a significant number of users are unlikely to multi-home even if Google were to degrade the quality of its general search service".[10] Thus, Google currently is in the position of a *de facto* monopolistic company because thanks to its initial advantage (based on merits), now the search engine operator has taken a very large portion (if not all) of users.

In general, what is currently happening to metaverse has already happened for some of the services on the internet. In fact, investments to enter in the metaverse market are high and – indeed – especially so-called big tech companies are trying to deal with this new dimension of providing services. As already said, Meta and Microsoft are one of the main providers of Virtual World platforms so far. In this sense, as occurred for search engine services, investments and costs to implement and develop a Virtual World platform could be so relevant that even an incumbent of the tech markets can find it difficult to succeed.

In effect, as argued by the European Commission in the *Google Shopping case* in 2017, "*since 2007, there has been only one significant entrant in the national markets for general search services, Microsoft, which launched the latest version of its general search service, Bing, in 2009. Since 2009, however, Bing's market shares have never exceeded 10% in any EEA country*".[11] That notwithstanding the

[8] *Ibidem*, para. 51.

[9] Commission decision of 27.6.2017 relating to proceedings under Article 102 of the Treaty on the Functioning of the European Union and Article 54 of the Agreement on the European Economic Area (AT.39740 – Google Search (Shopping)). The European Commission's decision was largely confirmed by the General Court of the European Union, judgment of 10 November 2021, *Google/ Alphabet vs European Commission*, Case T-612/17, ECLI:EU:T:2021:763.

[10] *Ibidem*, para. 312.

[11] *Ibidem*, para. 300.

fact that Microsoft invested a significant amount in R&D and capital expenditure in the development and maintenance of Bing.[12]

Thus, no one can rule out that one of the current providers of Virtual World platforms could become *de facto* a monopolist, making it hard – also for its stronger competitors – to challenge its position. In other words, it is not impossible for the Virtual Worlds market to tip in the years to come, just like the search engine market tipped years ago, and not only for merits of Google's management.

In conclusion, neither of the two possible evolutions analyzed in the current paragraph are satisfactory from an antitrust perspective. The first one, where each Virtual World could in the long run constitute a separate product market, is not acceptable because place for competition is limited at the very first step of the purchasing process (*i.e.*, when users decide which Virtual World to enter and use). The second one, where one Virtual World provider becomes the dominant company, is not adequate from an antitrust point of view because antitrust law has been created exactly to tackle monopolies. In other words, little or imperfect competition is better than no competition at all, according to antitrust policy and enforcement.

But, in our crystal ball we not only saw the search bar of Google. Indeed, we also saw a payment card, which is the symbol of a competition among competitors that is not limited to the first phase (*i.e.*, when the customer purchases the product), but it is rather extended throughout the entire life of a product. And that was made possible due to interoperability rules.[13] Without interoperability, as already said, payment cards market would be like that envisaged in Virtual Worlds' first phase of evolution analyzed above: each card would constitute a distinct product market.

3 The Importance of Interoperability in Antitrust Enforcement, as well as in Designing Virtual Worlds and the Metaverse Markets

Interoperability is fundamental to promote competition and to make markets more dynamic. As we will see below, not only authorities and courts agree on that, but also Mark Zuckerberg embraces the same view. Indeed, according to the Facebook's founder, "*[i] deally, you should be able to sign into any metaverse experience and everything you've bought should be right there. There's a long way to get there, but this kind of interoperability will deliver much better experiences for people and larger opportunities for creators. That is, the more places you can easily use your digital goods, the more you'll value them, which creates a bigger market for creators. The more easily you can transact, the bigger the opportunity for creators should get as well. We're looking forward to building this out*".[14]

[12] *Ibidem*, para. 286.

[13] *Infra*, paragraph 4.

[14] Zuckerberg (2022).

As it is well known, the leading case on interoperability at the European Union level is the *Microsoft* one of 2004.[15] In that competition saga, the European Commission concluded that Microsoft reserved interoperability with Windows personal computers (PC) only to its own work group server operating system products, while it refused to supply interoperability information to competitors. Such a behavior basically drove customers towards Microsoft's work group server operating system products and constituted an exclusionary abuse of dominance according to the then Article 82 of the Treaty on the European Community (TEC, now Article 102 of the Treaty on the Functioning of the European Union, TFEU). Thus, the European Commission established that the interoperability information is indispensable to be able to viably compete in the work group server operating system market, requiring Microsoft to share such interoperability information with actual and potential competitors.[16] The decision of the European Commission was later confirmed by the then Court of First Instance (now General Court of the European Union).[17]

Still recently, the importance of interoperability has been underlined by the European Commission in its enforcement practice for merger control. In fact, in authorizing the acquisition of Fitbit[18] by Google, the European Commission – after a market test conducted during phase II of the investigation – was concerned that Google could have had "the ability and incentive to degrade interoperability between third-party wrist-worn wearable devices and Android OS by selectively degrading Android APIs vis-à-vis Fitbit's competitors".[19] According to the European Commission, the only way to avoid such an exclusionary conduct by the post-merger entity was to ensure interoperability between Android OS and wrist-worn wearable devices produced by Fitbit's alternative providers. Thus, Google decided to adopt a specific commitment according to EU merger control rules[20] aiming at guaranteeing third parties' access to the same Android APIs that Google used to implement its proprietary integrations on top of Android, therefore ensuring that rivals can also develop competing integrations that interoperate with Android via the same Android APIs (the so-called Android APIs commitment).[21]

---

[15] Commission Decision 2007/53/EC of 24 March 2004 relating to a proceeding pursuant to Article 82 [EC] and Article 54 of the EEA Agreement against Microsoft Corp. (Case COMP/C-3/37.792 – Microsoft), OJ 2007 L 32, p. 23. On this case, see Andreangeli (2009).

[16] Banasevic et al. (2004).

[17] Judgment of the Court of First Instance, 17 September 2007, Case T-201/04, *Microsoft vs European Commission*, ECLI:EU:T:2007:289.

[18] A technology company that develops, manufactures and distributes wearable devices, software and services in the health and fitness sector.

[19] Commission Decision of 17.12.2020 declaring a concentration to be compatible with the internal market and the EEA agreement, Case M.9660 – GOOGLE/FITBIT, https://ec.europa.eu/competition/mergers/cases1/202120/m9660_3314_3.pdf, para. 985. Accessed on December 1, 2025.

[20] Council Regulation (EC) No 139/2004 of 20 January 2004 on the control of concentrations between undertakings (the EC Merger Regulation), OJ L 24, 29.1.2004, pp. 1–22, in particular recital (30) and article 6.

[21] *Ibidem*, para. 998.

The pro-competitive relevance of interoperability has a very important place also in the new guidelines on horizontal agreements among competitors released by the European Commission in June 2023. Indeed, the European Commission clearly states that "*[s] tandards which establish technical interoperability and compatibility often encourage competition on the merits between the technologies of different undertakings and help prevent lock-in to a particular supplier. Furthermore, standards may reduce transaction costs for sellers and buyers*".[22]

In this regard, although standard setting among competitors could entail some antitrust risks (such as collusion to limit innovation), it cannot be denied that – as argued by the founder of Meta – it is indispensable to have a common standard in the metaverse market, so as to ensure a plurality of Virtual Worlds continuously in competition among them, thus avoiding lock-in effects to the detriment of users and ensuring multi-homing.

As argued by the World Economic Forum in mid-2022, big tech companies are driving the evolution of the metaverse, also building walled-garden ecosystems, *i.e.*, horizontally integrated ecosystems that are "*basically copying the Apple ecosystem of the smartphone era, characterized by one player controlling the entire value chain within a specific market segment, from hardware to operating system, to apps and services, and (the rules of) commercialization*".[23] However, despite the incentive of big techs – which should not be keen to standardization and interoperability – there are "*already initial attempts to facilitate a so-called 'open metaverse' by establishing common standards to enable information exchange and interoperability through initiatives like the Metaverse Standards Forum*[24] *or the World Economic Forum's Defining the Metaverse initiative*".[25] Other initiatives, such as the Open Metaverse Foundation, pursue the same objective of fostering interoperability standards in the metaverse.[26]

---

[22] Communication from the European Commission, *Guidelines on the applicability of Article 101 of the Treaty on the Functioning of the European Union to horizontal cooperation agreements*, para. 475, https://eur-lex.europa.eu/legal-content/EN/TXT/PDF/?uri=CELEX:52023XC0721(01). Accessed on December 1, 2025.

[23] World Economic Forum (2022).

[24] Metaverse Standards Forum (2022): "[t]he Metaverse Standards Forum brings together leading standards organizations and companies for industry-wide cooperation on interoperability standards needed to build the open metaverse. The Forum will explore where the lack of interoperability is holding back metaverse deployment and how the work of Standards Developing Organizations (SDOs) defining and evolving needed standards may be coordinated and accelerated".

[25] *Idem.*

[26] Open Metaverse Foundation (2022).

4 Best Practices: Interoperability in Banking

As already said (above, para. 1), the banking industry – and, within this sector, payment services – represent a perfect example of how interoperability fosters competition between different players and avoids lock-in effects and single-homing.

As clearly stated also by the European Court of Justice in the *Carte Bancaire case* of 2014, banks establish payment schemes in order to achieve the interoperability for payment and withdrawal operations by bank cards issued by the members of the scheme. Basically, "*interoperability enables, in practice, a [scheme] card issued by a member of the [scheme] to be used to make payments to all traders affiliated to the [scheme] system through any other member of the [scheme] and/or to make withdrawals from automatic teller machines (ATMs) operated by all other members*".[27]

The same can be said for all payment schemes, not only for the most globally known (such as Visa and Mastercard) but also for the domestic schemes, such as the already mentioned Carte Bancaire in France, Bancontact in Belgium, and Bancomat in Italy. Those players are usually associations of undertakings according to antitrust law (Art. 101, TFEU); and they can be so considered even after an initial public offering that produces a change in the shareholders' structure of the schemes. Thus, they naturally entail some competition risks (just like all associations of undertakings or all other forms of horizontal cooperation).[28] However, their fundamental aim is to ensure and stimulate competition, as argued above (para. 1).

Interoperability is so important for the payment industry that the European Commission – in its last study on the matter[29] – has recommended to consider "*the need for harmonizing formats, standards, technical protocols and rules set by card schemes in order to improve interoperability, also for new digital payment instruments*", with regard to the processing activities carried out by the schemes.[30]

But interoperability in the banking sector is not limited to payment schemes. At the very beginning of the e-commerce, for example, a large number of banks[31] agreed on the establishment of a joint venture (Identrus) for the "*promotion, operation and management of an infrastructure for securing electronic commerce transactions. That infrastructure [was] intended to enable the Participants in the system*

---

[27] Judgment of the Court of Justice, 11 September 2014, Case C-67/13 P, *Groupement des cartes bancaires (CB) v European Commission*, ECLI:EU:C:2014:2204, para. 3.

[28] For the most recent case at the EU level, see Commission Decision of 29.4.2019 relating to a proceeding under Article 101 of the Treaty on the Functioning of the European Union and Article 53 of the EEA Agreement, Case AT.40049 – MasterCard II, https://ec.europa.eu/competition/antitrust/cases/dec_docs/40049/40049_4172_3.pdf, paras. 30–32. Accessed on December 1, 2025.

[29] European Commission (2020).

[30] *Ibidem*, p. 26.

[31] ABN AMRO Holding NV, Bank America Corporation, Barclays Bank PLC, Bayerische Hypo- und Vereinsbank AG, Chase Manhattan Corporation, Citigroup Inc., and Deutsche Bank AG.

to operate as individual and competing Certification Authorities".[32] The aim of the cooperation was to give an answer to the increasing necessity for e-commerce operators to develop "*systems to prevent the transmission of unauthorised, fraudulent, or corrupted messages*".[33]

According to the European Commission's decision, Identrus System specifications provided "*interoperability in order to enable each Participant to develop its own technology independently*".[34] Thus, also in the *Identrus case*, interoperability basically increased competition. In fact, each participant in the Identrus System would have offered its own, independently created applications for certification and authentication services to end-users, built upon the Identrus System infrastructure, in competition with other Participants, considering that they were free to set their prices charged to end users.[35]

From a competition point of view, the establishment of such an interoperability system to securing e-commerce transactions did not entail antitrust infringements. Indeed, participating banks did "*not extend their cooperation to the market for the provision of certification and authentication services to end-users*", nor did they extend "*it to cooperation between the Parties in the financial or banking services sector*", where they remained independent competitors.[36] Therefore, no risk of coordination occurred. At the same time, on the one hand, the Identrus System was open and, thus, there were no risks of foreclosure of non-participating banks.[37] On the other hand, the Identrus agreements did not encompass exclusivity clauses (or exclusivity incentive). Thus, no foreclosure of potential competitors of Identrus was possible.[38] In conclusion, there was no risk of adverse effect on the markets of inputs.[39]

So, the banking industry has demonstrated that interoperability is the key to ensure both competition and the technology progress. In fact, these two public interests can perfectly coexist. And if that was (and still is) possible for credit institutions, it should also be possible for the metaverse operators.

---

[32] Commission Decision 2001/696/EC of 31 July 2001 relating to a proceeding under Article 81 of the EC Treaty and Article 53 of the EEA Agreement (Case No COMP/37.462 — Identrus), https://eur-lex.europa.eu/legal-content/en/TXT/HTML/?uri=CELEX:32001D0696&from=EN, para. 9. Accessed on December 1, 2025.

[33] *Ibidem*, para. 43.

[34] *Ibidem*, para. 11.

[35] *Idem.*

[36] *Ibidem*, para. 43.

[37] Indeed, Identrus had "*no incentive to exclude potential Participants, as it is inherent in the Identrus System to attract as many Participants as possible. Identrus's revenues increase with the number of electronic commerce transactions covered by the Identrus System*" (*ibidem*, para. 46).

[38] *Ibidem*, para. 51.

[39] "*The Notified Agreements are unlikely to affect markets for inputs that are necessary for companies operating in the relevant markets. As a matter of fact, Identrus will not engage in software development, it will only set up specifications which will be given free of costs to Participants and software providers. There is no exclusivity as to which software will be used as root software and which software Participants can choose. In practice, many different vendors could be used by the Participants, provided those vendors meet the Identrus standards that have to be developed. Participants can change vendors if they so wish*" (*ibidem*, para. 52).

5 The "Inevitability" of Interoperability in the EU: The Digital Markets Act

Apart from antitrust enforcement (*e.g.*, in the case of an abuse perpetrated by a dominant metaverse platform) or antitrust-compliant agreements among metaverse operators (such as standard setting cooperation to ensure interoperability among Virtual Worlds), in the European Union interoperability should be guaranteed in the metaverse field also through the application of the so-called Digital Markets Act (DMA).[40]

Such a new set of rules – entered into force in October 2022 – basically complement the competition provisions of the TFEU. Indeed, the DMA pursues an objective which is different from that of protecting undistorted competition, "*which is to ensure that markets where gatekeepers are present are and remain contestable and fair, independently from the actual, potential or presumed effects of the conduct of a given gatekeeper covered by this Regulation on competition on a given market*".[41]

Gatekeepers are undertaking that provide core platform services and which are designated by the European Commission according to the provisions of the DMA.[42] Core platform services include (among the others) online intermediation services, online search engines and online social networking services.[43] Thus, metaverse platforms could fall under the scope of application of the Digital Markets Act, giving that they belong to both "online intermediation services" and to "online social networking services" categories.

Such gatekeepers must respect the obligations established by the Digital Markets Act under articles 5 and 6. Obviously, such obligations are directly applicable – as it usually happens for all the provisions included in a regulation under EU law –, even though those within the scope of article 6 can be further specified by the European Commission.

---

[40] Regulation (EU) 2022/1925 of the European Parliament and of the Council of 14 September 2022 on contestable and fair markets in the digital sector and amending Directives (EU) 2019/1937 and (EU) 2020/1828 (Digital Markets Act), OJ L 265, 12.10.2022, pp. 1–66.

[41] *Ibidem*, recital (11). The EU lawmakers decided to strongly highlight the difference (and complementarity) between competition law and the DMA, in terms of legal interests protected by the two sets of rules, also to avoid a misinterpretation of the relation between antitrust and DMA rules which could raise concerns regarding possible violations of the *ne bis in idem* principle.

[42] According to Article 3 DMA: "*[a]n undertaking shall be designated as a gatekeeper if: (a) it has a significant impact on the internal market; (b) it provides a core platform service which is an important gateway for business users to reach end users; and (c) it enjoys an entrenched and durable position, in its operations, or it is foreseeable that it will enjoy such a position in the near future*". The provision also sets some presumptions according to which a provider of a core platform service is designable as a gatekeeper (*i.e.*, turnover thresholds and monthly active end users thresholds).

[43] The other core platform services mentioned by article 2 of the DMA are: video-sharing platform services, number-independent interpersonal communications services, operating systems, web browsers, virtual assistants, cloud computing services, online advertising services, including any advertising networks, advertising exchanges and any other advertising intermediation services, provided by an undertaking that provides one of the others core platform services listed by article 2.

Among those duties for gatekeepers, interoperability has an important place especially under article 6. In fact, for example, such provision requires gatekeepers to allow the installation of third-party software applications using, or interoperating with, its operating system.[44] Moreover, gatekeepers "*shall allow business users and alternative providers of services provided together with, or in support of, core platform services, free of charge, effective interoperability with, and access for the purposes of interoperability to, the same operating system, hardware or software features, regardless of whether those features are part of the operating system, as are available to, or used by, that gatekeeper when providing such services*".[45]

The last obligation is more than a mere neutrality rule for gatekeepers that compete with their business users on a specific service on the gatekeeper's platform. Indeed, the interoperability rule at issue applies irrespective of the fact that the gatekeeper competes with the business users that have the right to interoperability. A gatekeeper can deny interoperability to its business users only in exceptional and specific cases in order to protect the integrity of the platform.[46]

The fact that the Digital Markets Act will apply to Virtual World platforms has been confirmed even before the entry into force of the DMA by EU Commissioner Breton, according to whom "*the Digital Markets Act and the Digital Services Act [...] provide the appropriate framework and the necessary tools to tackle issues concerning metaverse. The Digital Markets Act [provides] tools to foster contestability in the metaverse, either because the relevant services are within its scope or through the provisions that ensure future proofing of the Digital Markets Act*".[47]

Therefore, even though our crystal ball may be too little or opaque to see all the possible outcomes of the metaverse market's development in the future - and there can be also different evolutions that we did not see - the willingness of the European Commission to strongly apply EU rules – including the Digital Markets Act – to the metaverse is undoubtful. And provided that the DMA requires gatekeeper to guarantee and offer (free of charge) interoperability in favor of their business users (and to the final benefit of end users), perhaps interoperability in the metaverse will be inevitable, irrespective of the willingness of Virtual World platforms. Such obligation for platforms could be implemented by a standard setting agreement among Virtual World providers, in line with competition rules (especially Article 101 TFEU). Indeed, nothing under the DMA precludes the European Commission to collectively require gatekeepers in the metaverse to collaborate in order to establish a common standard for the interoperability of their virtual spaces.

That will basically avoid both the emergence of a dominant metaverse – through a tipping effect of the market – and the lock-in of consumers (and business users),

---

[44] Digital Markets Act, *cit.*, article 6, para. 4.

[45] *Ibidem*, article 6, para. 7.

[46] *Ibidem*, article 6, para. 7: "The gatekeeper shall not be prevented from taking strictly necessary and proportionate measures to ensure that interoperability does not compromise the integrity of the operating system, virtual assistant, hardware or software features provided by the gatekeeper, provided that such measures are duly justified by the gatekeeper".

[47] European Parliament (2022).

forcing them to single-homing. So, hopefully, the Digital Markets Act will really ensure interoperability (*rectius*, competition) in the metaverse market. If this will be the case, antitrust rules – especially Article 102 TFEU – basically will not have room to be applied to the metaverse in order to enforce interoperability. However – as stated by the regulation itself – the DMA is without prejudice to the application of EU antitrust rules.[48] Thus, if the DMA will not be enough, we will fortunately have traditional competition tools which have widely demonstrated their value during the last decades.

References

Andreangeli A (2009) Interoperability as an "essential facility" in the Microsoft case: encouraging stifling competition or innovation? Eur Law Rev 4:584–611

Banasevic N et al (2004) Commission adopts decision in the Microsoft case, Competition Policy Newsletter, Number 2 — Summer 2004. https://www.dse.univr.it/documenti/OccorrenzaIns/matdid/matdid978033.pdf, last accessed December 1, 2025

Di Benedetto F, Moscianese J (2022) Il diritto antitrust nel metaverso: spunti di riflessione su quel che verrà. https://www.medialaws.eu/il-diritto-antitrust-nel-metaverso-spunti-di-riflessione-su-quel-che-verra/ , last accessed December 1, 2025

European Commission (2020) Study on the application of the interchange fee regulation (final report). https://ec.europa.eu/commission/presscorner/detail/en/ip_20_442, last accessed December 1, 2025

European Parliament (2022) P-000656/2022, answer given by Mr Breton on behalf of the European Commission (1.6.2022). https://www.europarl.europa.eu/doceo/document/E-9-2022-000656-ASW_EN.pdf, last accessed December 1, 2025

Metaverse Standards Forum (2022) The Metaverse Standards Forum. https://metaverse-standards.org/ , last accessed December 1, 2025

Open Metaverse Foundation (2022) Building an open, accessible, interoperable metaverse for all. https://www.openmv.org/, last accessed December 1, 2025

Petit N, Moreno Belloso N (2021) A simple way to measure tipping in digital markets. https://www.promarket.org/2021/04/06/measure-test-tipping-point-digital-markets/, last accessed December 1, 2025

World Economic Forum (2022) The metaverse paradox: why the industry needs standardization. https://www.weforum.org/agenda/2022/07/the-metaverse-paradox-why-we-need-standardization/, last accessed December 1, 2025

Zuckerberg M (2022) Facebook Post. https://www.facebook.com/zuck/posts/pfbid021Q1ZMJFWcXBvPcaqpLWgp3x5HTMD3vyVNbPB17BcuX6n1UmAKh7Kyv6dUb6oKP7Nl, last accessed December 1, 2025

[48] Art. 1(6), Digital Markets Act.

Metaverses, Digital and Competition Law: What's New?

Andrea Pezzoli

Abstract *Is metaverse just a new and fashionable word or is a new challenge for competition policy?*

This brief contribution will focus on the main competition issues which will be raised in the near future by the development of metaverses and will try to discuss if the theoretical tool-kit at disposal of the competition authorities is still appropriate and self-sufficient. Most of the challenges Competition Authorities will have to deal with seem to be quite similar to those they are facing with digital platforms. The author does not question the need for a "more economic approach" but such an approach should not be focused solely (and ideologically) on static efficiency. It should not ignore economic freedom, market structure and dynamic efficiency. On the contrary, the temptation of a per se *regulation might be at the same time too ambitious and quite risky.*

1 Introduction

In the current (and never-ending) debate about the goals of competition policy we observe (mainly because of the digital revolution) a continuous tension between public interest goals and more traditional goals such as the consumer welfare standard, more or less "enriched". Competition concerns are often intertwined with other issues concerning privacy, pluralism, democracy, sustainability or inequality. It cannot be denied that this intertwining does affect the attitude towards big tech, digital platforms and - why not? – metaverses.

On the one hand we can appreciate a strong desire to assign to antitrust enforcement a number of different goals, absolutely noble goals but possibly too many and for whose achievement antitrust is not necessarily the most appropriate tool. On

The views and the opinions expressed in the article belong solely to the author and do not necessarily reflect the view of the Italian Competition Authority.

A. Pezzoli (✉)
University of Tor Vergata, Rome, Italy
e-mail: andrea.pezzoli57@gmail.com

F. Di Porto and O. Pollicino (eds.), *Law and Politics of Virtual Worlds*, Law, Governance and Technology Series 79, https://doi.org/10.1007/978-3-032-08541-2_14

Fig. 1. Competition authorities need constant update. *Source* Jenny (2018), *The digital sector: Challenges for Competition Law and Policy*, Mannheim Center for Competition and Innovation Annual Conference

the other hand, there is a strenuous defence of the purity of competition law. The contribution of economic analysis seems to be confined to the assessment of efficiency, more often than not identified with static efficiency, today's efficiency, which is nothing but the efficiency of the past.

This brief contribution will focus on the main competition issues which will be raised in the near future by the development of metaverses and will try to discuss if the tool-kit at disposal of the competition authorities is still appropriate and self-sufficient.

Figures 1 and 2 below synthetize the main contributions of this chapter: first, that Antitrust policy needs continuous updating; and second, that Antitrust enforcement is not self-sufficient, meaning that market friendly public policies are (more than) welcome,[1] as the market is a "human creation"[2]!

Though not self-sufficient it is worth noting that the theoretical tool-kit of antitrust is still largely appropriate!

In this perspective this contribution will deal with the challenges raised by new phenomena (NFT, metaverses) for the application of competition rules.

Let's start with a simple question: from an antitrust perspective is metaverse just *name changing*?

In other words, are the challenges raised by metaverses "by and large" the same as those raised by the Digital Economy?

Though scepticism about the new fashionable issues that become suddenly popular in the antitrust discourse and about some "nebulous" concepts as gatekeepers, ecosystems and metaverse itself, may be justified, it cannot be denied that competition law needs to be updated. Nevertheless, a better understanding is needed[3] before arguing (sometimes, shouting) that: (i) the traditional antitrust theoretical tool-kit is no more

---

[1] See Pezzoli, 2019.

[2] *«il mercato è una creazione umana e l'intervento pubblico ne è una componente necessaria e non un elemento di per sé distorsivo e vessatorio»* which may be translated as "the market is a human creation and public intervention is a necessary component of the market, as such neither distorting nor oppressive". See. Caffè, 1974.

[3] Jenny (2021).

Fig. 2 Competition Authorieties need to combine enforcement with market-friendly policies. *Source* Lennon and McCartney (1967), *Sgt. Pepper's Lonely Hearts Club Band*

sufficient; (ii) updating the tool-kit is not enough; (iii) we must move towards a more regulatory approach; (iv) we must anticipate with *ex ante* regulation phenomena (as NFT and metaverse) that we don't fully understand and that change continuously.

The Italian comedian Maurizio Ferrini used to say "I don't understand but. still, I conform".

Today Ferrini's slogan could be changed with "I don't understand but still I regulate"!

In this regard, even if it is not worth re-opening here the discussion on the DMA, it may be pointed out that it is really hard to argue that the regulatory approach privileged by the DMA is actually future-proof. "Quick and timely response" has been the mantra that pushed the quick approval of the DMA. Now that the train has finally left the station we all hope that the new regulation will actually be self enforcing and could guarantee quick and effective response, but the complexity of the designation process, the lack of flexibility which characterizes the list of DOS and DON'Ts included in artt. 5, 6 and 7 and the difficulties to enrich or integrate that list may make the functioning of the new regulation quite complex.

After these preliminary and not so articulated considerations in the following paragraphs the paper will follow a more rational order, focusing on 5 basic topics: (i) metaverse and market definition; (ii) metaverse and market power (more specifically, to which extent the essential facility doctrine could be helpful in dealing with NFT and metaverse?); (iii) metaverse and collusion; (iv) metaverse and mergers review; (v) metaverse and data.

The discussion will be very sharp and assertive, no more than remarks in a nutshell, whereas each of the topics would deserve a much wider (and serious) debate. There will be time for a deeper understanding. Indeed, we cannot ignore that the time required for the diffusion of metaverse might be longer than expected. At present *World Horizon*, a virtual environment developed by Meta, registers less than 300 thousand users per month and other well-known metaverses as *Decentraland* and *The Sandbox* have 38 and 500 users, respectively.

2 Market Definition

Relevant market is still relevant, even in a virtual world. I'd say, not only for real consumers but also for avatars - though much less relevant as a tool to assess market power - in a digital world and *a fortiori* in a metaverse context market shares are not that useful and sometimes may be quite meaningless. Market shares held by the owner of the metaverse on any particular market (and even the existence of entry barriers on specific relevant market) may not be an appropriate indicator of market power. This may be particularly true if we have to cope with competition between metaverses.

More generally when we deal with Big Tech it is not that easy to disentangle market power from bargaining power, economic power and power *tout court*.

Nonetheless market definition is still useful to understand how the competitive process works in the new environment, the possible anti-competitive effects and, ultimately, the competition theories of harm. For instance, it is quite interesting to understand if we can look at metaverses just as a new type of market-place, within which horizontal and vertical relationships take place.

What can be seen as a quite traditional view does not arise from the natural resistance to change, typical of practitioners of competition law, who are afraid to abandon tested tools (the old slippers) and to deal with new analytical concepts. And it does not depend on the still fragile knowledge of new concepts as gatekeepers, multi-actor or multi-product ecosystems, NFT or metaverses. Some important steps forward have been made and the learning process is developing. This volume could be a qualified example!

The main reason why market definition is still important is that even in a digital environment we have to pay wider attention to the structure of the markets and to freedom to compete.

The criticisms to the consumer welfare standard and to an economic approach based solely on static efficiency (the outcome of competition of the past) - do not belong only to the so-called Neo-Brandeisian world.[4] The criticisms (quite often constructive criticisms) come also from those economists and lawyers who call for a higher attention to the competitive process, the structure of the markets and economic freedom.[5] The protection of the competitive process among a significant number of

[4] See Kahn (2017), Wu (2019); Tepper e Hearn (2018), and CPI, 2018.

[5] See for example Hovenkamp (2019), or Shapiro (2018). For an interesting discussion about the protection of the competitive process and about the relationship between liberty and efficiency (two sides of the same coin) see, doi:10.1177/0003603X18756130 and Grillo (2023).

rivals in free and open markets is a goal that can be framed in a sound economic approach equally sensitive to efficiency.[6]

Disregarding the structure of the market, the competitive assessment may risk to consider today's efficiency as the best predictor of tomorrow's efficiency and to underestimate the future competitive constraints that may derive from today's less efficient competitors. This could be particularly distorting when we cope with innovative markets, and metaverses are by no means innovative!! It may provide a great justification for not contestable monopolies. Freedom to compete and efficiency are strictly intertwined.

In this perspective (which is more focused on the protection of the competitive process rather than on the consumer welfare standard) market structure matters and consequently market definition continues to matter and to play a crucial role.

In this perspective the updating of the Market Definition Notice is very welcome and hopefully very helpful.[7]

3 Market Power

In the realm of the Big Tech market power continuously blurs with economic power and takes new forms.

When we cope with metaverses a more specific question may concern the possibility to apply the essential facility doctrine. In principle even if metaverses and NFT should guarantee a decentralized world, the risk of centralization and competitive concerns related to centralization may arise.

The essential facility may be represented by the infrastructure and the underlying platform on which metaverses could be based.

But what about the haptic gloves, the smart glasses? When I read on the newspapers about a possible agreement between the most powerful glass distributor and Metaverse I'm seriously curious (or should I say concerned?).

As in the whole digital world network effects, low incentives to change ecosystems and high switching costs may also play an important role when you have to assess market power.

There is no time to recall the cumulative conditions required to apply the essential facility doctrine[8] but it is worth recalling that the essential facility doctrine has to be handled with care because it could be a dangerous short-cut and the competitive assessment might be significantly distorted.

More generally, it must be stressed that there is still a number of issues about which further economic thinking is required before Competition authorities can make some decisions concerning new phenomena as metaverses.[9] The scope for competition

[6] See Fox (1981).

[7] See European Commission (2022).

[8] See the recent contribution by Hovenkamp (2022).

[9] It seems to the author that the approach suggested in Jenny (2021).

among metaverses and within metaverses, data and privacy issues,[10] the role played by interoperability and data portability do require a better understanding.

4 Collusion

As far as competition among metaverses is concerned we might argue that cooperation and interoperable metaverses may have clear and procompetitive potentialities. According to some experts the technology would even favour the presence of multiple metaverses and specialised metaverses may have weak incentive to compete with generalised platforms. In this case, we may ask ourselves if we are dealing with collusion or, more probably, if specialised and generalised platforms do not belong to the same relevant market.

As far as for the assessment of competition of ecosystems and/or multiproduct platforms the standard analysis traditionally used in the application of antitrust rules becomes quite difficult to apply to competition between metaverses.

And what may happen within the metaverse?

When the metaverse is competing with some of the business users of the metaverse itself or with some of the providers of the complementary services, antitrust issues may arise, mainly the risk of abuse of dominance (e.g. refusal to deal, discriminatory behaviour, self-preferencing…) but also the risk of collusion.

In this perspective we have to focus on the relationships between the users of the metaverse and the metaverse itself, which could be both vertical and horizontal, and try to isolate the collusive component of the relationship.

Furthermore, the thin line between tacit and explicit collusion, by rational adjustment (which is not an "antitrust sin") and restrictive coordination may be easily obscured by the use of algorithms and in particular by machine learning algorithms. It won't be easy to distinguish a cartel between human beings from a "cartel among robots" for which identifying a proper exchange of minds and the attribution of liabilities may be a difficult task.

5 Mergers

Some of the main recurring issues typical of mergers in the digital era may affect the assessment of mergers involving metaverses. On the one hand the well-known phenomenon of the so-called killer acquisitions and the challenging problem of the

---

[10] Dealing with the new digital world, competition authorities have had limited occasions to cope the role played by data. Two meaningful examples may be found in the decisions made by the French authority in the *GDF/Suez* case (Décision n° 14-MC-02, 9 September 2014) and by the Italian competition authority in the *Enel/Sen* case (AGCM, A511 - *ENEL/condotte anticoncorrenziali nel mercato della vendita di energia elettrica* - Provvedimento n. 27,494 and CJEU, 12 May 2022, C-377/20)

counterfactual: what would have happened in the absence of the merger? Would the small and innovative company become an effective competitive constraint for the metaverse? Or will the target company fully develop its innovative potentialities only because of the merger?

Is it really true that the big players, after the merger, would continue to encourage the small firms to innovate and to guarantee decentralized strategies? Or it is just a wishful thinking? And laziness and short-term profits may prevail?

On the other hand, we cannot ignore the increasing difficulties in the assessment of market power that I just briefly mentioned before (par. 2). Just to mention two of them:

(i) Market shares are a poor indicator and the application of the more traditional tests is not so clear-cut;
(ii) Conglomerate effects, in the past considered absolutely harmless, in a metaverse environment may become crucial because of the role played by data. We have to look at data as a sort of glue that allows to extend market power from a market where the platform is already strong in another market where the platform is not present yet.

6 Data

Finally, data. Shall we say that data are the origin and the very end of Metaverse? And that "Old social networks" are no more effective for data collection? The essential facility issues might come on stage again, together with the role which can be played by data (Big Data?) as a barrier to entry, or as a quality competitive factor. Pretending to be more sensitive to privacy issues metaverses might be more attractive for consumers.

At present, however, the number of users (and, hence, the amount of collected data) does not seem to be particularly large.

Antitrust enforcers might also be concerned of data exploitation, which can be theorized as a sort of "excessive data" abuse. For instance, in 2019 the *Bundeskartellamt* observed that Facebook's terms of service and the approach followed for the collection and use of data violated European Data Protection rules and hence could be assessed as an exploitative abuse: too much data and collected in a not sufficiently transparent manner.

It is not widely accepted that competition law is the most appropriate tool to cope with privacy violations. It seems still quite controversial how data and privacy issues can be integrated in a sound antitrust assessment and it is still controversial whether they should be. On the one hand, what could be read as an exploitative abuse, could be read also as a lack of transparency issue. For instance, coping with a case which was quite similar to the German Facebook's case, the Italian Competition

Authority privileged the application of Consumer Protection rules and the outcome was substantially the same.[11]

On the other hand, in the near future the need for cooperation between antitrust authorities and data protection agencies will be increasingly important, since data, exchange of data, data portability, data sharing will be increasingly key for the competitive process. It will not be an easy task, since the cultural backgrounds of the two institutions are quite different.

7 Concluding Remarks

The challenges that might be raised by metaverses are quite intriguing for competition law, even if not necessarily so different from those raised by the digital platforms, unless we are eager to enrich the endless debate about the goals of antitrust law with a new standard, the "avatar welfare standard".

Seriously speaking, times they are a'changin' (see Fig. 3). The world moves on and Competition Agencies need to understand the continuous changes. Their tool-kit needs continuous up-dating, though it is still quite sound especially if the so-called "more economic approach" is not merely (and ideologically) identified with an approach focused solely on static efficiency and much less interested in economic freedom and market structure.

In the new digital era cooperation among different institutions will be crucial both at the domestic and international level. For the implementation of the DMA the degree of cooperation between the European Commission and the National Competition Authorities has to be even higher. Speaking of metaverses, even the need for a global antitrust agency has been proposed again, though the new phenomenon might require quite a long time to reach significant dimension.

However, after having learned how to cooperate among themselves and with sectoral regulators, the new challenge for Competition Authorities will be to learn how to collaborate with Data Protection Agencies. Data and privacy issues are increasingly central in the application of competition rules and metaverses might make these issues even more crucial.

Therefore, better understanding of the new phenomena and institutional cooperation are key for an adequate antitrust enforcement whereas the temptation to run before having learned how to walk, the temptation to anticipate through *ex ante* regulation the future developments is quite risky and, I'd say, might be too ambitious. Especially if the temptation is a "*per se*" temptation. Don't forget that if there is a temptation, somewhere there is a sin!!

[11] See Agcm (2018) and Bundeskartellamt (2019).

Fig. 3. Competition Agencies need to adjust to continuous change. *Source* Dylan (1965), *The times they are a'changin'*

References

Agcm (2018) PS11112 – Facebook – Condivisione dati con terzi, Provv. 27432. Garante della Concorrenza e del Mercato (AGCM), Rome

Bundeskartellamt (2019) Facebook, B6-22/16. Bundeskartellamt, Bonn

Caffè F (1974) Lezioni di politica economica. Boringhieri, Torino, p 38

Competition Policy International (2018) Hipster antitrust. Competition Policy International

CPI (2018) Antitrust chronicle–hipster antitrust. CPI

European Commission (2022) Commission notice on the definition of the relevant market for the purposes of Union competition law. Directorate-General for Competition, European Commission, Brussels

Fox E (1981) The Modernization of antitrust: a new equilibrium. Cornell Law Rev 66:1140–1192

Fox E (2018) Competition Policy at the intersection of equity and efficiency: the developed and developing worlds. Antitrust Bull 63(1):3–6

Grillo M (2023) Competition, efficiency and liberty. Intern Rev Econ 70(4):437–456

Hovenkamp E (2022) The antitrust duty to deal in the age of Big Tech. Yale Law J 131(5):1483–1718

Hovenkamp H (2019) Whatever did happen to the antitrust movement? Notre Dame Law Rev. 94(2):583–622

Jenny F (2018) The digital sector: challenges for competition law and policy, presentation at the Mannheim center for competition and innovation. Annual Conference.

Jenny F (2021) Competition law and digital ecosystems: learning to walk before we run. Ind Corp Chang 30(5):1143–1167. https://doi.org/10.1093/icc/dtab047

Kahn L (2017) Amazon's antitrust paradox. Yale Law J 126(3):710–805

Pezzoli A (2019) With a little help from my friends: quale politica della concorrenza per l'economia digitale? Econ. Ital. 2:1–23

Shapiro C (2018) Antitrust in a time of populism. Int J Ind Organ 61:714–748

Tepper J, Hearn D (2018) The myth of capitalism: monopolies and the death of competition. Wiley, Hoboken
Wu T (2019) The curse of bigness: antitrust in the new gilded age. Columbia Global Reports, New York

Privacy and Data Protection

Data Protection Challenges and Privacy Issues in the Metaverse dimension

Laura Greco

Abstract *The rise of the Metaverse introduces significant challenges to existing data protection frameworks, notably the EU General Data Protection Regulation (GDPR). This chapter explores how the immersive and data-intensive nature of the Metaverse may exacerbate privacy risks through the large-scale collection and inference of personal data, including emotional and behavioral attributes. Key concerns include the regulation of profiling and automated decision-making, transparency of data processing, identification of data controllers, and the evolving nature of user consent. It also questions whether inferred data should be granted the same legal protections as traditional personal data. Moreover, the chapter considers different models of data controllership and reflects on the implications for user autonomy, consent validity, and the effectiveness of rights such as data portability. Concluding, the author urges the need for a coordinated legal response to ensure accountability and protect data subjects in an increasingly complex digital environment.*

1 Introduction

Data protection applies to off- and on-line life.[1]

Nowadays an assessment of privacy aspects is essential with respect to every activity of the real world and of the digital one, where implications have a greater impact because of a weaker control over data and better opportunities of data collection and elaboration.

We already know that technologies give rise to new challenges for the law. In the data protection field, the technological development has increased the opportunities

L. Greco (✉)
Free University of Bozen-Bolzano, Bozen, Italy
e-mail: lagreco@unibz.it; l.greco@studiolegalegreco.net

[1] Perhaps it is more appropriate today to talk about "on-life", using a neologism created by Floridi 2015. With this neologism the Author points out the blurring of the distinction between reality and virtuality in the current society where life is nestled in the confluence of these realities.

F. Di Porto and O. Pollicino (eds.), *Law and Politics of Virtual Worlds*, Law, Governance and Technology Series 79, https://doi.org/10.1007/978-3-032-08541-2_15

and the ways of data processing, cyber threats, cross-border data transfers and the need for more caution regarding security issues.[2]

For these and other reasons, which can not be described here for the sake of brevity, the European lawmaker adopted the Regulation (EU) 2016/679 "on the protection of natural persons with regard to the processing of personal data and on the free movement of such data",[3] also known as "General Data Protection Regulation" (hereinafter "GDPR"), born from the experience of Directive 95/46/CE[4] and created with the aim and the need to regulate a new reality based on data sharing models and joint management of data, which are meant for a worldwide movement from the start.[5]

The Metaverse represents a new challenge which data protection law, as well as other fields, must face.

So far the GDPR has proved adequate in relation to the technological evolution.[6] Technical progress is undeniable with regard to information society services, payment services, blockchain, smart contracts and, lastly, Artificial Intelligence applications:. Notwithstanding, GDPR's rules, principles and legal categories have been able to adapt and did not require a review.[7]

However, the Metaverse could have such resources, yet to discover, as to fuel what Rodotà described as "electronic double" back in 2005.[8] The digital world managed to create a copy, a duplicate of people through the collection of pieces of data, like

---

[2] "Rapid technological developments and globalisation have brought new challenges for the protection of personal data. The scale of the collection and sharing of personal data has increased significantly", recital no. 6 of the Regulation (EU) 2016/679.

[3] Regulation (EU) 2016/679 of the European Parliament and of the Council of 27 April 2016 on the protection of natural persons with regard to the processing of personal data and on the free movement of such data, and repealing Directive 95/46/EC (General Data Protection Regulation), published in the Official Journal of the European Union, L 119/1 of 4 May 2016. For further information on the GDPR, see D'Orazio et al. 2021; Finocchiaro 2019a; Kuner et al. 2019.

[4] Directive 95/46/EC of the European Parliament and of the Council of 24 October 1995 on the protection of individuals with regard to the processing of personal data and on the free movement of such data. The Directive regulated data protection before the adoption of the GDPR, which has repealed the Directive with effect from 25 May 2018.

[5] See Finocchiaro 2017.

[6] The widespread availability of new technologies, such as smart contracts and Artificial Intelligence systems, has been a "stress test" to verify the endurance of Regulation (EU) 2016/679. It has been "the litmus test of the foresight of rules that the European lawmaker introduced not so long ago in order to overcome a state of standstill where it was hard to interpret the level of individual's protection between national and international regulations", see Bassini and Pollicino 2022 (the translation from Italian was freely made by the Author of this Chapter).

[7] Every new innovation does not necessarily require the creation of new rules, as long as the existing rules can properly adapt and regulate the new situation. This concept is well explained by Finocchiaro 2019b: "there is a widespread tendency, exalted by the media, of requiring a new rule for each new phenomenon. The social alarm, absolutely acceptable in many cases, almost automatically produces the request for *ad hoc* regulations. (…) the need to provide for a specific rule for each new case appears to be the result of a methodological deficiency" (the text was translated by the Author of this chapter).

[8] In 2005 Stefano Rodotà was already talking about the "electronic double": "*We are now faced with a double body, physical and electronic, which modifies the sense of the self and the relationship*

fragments of pottery, spread across the web by themselves. The Metaverse could manage to accomplish this operation in exponential ways through the collection of data and inferences and the creation of increasingly sophisticated profiles, supported by the spontaneous, but not aware, cooperation of users themselves.[9]

Talking about Metaverse, a preamble should be made: today it is hard to understand the real impact of the Metaverse and whether it will be an actual innovation, which will deeply change the relationships and the way people connect, or maybe "something of an empty shell".[10]

Today we may well not see the full extent of its potential and may not have a clear idea of the full range of potential opportunities.

Nevertheless, it can be easily imagined that the Metaverse could raise issues around state sovereignty[11] and this paper aims at offering some ideas and viewpoints about which possible data protection implications the Metaverse dimension could entail.

The aim of this chapter is to try to wonder how the main principles and rules on data protection may apply in the context of the Metaverse. How materially could information on data processing be given to the data subject? Who will be the Data Controller in the Metaverse? How to regulate and perhaps prevent from unlawful profiling activities in the Metaverse? The chapter addresses this kind of questions, wondering if data protection law may need to adapt or may be disrupted by this new Reality.

---

with others. (…) pieces of each of us are stored in several databases, where our identity is dissected and broken down, where we appear now as consumers, now as voters, debtors, workers, highway users" (our translation from Italian): Rodotà 2005, available at the following link https://www.privacy.it/archivio/rodo20050504.html (acccsscd on 3.10.2022). Haggcrty c Ericson 2000.

[9] "We submit our rights to privacy for slaughter of our own will. Or perhaps we just consent to the loss of privacy as a reasonable price for the wonders offered in exchange", see Bauman and Lyon 2013.

[10] This is how the Council of the European Union defines the possible outcome of the Metaverse in its paper "Metaverse – Virtual world, real challenges" of 9 March 2022, p. 1, available here https://www.consilium.europa.eu/media/54987/metaverse-paper-9-march-2022.pdf (accessed on 3.10.2022). So far, also the European Commission does not seem to be keen "to launch a specific study into the functioning of the metaverse, but such a study is not excluded at a later stage. The Commission has also no immediate intention to propose specific policy or regulatory measures concerning the metaverse, in particular since the existing regulatory framework also applies to metaverse" (see "Answer given by Mr. Breton on behalf of the European Commission", 1 June 2022, document no. P-000656/2022, available here https://www.europarl.europa.eu/doceo/document/E-9-2022-000656-ASW_EN.html (accessed on 3.10.2022).

[11] "Absence of borders and rules in the Metaverse is likely to constitute a further challenge to the existing notion of territorial sovereignty", according to the Council of the European Union in its paper of 9 March 2022 (see footnote no. 10). About digital sovereignty, Floridi 2020, states: "Sovereignty is a form of legitimate, controlling power [...] we can now qualify as national sovereignty the controlling power exercised by the State on its territory, on the resources that are found in it, and the people who live there. The digital age is forcing us to rethink the nature of sovereignty. But who should exercise it *de facto* and *de jure*? (…) Today, the fight is not over secular and spiritual power, but over corporate and political power over the digital" (p. 372 and p. 377).

2 Personal Data and Inferences

As disclosed in the Introduction, data subjects, namely natural persons who can be identified directly or indirectly,[12] represent the category that is more likely to be affected by the Metaverse.

This prediction seems to be quite certain, considering that the Metaverse calls for a massive use of personal data. Besides, the use of augmented reality (AR) technologies and the multiplication of possibilities to forge facial features, footage and voice will lead to the acquisition of much more data than today, including insights into emotions through visual interpretation of facial muscles, for instance.

Data is in inferences,[13] especially in the Metaverse dimension. This concept is not new: inferences and the economy of inferences have been already debated talking about Big Data and more recently with regard to Artificial Intelligence and machine learning (ML) mechanisms.[14] It is about the possibility to deduce, with significant probability, the value of an attribute from the values of a set of other attributes.[15]

In other words, through the processing of known data and the observation of characteristic elements of a person or groups, it is possible to derive and infer new information that was previously unknown and has not been shared by the data subject himself/herself.

---

[12] Pursuant to Article 4, par. 1, no. 1) of the GDPR, "an identifiable natural person is one who can be identified, directly or indirectly, in particular by reference to an identifier such as a name, an identification number, location data, an online identifier or to one or more factors specific to the physical, physiological, genetic, mental, economic, cultural or social identity of that natural person".

[13] This is also what Mrs. Kavya Pearlman (founder and CEO of the XR Safety Initiative, a global non-profit Standards Developing Organization (SDO) that promotes privacy, safety, security and ethics in immersive environments and technologies) claims. The full interview is here available: https://venturebeat.com/cloud/metaverse-vs-data-privacy-a-clash-of-the-titans/ (accessed on 5.10.2022).

[14] See Solow-Niederman, 2022: "machine learning facilitates an inference economy in which organizations use available data collected from individuals to generate further information about both those individuals and about other people. (…) This result disempowers individuals who seek to shield their personal data, yet can no longer know what needs protecting" (p. 361). The Author goes on and affirms: "The term inference economy underscores how machine learning generates information from bits of data. It also highlights how this threat to information privacy protections runs in parallel to surveillance capitalist concerns with platform firms' manipulation of user autonomy and preferences, as well as informational capitalism's concern with property law's role in facilitating the exploitation of data" (p. 363). The European Parliament warns against the power of inferences as well: "data collected from the digital traces of individuals can be mined in ways that allow for a highly accurate inference of very intimate personal information, especially when such data is merged with other data sets" (see *Resolution of 20 October 2020 on the Digital Services Act and fundamental rights issues posed*, available here https://www.europarl.europa.eu/doceo/document/TA-9-2020-0274_EN.html, accessed on 5.10.2022).

[15] This is how the Article 29 Data Protection Working Party (hereinafter "WP29"), which has been now replace by the European Data Protection Board pursuant to Article 94 GDPR, defines inference in its *Opinion 05/2014 on Anonymisation Techniques*, adopted on 10 April 2014. The WP29 goes on: "it must be clear that 'identification' not only means the possibility of retrieving a person's name and/or address, but also includes potential identifiability by singling out, linkability and inference" (p. 10).

Hence, one could consider inferences, together with personal data, as raw materials of the Metaverse, which represents an immersive experience[16] and could lead to the next generation of the so-called "Internet of sense".[17]

Under this perspective, it seems that the category of personal data is bigger than what is currently protected by the letter of the law and there may be the need to expand it. Indeed, the GDPR does not consider inferred data (or "economy class" data, as they are commonly referred to[18]), which instead could be the fortune of many providers of the Metaverse, who may take advantage of the exclusion of this category from the scope of the GDPR.

Extending the personal data category to include inferences could lead to a series of consequences.

2.1 *Profiling and Decision-Making Process*

As already stipulated by the GDPR, profiling is "*any form of automated processing of personal data consisting of the use of personal data to evaluate certain personal aspects relating to a natural person, in particular to analyse or predict aspects*

---

[16] The European Parliament Research Service' briefing, *Metaverse. Opportunities, risks and policy implications*, 24 June 2022, defines the Metaverse "as an immersive and constant virtual 3D world where people interact by means of an avatar to carry out a wide range of activities" (full text is here available https://www.europarl.europa.eu/RegData/etudes/BRIE/2022/733557/EPRS_BRI(2022)733557_EN.pdf accessed on 7.09.2022).

[17] Following the Internet of Things, the Internet of Sense will be the next generation of virtual and web experience. According to the 9th Edition of "Hot Consumer Trends" report by Ericsson, the various trends are clustered under the name of Internet of Senses, a new service economy based on sensorial experiences in a digital context. Ericsson describes the Internet of Sense as follows: "In the Internet of Senses, visual, audio, haptic, and other technologies allow human beings to have digital sensory experiences similar to the ones we experience in the physical world. The Internet of Senses augments our senses beyond the boundaries of our bodies, giving us augmented vision, hearing, touch, and smell. It enables us to blend multisensory digital experiences with our local surroundings and interact with remote people, devices, and robots as if they were right beside us" (the full report is available here https://www.ericsson.com/en/reports-and-papers/consumerlab/reports/10-hot-consumer-trends-2030, accessed on 4.10.2022).

[18] See Wachter and Mittelstadt, 2019, available at SSRN: https://ssrn.com/abstract=3248829: "inferences are treated as 'economy class' personal data that are afforded little meaningful protection, and certainly less than personal data provided by the data subject or sensitive personal data. In part, third parties may have an interest in inferences and derived data and the techniques used to create it (e.g. trade secrets) due to their value or the costs involved" (p. 611) and "Given the novel risks of Big Data analytics and algorithmic decision-making, inferences cannot justifiably remain 'economy class' personal data. Data subjects' privacy interests require renewed protection to restore the fair balance between individual, public, and commercial interests that inspires data protection law. The current remit of data protection law works well to govern input data, but fails to provide meaningful control over how personal data is evaluated. A right to reasonable inferences is a first step to correct this imbalance" (p. 620), accessed on 29.09.2025.

concerning that natural person's performance at work, economic situation, health, personal preferences, interests, reliability, behaviour, location or movements".[19]

Sometimes, but not always, profiling is used in the context of automated decision-making processes, namely decisions, which may include a measure evaluating personal aspects relating to a data subject, based solely on automated processing and which produces legal effects concerning him or her or similarly significantly affects him or her.[20]

These notions allow to understand the extent of how these processes exploit data. Hence, a bigger availability of data (and inferences) could lead to even more pervasive profiling activities, which could also have harmful consequences, such as loss of control over one's life and decisions or voter manipulation, in particular for vulnerable groups.[21]

Since 2017, the Article 29 Data Protection Working Party (hereinafter, "WP29") talks about inferences referring to profiling and automated decision-making processes. Specifically, in the Group of Data Protection Authorities' opinion, the process of profiling "*works by creating derived or inferred data about individuals – 'new' personal data that has not been provided directly by the data subjects themselves (…). Profiling can create special category data by inference from data which is not special category data in its own right but becomes so when combined with other data. For example, it may be possible to infer someone's state of health from the records of their food shopping combined with data on the quality and energy content of foods*".[22] Automated decision-making processes can be based on inferences too.[23]

So it is clear that the bigger the availability of (referred or inferred) data, the greater is the opportunity of finding correlations and links, allowing the identification, the analysis and the deduction of aspects about personality, behavior, interests and habits of people.[24] And these consequences could concern not only the single subject whose

[19] Article 4, par. 1, no. 4 of the GDPR.

[20] Recital no. 71 of the GDPR.

[21] In its resolution mentioned above in footnote no. 14, the European Parliament reminds that "*the Cambridge Analytica and Facebook scandals showed the risks associated with opaque data processing operations of online platforms by revealing that certain voters had been micro-targeted with political advertising and, at times, even with targeted disinformation*".

[22] See WP29, *Guidelines on Automated individual decision-making and Profiling for the purposes of Regulation 2016/679*, adopted on 3 October 2017 and then revised and adopted on 6 February 2018 by the EDPB, p. 15, here available https://ec.europa.eu/newsroom/article29/items/612053, (accessed on 7.09.2022).

[23] See the above-mentioned WP29's Guidelines, p. 8.

[24] Rodotà's view proves still valid today, especially when he talked about "*the controlled body*": "*(…) today tested controls and external conditioning go along with a construction of the body itself in forms that can make it compatible with the surveillance society. (…) the person, who is 'scrutinized' by means of video surveillance systems and biometric techniques can become a person 'modified' by the implantation of 'smart' chips and tags, in a context that increasingly identifies us as 'networked persons', bodies which are permanently on the Net, gradually configured in such a way as to emit and receive impulses that make it possible to trace and reconstruct movements, habits, contacts, thus modifying the meaning and contents of people's autonomy*" (our translation from Italian): Rodotà, above fn 8.

data and inferences are processed, but also groups, since "*data's significance is not just about how that data relates to any one person. It is also about population-level, group-based inferences that can be derived from individual data points*".[25]

These processes aim at targeting people in order to offer them products and services more suitable to their needs. But, at the same time, if these processes are used with malicious intents or serve spiteful scopes, they could, in extreme cases, undermine people's freedom to choose; lead to inaccurate deductions and inferences and perhaps, as a consequence, to the denial of services and goods and to unjustified discrimination.[26]

If these risks already exist in the real and virtual worlds (they have been regulated since 2016), the Metaverse might have a booster effect since it provides for an immersive dimension by means of the use of technologies (which nowadays we are not used to) capable to gather and draw the slightest emotion, tendency or even movement.

If not adequately projected and implemented by keeping in mind the greater possibilities and opportunities which Metaverse seems to give, these processes could give rise to more intensive ways of surveillance and restriction of people's self-determination. Indeed, profiling – through the creation of accurate profiles, classification into categories and inference mechanisms – may have the effect of limiting one's control over his/her own data. In so doing, information and data take on a life of their own[27] and are used to predict future behaviours and addressing choices and decisions.

---

[25] A. Solow Niederman, *op. cit.*, p. 387, claims that "inferential capability introduces the risk of not only privacy invasions, but also 'discrimination by association' if individuals are not shielded from discriminatory inferences that are drawn based on their predicted affinity with a protected group". The so-called "relational theory of data governance" is also explained by Viljoen 2021, according to who dataflows entail not only "vertical relation[s] between a particular individual and a data controller, but also 'horizontal relations' between the individual and others [who] share relevant population features with the data subject".

[26] It is worth recalling an example offered by A. Solow Niederman, *op. cit.*, p. 402, which is referred to machine learning technology but it turns out to be applicable to the current issue as well: "Take, for instance, a hospital's turn to [machine learning] to determine which patients should receive extra medical care. The hope was that identifying patterns in medical data would allow the hospital to make better predictions about health needs. Instead, the running model's prediction on health needs [wa]s, in fact, a prediction on health costs. And because it relied on past healthcare spending to assess need, and because, [a]t a given level of health, Black patients generated lower costs than white patients, the running model undercounted the actual needs of Black patients. The inferential patterns drawn from the data in this healthcare setting hurt those most in need. In other healthcare settings and in many other instances, the applied use of [machine learning] risks embedding long-standing racial and socioeconomic inequity". See also Gandy 2010; Lyon 2002.

[27] "Our electronic body, meaning the set of data concerning us, is the subject of increasingly aggressive and pervasive data mining on grounds of security or else for market purposes. Social surveillance avails itself of increasingly sophisticated electronic leashes. The human body is being equated to a moving object that can be controlled remotely via satellite, or by means of electronic devices", see Stefano Rodotà's conclusive Remarks at the 26th International Conference on Privacy and Personal Data Protection", Wroklav, Poland, 14–16 September 2004, available at: https://www.garanteprivacy.it/home/docweb/-/docweb-display/docweb/1049293, accessed on 03.09.2022.

Under this perspective (maybe a little dramatic, but not too visionary), the Metaverse could represent the expression of the "post-panopticon digital" world, theorized by Bauman and Lyon. In the Authors' opinion, we live in a world where surveillance and control have the mask of the entertainment and mass consumption[28] and where digital natives voluntarily abandon their own personal data and spontaneously accept and submit themselves to surveillance.[29]

This situation and human tendency have developed thanks to social networks, which have paved the way for this common habit of sharing, exposing, displaying, without realising the consequences of this exhibitionism.[30]

Is the Metaverse an evil impossible to defeat? Still early to say. But today we have some tools, like data minimization, purposes limitation and transparency principles, which – if strengthened enough – could represent an initial arsenal.

2.2 Transparency

Another issue, strictly connected to the previous one, is that of transparency.

Transparency is a key principle in the GDPR, it is an attribute attached to processing; transparency of purposes, means and information; transparency in the management of data breach and data subjects' requests.

First of all, transparency is a a rule of conduct of the data controller, who determines the purposes and means of the processing of personal data: pursuant to Article 5(1)(a) GDPR, the data controller is required to process personal data in a lawful, fair and transparent manner towards the data subjects.

But at the same time this principle produces a very precise result for the data subjects. Indeed, the latter acquire a powerful tool to control their own data, since, as a consequence of data controllers' obligation of transparency, they shall be informed of the existence, purposes and methods of the processing of personal data.

The principle of transparency is thus inevitably linked to the very essence of the right to protection of personal data, consisting in the right to have control over these data: the recognition of this right, as well as its practical implementation, are indeed possible only if there is a general obligation to provide information to data subjects.

Therefore, the communication of information is crucial for data subjects to be fully aware of what happens to their personal data and to learn the essential elements for the exercise of their rights. However, in order for this tool to be effective, information

[28] It is not by chance that first attempts at building a Metaverse concerned the gaming experiences in virtual world, like Second Life and Club Penguin, the first two online multimedia platforms that allowed people to create an avatar for themselves and then interacted with other users.

[29] In according to Z. Bauman and D. Lyon, *op.cit.*, p. 7: "*Social media depend for their existence on monitoring users and selling the data to others. (...) surveillance power within social media is endemic and consequential*"

[30] "The private is public, to be celebrated and consumed by countless 'friends' as well as casual 'users'", see Z. Bauman and D. Lyon, *op.cit.*, p. 14.

intended for data subjects must be concise, easily accessible and intelligible, by using plain and clear language and, where appropriate, standardised icons.[31]

The main question is if in the Metaverse this rule can be effectively pursued. In this case the issue is partially connected to inferred data as well.[32]

The informational requirement and the whole individual-centered model of data protection are based on the need that people, at the time they are presented with a privacy policy, are capable to assess the consequences that might flow from releasing personal data. In the Metaverse dimension are these consequences really predictable, since data subjects cannot have the control on their own emotional and physiological responses? The projection of small bodily variations will be translated into the avatars of people with whom one interacts in the virtual world, revealing information in an undesired way that can even be exploited by automatic means. And of course new and advanced techniques, like novel neuromarketing,[33] could be employed with great precision.

For this reason, the principle of purposes limitation seems to acquire utmost importance in this context. Indeed, the previous identification of legitimate, specific and precise purposes could properly protect data subjects even in the case they involuntarily reveal personal data (including inferences), since their use would be limited to those specific purposes.

The transparency principle is fundamental also regarding profiling and decision-making processes. Indeed, pursuant to Article 13(2)(f) GDPR, data subjects must be informed about "*the existence of automated decision-making, including profiling, referred to in Article 22(1) and (4) and, at least in those cases, meaningful information about the logic involved, as well as the significance and the envisaged consequences of such processing for the data subject*". However, it is widely known that profiling "*is often invisible to the data subject. Individuals have differing levels of comprehension and may find it challenging to understand the complex techniques involved in profiling and automated decision-making processes*", and that's why "profiling can be opaque".[34]

[31] Recitals no. 58 and 60 and Article 12 of the GDPR. About this issue, see WP29, *Guidelines on transparency under Regulation 2016/679*, adopted on 29 November 2017, as last revised and adopted by EDPB on 11 April 2018, here available https://ec.europa.eu/newsroom/article29/items/622227, accessed on 04.09.2022.

[32] A. Solow Niederman has been already wondering about this concern with regard to machine learning and Artificial Intelligence: "seemingly innocuous or irrelevant data can generate machine learning insights, making it impossible for an individual to anticipate what kinds of data warrant protection. Moreover, it is possible to aggregate myriad individuals' data within machine learning models, identify patterns, and then apply the patterns to make inferences about other people who may or may not be part of the original data set" (*op. cit.* p. 357).

[33] Neuromarketing means the discipline that relies on the exploration of brain reactions to some stimuli in order to delineate the cognitive mechanisms and dynamics that influence one's preferences and behaviours. See, among others, Garczarek-Bąk et al. 2021.

[34] See WP29, *Guidelines on Automated individual decision-making and Profiling*, cit., pp. 9 and 13. Besides, according to WP29, profiling often "relies upon data that is derived or inferred from other data, rather than data directly provided by the data subject".

If the prediction about greater opportunities of pervasive profiling will be true, greater attention shall be paid to the transparency principle as well.

But in addition to a strengthening of the informational contents to be provided to data subjects, also "when" and "how" to inform people should be re-considered or, at least, studied.

Regarding the timing, there are several scenarios depending on the purposes of the processing of personal data. Information about why and how their data would be processed for the enrollment on a Virtual World platform could be provided when data subjects join the platform and create their own avatars. Other information could be given by each business user every time data subject enters into a contract or, in general, interacts with him/her. Actually, this aspect will depend on the architecture and the definition of roles and responsibilities of the actors involved in the Metaverse.[35]

As for the ways of giving information, one of the most favorable practices could be a "layered privacy policy", which are already performed in the virtual context. This approach enables data subjects to navigate specific sections of the privacy statement to immediately access to, rather than having to scroll through large amounts of text searching for particular issues. Especially in the Metaverse, this method could include "just-in-time" contextual pop-up notices, 3D-touch or hover-over notices, privacy dashboards, cartoons, infographics or flowcharts.

One last, but not the least, thought concerning this issue is about the effectiveness of consent as condition of lawful processing.

As it is widely known, consent should be given by a clear affirmative act establishing a freely given, specific, informed and unambiguous indication of the data subject's agreement to the processing of personal data relating to him or her.[36] In particular, for consent to be informed, it is necessary to inform the data subject of certain elements that are crucial to making a choice. As described above, providing information to data subjects prior to obtaining their consent is essential to enable them to make informed decisions and understand what they are agreeing to. If the data controller does not provide accessible information, data subjects' control becomes illusory and consent would be an unvalid basis for processing.[37]

Hence, if in the Metaverse transparency is not fully guaranteed, consent will not be a valid condition for lawful processing as well.

"A state of conscious and permanent visibility": this how Michel Foucault's theory of panopticon depicts people who are subject to continuous surveillance, where only the guard can see prisoners without being seen himself.[38] In the Metaverse if visibility is certainly a main quality for the above-described reasons, then awareness of being constantly observed may not be taken as a given. For this reason, it is of utmost importance to strengthen methods and obligation to provide information, as well as

---

[35] About this issue, please see the next paragraph 4 of this Chapter.

[36] Recital no. 32 GDPR.

[37] EDPB, *Guidelines 5/2020 on consent under Regulation 2016/679*, adopted on 4 May 2020, par. 62, p. 15, available here https://edpb.europa.eu/our-work-tools/our-documents/guidelines/guidelines-052020-consent-under-regulation-2016679_en, accessed on 08.09.2022.

[38] Foucault 1975.

to develop a cultural and technological maturity which will allow users and data subjects to understand the surroundings where they move.

2.3 *Right to Data Portability*

If, as already mentioned, the notion of personal data is to be expanded in such a way as to include also inferences, this could have important consequences on the right to data portability.

Article 20(1)GDPR recognizes, under certain conditions, "*the right to receive the personal data concerning the data subject, which he or she has provided to a controller, in a structured, commonly used and machine-readable format and have the right to transmit those data to another controller without hindrance from the controller to which the personal data have been provided*". But, as of today, inferences are expressly outside the scope of this new right[39].

However, it can be easily imagined that the Metaverse will be populated especially by this category of data and therefore the question is if the implementation of this right will need a new interpretation that extends to inferred data too.

Nevertheless, the Metaverse will not necessarily have a booster effect on the right to data portability. It depends on the – currently lacking[40] – awareness that users might develop about their right to data portability, on the adoption of tools which could facilitate the effective exercise of this right[41] and on the upgrade of the infrastructure aimed at the transmission and reception of portability requests, which today are considered insufficient.[42]

---

[39] "*Inferred data and derived data are created by the data controller on the basis of the data 'provided by the data subject'. For example, the outcome of an assessment regarding the health of a user or the profile created in the context of risk management and financial regulations (e.g. to assign a credit score or comply with anti-money laundering rules) cannot in themselves be considered as 'provided by' the data subject. Even though such data may be part of a profile kept by a data controller and are inferred or derived from the analysis of data provided by the data subject (through his actions for example), these data will typically not be considered as 'provided by the data subject' and thus will not be within scope of this new right*", see WP29, *Guidelines on the right to data portability*, adopted on 13 December 2016, as last revised and adopted by EDPB on 5 April 2017, p. 10, here available https://ec.europa.eu/newsroom/article29/items/611233, accessed on 08.09.2022.

[40] According to Exposito-Rosso et al. 2021, p. 21 "People have little interest in portability law. They are not aware of this right. They do not know how to exercise it. They are unaware of the opportunities data portability offers them" (the full text of the report is here available https://cellar-c2.services.clever-cloud.com/alias-code-is-law-assets/static/report/gdpr_data_portability_the_forgotten_right_report_full.pdf, accessed on 15.09.2022). See also European Commission 2019, which shows data about the level of awareness on the right to data portability among EU citizens.

[41] Kuebler-Wachendorff et al. 2021. See also Wong and Henderson 2019.

[42] Syrmoudis et al. 2021.

3 Data Controllership

Among all the critical issues, one of the greatest may arise with respect to the identification of subjects involved in the processing and their roles. As brief as the question is, the matter is quite complicated: who is the data controller?

As we know, the data controller is the subject whom the GDPR (and, even before, the Directive 95/46/CE) entrusts to guide the processing and whom determines purposes and means of the processing itself. He/she has a primary role in the data protection architecture and is responsible for respecting data protection law and carrying out the processing of personal data with the guarantee of safeguarding data subjects' rights.

Except when data controllership is provided by law,[43] the data controller is identified through a factual approach which inspects who processes data and how processing is carried out. In other words, whoever actually holds the power of defining purposes and means of processing is considered the data controller.

Before examining who the data controller could be in the Metaverse, it is worth recalling the concepts of purposes and means of the personal data processing.

"Purpose" means the scope that the data controller wants to achieve by processing personal data, therefore the objective which the processing aims at and due to which the data controller arranges his/her activity.

As for the processing "means", this notion includes both technical and organizational measures used to process personal data. Data controller determines which data shall be processed; which electronic or analogic tools to use; which security measures to adopt; and so on.

In light of this, it is possible to make some assumptions about who holds the power of determining purposes and means of personal data processing of in the Metaverse, where the main actors involved could be the Metaverse platform keeper, who creates the technological platform and puts it at others' service, and the business users which operate and offer their products and services through the Metaverse platform.

3.1 *Case 1: Business Users are Data Controllers while the Virtual World's Provider is the Data Processor*

In a first case-scenario, business users could be considered as autonomous data controllers, while the platform keeper could be their data processor, namely the entity which processes personal data on behalf of the controller.[44]

[43] This is the case considered in the same notion of data controller at Article 4, par. 1, no. 7, which provides as follows: "where the purposes and means of such processing are determined by Union or Member State law, the controller or the specific criteria for its nomination may be provided for by Union or Member State law".

[44] Article 4, par. 1, no. 8 GDPR.

Indeed, the platform keeper offers his/her service (namely, a Virtual World platform) which users exploit to pursue their autonomous scopes. Therefore personal data processing is carried out by the data processor solely on behalf of users/data controllers and in order to achieve purposes determined by each user.

To assess whether this scenario could be feasible, it is necessary to examine if the means of processing, provided for by the platform keeper, are essential or not. This distinction is useful to determine the role of the platform keeper in relation to the users. Indeed, only non-essential means can be left to the processor, while a controller must decide on both purposes and essential means of the processing, as explained above.

As the EDPB states,[45] "essential means" are means that are closely linked to the purpose and the scope of the processing, such as the type of personal data which are processed, the duration of the processing, the categories of recipients and the categories of data subjects. "Non-essential means" concern instead more practical aspects of implementation, such as the choice of a particular type of hard- or software or the detailed security measures.

According to these notions, the platform keeper may be qualified as data processor as long as he/she does not determine other elements of the processing, beyond technical and practical means. But this will clearly depend also on how the Virtual World platfom will be designed and set up.

Usually, the outsourcing or the hiring of hosting services entail this kind of relationship between the actors involved in the processing. This scheme is similar to that one used in the cloud computing context as well, where the cloud provider is the data processor designated by the subject who uses his/her services.[46]

However, criticism of this model can be foreseen in relation to the concrete power that users can actually exercise on the Virtual World platform. Indeed, the data controller has the right and duty to give instructions, supervise and inspect the data processor's activities, but it is unlikely that, in the context of the Metaverse, each user could carry out this sort of surveillance, with the consequence that the effectiveness of the data controller's supervision may fade.

---

[45] EDPB, *Guidelines 07/2020 on the concepts of controller and processor in the GDPR*, adopted on 7 July 2021, p. 15, here available https://edpb.europa.eu/system/files/2021-07/eppb_guidelines_202007_controllerprocessor_final_en.pdf, accessed on 15.09.2022.

[46] This model was embraced by the WP29 itself, even if the Working Party recognized as well that "In the current cloud computing scenario, clients of cloud computing services may not have room for manoeuvre in negotiating the contractual terms of use of the cloud services as standardised offers are a feature of many cloud computing services. Nevertheless, it is ultimately the client who decides on the allocation of part or the totality of processing operations to cloud services for specific purposes; the cloud provider's role will be that of a contractor vis-à-vis the client, which is the key point in this case" (see *Opinion 5/2012 on cloud computing*, 1 July 2012, p. 8).

3.2 Case 2: Business Users and Virtual Worlds' Providers are Joint Data Controllers

In a second scenario, business users operating through the platform and the platform keeper could be considered as joint data controllers.

Joint controllership exists when two or more actors determine jointly the purpose and means of the processing activity.[47] However, as the EDPB explains,[48] joint participation can take the form of a common decision taken by two or more entities, but it can also result from converging decisions by two or more entities as well, where the decisions complement each other and are necessary for the processing to take place in such a manner that they have a tangible impact on the determination of the purposes and means of the processing.

Therefore, to assess whether joint controllership could exist in the Metaverse, it is necessary to figure out if the processing would not be possible without both users' and the Virtual World provider's participation, in the sense that the processing by each party is inseparable and inextricably linked. Also in this case, the assessment of joint controllership should be carried out by means of a factual approach and an analysis of the actual influence on the purposes and means of the processing.

In the Metaverse, the Virtual World provider sets up the means for the processing of personal data, such as the technical system and infrastructure, allowing users to process personal data through it.

Two elements need to be explored further: on one hand, we should assess if users of the Virtual World platform can decide on the processing of personal data to be performed in this context; on the other hand, it should be ascertained if the processing carried out by users is not separable and could not be performed without intervention from the Virtual World platform provider.

If the answers are positive, then joint controllership may be a solution for the definition of roles and the allocation of responsibilities under data protection laws.

Furthermore, the existence of joint responsibility does not necessarily imply equal responsibility of the various operators involved in the processing of personal data: operators may be involved at different stages of that processing and to different degrees, so that the level of responsibility of each of them must be assessed with regard to all the relevant circumstances of the particular case.

It is worth noting that this model has been already used in the case law of EU Court of Justice, where web operators and users were considered joint controllers with a social network provider as long as, according to the Court, they jointly determined purposes and means of the processing.[49] Besides, the European lawmaker seems to be

---

[47] Article 26 GDPR, which reflects the definition in Article 4, par. 1, no. 7) GDPR, provides that "[w]here two or more controllers jointly determine the purposes and means of processing, they shall be joint controllers".

[48] EDPB, *Guidelines 7/2020*, cit., p. 19.

[49] In the case C-40/17, *Fashion ID GmbH & Co. KG v. Verbraucherzentrale NRW eV,* with intervention of *Facebook Ireland Ltd,* 29 July 2019, ECLI:EU:C:2019:629, the European Court of

inclined to adhere to the joint controllership model as well: indeed, this configuration is the one frequently suggested in the context of the European Health Data Space.[50]

3.3 *Case 3: A Network Perspective*

One last scenario may concern the creation of a new relational model which focuses not on the single entity that processes personal data, but instead on the whole network.

This scheme could result from the ascertainment that the multitude of entities populating the Metaverse will create a web of relationships, making it very difficult to determine responsibilities and liabilities.[51]

Hence, the Metaverse could lead to the establishment of a new accountability system, whereby the party responsible for the infringement of data protection rules would not be the single entity but the network, and the accountability scheme would result in the joint liability.

4 The Data Subject

Beyond the above-examined cases, one last figure must be considered: the data subject.

Data subjects are easy to identify: they are natural persons whose personal data are processed or, from a different perspective, the natural persons who are identified or identifiable through their information.

Justice has stated that the operator of a website that features a Facebook 'Like' button can be a controller jointly with Facebook in respect of the collection and transmission to Facebook of the personal data of visitors to its website. By contrast, that operator is not, in principle, a controller in respect of the subsequent processing of those data carried out by Facebook alone. Likewise, in the case C-210/16, *Unabhängiges Landeszentrum für Datenschutz Schleswig-Holstein* v. *Wirtschaftsakademie Schleswig-Holstein GmbH,* with intervention of *Facebook Ireland Ltd*, 5 June 2018, ECLI:EU:C:2018:388, the Court affirmed that the administrator of a fan page on Facebook is jointly responsible with Facebook for the processing of data of visitors to the page. For further details, see Blanc 2018; Lynskey 2018.

[50] The reference is to Regulation (EU) 2025/327 of the European Parliament and of the Council of 11 February 2025 on the European Health Data Space. In this context, the European legislator introduces the joint controllership scheme with regard to the new health data platforms and the secondary use of data. Specifically, Article 23, par. 7 provides as follows: "The national contact points for digital health shall act as joint controllers of the electronic health data communicated through 'MyHealth@EU' for the processing operations in which they are involved. The Commission shall act as processor". Likewise, Article 76, par. 10 with regard to secondary data use.

[51] "Defining the distinction between data controller and data processor in the metaverse might become a big challenge as the entities present in a particular universe will be highly intermingled. Defining who does what on behalf of whom will not be easy", see European Parliament's briefing *Metaverse. Opportunities, risks and policy implications*, cit., p. 5.

In the Metaverse, a data subject could be allegedly a person who, through his/her avatar, purchases products or services which business users offer him/her on the Virtual World platform. In this case, the data subject acts in the course of a purely personal or household activity. But, as already explained, the Metaverse could allow to build personal connections and tangled networks by increasing the opportunities of interactions among users and data subjects.

How can we ascertain when the personal or household purpose – which falls outside the scope of data protection law – comes to end and a professional or business use of personal data begins? This could be the event where the same subject is – or rather, the same avatar represents – a customer and, at the same time, the legal representative of an entity.

It is advisable that the qualification of a user who wants to enroll on a Metaverse platform be determinable in advance and decided at the time of registration. But this takes to other questions that are left to readers as hints for future debate: who shall control and verify the identity of users? Which identification systems could be used? Should multiple avatars be allowed to exist for the same user/data subject, if this latter has more than one role or qualification?

5 Conclusions

Whichever architecture will be chosen and whether data protection law will need to be reviewed, it is hard to imagine the Metaverse like a space to be left to the free private initiative. A legal framework should be drafted and access, technical, security, ethical requirements should be defined in order to minimise risks of surveillance, monitoring and hidden influence to which data subjects may be exposed.

This regulation could be stricter or lighter. In any case, being the Metaverse materializing, the legislator cannot refraing from action as users and data subjects cannot be left defenseless.

So far European regulators have intentionally decided not to draw a legal framework in order to facilitate technological progress and the free movement of people, goods, services and data, with the consequence of letting privates and Big Tech free to regulate the virtual world, impose their own rules and build their own tribunals.

But it is time that legislators realise that today dimensions are different. There is not a territoriality concept anymore, but a globalized dimension. "*Power now exists in global and extraterritorial space, but politics, which once linked individual and public interests, remains local, unable to act at the planetary level*".[52] Perhaps the Metaverse will manage to require the participation of the public power, which has been missing for a while.

---

[52] Z. Bauman and D. Lyon, *op. cit.*, p. 5.

References

Bassini M, Pollicino O (2022) Intelligenza artificiale e protezione dei dati personali. In: Pajno A, Donati F, Perrucci A (eds) Intelligenza Artificiale e diritto: una rivoluzione? Vol. 1 Diritti fondamentali, dati personali e regolazione. Il Mulino, Bologna, pp 270–271

Bauman Z, Lyon D (2013) Liquid surveillance: a conversation. Polity Press, Cambridge, p 21

Blanc N (2018) Wirtschaftsakademie schleswig-holstein: towards a joint responsibility of facebook fan page administrators for infringements to european data protection law? Eur Data Prot Law Rev 4(1):120–126

D'Orazio R, Finocchiaro G, Pollicino O, Resta G (2021) Codice della privacy e data protection. Giuffrè, Milano

European Commission 2019 Special eurobarometer 487a. The general data protection regulation

Exposito-Rosso S, Cao FX, Piquet A, Medjaoui M (2021) GDPR data portability: the forgotten right. ALIAS

Finocchiaro G (2017) Introduzione al regolamento Europeo sulla protezione dei dati. Nuove leggi civ comment 1:1–18

Finocchiaro G (ed) (2019a) La protezione dei dati personali in Italia. Regolamento UE n. 2016/679 e d.lgs. 10 agosto 2018, n. 101. Zanichelli, Bologna

Finocchiaro G (2019b) Intelligenza artificiale e protezione dei dati personali. Giurisprud. Ital 2019:1670–1677

Floridi L (2015) The onlife manifesto. Being human in a hyperconnected era. Springer Nature, Cham

Floridi L (2020) The fight for digital sovereignty: What it is, and why it matters, especially for the EU. Phil Tech 33(2):123–145

Foucault M (1975) Surveiller et punir: naissance de la prison. Éditions Gallimard, Paris

Gandy OH (2010) Engaging rational discrimination: exploring reasons for placing regulatory constraints on decision support systems. Ethics Inf Technol 12:29–42

Garczarek-Bąk U, Szymkowiak A, Gaczek P, Disterheft A (2021) A comparative analysis of neuromarketing methods for brand purchasing predictions among young adults. J Brand Manag 28(2):171–185. https://doi.org/10.1057/s41262-020-00221-7

Haggerty K, Ericson R (2000) The surveillant assemblage. Br J Sociol 54(1):605–622

Kuebler-Wachendorff S, Lusza R, Kranz J, Mager S, Syrmoudis E, Mayr S, Grossklags J (2021) The right to data portability: Conception, status quo, and future directions. Inform Spektrum 44:264–272

Kuner C, Bygrave LA, Docksey C, Drechsler L (2019) The EU general data protection regulation (GDPR): a commentary. Oxford University Press, Oxford

O Lynskey 2018 Another turn of the screw? The 'Facebook Fanpages' Judgment, in "*European Law Blog*", 25 June 2018

Lyon D (2002) Surveillance as social sorting: Privacy, risk and automated discrimination. Taylor & Francis Ltd, London

S Rodotà 2005 Speech at the conference "Transformations of the body and dignity of the person", Rome, 4 May 2005

Solow-Niederman A (2022) Information privacy and the inference economy. Northwest Univ Law Rev 117(2):357–423

Syrmoudis E, Mager S, Kuebler-Wachendorff S, Pizzinini P, Grossklags J, Kranz J (2021) Data portability between online services: An empirical analysis on the effectiveness of GDPR art. 20. Proc. Priv. Enhancing Technol. 3:351–372

Viljoen S (2021) A relational theory of data governance. Yale Law J 131(2):573–654

Wachter S, Mittelstadt B (2019) A right to reasonable inferences: re-thinking data protection law in the age of big data and AI. Columbia Bus Law Rev 2:495–620

Wong J, Henderson T (2019) The right to data portability in practice: exploring the implications of the technologically neutral GDPR. Int Data Priv Law 9(3):173–191